LANGUAGE AND LITERACY

LANGUAGE AND LITERACY

Studying Discourse in Communities and Classrooms

Eleanor Kutz

BOYNTON/COOK PUBLISHERS
HEINEMANN
Portsmouth, NH

Boynton/Cook Publishers
A subsidiary of Reed Elsevier Inc.
361 Hanover Street
Portsmouth, NH 03801-3912
Offices and agents throughout the world

Editor: Scott Mahler
Production Editor: Renée M. Nicholls
Cover Designer: Tom Allen/Pear Graphic Design
Manufacturing Coordinator: Louise Richardson

The author and publisher wish to thank those who have generously given permission to reprint borrowed material:

Library of Congress Cataloging-in-Publication Data

Kutz, Eleanor.
    Language and literacy : studying discourse in communities and
classrooms / Eleanor Kutz.
        p.   cm.
    Includes bibliographical references (p.   ) and index.
    ISBN 0-86709-386-2
    1. Language and languages.   2. Literacy.   3. Discourse analysis.
I. Title.
P106.K86   1997
400—dc21   96-39569
                                                                    CIP

Printed in the United States of America on acid-free paper
99 98 97 DA 1 2 3 4 5 6

CONTENTS

ACKNOWLEDGMENTS

I would like to thank my husband, Ron Thornton, always my best reader, who shares my interest in creating effective disciplinary-based pedagogies; my children Kenny and Karen, who have tolerated with good humor the intrusion of their mother's research into their lives; the friends and neighbors who have helped us appreciate our community's rich diversity, particularly Melanie Brown and Shanna Higgins Bearfield and their families, as well as my long term friend and ally, Joann Brown; the colleagues at UMass/Boston who have shared an ongoing commitment to studying and valuing multiple literacies and diverse linguistic communities, including Elsa Auerbach, Donaldo Macedo, and especially Chuck Meyer and Vivian Zamel, as well as other friends, Maureen and Barry Kolb who read and responded to this manuscript; and the many students and teachers who have explored the study of language and literacy in their own lives and classrooms, including those who contributed to this book: Eliot Adelstein, Mike Arsenault, Antonio Ayatala, Florence Banks, Michael Bradley, Lorraine Cecere, Rebecca Day, Joseph DelRosso, Sandra Dionne, Patricia Doherty, David Dorsey, Kevin Dotson, Kerry Frye, Elaine Hays, Paul Joseph, Stan Kaplan, Joan Kingsbury, Ellie Klauminzer, Margaret Lombard, Melissa Marotto, Nicole Nadeau, Nilda Ocasio, Stephanie Pegorier, Justine Rowland, Sue Szottfried, Gilbert (Andy) Thompson, Zina Venezia, and Kevin Young.

INTRODUCTION

This book is about language and the study of language, but I hope it will be different from other books you've encountered on these subjects. I begin in the world my students and I inhabit as learners and teachers, friends, family members, and residents of a city that's increasingly linguistically and culturally mixed. I explore the questions and concerns about language that emerge in our daily lives, as we observe the words spoken by our young children, nieces, or nephews; the different ways people speak as we move from one setting to another; the written texts produced by the students we teach, or will teach; and the debates about educational practice or language policy that are played out in the media. I've used the conversations, stories, and writings that my students and I collected in our different roles as a starting point for considering formal knowledge about language and how it can help us explore the issues that arise in our lives. I believe that developing a coherent framework of knowledge about language should be an important part of education at all levels of schooling, but that it's one in which our current practices have failed.

In this book I've called for, and tried to model, a new approach to the ways that we learn about language. This approach begins not with the memorization of key terms and concepts, but rather, with our personal and social experience of how language is used in the world, and the sorts of informal knowledge and preliminary questions this experience generates. I've used this framework as a means of reexamining our understanding of literacy as well, exploring what it means to acquire the language of literacy: to speak and write as a member of particular literate communities. In each chapter, I've begun with examples of actual discourse recorded in natural conversations, or produced in writing for real audiences and purposes. I've included an introductory exploration describing what those texts show us about particular issues in language and literacy, and what our research in language and literacy can contribute to our understanding of those texts. I have also introduced the formal methods of discourse analysis I've found most useful, for those who want to study how language works in particular contexts, such as classrooms, or in particular texts, like students' writing. (A separate "Guide" in the appendix gives detailed suggestions for the sort of inquiry represented in the chapters.) Before I turn to the specific aspects of this study, I want to explain why the ability to talk and think about language in knowledgeable ways is important to the roles we play as parents, citizens, policymakers, and above all, as teachers. I want to look briefly at the prior knowledge about language we're likely to be bringing to those roles.

Language in society

In American society, concerns about language and literacy have long been at the center of public discourse. We have responded to successive waves of immigration with conflicting models for how to create a functioning society across differences of language and culture. Our social attitudes and educational policies have swung between perceiving a primary need to assimilate newcomers into a larger, coherent culture, and responding to an equally strong need for that society to accommodate its diverse multilingual and multicultural members. Differences in our common language, American English, as it is used by groups of speakers from different regions with different educational or socioeconomic backgrounds, contribute to the complexity of the problem.

As I read the newspaper, I find these broad social concerns showing up repeatedly in relationship to local issues. My daily paper, *The Boston Globe,* recently reported on a controversy that broke out in a small Massachusetts community. In response to a report that an elementary school teacher whose first language is Spanish was being moved from a bilingual classroom to a regular classroom, parents in the town of Westfield submitted a petition to the school board that called on local and state officials to prohibit hiring any elementary school teacher who speaks English with an accent. The teacher was considered by colleagues to be an excellent teacher, and concerns about the move seemed to focus entirely on issues of language.

The petitioners in Westfield included parents who themselves had learned English as a second language and who spoke with an accent. The four-term mayor of the city, whose first language was Greek, supported their position, saying that he would not feel qualified to teach young students "because of my accent," and in a later interview went on to say that he wouldn't even have hired Einstein, for the same reason. As might be expected, reports of the petition led to a great deal of controversy. In letters sent to the editor, people speculated about the effects of a teacher's accent not only on children's spoken language, but also on their learning to read and write. They raised questions about how language and literacy are acquired. Some wondered whether a native speaker of English from a different region would be seen as having an accent that precluded teaching in Westfield, while others recalled their own confusion when they came to New England classrooms from other parts of the country and found that *Korea/career* or *often/orphan* were pronounced alike and treated as homonyms. Their concerns raise questions about language variation: how different dialects of a language arise and are maintained. Others wondered how people learn to use language in different contexts. In one letter to the *The Boston Globe* a parent from another Massachusetts town (after describing his own midwestern accent as "perfectly neutral") said that he'd noticed his own children developing two accents: they used one with their playmates, but switched to his style of pronunciation and syntax when speaking with him. "Where did they learn this?" he asked.

The *Globe* reporter who had written the original news account sought to answer the many questions that had been raised by turning to an authority—in this case my colleague Donaldo Macedo, director of the graduate program in Bilingual Education at UMass/Boston. Macedo responded to the immediate concern by pointing out that the linguistic research has found no evidence that children raised by someone with a heavy accent will acquire that accent, explaining that many immigrants who learn English as adults have a permanent accent (sometimes referred to as the Kissinger effect, from the accent retained by former Secretary of State Henry Kissinger) but that this does not reflect diminished mastery of the language.

But Macedo's response didn't settle the issue. The discussion of these events continued in different arenas, and the debate moved on to legal issues of discrimination, moral concerns about racism and prejudice, and economic concerns about priorities in funding and budgeting in education. What began as an apparently straightforward argument about language was soon seen as connected to broad social questions, drawing in many people who would not have anticipated that their own lives and work would require them to think, in any significant way, about language and how it works, or to act based on an understanding of linguistic issues.

Language in school

While we are often confronted with issues about language in our society, our typical language education leaves us unable to formulate the questions and answers we need about language: how it's acquired or learned, how it varies among regions and social groups, how it affects and is affected by literacy. (Just as our typical science education leaves us unable to answer, or even to ask, probing questions about technology, the environment, or genetic engineering.)

Our schools, by and large, teach traditional, prescriptive "school grammar," a confusion of structural terms and stylistic rules, with the production of "correct" forms in speech and in writing as the intended effect. Recent, and often controversial, whole language approaches to the teaching of reading and writing have downplayed the study of grammatical rules and the focus on correctness, replacing the completion of sentence exercises with ongoing writing and reading for authentic purposes and presenting writing as a process for formulating ideas as well as reporting on them in final, edited form. These approaches have done much to support the development of young writers. But they ignore most explicit questions about language and how it works. Rather than replacing traditional school grammar with more effective approaches to the study of language—ones that more accurately reflect the state of current knowledge—many of our schools have displaced this area of formal study entirely, bypassing the opportunity to build on the implicit knowledge of language that young learners bring to the classroom and missing the chance to create a foundation for their later understandings of language-related social issues.

In college, a few students do go on to take introductory linguistics courses (and these may even be required of those planning to teach English). But again, there is a mismatch between what is offered and what will be needed by the majority of students who will not go on to advanced study in this discipline. The formal study of language, as carried out by linguists, covers a vast field of inquiry: Some of it is highly theoretical and technical, and apparently isolated from social concerns; some provides a great deal of research in areas that can contribute to the public inquiry in cases like Westfield's. But while typical introductory courses present concepts that are central to work in linguistics, they tend to focus primarily on terms to be memorized and models to be learned—as a self-contained system to be mastered. These linguistic concepts hold more explanatory power than school grammar, but are typically taught in ways that provide little connection with what learners might need to know about language in the world, and little connection to what they already know about language from their daily lives. As a result, the formal study of linguistics has been treated as irrelevant, not only at the elementary or high school level but even as part of a college general education—even in a society that is continually dealing with public policy around language issues.

Common knowledge about language

As humans we are language users, and we use language not only to represent things in the world, to convey information about them, or to motivate others to act in some way on those things, but also to reflect on all of these activities. We use language to think about language and how we use it. And so most of us have formulated ideas about language, about how it works, about how we and people around us use it. Anthropologists refer to the ideas that people in a particular cultural group share about how something in the world works as "cultural models" or "folk theories." Our folk theories about language provide a common fund of knowledge, with some fairly accurate pictures of the way language works—and some misleading ones. But our existing common knowledge about language can provide an important starting point for further study.

The Westfield parents were taking action in an area of common concern—their children's education—based on their common knowledge, on their folk theories of how language and literacy are acquired. As linguist Jim Gee points out in *The Social Mind* (1992), folk theories often provide a rationalization of a particular action or set of practices, even when the practice doesn't actually follow the folk theory. People then judge others, in part, on whether they have allegiance to the same theory. A theory that having a teacher with an accent will interfere with children's learning in first grade, for example, provides a rationalization of the practice of not allowing bilingual teachers to teach in regular classrooms. So what folk theories about language were the Westfield parents, the mayor, and the others who entered the debate likely to be drawing on? What do most people think they know about language—its structure, acquisition, use, and its variation—and how do they know it?

One folk theory about language resides in the notion of "The King's English," a better, "more correct" English than commoners and ordinary people speak. In our contemporary society it is more often teachers who are assumed to be the nobility in this regard (hence the Westfield controversy) and students who are seen as smart, or good in school, are those who seem to emulate them, to learn their ways. Many people hold a version of this theory and it helps them to explain much of their own experience. As the father of my daughter's friend told me recently, "I might have tried to stay in school, but I was just so bad at English." He is an intelligent man who had to discover his own competence sometime after his high school years yet he had both imagined and confirmed himself as a failure. Why? Because the forms of his native English language as it was spoken in his working-class white community did not match the standard English of his high school teachers.

But why should speaking nonstandard English cause his overall failure in school? The answer lies in another folk theory. An important part of the school's business is to teach literacy, and literacy is intertwined with particular forms of the language in the minds of most people, including teachers. While the "standard" forms of English have been established as those used by those who hold power in our society—middle- and upper-class white Americans who really learn them at home, not at school—the responsibility of schools has been seen not only as teaching children to read and write, but to use these standard forms in speaking as well, so that the two endeavors have been confounded. *The Harbrace College Handbook,* in an old edition I've had since my own college days, makes explicit the view that use of a standard form of English is a sign of literacy: non-standard forms ("Where is she at?" or "She sang good") are labeled *illiterate,* and readers are told that "*Illiteracies* are the crude expressions of uneducated people." (More recently these labels have been changed to simply "correct" and "incorrect," but the problem, and the folk theory that underlies it, remains the same.) In fact, belonging to a group that uses one set of forms rather than another has nothing to do with literacy, if literacy is defined in terms of one's competence and fluency as a reader and writer (though we will explore that definition). The "illiteracies" that were pointed out in the old handbook are really an aspect of language variation—of the ways in which the forms of one language will differ as it is used by different communities of speakers. People can learn to read and write using any of these variants, any linguistic code.

Related folk theories govern much of our schools' instruction in English and in foreign languages. People remember the study of grammar from their own schooling, with the memorization of labels and rules and the completion of endless sets of exercises, and they probably remember it so well because these activities were so painful and boring. In the process, they gained some conscious (if sometimes erroneous) knowledge about grammatical forms and structures, and they assume that it was through that study that they learned to use standard forms in English. Yet, though my neighbor's high school offered plenty of text-book exercises in the more "literate" forms of standard English (the student teachers I sometimes supervise at his old high school must still follow essentially the same curriculum), these made no difference to his actual ability to use those forms, because we don't actually acquire new languages or uses of language through this sort of formal instruction. The lack of a relationship between such study and the actual ability to use a new language or new forms is seen more clearly in the failure of our typical foreign language instruction where, after memorizing grammatical rules without the opportunity to use the new language in meaningful conversations, most Americans fail dismally when called upon to speak or write it.

An analogous folk theory governs our beliefs about the acquisition of literacy and affects the still dominant ways of teaching reading and writing in schools. Because it is possible to analyze the structure of larger units of language in terms of component parts, people have too often assumed that explicitly teaching those parts will support their acquisition, whether these are forms for the declension of nouns in German or the sound-letter correspondences of written language. Phonics-styled approaches in first- and second-grade class-rooms often drill these relationships to the exclusion of meaningful reading that would support the development of reading competence. Soon the drills and worksheets become "reading," as was the case for one of my students who had long remembered, with pain, the fact that she had nearly failed reading as a child, until she found, on her old report card, the explanation that she had been rushing carelessly through her worksheets because she was too eager to get to her library book. The folk theory also says that children who don't learn to read need more drills, although research with children and adult literacy learners shows that treating reading and writing as a meaningful extension of other language use— not more of the same school stuff—is what makes a difference.

Outside of schools, folk theories about language shape the ways in which adults treat their children and interpret their own experience. Adult immigrants of an earlier generation, believing that children would not acquire the English language if they heard their first language spoken at home, struggled painfully to confine their conversation to what they themselves could say in their limited English. In *The Hunger of Memory* (1982), Richard Rodriguez tells how, on the advice of his teachers, his parents stopped speaking Spanish to him at home. While crediting his own learning of English to this event, Rodriguez describes the new silence that appeared at home:

> The family's quiet was partly due to the fact that, as we children learned more and more English, we shared fewer and fewer words with our parents. Sentences needed to be spoken slowly when a child addressed his mother or father. (Often the parent wouldn't understand.) The child would need to repeat himself. (Still the parent misunderstood.) The young voice, frustrated, would end up saying, "Never mind"—the subject was closed. (23)

Rodriguez' mother kept trying to join her children's conversations, "but her intrusions often stopped her children's talking" (24). His father said less and less, and the silence became increasingly profound.

Rodriguez' rationalization of his own experience has made him a spokesperson for those who oppose bilingual education, arguing that "the bilingualists simplistically scorn the value and the necessity of assimilation" (26). Yet, from recent research with bilingual children there is no evidence that speaking another language fluently at home is more harmful than speaking limited English for a child's acquisition of English. Rather, it seems the children who have limited use of a first language at home are less likely to have the full linguistic foundation needed for full acquisition of other languages. (See Cummins, 1981.) Again, as in the Westfield situation, the debate becomes polarized, and the folk theories governing the public response to the question of bilingual education mostly serve to help people judge who is in their camp, rather than weigh complex evidence and develop flexible educational responses.

As adults, we often use the rationalizations we've created from our own experiences with language and the prevailing folk theories of the larger community to evaluate the new circumstances we encounter. Our theories also affect the ways we interact with our own children: whether we use baby talk with them, how we prepare them for the language of school, whether we correct the forms they use, when and how we expose them to a second language. And they affect the ways in which we respond to others in our communities and workplaces as well. The young black man in the courtroom who suddenly shifts language into full street style may be seen by a judge as hostile and aggressive, by a middle-class lawyer as stupid, by a social worker as needing to affirm his identity in a moment of powerlessness, though his use of street style may simply indicate his lack of experience in the formal context of the courtroom (and thus could be taken as a point in his favor). Or if, like the young white offender who follows him, he falls silent, he may be considered sullen and uncooperative, rather than scared and uncertain. Similarly, the half-truths of much political discourse may be seen as pragmatic and effective by some members of the electorate, and as lies by others.

What we think we know about language (our folk theory or cultural model) helps us to rationalize our practices with language. But these practices are learned and passed on within the communities that we're part of, with or without our articulating a conscious theory. As Shirley Brice Heath has shown in *Ways with Words* (1983), her study of the language practices of different communities in the Piedmont area of the Carolinas, children learn to use language in the ways that the adults around them use language—to value what the adults value. If the adults value verbal cleverness and invention, these are the practices that children will perfect. If the adults value factual accounts of events, accounts that end with a moral, children will develop skill at offering such accounts. But all of this is done unconsciously. And, as Heath found, when children from these different communities enter school, the teachers' own experiences and rationalizations shape their responses to the children's language practices: When "Trackton" children carry their verbally inventive games into the classroom, their teachers see them as aggressive and disrespectful; "Roadville" children, who have learned to be quiet and fact-oriented with adults, appear to their teachers to be lacking initiative and creativity.

In fact, when it comes to our own reflection on language practices, or generating theories of why we do what we do, schools typically play an important role because they call our conscious attention to the ways we use language, imposing a particular shape or a particular model on what we've been doing. We've seen some of the common folk theories that have been shaped, for most people, by their long experience (seventeen or more years) with the language practices and ways of talking about those practices that schools require. When classes focus on grammar book drills and teachers respond to students' writing primarily by correcting errors, school practices inadvertently end up compounding the folk theories many of us hold, including the idea that some forms of language are inherently better than others; that it is through exercises that these better forms are learned; and that literacy itself is tied to discrete names and labels, and to compliance with particular linguistic conventions.

Grammar and school grammar

The grammar most of us have been taught in school is received knowledge that comes weighted in tradition, rather than knowledge that is generated from the current study of language. School grammar is descended from the grammar that was one of the seven areas of study in the medieval university, and it has inherited the terms and categories that had been used to describe Latin and then applied to the evolving vernacular languages—French, German, English. The vernacular languages were shoehorned into the existing grammatical model, and the fit wasn't exact. But the model provided a way of describing these languages, while asserting their legitimacy, alongside Latin, as a medium for learned exchange—for literature, for history, and after the Reformation, for reading and commenting on the scriptures. The description of a fixed grammar had a conservative effect on Latin. It established a stable form of the language, a "correct" form that could be maintained through teaching, despite the changes that would naturally occur in the spoken language. Correct, formal Latin was also associated with education in letters—with literacy. In the early medieval period the term *literacy* was seen as related exclusively to knowing Latin, and to be a *literatus* was to be able to read and write that language. Over time, the distance between the fixed and unchanging forms of literate Latin and the fluid forms of a spoken language increased, while the central political authority of the once Latin-speaking world broke up. Eventually, even in Italy where there was the least pressure from the languages spoken by other migrating peoples, Latin and Italian soon became different and mutually incomprehensible languages.

Using the categories derived from Latin grammar to describe the vernacular languages of Europe defined them formally in terms that would remain relatively unchanged over time, despite the changes that were always occurring in spoken languages as people actually used them. The invention of the printing press brought increasingly regularized conventions of spelling and orthography as well, creating a standard written language that, while it changed slowly over centuries, was much more stable than spoken forms. In each country, this standard was greatly influenced by the spoken dialect of those who had wealth and power as well as access to the means of literacy—as the Southeast Midlands' dialect of London's merchants and bankers became the standard for English. Describing a grammar that fixed a standard had a conservative effect on much thinking about language, as language came to be seen as what was written about grammar in books, rather than what people actually said. And, over time, its political effect was also conservative, as the forms and usages of a particular class of speakers were codified as correct, while those of others were seen as incorrect and inferior, as disqualifications for positions of public power.

Despite efforts to fix a grammar, language (even in written texts) kept on changing. Coincidentally, the descriptive categories of a formal grammar derived from Latin aided historical linguists in their study of such change, providing a framework against which the differences between languages and changes in languages over time could be seen. Since much of that study focused on languages that had the same Indo-European roots, the grammatical model fit reasonably well. But, the application of a top–down grammatical framework to the data of languages effectively eliminated any attention to those details that didn't fit the framework.

Modern linguistics

Twentieth-century linguistics has moved away from the traditional approach to grammar in two ways: First, fueled by the need to describe nonIndo-European languages with no written traditions (like the many Native American languages), linguists began to work from the bottom up, from the observation and description of linguistic features to the creation of categories that will explain those features. Grammatical categories have been found to vary across languages, and categories have been discovered that do not exist in Indo-European languages. (For example, a category appears in some languages to indicate whether the speaker is offering an utterance on his own authority or is referring to another authority.) Secondly, linguists have drawn on the implicit grammatical knowledge held by any speaker of a language. When the linguist wants to know if a construction is grammatical in a particular language, she asks an informant who is a native speaker of that language whether the construction could be used, and whether it would be understood and make sense. (If, as speakers of English, we were asked whether one could say, as Lewis Carroll did in *Jabberwocky,* "All mimsy were the borogoves,/ And the mome raths outgrabe," we would say yes, even though many of the words are nonsense words, while "Mimsy the were borogoves all," wouldn't make sense to our deeper grammatical understanding. Grammar becomes a description of the language, as it is implicitly understood by those who speak it, rather than an a priori set of categories and correct forms. And not all of this implicit knowledge has yet been discovered for any language.

A further step is to move from the description of what is in the grammar as it exists in the minds of individual speakers to a larger theoretical model of the grammar of any one language across its common variants and of languages in general. Several such theoretical models are competing for the allegiance of linguists at the moment: Some focus on the formal linguistic structures underlying words and sentences; others try to account within the grammar for the ways that people can use those structures and for the functions they can be used to serve.

We can see here that a different definition of grammar has developed for linguists, versus the general public and its teachers. For the linguist, grammar refers to the structure of a language, to an area of study that includes the formal description of a language's components and the relationships between these components: the study of the sounds its words are built from (its *phonology*) and the ways its words, in turn, are combined in larger units like sentences (its *syntax*). Modern theories of grammar vary in what they attend to beyond these structures. Some focus on syntactic structures alone, like the Transformational/ Generative Grammar or Universal Grammar associated with the work of American linguist Noam Chomsky; others consider the study of semantics or meaning as well; while still others (like the Functional Grammar associated with Australian linguist, M.A.K. Halliday) look at how the language is structured in relation to the functions it serves as it is used in social contexts. But in all cases, the term as it is used by linguists excludes the study of rules of "correct" usage that are so much the focus of school grammar (though the effect of such notions of correctness is of great interest to sociolinguists, who study the relationship between social roles and the forms speakers use). For the linguist, a grammar offers a descriptive model of language as it is used, rather than a prescriptive model that calls for language to fit established rules and categories. To the modern linguist, nothing that a native speaker says that is understood by others can be considered ungrammatical. Even the "errors" made by second language learners are systematic in a way that shows how the learner has created a coherent grammatical system, an "interlanguage" that functions as a fully grammatical language even though it has forms and structures that do not exist in either the learner's first language or the target language.

Although linguists consider the structure of language, the way the structure operates, and the things the structure and its operation tell us about the nature of language and of the human beings using it, modern linguists are also interested in much that traditional grammar left out, much that is important to a larger understanding of language and its use. This includes the study of how language functions as a mode of communication, a way to get things done in the world, *pragmatics*; how a particular language varies among the different communities that use it, *language variation*; how both first and second languages are acquired and learned, *language acquisition*; and how language is used in, and affected by, social context, *sociolinguistics*. Linguists are also looking at the structure of larger units of language beyond the sentence *(discourse)* in either writing or speaking, focusing on the processes involved in producing and comprehending discourse, and at the social and cultural knowledge the users of particular styles of discourse (members of a discourse community) must share in order to communicate effectively. The study of discourse, *discourse analysis,* is leading to new discoveries about the ways that language works in particular contexts and provides much of the basis of inquiry for this book. Finally, the study of language and our ability to use it necessarily crosses disciplinary boundaries into the fields of psychology, sociology, and anthropology.

Like any formal discipline, linguistics offers both method and theory: formal methodologies for observing, in a systematic way, the workings of real language in the world around us, and scholarly or "scientific" theory that involves (ideally) ongoing inquiry: gathering data, generating hypotheses about those data, testing those hypotheses with the gathering of new data, revising the model that's being created to accommodate bits of data that don't fit an earlier version. Linguistics is unlike our folk theories about language, in that, while folk theories—as rationalizations created for social practices—are rarely challenged or questioned by those who share those practices, it is through questioning, challenging, and reexamination that scholarly theory (again, ideally) comes to provide a more coherent picture of its object. Of course, communities of scholars also share social practices around their research in ways that give them a theoretical bias, but other researchers challenge them in ways that at least lead to ongoing discussion of what those biases are, how they shape what is looked at and what is seen, and what other questions might be asked.

Connecting folk theories, formal knowledge, and experience

Our folk theories do have value, though, in helping us articulate what we think we know about language—as long as we use them as a basis for asking questions rather than asserting answers. If we think, as the Westfield parents did, that children will acquire an accent or even some slightly different phraseology or grammatical constructions from their daily interaction with one adult whose English varies from that of their wider community, and we wonder whether this will affect their learning to read and write, we can ask whether this is really so, and why, or why not. We'll need to learn about speech communities, language acquisition, language variation, and the grammar of a language and how we know it. We'll want to observe the world around us carefully: to see how children use the language they hear around them; to discover the range of styles people draw on and when and how they use them; to find out what it means to be competent in a language, whether that is in the style of a local speech community (a neighborhood, a church) or the style of the school.

If we look at the language we use and the ways we use it with fresh eyes (not our school-jaded eyes) what will we see? To start with, we'll find much evidence that contradicts what our school-based folk theories would say about language and how it is learned. School grammar has suggested that language occurs in discrete bits (subjects, verbs, objects, etc.), that our knowledge of how to put these bits together grammatically is gained through memorizing rules and practicing exercises, that there are correct and incorrect forms and constructions and the ones labeled incorrect in school are inferior and even ungrammatical, and that people who use those forms are illiterate or stupid. We'll discover that the real story about language is quite different. We'll find that language occurs in a fluid whole, that children produce comprehensible grammatical constructions that they've never heard, much less practiced, that people come unconsciously to use the forms that are most effective in establishing their membership in particular communities and in getting things done there, and that none of these naturally occurring forms are inferior for the context in which they naturally appear. We will see that reading and writing are used in many different settings, reflecting many different literacies, and that acquiring the particular literacy practices of any literate community is much like the process of acquiring a language—that it proceeds, to a great extent, unconsciously, through ongoing participation in the community.

We cannot of course discover everything about language through our individual observations. In fact, as with anything that goes on in our minds, we can't observe a person's linguistic knowledge directly, but can only theorize about that knowledge based on what people do in the world. The work of expert theorists and researchers can help us make sense of the world's data. But by observing and questioning we can begin the process of creating a framework that will allow us to understand and begin to use those theories and that research, so that we can evaluate the conflicting opinions of the authorities whom we call on in cases like Westfield's. Such a framework of understanding about language is one which we need as responsible participants in a society that is multicultural and multilingual, a society in which folk theories about language have helped many people to rationalize the displacement of those who have been marginalized in our social and economic structures.

However, it is not enough for me to tell these things to the readers of this book. To become literate *about* language, we'll have to try out new practices, to discover how to look at the data of the world and ask questions about these data, as we begin to build a conceptual framework about language that connects our data and our questions to the findings and theories of others.

The most useful linguistic data to begin with are those that are immediately at hand—those of our daily lives as students, workers, family members, friends. To ask questions of these data, we need also to place these experiences and our understandings of them in the larger context of our past theory-building about language and the things that shaped these theories, to discover what we think we know about language and why.

Some of the data this book will examine and many of the questions it will ask have arisen from my own experience. But they are questions I've heard echoed by others—my students, teachers, and friends in my community. It was a midwestern graduate school professor's embarrassing selection of me, with my Boston accent, to illustrate phonological variants (particularly the glottal stop)—and my desperate attempt to lose that accent over the next few years as fellow students took to calling me "Hey, Boston!"—that led me to wonder why language variation remained so strong in American society, despite the influence of mass media, and to be sensitive to the variation my students brought to the classroom. It was my own excessive concern for correctness, seen not only in my attempt to lose my Boston accent, but also in my own learning of other languages, that shaped some of my questions about the acquisition of a new language or new uses of language. Raising my own children in a racially and socio-economically mixed neighborhood, I was impressed by their fluent control of a number of different styles as they moved from community-center play groups and day care to neighborhood peer activities and in and out of their friends' homes, and I began to study the relationship between language and social context. But above all, my questions have come from my work as a teacher.

For a number of years I have been trying to bridge the gap between the folk theories that I've described and a deeper understanding of language acquisition and social context in my own teaching of freshman writers at an urban university, where students bring a variety of linguistic codes and academic experiences to the classroom. For a long time, knowing that learners acquire most of their important linguistic knowledge unconsciously in an environment that provides rich examples, I concentrated on creating a language-rich classroom where students could engage in real acts of communication, and I ignored "grammar," or any formal study of language entirely (except to provide the information that would help a student with the editing of a final paper). But as I began to look systematically at my students' writing for evidence of their acquisition of the new, written discourse of the academic community (and sometimes for their acquisition of English as a second language as well), I became increasingly interested in the linguistic repertoire they had already acquired—a repertoire that would provide the foundation for whatever they would learn in my classroom. As I found that learning about the power and variety of that repertoire was useful to me, their teacher, I also discovered that becoming conscious of what they already knew was valuable to my students, allowing them to see themselves as fluent rather than deficient in their own language use, and to understand the nature of the process they would go through in acquiring the new discourses of the university. So it made sense for us to begin to study language, and how it was used in the different contexts of our lives together. Over the last ten years, then, with freshmen writers (see Kutz, Groden, and Zamel, *The Discovery of*

Competence 1993), but also in introductory linguistics courses, advanced courses on language and literature, and graduate courses on literacy and discourse analysis, my students and I have collected data about language and have worked together to make sense of what we found there—to learn more about language in the contexts of our lives. What follows is a reflection of that work.

CHAPTER 1

Studying Language in Speech Communities

Let us begin with the most common linguistic data we can find—the conversations that take place among friends in an informal setting. The particular conversations we'll look at involve three young teenaged girls (ages twelve to fourteen) who have grown up on the same street in a racially mixed community and have been close friends since early childhood. From the perspective of where they live, they are members of the same speech community, but each of them belongs to other communities at the same time. They are in different classes, in different schools. Their families belong to different organizations. One family participates actively in a racially mixed church and a wider black community. Another is deeply connected to the father's roots in a white, working class community, a community which provides a center for many of the family's social activities. Five of the six parents have at least a college education; three are teachers.

The conversations Karen, Melanie, and Shanna have are typical for girls their age. They talk about clothes, favorite music, videos, teen stars, stores. They plan their next sleep-overs and shopping trips. They participate in a larger, constantly changing teen culture—one that values, at the moment, 24 hole boots, Luke Perry posters, and MTV videos—while continually negotiating the meaning of that culture in their own world. At the same time, their immediate concerns are framed by references to a wider world: Melanie, for example, is a gymnast, and they dream of her participation and their attendance at the next Olympics. Their language is embedded in a rich communicative and social context.

As the girls sit in my kitchen eating pizza one night, their talk turns to boys. As is often the case, Melanie, who is the oldest, introduces the topic, while Shanna, the youngest, tries to keep up, to assert her place in the conversation. Karen, silent for the moment, occupies a middle ground.

MELANIE: Well anyway . . . OK. I was down . . . I was at the Museum of Science with my mother, right? I saw these f-i-n-e boys. I was like . . . oh my gosh. I was like . . . I wish my mother wasn't here. This boy was so cute . . .

SHANNA: Why? So you could follow them around?

MELANIE: No no no. The one of them was looking at me and probably wanted to get my number but my mother was standing right there smiling. I was like . . . MOM!

SHANNA: What? Did he keep looking at you or something?

MELANIE: Shanna, be quiet! You don't know nothin you're talkin about. Anyway, we're too mature for you.[1]

This brief excerpt is typical of conversational discourse, where participants must try to convey their meanings and take part in a complex social interaction at the same time. Melanie starts, hesitates, revises her thought, and starts again, but she has something she wants to tell, and she keeps her focus. Shanna jumps in, asking questions that are relevant but distracting to Melanie, until finally Melanie addresses these interruptions directly, declaring Shanna's lack of authority and, by implication, asserting her own. There's a larger conversational structure, with speakers who take turns. But these speakers, though they've been friends for a long time, still collide sometimes in their conversations, disagreeing about how long a turn should be and what sorts of interruptions are allowed. Melanie wants to tell a story and to have the other participants remain quiet until she's finished (something Karen implicitly agrees to). Shanna wants to get all of the facts and an explicit interpretation of those facts before the story goes on. Nevertheless, though their conversational styles differ and often clash, they keep finding ways to negotiate those differences and continue the conversation, and that, in itself, is a mark of their competence in carrying out acts of communication.

Here Melanie is engaged in a process of representing her world and the events that have taken place in it, but she is also commenting on it and presenting her attitude toward the event she is describing, while defining herself in relation to it. At the same time, she is signaling a complex set of social meanings and trying to get the others to respond in particular ways. And she's offering what she sees as a coherent narrative that provides just enough information and not too much (though her sense of this is not shared by Shanna, who wants her to be more explicit in explaining the meaning of the events she's describing). She is using the same words—the same stretch of connected discourse—to do all of this at once.

One way of looking at how language works and what speakers like Melanie must know to use it is to consider the functions that language serves in human communication. In *Language as a Social Semiotic* (1978), Halliday describes the functions that language must fulfill in all human cultures, despite differences in the physical environment:

---

1. Excerpts from conversations are represented throughout this book with standard punctuation, with the exception of ellipses (. . .) to indicate longer pauses. For one set of more formal conventions that are commonly used in transcribing speech, see Gumperz 1982a, prefatory note.

1. Language has to interpret the whole of our experience, reducing the indefinitely varied phenomena of the world around us, and also of the world inside us, the processes of our own consciousness, to a manageable number of cases of phenomena: types of processes, events and actions, classes of objects, people and institutions, and the like.
2. Language has to express certain elementary logical relations, like 'and' and 'or' and 'if', as well as those created by language itself such as 'namely', 'says' and 'means'.
3. Language has to express our participation, as speakers, in the speech situation: the roles we take on ourselves and impose on others, our wishes, feelings, attitudes and judgements.
4. Language has to do all of these things simultaneously, in a way which relates what is being said to the context in which it is being said, both to what has been said before and to the 'context of situation'; in other words, it has to be capable of being organized as relevant discourse, not just as words and sentences in a grammar-book or dictionary. (21–22)

Halliday goes on to refer to functions one and two together, as the *ideational* function of language (sometimes called its *propositional/referential* function), the function that allows us to name and make statements about the world. He names *#3* the *interpersonal* (often called the *pragmatic*) function, that which allows us to act, maintain relationships, and place ourselves in the world through language. And he refers to *#4* as the *textual* (or *discourse*) function, that which allows us to carry out each of these functions simultaneously in a discourse context.

Within these generalized functions are many more specific uses of language. For example, language can be used not only to think about the world, but to accomplish a variety of actions like requesting or apologizing, or more generally regulating the behavior of others. We'll look in detail at how the girls build a world of shared ideas and meanings in Chapter Three, the ways they carry out particular acts and intentions with language in Chapter Four, and at how they realize these functions in a coherent text in Chapter Five, seeing what they must be able to do with language to be successful in their most immediate community before turning, in later chapters, to what participants must do to carry out these functions in more public settings like classrooms, and in written texts.

Another way of understanding what speakers like Karen, Melanie, and Shanna must know to be able to engage in any act of communication is to infer, from the sentences they say, the underlying structures of the linguistic system that is available to them and the *grammatical competence* that they must therefore possess as users of the system. That competence—their knowledge of the grammar of their native language and their ability to use its grammatical structures—is mostly unconscious, but clearly present in their conversations. Though they may back up and start a sentence again as they find their direction, they don't construct sentences that sound like nonsense or that seem fundamentally ungrammatical to their listeners. But the grammatical system offers them a great variety of structures that can be used in making any particular statement, and they must be able to choose—from all potential ways of expressing an idea allowed by the grammatical structures of their language—the most appropriate way for the immediate situation they're in: the way that best expresses their own meanings, that's most likely to be understood by their listeners, and that's likely to have the effect they intend. They must also know how to engage in a conversation—how to manage turns and build on what the others say, knowing when it is appropriate to shift styles. So we'll want to discover, as well, something about the girls' *communicative competence*, what they have to know in order to use language appropriately in particular communities of speakers. These two aspects of competence will be the focus of this chapter and the next—the underlying knowledge or potential that is always present but that we can see only a tiny bit of in any actual language act, as language is used for the several functions named above.

W hether we describe what speakers know and can do in terms of these two aspects of competence, or in terms of the functions for which they're using language, the object of our study remains the same, and what we can see through the different lenses will be complementary. In my own study, I began with a focus on grammatical and communicative competence. This helped me to see that the students who came to my freshman writing classrooms (or the classrooms of the public school teachers with whom I've been working) brought competence in the full grammatical and communicative resources of the dialect of their native language used in their home communities. Nothing that these competent language users said or wrote was inherently ungrammatical, but simply appropriate to a different community (an understanding that's explored more fully in Chapter Six). But to understand better the demands that would be placed on my students as they entered into extended discourse in new communities (including the academic discourse community), I drew on Halliday's framework to see the several functions of language that must be carried out simultaneously by a speaker or writer within one text. As I began to analyze the different ways in which these functions were realized in the larger discourse structures that were characteristic of different contexts (such as classrooms at different levels, or in the writing produced in different disciplines) I came to understand more about what speakers and writers had to be able to do to function effectively in these contexts.

These two complementary ways of framing and describing what speakers and writers know and can do are woven throughout this book. But I will begin, in these first two chapters, from the perspective of competence with language, both grammatical and communicative.

Grammatical competence

Karen, Melanie, and Shanna are developing their competence as language users with every interaction, a continuing process that began with their birth. The girls weren't born speaking in words and sentences, nor did they immediately use full grammatical structures of their native language when they began to talk; however, they acquired those structures in a predictable way. For example, as toddlers who were learning to share toys at the baby-sitter's house, Karen and Melanie moved through regular stages in saying no. Although I didn't record these early interactions (and we'll look in the next chapter at some my students did record) the pattern of development would have been a regular one, in which they first put the negative in the initial position in the sentence *No take Karen's truck;* then put the negative between the subject and verb *Melanie not take Karen's truck;* and finally placed it in the standard position after the first auxiliary verb, (such as the auxiliary do) *Don't take my truck.*

Over the same period, of course, they were acquiring other features of the linguistic system, such as pronouns. And they used these structures to produce sentences they would not have heard from those around them. This early linguistic competence has led many linguists, particularly Noam Chomsky, to theorize that we are born with much of our ability to process language—that our brains are structured with much language competence built in, waiting to be activated through use in communication. Where similar structures appear in different languages, they appear at roughly the same time in a child's development, and from this it appears that the capacity to understand and use these structures is an innate and universal feature of the human brain. Chomsky refers to his theory as Universal Grammar.

There is a debate about how much actual learning is involved in activating or developing this linguistic competence. Some developmental psycholinguists have argued that the child does actively, though unconsciously, *learn* language. The child receives rich data from her social and cultural context; that is, she hears language spoken, and from what she hears is able to infer the rules. But Chomsky argues that the data received can never be rich enough to account for all of the language that the child knows. For instance, early on the child has a great deal of knowledge about negative features of language—syntactic constructions that would not be used, that are ungrammatical—while having heard very few of these unacceptable constructions. Such evidence leads Chomsky to theorize that language is not learned wholly by deducing rules from the language data received, but that there must be some form of preexisting language mechanism in the brain, whose parameters can be set on the basis of relatively little selected information. (Halliday and other functionalist grammarians, would add that it is in our *use* of language that we find the origins of grammatical categories and structures—that the structures aren't arbitrary but arose out of common human needs to use language to perform particular functions, and that this process is replicated in the child's language learning.)

Although much of the girls' potential linguistic competence may have been innate, this potential would not have been realized if they hadn't been involved, through their early years, in actual human communication. Like other children, Karen, Melanie, and Shanna were part of a world of language from their earliest moments, a world of parents, aunts, uncles, grandmothers, siblings, cousins, and playmates.

Because virtually all children grow up in language-rich environments, it is hard to imagine what they would be like if raised in a world without language, but we do have some accounts of feral children who were somehow separated from human society when they were very young and were most likely cared for along with the young of some animal like a wolf. In one famous case, that of the wild boy of Aveyron (whose story was told in Francois Truffaut's movie *Wild Child*), a twelve-year-old boy was found in 1800 in southern France, with scars that indicated that someone must have cut his throat and left him to die when he was a baby. He had no language when he was found, and though, with intensive teaching he learned to spell out words with alphabet letters, he never learned to talk (Itard 1962).

A more recent and disturbing case was that of Genie, a girl who was locked in a room from infancy, fed but not talked to, and not discovered until she was thirteen. With a careful program of instruction over several years she gained increased cognitive functioning (as measured by standard intelligence tests) and a fairly extensive vocabulary. Over time, she became able to string words together, but she was never able to acquire the full syntactic structures of the language (such as the rules for forming tenses or showing plurals or possessives), and her speech remained like that of a very young child who says "Me big boy" (See Curtiss 1977; Rymer 1993). Studies of Genie seemed to refine Chomsky's evolving theory showing that if there is an inbuilt human linguistic competence, it must be brought out during a critical period of a child's development. During this period, those structures that are part of the child's native language seem to be activated as others talk to the child, and they become part of the child's underlying language competence.

The stories of feral children and Genie may illustrate something about our innate grammatical potential and the period in which this must be activated, but they also point out that language development takes place only in human communities, in the child's interaction with others. Grammatically developed language appears in all human communities, even in situations where there would seem to be barriers to communication. In deaf communities all over the world, sign languages have evolved—languages that have now been discovered to carry all of the grammatical resources of spoken languages (Bellugi 1980). Hearing children who are born to deaf parents may not hear much spoken language in their earliest childhood, but they learn to sign as a first language. Since sign languages reproduce spatially the full grammatical structures and categories of human language, these structures are activated and wholly available when hearing children later learn spoken language. For deaf children of signing parents, the linguistic resources are the same, ready to be transferred to the production and reading of written versions of spoken languages. But often deaf children of hearing parents have been deprived of this critical early communication if their parents have not learned to sign, and these children may have more problems in developing their full linguistic competence.

Recent work with other children who might seem to be linguistically deprived—autistic children and others with communication disorders—shows the power of existing within a world of communication for language development, even when the child does not seem to be a direct participant. Using Facilitated Communication methods, in which an adult supports the child's use of a keyboard or letter board, even some children thought to be profoundly retarded have been found able to use literacy as a means of communication—and to have learned, from hearing language spoken around them, to produce rich and syntactically developed language in writing (see Biklen 1993).

Another kind of unusual language acquisition experience has occurred for whole groups of children in areas of the world where large numbers of speakers of different languages were brought together to provide labor in a new place, and it further supports the idea that some sort of predisposition to create grammatical structures is part of being human. In such settings—places like the islands of the Caribbean, Cape Verde, Hawaii—immigrants from different language backgrounds learned to communicate with each other quickly through use of a pidgin.

In a pidgin, the words of one language (usually that of the dominant group, most often the colonizers) are used in very rudimentary combinations that are based on the syntactic structures from different native languages, so that a Filipino speaker of English pidgin might say the equivalent of "Work hard these people," while a speaker who had come from Japan says, "These people hard work" (in Japanese, the verb is often placed at the end of a sentence). Unlike natural languages, pidgins vary in syntax as they are used by different speakers who bring different native languages to one setting. While they work well enough for communicating simple information, they are hard to use for expressing complex ideas; pidgins have only a simple grammar, with few articles, prepositions, auxiliary verbs, and no subordinate clauses.

But something amazing happens to the children of immigrant pidgin speakers who grow up in a community where the adults around them speak many different languages, but much communication takes place in pidgin, where their parents may be native speakers of different languages who use pidgin to communicate. According to linguist Derek Bickerton, these children actually seem to create full new languages from the pidgin base—creole languages that have all of the syntactic features of other natural languages. Bickerton (1981) has carried out extensive studies of the creoles that have developed in different parts of the world, including the creole that developed in Hawaii among the first generation of children born there after a major wave of immigration around 1900. Although the working-class Hawaiian immigrants all spoke some form of pidgin, their children born in Hawaii spoke a uniform Hawaiian creole, with complex verb tenses and all of the other features of a full grammar.

Bickerton argues that such full creole languages could not develop in just one generation if it were not for an actual inbuilt grammatical model common to all children. He finds further evidence for such a model in the fact that different creole languages, which have developed among different populations and on different language bases in different parts of the world, have some key grammatical features in common (as do sign languages)—particular features that may not exist in any language contributing to the creole environment, but that often exist in children's linguistic structures. One such feature, a negative subject combined with a negative verb as in "Nobody don't like me," is commonly used by children, even though it doesn't typically appear in the language of adults, except in creoles and in some dialects. Bickerton hypothesizes that "It was only in pidgin-speaking communities, where there was no grammatical model that could compete with the child's innate grammar, that the innate grammatical model was not eventually suppressed. The innate grammar was then clothed in whatever vocabulary was locally available and gave rise to the creole languages heard today" (1981, 147). Children everywhere realize or discover a version of a common human grammar as others speak to them and carry on conversations around them, without any explicit teaching about grammatical rules.

Communicative competence

While Chomsky's work has focused exclusively on the grammatical underpinnings of linguistic competence, other researchers, particularly sociolinguists, have been interested in the ways people learn to use these grammatical structures in order to communicate in real settings, what Dell Hymes (1972) has described as "communicative competence." While Chomsky focused his attention on describing the syntactic structures and rules that constitute the grammatical resources of an adult speaker of the language, Hymes and others have looked at the ways in which these linguistic resources are used differently in different social contexts, studying the sociolinguistic principles that lead people to use language in ways appropriate to the styles of communication in different communities, and to do so flexibly, in response to a range of intentions and purposes.

Because Karen, Melanie, and Shanna acquired the grammatical structures of English through hearing speech in ordinary family and community contexts, they also inferred the rules for how to actually use this language in these contexts. There were different rules for how to refer to adults, for example. Some adults, like the baby-sitter, Annie, were to be called by their first names. Others were referred to as Mr. or Mrs., others by kinship terms like aunt or uncle, whether or not they were actual relatives. The rules weren't consistent— Melanie knew that Karen's parents were Ellie and Ron, but the parents of another friend were Mr. and Mrs. Roberts. Yet somehow the girls grew up knowing what terms to use when, what words could be said with friends but not with parents, or with parents but not with grandparents. They learned, early on, how to take turns in conversation, how long a turn they could expect to have with their baby-sitter Annie or with their parents or with a sibling, and when they might interrupt. Sometimes they learned these things through explicit instruction: "Wait your turn," "Say 'Please!' " "This is Mr. Hunter." But much more of their knowledge of how to communicate in particular situations was acquired naturally and unconsciously.

At the same time, much of the language the girls received from the adults around them was appropriate. That is, while their general language environment was rich in its variety of forms and expression, some of the elements of the environment were selected and focused for them by adults. Studies of motherese or caretaker language have highlighted several common features of adults' communication with children that were part of the girls' early language experiences (see Snow 1977). One is that the adult caretakers elicit language, in early years, by focusing on the child and on things in the immediate environment that are of interest to the child: Our neighborhood sitter, Annie, always greeted the children who arrived at her house each day with talk about the clothes they were wearing, the toys they brought, and the food they'd be having for snack. Adults are also likely to repeat and extend the child's utterances, validating them and showing how they might be extended. Karen and Melanie took particular delight in running full speed down the block to greet whatever parent was arriving home from work, screaming "Daddy home" or "Mommy home" in unison, while leaping together into the Mommy's or Daddy's arms in a tangle of limbs. The utterance "Daddy home" might have been a wish or a demand or a question, but it was always treated as a genuine act of communication deserving a real response from the other parent: "Is Daddy home now? Should I open the door?" At the same time, adults typically focus their attention on the meaning, not the form of a child's words. If Melanie said, "Me want Daddy," her mother would not reply, "Wrong, say *I* not *me*," but would continue the conversation, finding out why Melanie wanted her father or explaining that he wouldn't be home until later. And finally, adults respond to these genuine conversational interactions with delight in the child's expanding linguistic ability, and with further conversation. Upon her father's arrival, Melanie's mother was likely to say: "Melanie's been waiting for you all afternoon. Melanie, tell your father what you told me about what happened at Annie's today. What happened at Annie's?" encouraging Melanie to continue using language to comment on the world around her.

The patterns of caretaker communication described here are typical of middle-class English-speaking parents in the United States. Different cultures, with differing expectations of the child's participation in conversation, have different patterns of parent-child linguistic interactions, as did the Cape Verdean and the Haitian families on our block. But the focus of attention in all parent-child interactions is on meaningful communication rather than grammatical forms, and all children learn to use their home language correctly and appropriately without being aware of its rules. In other words, language acquisition takes place within the normal cultural and social patterns for child-adult conversational interaction within a particular community, and virtually all children grow up to be competent language users within their communities, knowing not only the grammatical structures of their dialect, but also all of the complex rules for its social use.

Speech communities are formed in settings like families or churches or workplaces, where people come together over long periods of time and develop particular ways of using language to interact with one another. Children learn the ways that language is used within their own home communities, and if they move among different communities—as Melanie did between the home of her white working-class baby-sitter, her black middle-class family, and the larger community of a racially mixed Baptist church; or as Karen did as she attended services with Melanie, with her Catholic grandmother, or with her Methodist minister grandfather—they learn to shift their ways of using language to suit the many different styles of the communities in which they participate. Through such genuine interactions, in different speech communities, they enhance their communicative competence.

Speech communities

As linguists began to focus on communicative competence—on the ways that people use language in particular social contexts—the differing demands of different communities of language users became more apparent. Studies of language variation focus on the different forms produced by speakers of the same language who come from different regions or from different social classes. Melanie's mother, having been raised in the South, still says bucket when I say pail, and pronounces aunt in the same way as ant. Distinct speech communities have been shaped by the relative isolation or separation of groups of speakers from each other—most obviously by geography, but also by social class, and by racial or ethnic background. As such social and geographical isolation breaks down (particularly as people move from one region to another) people often maintain aspects of their home language (especially pronunciation and vocabulary) as a way of holding onto important aspects of their identity. As a graduate student in the Midwest, I worked hard to lose certain aspects of my Boston accent: to put *r*'s in appropriate places in words and not to put them in where they were not commonly expected. But I held onto my New England pronunciation of "aunt," never wanting to merge the people I loved with the name of an insect I disliked, though this continued to mark me as an outsider.

While the language of different speech communities may be distinguished by the words that are used or the ways they are pronounced, it is also distinguished by the sorts of subjects talked about, by who gets to ask and answer questions, by what things are stated explicitly and what implications might be understood. Speech communities are formed anywhere that people come together on a regular basis and develop characteristic ways of using language—in schools and workplaces and churches as well as in homes and neighborhoods. The term can also be applied to professional communities that carry on their conversations in writing, through newsletters and journals, though the more inclusive term *discourse community,* covering both spoken and written discourse, is usually used to refer to such contexts.

One of the most extensive studies of what it means to grow up in different speech communities, which have their own characteristic ways of using language, is described in Shirley Brice Heath's *Ways with Words*. Heath studied the ways in which language was used in three different speech communities in the Piedmont area of the Carolinas: a rural white community, a rural black community, and a community made up of middle-class townspeople, both white and black. Participating in the lives of members of these communities over a period of ten years, she observed the ways they communicated with each other and with their children—their communicative competence, or "ways with words."

Heath's ethnographic study provides a detailed picture of the way in which all aspects of a community's life and values are extended and reinforced in its members' linguistic behavior, both oral and literate. She argues that "the place of language in the cultural life of each social group is interdependent with the habits and values of behaving shared among members of the group" (1983, 11). Particular ways of using language are part of the process of "gettin' on" in these communities, and these ways are shared by the community's adults and learned by the children.

In the rural white community of Roadville, the adults typically gather in each other's living rooms or at church for scheduled events like Bible study, or else talk on the phone. The Bible stories they study provide models for their own talk, as they offer factual accounts of events that happened and follow these with the moral of the story or the lesson that they learned. Adults in the rural black community of Trackton are more likely to gather on their front porches in a rather free-flowing and unscheduled way, sharing gossip and stories. Verbal cleverness and invention (talkin' junk) are rewarded. Nobody's much interested in the facts alone but rather in the way they're told, and many stories, though they're called "true stories," begin in reality but take off into high fantasy. And Maintowners, both black and white, tend to gather in organized groups (tennis clubs, town councils, and voluntary associations) with formal rules and processes. They identify themselves as having mainstream values and behaviors, defining these with reference to a larger society outside of their immediate community—the American middle class—and their views are shaped not as much by telephone or front porch conversations as by the public media and by the books they read.

As Roadville children are "brought up" by their parents, they are *taught*, explicitly, the ways of the community from babyhood (though they would acquire these patterns unconsciously even without explicit instruction): "We learned at church and at home too that things were either *right* or *wrong*; you did things the *right* way and you were *right*; you did wrong or said wrong and everybody *knew* it was wrong" (143). They're taught not to interrupt or question adults but to speak when spoken to, to recite in response to adult questions with information that's requested (their names, the alphabet, prayers and Bible verses, factual accounts of events) and no more. On the other hand, Trackton children are said to "come up" rather than being "brought up," suggesting that the process is less under parental control, and they *learn* from observing and participating rather than being told explicitly many of the ways of their communities. In fact, children in Trackton have to learn to speak up aggressively and to be clever and creative, in order to get adult attention. But Maintown children are involved in conversations with their parents from babyhood, encouraged not only to answer questions, but to ask their own questions as well, to respond to and make up stories, to connect their own experiences with the experiences described in books, to think not only about what things are called but also about how they work.

The language practices of these communities extend to the ways they use written texts—reading them as a representation of external authority to be turned to for the "right" answers (Roadville); working out their meaning through oral reading and communal discussion based on personal experience (Trackton); or seeing them as a source of others' authority and knowledge that can be questioned and interpreted based on one's own knowledge, that can be used for many purposes, for pleasure as well as information, and that can be written as well as read (Maintown). Maintown ways of using both spoken and written language turn out to be very similar to school ways (not surprising, since most teachers identify themselves as members of the mainstream community), and Maintown children, like middle-class children everywhere, generally have an easy transition from home to school. (We'll look at school language and at classroom discourse practices in a later chapter.) But Maintown ways of communicating are not inherently better than those of the other communities; they are just different.

Heath's study shows how distinctive the ways of a speech community may be, even from those of a neighboring community. But in urban areas, people who may have grown up in communities whose language practices are much like those in Roadville, Trackton, or Maintown are likely to move in and out of a number of smaller and overlapping speech communities in their daily lives, shifting their styles and switching their ways of using language as they step from one to another. Karen, Melanie, and Shanna, for example, are part of a neighborhood peer group of teenage girls that is mixed by race and class. They bring some of the features of their home practices to their conversations, but they're involved in a constant process of negotiating these differences. Their language also has a number of distinct features that are part of a larger teen culture (for example, the word *like*). Though the girls carry out their conversations in standard English, they may occasionally shift into one of the variations allowed by a dialect.

In the segment of conversation that begins this chapter, Melanie shows her exasperation with Shanna by switching to Black English (You don't know nothin you're talkin about) with its characteristic pronunciation and intonation as well as a particular syntactic feature—a double negative. As we'll see, these are regular and grammatical linguistic features in Black English, and the variety of English Melanie shifts to here is part of the repertoire of most participants in a larger black culture, one that they can draw on to assert common bonds and create a kind of intimacy. Karen often echoes such shifts in intimate conversations with Melanie, her best friend. But she confided to me one night: "I worry that some of the other kids won't like it." As a white child, growing up in a racially mixed neighborhood, Karen has picked up the subtle nuances of what is appropriate in different groups of peers.

The girls' style is also distinguishable from the boys' style that Karen's and Melanie's older brothers (who were also close friends) used at the same age—a style heavily influenced by rap music and black street language, with common obscenities punctuating pauses and filling much the same linguistic function as the girls' recurrent "like." It's different, as well, from the more distinct dialects of their parents' home communities, which were separated by region (South, North, East, West, Midwest) as well as by race. At the same time, the girls move in and among several other speech communities, some distinguished by race and class, some by education or parents' professional associations, some by their family's roots, both regional and social. With each of these moves they use language in ways that show their membership in those communities, just as they switch from jeans to dresses, from sneakers to 24 hole combat boots, with subtle but precise variations along the way.

Like Karen, Melanie, and Shanna, the students in my classes come from many different home speech communities, and they typically move through several others during the course of a day. They've grown up in different neighborhoods of Boston or have come to Boston from other parts of the United States or from other countries. They bring a variety of ethnic backgrounds and some differences in social class. Some are raising families of their own. Many work in fast-food restaurants, grocery stores, offices, as policemen, heating contractors, teachers, or teachers' aids. They socialize in different groups, sometimes single sex groups of young men drinking beer on a Friday night, or young women shopping, or in couples or extended families. All are members of the particular academic community that makes up our university, but within that academic community they take courses in different disciplines, each of which has its own terminology and style of discourse. And they have different educational goals, from working slowly toward an undergraduate degree to planning for law school, teaching, or enriching an already defined working life through the study of literature, philosophy, or political science. At the beginning of each semester, we tape-record conversations that go on in one or more of the speech communities we regularly spend time in, just as I recorded the conversation that took place between my daughter and her friends as they were sitting around my kitchen table eating pizza. We transcribe the conversations we've recorded and create a common collection of these many different exchanges, with their many different participants—from toddlers to grandparents in different relationships, from intimate parent-child exchanges to the sorts of public but often casual mini-conversations that take place in a checkout line.

The worlds my students bring into the classroom in this way are very different, but also quite similar. Each small community might have a different way of expressing meanings and getting things done with words, even different conventions about who gets to speak and who should listen and for how long, or about what can be talked about and what words can be used to talk about it, but each of these communities has *some* way of doing these things, and from the exploration of the differences comes an understanding of the commonalities as well. We are all insiders to some communities and outsiders to others. Discovering the nature of our knowledge as insiders can help us to develop strategies for moving outside of our primary communities and into new ones. Discovering the nature of others' knowledge about language and how to use it in the communities to which they are insiders and we are outsiders can help us to see the way it is, in substance and function if not in surface details, like our own. Though our studies of speech communities may sometimes highlight differences, those differences can help us to understand commonalities as well, the ways in which the things we all know as human beings and language users can support a concept of a common language that does not deny our differences but that includes and transcends them.

CHAPTER 2

Acquiring Language

It's Saturday morning, and the students in my sophomore course have spread out across the city in search of young children (under the age of five) to record, with tape recorder or pencil, their typical utterances. Eliot stops by to see his ten-month-old granddaughter. Zina turns on the tape recorder, grabs a book, and sits down with her grandchildren, a boy and a girl, ages one-and-a-half and four. Sue goes into a downtown toy store, explains her class assignment to a mother who comes in with a boy of about fifteen months, and with the mother's permission, positions herself to discretely record their interactions. Stephanie baby-sits for a two-year-old. Melissa pays a visit to her young friend Elyssa, also two. Justine spends the morning bathing and playing with her three-year-old son, Matthew. David drops in on some Spanish-speaking friends whose three-and-a-half-year-old daughter is bilingual in Spanish and English. Stan spends a couple of hours at a fast-food restaurant, carefully noting the exchanges of several groups of parents and kids who sit in the booth next to his, particularly some four-to-five-year-olds. And I have a phone conversation with my two-year-old nephew and five-year-old niece. On Monday, we have data from more than twenty-five children to bring to our discussion: recordings of their actual utterances, accounts of the interactions in which these utterances were spoken, and descriptions of the contexts in which those interactions took place. As we share our data we can see that the older children use more actual words in their communication and demonstrate a greater range of communicative strategies. But we also see the beginnings of these communicative strategies in the interactions of the youngest, even pre-verbal children with those around them. Children may have an innate propensity toward grammatical structuring that allows them to acquire easily the grammatical structures of their native language, but that latent ability can only be realized in the context of actual language use, and it is within particular ways of using language—as children acquire communicative competence—that all grammatical competence is shown.

We can see both aspects of a child's competence in Justine's transcription of a typical exchange that has taken place a few nights earlier between herself and her son Matthew:

MOTHER: It's time to put your toys away.
MATT: Not time put toys way . . . play trucks!

MOTHER: You can play with your trucks tomorrow, right now you have to
   get ready for bed.

MATT: Not go bed. . . . Play trucks!

MOTHER: Matthew, mama said *now*.

MATT: Just go a—way.

MOTHER: Don't tell mama to go away . . . you have to put your toys away so
   you can have a bath and get ready for bed.

MATT: Don't want take baf now.

MOTHER: Matthew!! It's almost eight o'clock and you have to go to bed so
   you can wake up and go to school tomorrow.

MATT: Go see Nana?

MOTHER: Maybe after school we can go see Nana. Now help me clean up.

MATT: Baf time. [*He starts to leave the room.*]

MOTHER: Matthew, you have to help pick up your toys first.

MATT: O.K. Time clean up guys. [*Picks up toys.*]

MOTHER: Good job. Mama loves you. Now we can have a bath and then I'll
   read you a story.

MATT: My goodnight book.

MOTHER: We always read that one.

MATT: "When mummy says it's time for bed I go upstairs and get undressed."

MOTHER: You are so smart, sit down so mama can take your shoes off.

MATT: Baf time.

MOTHER: That's right . . . *bath* time. Let's get these dirty clothes off so we can
   go and take a bath.

MATT: Baf time, Baf time [*jumping on the bed*].

MOTHER: Sit down so I can take off your clothes.

MATT: Gimme a huggie.

MOTHER: I love you to pieces.

MATT: I wuv you too mama.

Justine is a young mother whose son was born prematurely and was diagnosed
as having a "Global Development Delay." He began to speak later than her
friends' children, and they seem to Justine to show greater linguistic competence. Because of this, Justine finds that she's very careful about how she talks
to him, always speaking to him in complete sentences, giving him full explanations for her requests, letting him finish his thought before she responds, and
often repeating what he says if he mispronounces a word like *baf*. But she worries that she might be too careful and overly corrective.

   As parents, we are likely to hold different models of how our children get
to speak the language we speak, drawn largely from the beliefs of those around
us. We've seen from Heath's study that Trackton parents see their children as
not able to understand much and not able to participate in conversations until
they're quite verbal, whereas Maintown parents treat their children as conversational partners from the very beginning, though they use somewhat abbreviated syntax and altered intonation with them, and Roadville parents more often

direct a special "baby talk" to the child. Bambi Schieffelin (1990) has studied Kaluli children in New Guinea, whose mothers *teach* them to speak by holding the babies up in front of them and speaking for the child in high, nasal voice, while moving the child as if it's conversing. Nancy Smith Hefner (1988) has studied a similar pattern among the Javanese, where mothers model a special child language register that's very complex morphologically and lexically—a register that includes intricate forms of the polite honorifics that Javanese children are expected to use in addressing adults (who have greater status in the society). These beliefs and practices have little to do with children's acquisition of their native language, but a lot to do with cultural norms for how adults should behave toward their children in this regard.

Children are seen by most linguists as coming to the adult language through a process of *acquisition*—a process that is subconscious and occurs without explicit teaching. Some, like Chomsky, believe that the process of being exposed to a native language allows the realization of a grammatical potential that's genetic and independent of any particular knowledge of the world. Others, like Halliday, argue that the initial forms, at least, of a child's language are determined by functions for which the child (in a social context) is using language, though these forms are eventually restructured to fit the syntactic patterns of the adult language (patterns which could still be innately preset). From either perspective, it seems clear that children *acquire* the grammar of their language and most of their implicit knowledge of its use unconsciously, as they hear and increasingly take part in verbal interactions, rather than *learn* it consciously through explicit teaching. Justine's corrections of *baf* are unlikely to have any effect on Matt's pronunciation, nor would an attempt to turn "Not go bed" into "I don't want to go to bed" be successful. As his phonetic articulatory system develops, Matt will be able to pronounce *th*, and as he refines his unconscious understanding of how to form negatives, he'll be able to say, "I don't want to go to bed," no matter what his mother does now. He will catch up with his peers in the grammatical structures he can produce. But by involving Matt in conversations like these, Justine is helping him acquire and practice a style of discourse (involving full sentences and elaborated explanations) that will be important to his membership in the particular discourse community they belong to. Already she feels that his ability to communicate—his communicative competence—is "pretty good."

As children acquire their language, they are unaware of either the complex rules they've acquired or the acquisition process itself. Yet they are able, over a short time, to generate grammatical forms that show a deep understanding of the complex rules governing language (rules that linguists are still trying to work out), so that they can generate an infinite number of correct utterances that they've never heard before. Over time, they seem to formulate hypotheses about the grammar of the language as well as its uses, test these out, and then revise them. Although many of their early constructions don't match the adult grammar of their language, at any moment the grammatical system they're constructing is internally consistent and much like that of other children. In fact, many features of that early grammar, like its forms of negation, are similar across children's versions of different languages, and they are also common to the creoles created by children who are born into a language contact situation where the only language available to them is a pidgen that does not have an elaborate grammar. Children's acquisition of grammar is regular and systematic, and all children (even across languages) go through similar stages of production and attend to similar features at roughly the same age, creating a grammatical system that they keep revising until it matches the unique features of their native language. And this system is not responsive to adult correction or explicit instruction.

At the same time, children are learning how to use this evolving grammatical system to produce language that allows them to communicate with those around them. In fact, in most of their real communicative contexts, it matters very little that the grammar they are constructing is not yet complete from the perspective of the adult language. From very early on, they are able to use even one- and two-word constructions to interact with others, to make their intentions and purposes known, to comment on the world around them, and to contribute to an evolving text—to carry out the several functions for which all language is used. They acquire strategies that are appropriate to these functions, and communicative competence as participants in a social world that's at least partly constructed through language. In this communicative world, the focus of the participants is on the meaning of utterances, not on their surface forms, and Matt can negotiate about picking up toys, taking baths, and reading books with his mother perfectly well, even though he doesn't produce what she considers correct sentences. So it matters little that children are still refining their grammar once they're perceived as producing language that's intentional and meaningful, though that moment varies across cultures. (For the Kaluli, according to Schieffelin, it occurs only when the child begins to use two significant words— *mother* and *breast*.)

Grammatical competence and communicative competence aren't separable elements of children's language, but are acquired together through the ongoing interaction of the child with other participants in a particular social context. But because linguists have typically approached the study of child language from one perspective or the other, these two perspectives offer us clearly defined frameworks for describing what we see.

Grammatical competence

When my students and I look at the grammatical structures represented in the data we've collected, two things strike us: First, children of about the same age do show real similarities in the linguistic structures they use, and from our own data we can get a sense of what extended studies of children's language acquisition (following the same child over months and years) have shown—that there are similar patterns to the development or realization of grammatical competence for all native speakers of a language. Second, the amount of language that children can use productively and the complexity of their working grammatical system increases rapidly with their age. The most obvious variations from the adult system that we see among children of different ages appear in the sounds they produce and the sorts of syntactic structures they use.

Sounds

Children attend to the sounds of the language spoken around them early on. Most noticeable in young children is their responsiveness to the patterns of *into-nation* used by those around them. Eliot's grandchild, at ten months, is the youngest of the children this class observes. Although she seems to still be in a preverbal, babbling stage, she already shows the patterns of intonation that are characteristic of adult utterances: the rising intonation of questions (*o-a-a?* about a new food) or the falling contour of statements (*e-y-a-a!* when her grandmother points to the toy she is holding and asks: "What is that?"). In other words, like other young babies in the babbling stage (before they produce distinguishable words) she has already begun to acquire the information contours of the adult language. These information contours allow children to indicate the nature of an utterance, such as a question, long before they've acquired the full syntactic structure of that utterance, helping adults to interpret early babbling and to understand whether a reduced utterance like "Mommy book" is a command for the Mommy to read the book (typically shown by a falling intonation contour) or a question about possession "Is this Mommy's book?" (typically shown with a rising contour). When Matthew says "Baf time," his falling intonation shows that he is accepting his mother's version of what will happen next, not question-ing it as he might with a rising intonation.

Throughout most of their first year, children are equally responsive to the whole range of sounds that humans can articulate—the whole *phonetic* system. *Phonetics* refers to the study of all of the sounds that have been identified as occurring in language. Any language uses only some portion of the sounds it is possible to make with the human articulatory system. Different languages use different sounds and allow different combinations. (The International Phonetic Alphabet, which was created as a mechanism for recording accurately the sounds of all of the world's languages has many symbols for sounds that are not used in English. I'll use its symbols when the focus of our attention is on the articulation of different sounds, but for most of our transcriptions, my students use variations of conventional spelling to represent the sounds they hear.) Some languages, including many African languages, add tongue clicks to the sounds we perceive as meaningful in most European languages. Others, particularly Asian languages, add variations in tone, so that the word *ma* in the Mandarin dialect of Chinese, intoned in a higher or lower register, can mean *mother* or *horse* or *scold* or *hemp*. As nonspeakers of the !Kung language, my freshmen and I understand intellectually when we read Marjorie Shostak's book about a !Kung woman, *Nisa*, that when we say *Kung* without the preceding tongue click (represented orthographically as "!") we are saying a different word, not the real name of the African tribe. But we find it hard to perceive the click as necessary to the word. As a nonspeaker of Chinese, I don't perceive variations in tone as signaling different words with different meanings, but my son, who is studying Chinese, is learning to make these distinctions.

The sounds we use in English can be described in terms of where in the mouth and throat they are made, whether we actually use our voice in producing them, or whether we stop the flow of air or just control it in some way, etc. A thorough knowledge of the phonetic articulatory system is very important for the speech therapist who is trying to help a child learn to produce a sound correctly by helping her to use the appropriate combination of articulatory mechanisms. But it's the concept of the *phoneme*, a sound difference that is meaningful within a language because it distinguishes one word from another (as /d/ and /p/ distinguish "dig" and "pig"), which matters most to the questions that arise in our study of speech communities. (*Phonemics* refers to the representation of the sounds that are meaningful in a given language and there are some forty-four or forty-five such sounds in English.) The concept of the phoneme depends on our *perception* of differences between sounds (and we don't perceive all possible differences as meaningful). *Dig* is not a *pig* is not *big* because /d/, /p/, and /b/ represent different phonemes in English—they indicate differences in meaning. Although the sounds by themselves aren't meaningful, when they're combined with other meaningful sound-concepts like /i/ and /g/, a difference in this one phoneme represents a difference in the meaning of a word.

Babies up to about nine months will respond to many different articulated sounds, but suddenly, when they are about a year old, they stop attending to every spoken sound and notice only those sounds that are phonemes in the language spoken around them, noticing only those distinctive contrasts between sounds (like /p/ and /b/ in English) that can, by themselves, distinguish one word from another (*pat* and *bat*). It will be a long time still before they can actually produce accurately the full range of phonetic articulations of those phonemes, and they're likely to say *dat* for *that* and *fruck* for *truck*. By the time babies begin to speak words that others understand, they have refined their own phonological system to include only the phonemes of the language (or languages) they hear, and they'll accurately perceive the phonemic distinctions that others make and insist on them in their conversations with adults. Students of linguist Roger Brown (*A First Language*, 1973) tell the story of a time when he was talking to a child who referred to a "fis." Brown wasn't quite sure what the child meant to say, so he repeated *fis,* to which the child responded indignantly **fis.** This exchange was repeated several times before Brown tried *fish* and finally got an affirmative response from the child. (Children typically see adults who try to mimic their own early pronunciation as speaking either nonsense or baby talk, responding, in the latter case, with "I'm not a baby.")

Adults interacting with children in such exchanges usually do a better job than Brown did in understanding the child's meaning, at least when the potentially confusing word is embedded in a larger utterance. Part of what allows us to understand children whose pronunciation is different from that of adults is our own ability to perceive the important phonemic distinctions in a language and to ignore differences in their phonetic representation (in actual pronunciation) whether spoken by different speakers, in different social/geographical settings, or in different word contexts (whether the phoneme comes at the beginning, middle, or end of a word, and what other sounds surround it). Because some elements of the phonetic articulatory system are harder to master than others, a child may still say *d* (/d/) for *th* (/ð/) but if the child says "da book, da boat," regularly using *d* in contexts where the adult would say *th* we can surmise that the child perceives the *th* phoneme and the meaning distinction between words like *then* and *den* even though he is not able represent this distinction in his own speech. Our unconscious knowledge of the phonological system of our language allows us to filter out such variations as we process the meaning of utterances, and to communicate across them.

Justine sees her son Matthew's pronunciation of words as being affected by both the development of his phonetic articulatory system and the regional accent he is acquiring.

> He is able to perceive several phonemes of his native language (English) that he is not yet able to accurately produce. For example, he understands me when I say *bath,* but he says *baf*. He also has difficulty with the letter *a* at the beginning of a word when it has the *ah* sound. He understands me when I say *away* yet when he tries to reproduce this word he either drops the *a* entirely and says *way* or he pronounces it as two separate words *a* (with a long *a*) and *way*. The most obvious distinction to me however is Matthew's use of the letter *r*. Until recently he played *twucks,* he now plays *trucks*. Yet when the *r* is at the end of a word, Matthew drops it completely and pronounces *car* as *ka*. I know that this is regional in origin, because the rest of my family says it too.

The physical development that supports children's ability to phonetically reproduce the full range of sounds of their language seems to vary quite a bit, and it's not unusual for children to have particular difficulty with some sounds. This difficulty may persist into school age and ultimately require speech therapy. But their underlying linguistic competence is shown by their early recognition of the phonemic system that allows them to understand the significant sound distinctions made by others.

Syntax

Although there's some variation in the age at which children begin to say words or combinations of words, all children move through the same stages as they begin to put words together—to acquire the syntax of their native language. In our working model of language (our folk model) sounds combine to form words and words combine to form sentences. The concepts of the word and the sentence also provide a useful starting point for looking at the next level of the child's developing linguistic system. In describing the grammar of a language, linguists use two levels of description. One focuses on words and parts of words, or *morphemes*, the minimal units that in themselves carry meaning in a language (*morphology* is the study of such units). These can be divided into lexical morphemes (those that contain the basic content being expressed, nouns, verbs, adjectives, and adverbs) and grammatical or functional morphemes (those that show relationships between lexical morphemes and carry meaning about the grammatical relationships within a sentence, e.g., articles, prepositions, conjunctions). A second level of description focuses on the ways in which words (or combinations of morphemes) can be grouped together into phrases, clauses, and sentences, and is commonly referred to as *syntax*. But a grammatical concept such as possession may be represented by either the form of a word (the *girl's* book) or by a particular grouping of words (the book *of the girl*) and our understanding of the syntax of a language depends simultaneously on both levels of description. To see the many choices of wording available to adult speakers of English, we will need to know more about English syntax (see Chapter Five), but these working notions of morphology and syntax give us a starting point for describing what we see in the language of the children we're studying.

When my students sit at a fast-food restaurant on a Saturday morning and observe children of different ages, they find that the youngest children tend to use individual or two-word combinations of nouns, verbs, adjectives (and sometimes adverbs) to point to the world around them, with utterances like: *Truck, Truck go, Big truck*. Older children, around the age of three or so, begin to add other elements to their sentences—auxiliary verbs (Truck *don't* go), articles (*an, the,*), prepositions (*in, out*), conjunctions (*and, but*), and then forms for plurals (s), for tenses (crash*ed*, go*ed*, and eventually *went*), and for other verb forms (go*ing*). The child's use of morphemes gives a good picture of what this level of the grammatical system consists of and how it works. The first words the child acquires are nouns, verbs, adjectives, and adverbs—freestanding lexical morphemes—the words that allow us to point, successively, to a series of people or objects involved in various actions and processes and marked by particular qualities (Big truck, Truck go fast). These *content words* made up most of the content of messages on the telegrams that people used to send: Since the cost of a telegram was based on the number of words used, people typically omitted most of the *function* words or grammatical morphemes, sending messages like "Arrive tomorrow, train, 9 a.m." This early stage of child language is commonly referred to as telegraphic speech. (We practice a similar art, currently, in classified ads.)

Children can convey many of their meanings using only lexical morphemes because they share a physical context with their parents. When the child says, "Truck go fast," the parent can see whether the child is pointing to a truck currently in view or recapitulating an event that happened earlier, and any confusion can be cleared up with a few questions. But when people are less intimately involved in each other's daily lives, it helps their communication to have *tense* structures, for example, that allow them to place whatever actions are being described into a particular time frame from the perspective of the present conversation—to say that "the truck *went* fast"—or structures that we refer to in terms of *aspect*—that show whether an action was ongoing or bounded in time, as in "the truck *was going* fast until it came to the corner." And we can show these relationships with grammatical morphemes—some freestanding (like the auxiliary "was") and some bound (like the "ed" ending or the equivalent verb form "went" or "came" for past tense). Once a child uses a grammatical form to represent the concept of a discrete action that took place in the past, even if it is an invented form like *wented,* that child has acquired the syntactic representation of that concept in English.

Much of our sense that an older child has acquired the full, adult grammar of English is linked to her use of eight inflectional morphemes that are bound to words and that play an immediate role in our construction of grammatical sentences: those that show plural (girl*s*); possessive (girl*'s*); comparative (old*er*); superlative (old*est*); present tense in the third person singular (she kick*s*); past tense (kick*ed*—other past tense forms like *went* represent the same morpheme); the present participle (kick*ing*, go*ing*); and the past participle (kick*ed*, driv*en*, go*ne*). Each of these morphemes allows us to place an object, action, or quality in relationship to others systematically, and is most closely linked to other elements of syntax, to what allows us to form sentences. (Free grammatical morphemes tend to become bound to words in this way over time; it doesn't really matter grammatically whether a systematic form stands free, like the auxiliary *is* in "is going", or is bound to the verb as *ing*.) Children typically acquire free lexical morphemes first, then free grammatical morphemes, and finally these inflectional (bound grammatical) morphemes. Once they begin to use inflectional morphemes, they are particularly careful to include them wherever they seem to be needed, as we will see.

As children acquire the syntax of their native language, they extend the number of words they use (the mean length of utterance or MLU) from one word to two words and then enter a multiword stage, usually by the age of three. (In measuring MLU, all bound inflectional morphemes, as well as free grammatical and lexical morphemes, are counted: for "the boy hitted the doggies," the MLU is seven, with the past tense morpheme *ed* on "hitted" and the plural morpheme *s* on "doggies," counted as separate elements). We can see this progression as we look at the data my students have collected.

Pat starts us off with an overview from the baby books she kept when her own children were little, where, she discovers, she has recorded examples of each of these stages: one-word utterances like "dada," "wawa," "bawbaw"; two-word combinations like "me up," "no sleep," "more (with a number of other words)." And then, over time, "me up" became "me want up," then "me want get up," and finally "I want to get up." Pat inspires me to look back at the few notations I made about Karen's early language, and I find that at one-and-a-half she used a variety of two-word utterances, as well as sequences of related one word utterances: "Daddy's eyes," "Mommy's eyes," "Bear's eyes," "Shhh" (her bear was sleeping), "la-la-la-la" (a lullaby for the bear).

Likewise, in Zina's recording, we hear her one-and-a-half-year-old grandson Jordan as he points to pictures in his book and comments on them in one- and two-word utterances: "baby; baby see; baby wakeup." "That block; that book; that moon; that sunshine." He sometimes puts together what we would see as two separate words, but these probably include unanalyzed chunks that he has always heard in combination and that are effectively one word to him, like "wake up," "too hot", and "go out." At this stage of production, children often combine one fixed term (usually referred to as a "pivot") with one open one that can be changed, as Jordan does when he combines "that" with a series of other words or uses a number of different names with the fixed "go out" (as in "Tom go out").

The next stage in the acquisition of syntax is multiword, as children continue to link together nouns, verbs, adjectives, and adverbs (the content words, or free lexical morphemes, of the language), now in utterances of three-or- more words. This stage of "telegraphic speech" includes the essential content words while eliminating the function words like articles and prepositions. Justine's son is at this stage, stringing even four and five words together, but still in syntactically reduced constructions like "Go see Nana" for "I want to go to see Nana" and "Time clean up guys" for "It is time to clean up, guys."

Gradually children add grammatical function words (the free grammatical morphemes—articles, prepositions, auxiliaries, conjunctions, etc.) to the strings they produce. Finally, they use the inflectional features of the grammar that require changes in the forms of words (bound inflectional morphemes—verb tense endings, plurals, comparators like bigg*er*). Melissa finds, of the two year old she observes:

> Elyssa's language has definitely reached the multiple word stage. Amazingly enough, many of Elyssa's sentences contain correct verb tenses and function words. For example: "I'm cutting," or "Melissa's eating Elyssa's finger." Although in the second example she refers to herself and me in the third person (instead of saying, "You're eating my finger"), she succeeds at expressing the action as it takes place. Yet I found that her language was very inconsistent. She leaves the word "is" out of sentences quite frequently. "That Big Bird." "This my dinner." "Where Playdoh." In other sentences she was able to place it correctly. "Where's the Playdoh?" "Where's the book?" "Melissa's eating . . ." I did notice that the word "is" was not very distinct in these examples; instead it was attached to the end of the previous word.

Elyssa is also typical of most children in that, while there is a clear pattern of development from one stage to the next, there is also variation as a child begins to add new features. These features will be used in some linguistic contexts, but not in all, before the feature becomes regularized, as if the child is testing out a premise in particular areas before trying it out universally.

Dave's three-year-old bilingual friend, Bailey, uses most grammatical morphemes consistently in constructing syntactically complete utterances, as when she explains to Dave what the dog eats: "She doesn't have anything; she just has her dinner crunchies. . . . No not canine crunchy. Another one. In his little bowl . . . member?" Here Bailey uses auxiliary verbs (does) and prepositions (in), she refers to the dog with the correct form of the subject pronoun (she) and uses the appropriate possessive pronoun (her). She uses inflected forms to show the third person singular of the verb (does, has) and indicates the plural of nouns (crunchies). Bailey also produces occasional inconsistencies: she shifts the gender of the possessive pronoun in her second mention of the dog's dinner, from "her dinner" to "his little bowl." Dave thinks this might be a carry-over from Spanish, where the word "dog" is masculine, and it could indicate her sensitivity to the grammatical requirements of two different languages. She also sometimes produces syntactic structures that are correct but would probably not be said by adults, as in "I'm getting the smoke out of the way of us." Dave further hypothesizes that "being fluent in two languages could be helping her differentiate a larger range of grammatical structures."

At four, Zina's granddaughter Rebeka uses the full syntactic resources of the adult language, with both free and bound (inflected) grammatical morphemes in all of the places where they're needed, as she tells the story of the baby in the book she and her brother are reading:

> One day a little girl was putting her coat on. The little baby wanted to go with the little girl but the baby couldn't go. The baby waved good-bye while her mommy was taking her to school. Then the boy and the little girl hanged their jacket up and they went to school and the teacher was playing the piano, and they lookded at the little fishes.

There are two places where Rebeka's use of morphemes deviates from the adult standard: *hanged* and *lookded*. Here Rebeka, in a way typical of four year olds, has overgeneralized the use of the verb ending *ed* as an inflectional morpheme for past tense. She has acquired the underlying grammatical principle and the most common way of representing it, and she has begun to acquire the variations on that structure that exist in the adult language (went, could). But when she's uncertain about the past tense form of a particular verb, she goes back to the general pattern, overgeneralizing it. Occasionally, when she doesn't perceive that a form like *looked* already contains the past tense morpheme because of its pronunciation, she adds it again. She also leaves off the plural morpheme *s* on jacket, though she uses it elsewhere (fishe*s*). This is likely to be a performance error, where she's simply lost track of her plural subject in a long sentence, rather than a characteristic of her current grammar.

The grammatical features these children have acquired are productive, meaning that we can use them to form new words in the same category—we can always create new nouns and show their plural form by adding *s*, and we can form the past tense of unfamiliar verbs or newly created verbs once we know the *ed* morpheme. (New verbs added to the language always form the past tense with this morpheme, as in "I inputted the variables," or "they dissed his girlfriend." Other past tense forms are residual, from earlier periods of our language's linguistic history, but we no longer reproduce them as we create new verbs.)

Children attend to the underlying grammatical system, rather than its variations, so fully that they also tend to smooth out the irregularities of standard English. In a system that includes *his, hers, its, yours, theirs,* the first person possessive pronoun would logically be *mines,* and children frequently produce "It's *mines*" before "It's *mine*." In a system that includes *I sing, you sing, we sing, they sing,* the third person singular verb form would logically be *sing* as well—the pronoun (required in English) carries the information about person, and so the inflected ending *s* is redundant. Again children's developing grammar first shows the underlying pattern, with forms like "Mommy sing" appearing before the standard English exception to the pattern, with "Mommy *sings*." (The natural process of language change and simplification has already eliminated these irregularities from some non-standard dialects of English, as we will see in Chapter Six).

As we compare notes on our observations, we find other examples of children's attention to these grammatical features, to the point that they overgeneralize them. Pat recalls that one of her children's *more* became "more better" which became "more betterer" as the child began to infer rules and acquire the morphology of his language. And one of the five-year-old boys who sits at the table next to Stan at McDonald's follows a similar principle in creating a plural form when he says: "I'm not that hungry 'cause I ate two breakfastsez."

These older children speak in full sentences, although their sentences are often abbreviated as in "Know what?" and "Lookit!" That is a sign that their communicative competence is expanding and they know how to use an informal, abbreviated style when it's appropriate, not that they can't produce a syntactically complete sentence. Those sentences are characterized, not only by the inclusion of a full range of lexical and grammatical morphemes, but also by particular patterns of word order. As children put words together in longer and longer utterances, they do so not randomly, but in the allowable word order patterns for their native language. Word order plays a particularly important role in the grammar of English, because English does not encode as much grammatical information in inflectional morphemes as many other languages do. As the children we observe move into the multiword stage of their own language production, they are attuned to the word order requirements of English syntax, and again they move through predictable stages in their acquisition of the grammar of the adult language.

We can see these stages particularly clearly with children's acquisition of the adult word order for creating negative sentences and questions. Negation in English requires a particular, somewhat complex pattern. Children typically begin to express negation by placing the word *no* or *not* first, followed by any other words. Matt's "Not time put toys away," and "Not go bed," are examples, though he's creating a longer utterance than is typical for children using this pattern of negation. Generally, as children move from a two-word stage to a multiword stage, they include more subjects of sentences, inserting *no* or *not* between the subject and the verb. We might expect to see Matt saying, "Matt not take bath" or, "I no go bed" next. Around this time, children also begin to use *can't* or *don't,* as Matt does with "Don't want take bath now." (However, *can* and *do* don't appear as auxiliaries until later than these contractions, so it seems that children perceive them only as forms that can be used for negation, and not yet as contractions of *can not* and *do not*.) Later, there continue to be some irregularities in negation, and double negatives like "Don't nobody go" are likely for a while before they disappear for children whose dialects don't include them.

There are similar regularities in children's acquisition of the structure of questions in English. Early questions typically depend on two words spoken with rising intonation—a subject plus verb (Daddy shoe?) or verb plus object (Tie shoe?), or a noun or verb plus location (Shoe gone? Go home?). Matt's question to his mother, "Go see Nana?" is a three-word version of this pattern. Children then begin to use words beginning with *Wh* plus a subject and verb, spoken in rising intonation: "Where shoe is?" before they finally begin to invert the verb and subject as required in the adult grammar: "Where is the shoe?"

Lexicon

At the same time that children are expanding their grammatical competence, they are acquiring a vast store of words and understanding for each word, both what it means and how it is used grammatically within a sentence (e.g., whether it is a noun or a verb). They seem to extend their sense of word meanings gradually. When children first begin to say words, they frequently begin using a new word as a proper noun—as the name of a specific object—but they then quickly generalize it so that it applies to a whole set of similar objects. My nephew Benjamin was typical when he started out using his representation of *cat* (*at*) as a name for a particular cat in his neighborhood, and then moved to using *at* as a name for all small pets, including his grandmother's miniature poodle: "Nana at." Gradually the children's word meanings are narrowed until they conform with those of the adults, and Benjamin soon learned that "Nana at" was really a small dog, and used *at* only for the animals the rest of us would call *cats*. The three-year-old daughter of a student in another of my classes showed a similar overextension of a term one day when her mother brought her into our classroom. On arriving in the classroom, the student's daughter looked at another student in the class (a young white woman), and said to her mother "That a maryanne?" Her mother explained that they lived in a largely Jamaican community and that her only extended contact thus far with someone who was not black had been through the dancing lessons she took from a young white woman named Maryanne. At that moment, all young white women were, to this young child, "maryannes."

Children also acquire typically one of a pair of opposites before the other, overextending the unmarked term. The unmarked term is the one that's used more generally. *Big* and *tall* are unmarked terms about size, while *small* and *short* are marked: we say "how 'big' is your dog?" more generally, to ask about a dog of any possible size, but "how 'small' is your dog?" only if we already know that the dog is small. Stan finds an example of such overextension in one of the exchanges he observed at the fast-food restaurant, in which two five-year-old boys talk about what their families are going to do later that day.

Boy 1:   We're gonna see a movie.
Boy 2:   We aren't cause we have to go to the ball place first.
Boy 1:   Oh yeah. There's things that are free there . . . and red tags, but it pays money.

The conversation goes on about what *pays* money, and it becomes clear to Stan that the child's intended meaning is *costs* and that *pays* has been, at least momentarily, overextended to cover both terms. At the same time, "ball place" is nonspecific enough that Stan's never quite sure what the boys are referring to, though they share contextual knowledge that allows them to understand each other perfectly well. Like virtually all five year olds, these boys have acquired most of the adult grammar of English, with only occasional overgeneralizations of morphemes. But they will continue to expand their vocabulary and refine the semantic domain of the words they use over their lifetime.

Our Saturday morning observations have given us a sense of the general pattern of children's language acquisition and a framework for reading extended studies of first language acquisition focusing on specific areas of grammatical competence, such as those carried out by Roger Brown (1973), and the many others linguists who have built on his work (see Kessel 1988). Some studies look at large numbers of children of the same age in laboratory settings, but these are supported by studies of individual children over extended periods in home contexts. Our own observations show us how deeply any child's language use is embedded in particular contexts, in the rich, ongoing interactions of daily life. Children's developing grammar supports their expanding ability to communicate and participate in the ongoing life of a community.

Communicative competence

Stan finds that the conversations he listens in on have two threads: one goes on between parents and children in determining what everyone wants to eat, the other occurs mostly among the children themselves:

> The main theme of their conversations seems to have been social dynamics: getting attention, getting the floor, establishing a hierarchy within the group. There was much teaching and comparison and testing, and lots of attention getting and competitiveness. . . . It really is amazing that almost every utterance or exchange is loaded!

What allows these children to *load* their utterances so that they simultaneously serve several purposes, and what lets the children accomplish more obvious purposes like getting what they want to eat and more subtle purposes like placing themselves in a social hierarchy, is not their grammatical competence alone, but their ability to use the resources of the language in ways that are effective in their immediate context.

While Chomsky's work created a theoretical framework that fueled psycholinguistic studies focusing on children's acquisition of grammar, that acquisition could not be studied apart from real children using language in real social contexts (even if the context was the linguist's laboratory). And so the study of child language came to draw heavily on the framework created by the evolving field of sociolinguistics, focusing on language use in its social context, and taking into account a community's attitudes and beliefs about language socialization as well. It was sociolinguist Dell Hymes (1972) who coined the term "communicative competence" when he turned his attention to what speakers knew that allowed them to use their grammatical competence in their actual use of the language (in their *performance*, in Chomsky's terms).

Communicative competence involves a person's ability to use language, in actual interactions. It includes being able to use language for the several discourse functions described in Chapter One: to refer to the world and make statements about it; to get things done, interact with others, and take a stance; and to accomplish these things cohesively in an evolving text. It depends on the understanding that, in any act of communication, meaning must be shared and negotiated cooperatively, along with an increasing ability to imagine another's perspective and recognize that his or her perspective might be different from your own. It requires using a style that's appropriate to a particular interaction: whether it's informal or formal, and whether it should include the dialect features of vocabulary, pronunciation, or syntax common to a particular community. Communicative competence requires that speakers be particularly sensitive and responsive to actual communicative contexts. It demands a whole range of discourse skills.

Children growing up in a speech community learn the discourse skills necessary to participate in that community at the same time that they're realizing their grammatical competence, and they do so unconsciously and implicitly, in the context of actual communication in their communities and cultures. In cultures that treat the young child as a conversationalist, the skills necessary to successful participation in conversations are developed early, and include the ability to sustain conversational interaction—to initiate topics, take turns, and make repairs when the communication isn't successful. These communicative goals are supported by the language directed to the child by parents and other caretakers. Justine's interactions with Matthew as she gets him ready for bed may not hasten his acquisition of particular syntactic structures like the adult forms of negation, but they certainly contribute to his understanding of how to negotiate common meanings around bath time and bedtime. The fact that he says, "Not go bed," instead of, "I don't want to go to bed" makes absolutely no difference to his mother's ability to understand his meaning, nor in his comprehension of her response, and his offering of alternative possibilities like "Play trucks" and "Go see Nana" is a strategy that arises out of the sorts of communicative sequences that they create together. From their interactions, Matthew has learned how to take turns, how to add to a topic to create a cohesive text, as well as how to switch topics. With his mother, Matthew can create sequences that extend beyond what he could manage on his own at this point, as she echoes and recontextualizes his words ("Maybe after school we can go see Nana"). And their daily routines around picking up toys and reading books offer opportunities for adding other utterances, (and even for echoing the book language that's so different from Matt's own at this point: "When mummy says it's time for bed I go upstairs and get undressed)".

In *Child's Talk*, Jerome Bruner follows the prelinguistic and linguistic interactions of two children with their mothers, from the time they are a few months old until about two. Through early games like peekaboo and the formats that develop around particular speech acts like requests, the children gradually expand their linguistic repertoire, learning the discourse skills they will need to participate in extended interactions, and learning how to use language appropriately to accomplish their purposes. Most of their new communicative ability will be acquired unconsciously through their interactions with those around them, though sometimes parents will make their teaching explicit. For example, when Richard holds his cup out and says *more,* his mother focuses on the conditions that make such a request appropriate—that it has to be for something he doesn't already have, as she responds: "You've got some. You can't have more" (102). Bruner found that none of the mothers' responses to their one-year-olds focused on grammatical structures, but a third consisted of such lessons about speech acts—about how to use words to get the responses they want from the people around them. At the same time, Richard's mother extends his utterance, providing a scaffold on which he can build more language. Bruner concludes:

> Children learn to use a language initially (or its prelinguistic precursors) to get what they want, to play games, to stay connected with those on whom they are dependent. In doing so, they find the constraints that prevail in the culture around them embodied in their parents' restrictions and conventions. The engine that drives the enterprise is not language acquisition per se, but the need to get on with the demands of the culture. (1983, 103)

Interactions and games like the ones Bruner describes establish turn-taking patterns as part of a playful social interaction. They also point the child's and adult's attention to the same event, and can be considered a precursor to the notion of initiating and jointly maintaining a topic in conversation. Attention to an object can be signaled by looks or actions on the part of either child or adult, and the adult is likely then to comment on the shared topic (the object) in words, completing the statement that has been initiated. Or a child might respond to an adult-initiated topic nonverbally, perhaps by going to the object and picking it up. Catherine Snow's research (1977) shows that once a topic had been initiated, the adult caretakers she studied typically used questions, and tag questions at the end of a statement (It's a big dog, *isn't it?*) to get their children to respond in turn, and then responded by adding to the child's response.

Children use language to accomplish speech acts—to get things done in the world—and to interact with others. The situational context of any speech event also supports them in this effort. In many of our interactions we draw on patterns that are appropriate to the particular context we're in, (a common discourse frame allows us to accomplish a speech act like ordering food with a variety of other participants in many different settings), and much of a child's conversational interaction is supported by familiar patterns from a familiar environment. Let's look in more detail at the exchanges Sue recorded in the toy store between a fifteen-month-old boy named Bo and his mother. The toy store provides a familiar world of toy animals that provide topics for this conversation. The mother initiates the series of exchanges, but the boy quickly seizes control of the topic when he spots a monkey. The mother then picks up his topic and extends it with a series of questions and comments:

MOTHER: Where are you going? Aren't you going to play?
BO: Monkey [*points up*].
MOTHER: You want to look at the monkey? OK. Where's the monkey?
BO: Dhare
MOTHER: You love the monkey, huh? Look, she's got a telephone.
BO: I whan a monkey.
MOTHER: It's too high.
BO: High.

There's a regular pattern of turn-taking here: Each speaker responds to at least some of the other's comments about the topic of the monkey and adds new information. Bo offers mostly one-word responses until he asks for the monkey (and he may be treating "I whan a" as one word, an unanalyzed expression that precedes any object he wants) and he ends by repeating the final word from his mother's last comment on the topic of the monkey: *high*. So far, we can see that Bo is able to hold up his part of a conversation, interacting in regular conversational rhythms and using language to try to get what he wants in the world. At the same time though, his ability to do this is supported by a context in which both he and his mother can see the objects they're talking about, and by his mother's interest in sustaining the conversation by building on and extending his utterances. While he is immediately concerned with his own pragmatic purposes, in pointing out what he wants, she's trying to get him to extend his comments into several semantic domains, to comment on the monkey as an object—to name its location, and the other object (the telephone) associated with it—and to talk about his own feelings in response to it. The conversation continues, as his mother poses a series of questions that ask Bo to name and give information about other animals:

MOTHER: What's that?
BO: Iggy.
MOTHER: What does piggy say?
BO: Oink.
MOTHER: What does this kitty say?
BO: Meow, meow, meow.

A new sort of exchange follows, one in which the mother creates a new discourse frame, picking up a toy telephone and enacting a response to an imaginary phone call:

MOTHER: [*Holding a toy phone.*] Say "Hello"! Who's on the phone?
BO: Uh oh . . . uh oh . . . he right dhare.

This frame too is familiar, and Bo moves into it so easily that he doesn't answer his mother's question but responds directly to the imaginary caller with several unspecific utterances, as if he's listening to another speaker and confirming that he is paying attention. He then offers new information that it is someone known to him and the caller, an unspecified *he,* will be right *there* (referring appropriately to the caller's location and showing his control of perspective taking, or *deixis,* in language). Looking around, and following Bo's gaze, the mother tries to return to the topic of animals again, but this time Bo is distracted by a more interesting activity that another child is involved in. He pushes in to use an interactive toy, the "talking tree," initiating his interaction with the other child with the word *No.*

BO'S MOTHER: You want the rabbit? Look at the bunny, Bo, you LOVE BUNNIES.
BO: [*To another child who's taking a turn at the store's talking tree*] NO! NO!
JEFF'S MOTHER: Jeff, it's his turn now. Look at the raccoon. [*Bo hits the raccoon.*]
BO'S MOTHER: Did he say ouch? He's gonna cry.
BO'S MOTHER: OK, Bo, push the button. Your turn.
BO: Cry. [*To Jeff*] You turn now.
JEFF'S MOTHER: Say thank you.
JEFF: Thank you.
BO: Cry.
BO'S MOTHER: He's going to cry if you hurt him.

Here we have an exchange between the two children over a turn at the tree, but that exchange is mediated by the two mothers (so Jeff doesn't get to say *no* back to Bo, but has to relinquish his turn, and Bo hits the raccoon that Jeff's mother points to, the way he might have otherwise hit Jeff). The explicit naming of turns by the mothers is picked up by Bo, who offers Jeff another turn, and the requisite polite response is returned by Jeff. The topic of turns is interwoven with comments about the raccoon, who's going to cry if he's been hurt, providing a mini-lesson about social behavior which Bo seems to respond to, since he comes back to his mother's word *cry* after the switching of turns has been accomplished.

Children bring not only their present abilities to use the grammar of the language to construct utterances to exchanges like this one, but also their experiences in using language for similar intentions and purposes. The parents in exchanges like these support their children's expanding grammatical competence, by providing a bridge between the reduced sentences that the children can construct and the longer utterances that a meaningful conversation involves. The parents' input does not seem to affect directly how much of their meaning children can grammaticize at any age, as they come to rely increasingly on the grammatical structures of the language, rather than shared contextual knowledge for communication. But it does guide children toward using language to describe the world around them, express feelings, and resolve disputes, in ways that they could not manage on their own at this point. It helps them to use language in the ways that are valued in their discourse communities. The parents' scaffolding also allows them to participate in creating extended discourse in which utterances are linked across turns, and a longer coherent conversation on a topic is maintained. In extended discourse, each sentence typically names a topic and offers a comment on that topic, while subsequent sentences have, as their topics, either a topic or comment that was introduced earlier (see Chapter Five). At fifteen months, Bo has only a few utterances that extend beyond one word. When he introduces the topic *monkey*, that's all he says, and his mother guesses at the comment he intends when she asks, "You want to look at the monkey?" In this way, by offering either the topic or the comment themselves, the parents support children's evolving discourse skills. In the data we've collected, my students and I see a range of cooperative strategies from both parents and children that allow children to be conversational participants while their resources are still limited. Above all, the parents interpret their children's utterances as meaningful and intentional, creating an environment in which the children can safely try out new possibilities and negotiate to repair utterances that have led to misunderstandings.

Within their own families, linguists have also had extended opportunities to observe the development of language in particular children, and to see how cooperative discourse sequences can extend the grammatical resources a young child brings to a conversation. Ron Scollon (1979, 216), for example, was recording the language of his niece Brenda at one year and seven months to study her development of phonology, when he noticed something about her sequential one-word utterances that no one else had commented on in studies of child language—a syntactic feature that he referred to as a *vertical construction*. Brenda would repeat one word several times, and then, after a response from a parent, switch to another word that commented on the first:

Brenda: ka (car)
          ka
          ka
          ka

Father: What?
Brenda: go
            go.

In this way she was able to name a topic and then comment on it in two different clusters of one-word utterances, in a way that she could not yet do *horizontally*, in a two-word sequence: *ka go*. In sequences like these, the adult's questions have the effect of asking for a new constituent to complete a sentence that has been initiated, creating a bridge for the child between two words that she can't yet put together. Such support helps the child extend her present linguistic resources, so that she can participate in conversations and comment on the world in a way that exceeds what she could do without such interactions, allowing her to complete the topic-comment combination that is central to communicative discourse. Studying his interactions with Brenda led Scollon to conclude that "discourse structure is at the heart of sentence structure from the beginning of its development" (1979, 225) and highlighted for him the notion that a child's language development must be studied in its communicative context.

Studies of interactive book reading (Ninio and Bruner 1978; Heath 1984) also show such turn-taking and topic/comment cycles, where the parents' questions again support extended discourse, as they ask a series of questions that require only one-word responses: "What is that?" (Doggie) and "What is the doggie doing?" (Ball). Parents then combine those responses into a topic/comment sequence: "That's right, the doggie is playing ball." Once a topic is shared and turns are being taken, another discourse skill comes into play, as participants must attend to the other's comprehension and make repairs where there is confusion. Even very young children try to do this. At the time Brenda was offering her topic/comment *ka/go,* her uncle didn't really understand her and responded with a sound that indicated his lack of comprehension. At that point she introduced a new word *be*is* (bus), but Scollon, who didn't understand her word at that moment, responded "What? Oh, bicycle? Is that what you said?" To which Brenda replied, *na* for *no.* In listening to the tape afterward and hearing the sound of a vehicle in the street outside, Scollon decided that she had been trying to repair the conversation, by offering *bus* as an alternative to the word *car,* which he didn't understand, and letting him know that he has misunderstood again when he says *bicycle.* Children discover early on that, when others don't understand them, they have a range of strategies available, including saying *no,* repeating utterances, and even rephrasing them. Young children are also asked by adults whether they understand, and they learn how to respond as listeners to this question. These patterns are built on and extended throughout early childhood.

Over time, children lexicalize and grammaticize more of their meanings, so that the spoken texts they create carry more of their meanings. They rely less on shared contextual knowledge or on their parents' extensions of their utterances. Children gain a larger framework of knowledge about the world, and an understanding that such knowledge is likely to be generally shared, so that they begin to create a frame of reference that goes beyond the present context, bringing in past events, reported events, and things they've learned from other contexts and from books, television, and movies. They become increasingly able to consider the perspective of their listeners, see what knowledge is likely to be shared, what can be presupposed, and to explain what a listener is not likely to know. Over time, children also learn who gets the right to speak, when, and how discourse is constrained around social status.

Competence in social discourse outside of the home also requires the mastery of a repertoire of speech styles, and the ability to adjust these to different contexts and circumstances. By school age (as we will see in Chapter Eight) children are well aware of the nuances of different styles, and can identify quite clearly the differences between the ways something might be said at home and the way it is said at school. Even two-year-olds seem to be able to perceive differences in politeness (Bates 1976).

Discourse competence and the functions of language

The competence that children develop, both grammatical and communicative, is realized in a kind of discourse competence that allows the child to use language for the several functions it serves, and to do so simultaneously. In his study of his own son beginning when he was about nine months old Halliday (*Learning How to Mean* 1975) describes in detail the process Nigel goes through in constructing his own consistent system of sounds and meanings as he begins to use language for a number of functions, and gradually acquires the full system of vocabulary and grammar of the adult language. The functions Halliday observed in Nigel were instrumental (satisfying material needs); regulatory (getting others to do what the child wants); interactional (with exchanges like greetings and peekaboo); personal (to express awareness of self); heuristic (to find out about the world); imaginative (as in pretending); and, somewhat later, an informative function (to tell others something you know). From studying his own child, Halliday sees these functions operating quite distinctly at first, with each utterance serving one function. Over time, Nigel then seemed to regroup these into two functions, using *language as doing* (the pragmatic function) and *language as learning* (what Halliday terms the mathetic function). Gradually an utterance came to serve more than one function, so that Nigel could at once comment on the world and achieve pragmatic purposes.

Halliday suggests that over time, all children regroup those early functions until, when children are about two, they match those of the adult language: the ideational, interpersonal, and textual functions that we manage all at once with all of our utterances in a communicative context. Being able to mean in the adult system requires being able to refer to the world and convey information about it, but it also means being able to do so in ways that will be understood by others, that will achieve multiple communicative purposes. Creating an evolving text involves continually making choices about how to convey meaning, choices that are available, because meaningful within a particular situational context—a context that is social and cultural as well as physical, and where meanings must be not only represented but continually negotiated.

CHAPTER 3

Creating Shared Meanings

The children my students and I have been observing will soon become adolescents and adults who have realized their full competence in their native languages, both in their home dialects and in the dialects or styles of several other discourse communities. When we turn to the conversational data we have collected from our different speech communities, we see quickly that, like the children whose utterances we captured and analyzed in the last chapter, older speakers who have acquired the full range of structures used in their native language still tend to speak eliptically, in reduced sentences. Many of their utterances serve largely to evoke and confirm what is already known by others, and the participants in a conversation generally have little trouble understanding each others' meaning, though it is hard for us in the class, as outsiders to each others' communities, to follow a lot of the conversations. Much of any particular conversation builds on shared prior knowledge. Many connections are left unstated, and even where we understand all of the words and are familiar with all of the references, we don't always know the intentions behind them—though the participants generally seem to. But even people who know each other as well as Karen, Melanie, and Shanna do will have occasional moments of misunderstanding as they bring different frames of reference, from the different worlds they inhabit, to a common conversation.

We can see from another bit of Karen, Melanie, and Shanna's conversation the ways in which shared meanings are quickly evoked and affirmed, while those that aren't shared yet must be explored and explained. Each of their utterances serves, at once, the several functions of discourse: the propositional, referential, or ideational function of naming and commenting on the world; the pragmatic or interpersonal function of accomplishing particular purposes and maintaining interpersonal relationships; and the discourse or textual function of creating an ongoing and emerging text. In these next three chapters, we'll be looking at each of these functions. For the moment we'll focus on the first, looking to see how the participants in the conversations we've taped name objects and experiences, make statements about what they've named, define

terms, evoke particular frames of reference, and, throughout this process, negotiate shared meanings.

MELANIE: My favorite place to shop . . . is *down town* Boston.
KAREN: Downtown.
MELANIE: They have High Gear down there . . . fresh stuff. . . . They have
   these shoe boots I want. Combat boot shoes?
KAREN: Oh, those? What do you want?
MELANIE: The low tops.
KAREN: Doc Martens?
SHANNA: Do they call them that?
MELANIE: I don't call them that.
KAREN: Doc Martens is what they call them.
MELANIE: Yeah, I know that's what they call them. I just call them combat
   boots.
KAREN: My friend has 24 holes, up to here.
SHANNA: She has what?
KAREN: 24 holes.
MELANIE: Holes of what? Shoelace holes?
KAREN: Mmmm. They're called 24's, cause up to here is 24 holes—[*gesturing*]
   16, 9, and 6.
MELANIE: Mine are gonna be to here, for sure.
KAREN: What color, red or black?
MELANIE: Red, black, and orange.

The linguistic term for the study of meaning, *semantics,* comes from the Greek
word for sign, *sema.* Karen, Melanie, and Shanna are building a shared framework of signs (including objects and actions as well as words) and meanings. At
the moment, their world of teenage belonging is divided up semantically into
two large categories: what's in and what's out, or what's *fresh* and what's not,
just as the ideological world of world politics was divided for many years into
the categories of Democratic or Communist, or the freshman writers at my
university are divided into native speakers and English as a Second Language, or
the world of food might be divided into healthy or unhealthy. The boundaries
of these categories and the items they contain may shift, as coffee or olive oil or
wine or margarine have moved back and forth with each new health study, and
new categories may be invented. But some such categories are a necessary part
of the schemas through which we make sense of the world, the filters our culture leads us to impose on what's around us so that we can process quickly the
data our senses take in and know what to attend to and what to ignore.

   As children we learn to name the categories, and thus some of the fundamental meanings of our culture. We learn which animals are raised to be eaten
and which are pets, what sorts of activities are considered good or bad. We learn
other categories and distinctions—of religion, race, neighborhood—that help us
to divide the world into those like us and those different from us, those who are

insiders to our community and those who are outside. My colleague Suzy Groden argues that the process of education involves, in part, expanding the boundaries of the category of self and like-self so that there is "a growing sense that one is attached—by filaments of awareness, responsibility and caring—to an ever widening world of others" (Kutz, Groden and Zamel 1993, 177). As adolescents, Karen, Melanie, and Shanna are engaged in several parts of this process: defining self and like-self through their constant interplay and negotiation about what is in, awesome, or fresh and what is not. Part of being an insider to teenage culture involves keeping up with rapid changes in styles of clothing, music, and language. At the same time though, they are trying to refine their understanding of the larger culture's terms and sometimes to move beyond them.

Concepts of black and white, for example, must be redefined and renegotiated frequently in our racially mixed neighborhood—not so much among a group of friends as in their encounters with a larger world. When my son was very young, his best friend Toussaint told him you had to watch out for white kids because they would beat you up and take your toys. At this point, Kenny assumed that Toussaint's notion of white didn't apply to him but only to the kids on the next block who gave them trouble. At the community day-care center though, Kenny had a different model of black and white: he described as black any teachers he didn't like, no matter what their skin color. It turned out that his favorite, and coincidentally black, teachers were by his definition white, while he said of a young white male teacher whom he'd clashed with at first but who he had come to like, that he "used to be black." Kenny was beginning to pick up a sense of the larger society's meanings, including some that were wholly opposed to his parents' beliefs and values, but these implicit meanings matched imperfectly with his own experience of who was like-self and who was different.

For Karen and Melanie it was the explicit discussion of society's perceptions of race that challenged their early meanings: They were stunned to learn, with their first school celebration of Martin Luther King Day, about racism in American society. Since they'd always presented themselves to the world as sisters, as the two daughters of whichever Mommy or Daddy happened to be present, the understanding that the larger society separated people by the color of their skin had immediate and very disturbing implications. As I drove them to a lesson at the high school swimming pool one January day, they whispered intensely in the back seat of the car about what they had been learning in school, worrying that it meant people wouldn't really see them as sisters after all. Finally, six-year-old Melanie worked out an answer and broke out in a smile, saying: "It's OK, Karen. We're still sisters in God's eyes." What could have been a Sunday school piety had become for her a key to reframing the categories of black and white that had newly impinged on their concept of sisters as being fundamentally like-self, allowing her to reconcile her concept with the facts of the world, to apply a larger concept that embraced an apparent dichotomy. In the larger world, however, the old categories keep asserting themselves, as when, after a year of racial turmoil at the high school, Melanie the ninth grader had to explain to Karen, the eighth grader, that the high school isn't like the neighborhood—that there you have to be black or white and the kids in the other group don't talk to you. In that context, an overarching, unifying concept that is meaningful to everyone has not been found.

Elements of meaning

As my students and I study the conversational data we've collected from our different speech communities and compiled in a class data book, we begin, as outsiders to the the twenty or thirty other conversations in the set, with just the words on the page, not the background information that helps insiders to these communities interpret their meanings. As we list the words that appear in any particular conversation, we can see that the words do not represent the world directly, but rather they name our conception of it, most often in relationship to other words. Growing up as native speakers of English, conversationalists like Karen, Melanie, and Shanna have acquired the meanings the language is used to express in their immediate social and larger cultural world—as those meanings can be represented in the grammar of the English language. The words we find in our transcriptions connect the system of concepts and meanings offered by our culture with the system of sounds offered by our language, and we need to know something about both systems and how they are represented in our lexicon.

The semiotic system

Words function as part of the grammatical system of language, but they also function as part of a semiotic system of meaning that is socially determined, one that includes but is not limited to words. In studying his own son Nigel's development of language, which he sees as a process of "learning how to mean," Halliday points out that in each situation where the child uses language for a particular function, he also acquires a portion of the larger system of meanings of the wider culture.

> The meaning potential that a child learns to express in the first phase [of language development] serves him in functions which exist independently of language, as features of human life at all times and in all cultures. But, at the same time, and in the same process, he is constructing for himself a social semiotic, a model of the culture of which he is himself a member; and he is doing so out of the semiotic properties of situations, situations in which he is a participant or an observer. . . In this way a child, in the act of learning language, is also learning the culture through language. The semantic system which he is constructing becomes the primary mode of transmission of the culture. (1975, 66)

As he approaches age three, Nigel's utterances serve the several functions of adult language, but his world of meaning is still not that of the adults around him. He doesn't see relationships between events in the same way. His mother asks how he got sand in his hair, and Nigel responds, "I was just standing up and I threw the sand to it and it got in my hair." From his perspective, the sand got in his hair because that's the way things happen. He calls to his mother from the playroom asking: "Mummy where are the ones with green in?" He can't imagine that his mother doesn't understand what he's referring to, that she doesn't share the knowledge of what's in his mind at the moment, that she doesn't know what object is the focus of his attention. He asks his mother what day it is, but is surprised that the same day (Thursday) continues after he's been to school, adding that he can't "go to school on Friday yet." He understands that days follow one another and have different names, but he doesn't know when the changeover takes place. Through his interactions, Nigel is developing ways of talking and thinking about the relationships of physical events, of distinguishing between his own perspective and that of others, and of perceiving the world in the way that the adults around him perceive it. Halliday says:

> We can see all the time, if we pay attention to what is said by, to, and in the presence of a small child, how in the course of the most ordinary linguistic interaction he is constantly learning the structure of the environment in which he is growing up, in all its aspects, material, logical, institutional, and social. (122)

When my students and I observe young children, we too see them trying out the socially determined systems of meaning that their culture offers. My niece Molly, at about one, paid a lot of attention to dogs. Her family had a dog, so they were significant in her immediate environment. She would listen to dogs barking in the neighborhood and name the sound when she heard it: woof-woof. She used the sound to name her own dog and as a generic term for all other dogs that she saw or heard: all were *woof-woof*'s. Her term was repeated and echoed by the adults around her. At the same time, she had a lot of books with pictures of dogs, and when adults read to her, they named those pictures *dog*, so she too would use *dog* when she pointed to a picture. For a while Molly had two terms, one for the dogs in the world around her, based on the sound they made, and one for the dogs in books, based on the term her parents used. Eventually, she combined these understandings into a system in which the animal, whether in a book or in the world, was called a *dog*, and the sound that it made or was supposed to make was *woof*. But Molly's brother Benjamin, at about the same age, had a different system in place. For him, all small animals were cats, so his grandmother's small poodle became "Nana's cat," and the whole family adopted the term.

Children's namings are often picked up and echoed by others in the family, becoming markers of belonging and intimacy, of a shared experience that sets this group off from the larger world, and children quickly learn to move between private, family names and meanings, and those of the larger world. Growing up and moving beyond the immediate family involves a constant process of renaming—learning that the world can be named in many different ways, and ultimately learning to reconcile those new ways with familiar ones.

Meanings can be represented by more than words: in the girls' conversation, sneakers, hats, colors, all carry meaning beyond what they are. Doc Marten shoes are not just foot coverings—they are signs that point to attitudes about style and dress in the teen culture of the moment. The nuances of meaning may shift from one context to another, from school to street, from one school to another. And a particular item may share only some of the meanings carried by similar fashions from other time periods, like the combat boots of the late sixties and early seventies. But wearing or not wearing this style of shoe at this moment is almost always intended as a sign.

Signs can be *indexical,* drawing on an often observed connection (often physical) between the sign and its larger meaning—as with Molly's use of the sound "woof" to name the dogs in her world. They can also be *iconic,* representing an object with something similar—as with the drawings used to represent dogs in Molly's books. But most signs do not draw on such a relationship. They are, instead, *symbolic,* drawing on conventional understandings held within a community rather than on observed relationships or similarities. Symbols are, in fact, arbitrary, with no necessary connection between the symbol and the object or idea it represents. But they come to stand for a particular set of shared understandings in the way that our public symbols, like the American flag or the Statue of Liberty, are seen to stand for the United States and the values its citizens publicly profess. And words themselves are symbols in this arbitrary way.

There is no necessary connection between a particular set of sounds and the actual object or concept or event those sounds represent (the concept of *dog* is represented equally well by *Hund* in German or by *chien* in French). Ferdinand de Saussure, the turn-of-the-century French philosopher whose work provided much of the foundation for modern linguistics, built his study of the structure of language on the premise of the "arbitrariness of the sign," the notion that the words of a language are conventions that have significance only within a system of such relationships, not directly in terms of what they point to in the world. A language is a system of such relationships, and the structure of that system can be studied with reference to other parts of the system, not depending on either its reference to the world or its actual use by the world's speakers.

The grammatical system

Language, then, allows us to represent objects and ideas that exist in the world and in people's minds, within a culturally-derived semiotic system of meanings, but it does so within a grammatical system, and words are dependent on both of these systems for their meanings. The word is referred to in linguistics as the *signifier,* and the concept (not the actual object) it refers to as the *signified.* The combination of sounds that we spell as *dog* is a signifier that represents what we think of as a dog, either as a general category or as applied to a particular animal.

Both the system of meaningful sounds and the conceptual system these sounds name operate on the basis of difference. The signifier *dog* is not a *dig* and not a *hog* and not a *dot*. It depends, for its meaning, on a set of systematic differences from other sound combinations that are possible in English. Likewise, the concept of dog is not the same as the concept of cat because, though it shares similarities with other four-legged domestic animals that we have as house pets, it also has differences that we, unlike Molly's brother, perceive as significant. The grammatical system signals meaningful linguistic distinctions as they represent meaningful conceptual distinctions: sound differences distinguish one word from another, so that they can be used as signifiers for different concepts.

As we saw in Chapter Two, the grammatical system includes the regular and meaningful distinctions of sound (phonemes) that lead us to recognize *dog* (/d//o//g/) and *dig* (/d//i//g/) as different words in English, while ignoring differences in pronunciation between *dog* and *dawg*. It includes the meaningful components of words (morphemes) that allow us to use an essential concept of *dog* to create adjectives *dog-like* and their opposites *undog-like,* or verbs (he *dogs* her footsteps everywhere she goes), or to use these verbs in the present or past tense (he *dogged* her footsteps). The grammatical system also includes the syntactic relationships among parts of a phrase or a sentence that allow elements to be combined in particular ways: as the noun and verb in "The *dog dogged* her footsteps," or the adjective, noun, and verb in "The *dogged dog dogged* her footsteps." These grammatical elements function systematically. With our underlying knowledge of the system we can apply a finite set of rules repeatedly, to create a range of meanings (the *wolf wolfed* her food). Our sense that the grammatical system itself is an element of meaning is reinforced by the fact that we can so quickly guess at likely meanings for words or names we've never heard (Doc Marten's, 24's) if we hear them in the context of a sentence (I'm going to buy some Doc Martens; She's wearing the 24's). We can even substitute nonsense words (She sleked the zillies) and still feel that the sentence makes some sort of sense, even though we don't know at all what concepts might be signified.

Individual words allow us to name the salient features in our conceptualization of the world around us, but by themselves allow us only to point to a sequence of objects or ideas, a sequence of meanings, not to establish complex relationships among those meanings. The sequence of terms *shoe boots, combat boot shoes, Doc Martens, 24's* in itself offers a set of alternative names for a type of shoe, suggesting perhaps a relationship of equivalence. But to refine these terms—while at the same time expressing their attitudes toward the objects in question—the girls need to use more than such sequential pointing: They need to use their knowledge of the grammar of the language to build a set of relationships among the words. The sentence "*Doc Martens* is what they call them" does more than point to and name this style of shoe; it sets the name into a social world where other people (they) engage in an act of naming. "They call them" shows "them" (the type of shoes) to be an object that can be "called" or named by a generalized plural agent "they," while placing the name *Doc Martens* in the front of this sentence highlights the strength that this specific name, used by a generalized and unnamed group of people, has taken on in the mind of the speaker. All of these subtle nuances of meaning are supported by the grammar.

Another way in which grammar supports meaning is through the system of reference it allows. In their conversations, the girls point to objects in the world and to their prior namings of the objects within the discourse as well. As the girls offer assorted terms for *shoe boots*, their inability to agree on a term for the object in question doesn't interfere that much with their negotiation of a common meaning, because once these objects have been introduced to the conversation, they can be referred to with a pronoun—"they, them"—so that the whole conversation about what to call "them" can continue with a shared notion of the referent but without specific agreement on the appropriate term.

The lexicon

It is in the vocabulary, or lexicon, of a language that the semiotic systems and the grammatical systems of the language most clearly intersect. Words function at once in both of these systems, as shown in dictionary entries which indicate grammatical categories like noun or verb, give information about other grammatical relationships like the requirement that particular prepositions be used, and offer examples in syntactic structures—while at the same time listing a set of definitions and giving examples of ways the word might be used in different contexts. In my well-worn copy of *The Random House Dictionary*, the functions of the word dog in the grammatical system are clearly marked as *noun* and *verb*. The place of the word in the conceptual systems of the larger culture (its *sense*, in linguistic terms) is presented with definitions and examples:

> Dog: (dog, dog) *n, v* dogged, dogging 1. a domesticated carnivore; 2. any animal belonging to the family Canidae, including wolves, jackals, foxes, etc.; 3. the male of such an animal, . . .[but also] 5. "a despicable man or youth . . . 8. *Slang*. a. something worthless or of extremely poor quality," b. an utter failure; flop *a playwright with two dogs and one turkey to his credit,* 9. *Slang*. an ugly, boring, or crude girl or woman . . .

When I look up the word for another common animal, I find:

> Pig: (pig) *n, v* pigged, pigging 1. a young swine of either sex weighing less than 120 pounds; 2. any wild or domestic swine; 3. the flesh of swine, pork . . .

These animals are defined within a system of categories like *carnivore*, superordinates like *animal*, taxonomies that group similar types together. But *The Random House Dictionary* makes no reference to dog flesh, because the flesh of dogs isn't thought about separately, as meat, in this culture, while the flesh of pigs is. Cultures present consistent conceptual systems and ways of categorizing and defining meanings of lexical items in relation to each other. An English dictionary depends on the generally shared conceptual system or model of a larger English-speaking culture.

Linguists attempt to look at the meaning of a word in terms of the systems of related words in which it's imbedded. Any domain of our experience will be specified through sets of related words, such as the many terms for different breeds of dogs, for example, in what is termed a *semantic field*. The more general terms in the field are likely to connote the elements most common to our cultural experience of all possible related terms, so that the particular image that comes to mind when someone says the word *dog* is likely to derive from the dogs that are most familiar. Dogs are typically larger than cats, so for Benjamin, whose general image of dog included the property of size, Nana's miniature poodle puppy was too small to fall into the domain of meaning generally covered by the term. (Children often acquire the stereotypical or unmarked meanings of their culture before they begin to acquire more marked or less common ones).

What allows one word to substitute for another meaningfully? First, they have to fit into the same grammatical category—nouns replace nouns, verbs replace verbs. But not all words in the same category can replace all others and still be meaningful. In analyzing the systematic relationships that underlay meaning, linguists have focused on the *semantic features* or *semantic properties* that words must share to allow one word to replace another plausibly. Most analyses of semantic features have focused on a binary system—one where words show distinctions between animate and inanimate, concrete and abstract, human and non-human, male and female. Because cats and dogs share the feature of being animate, it's not so surprising that Benjamin called Nana's poodle a cat, but it would be startling if he labelled it a stone.

The ways in which we use words to represent meanings depends on a system of semantic relationships that carve up the world in particular ways, and not in others. Some of these relationships include taxonomies, or heirarchical classifications, and sets of terms that are at the same level of such a heirarchy, such as the names of different breeds of dogs (hyponyms), terms that are approximate equivalents like dog and canine (synonyms), terms that are opposites like carnivore and herbivore (antonyms). Analogy questions on standardized tests draw on an understanding of such semantic relationships, which is why they're often hard for students whose cultures don't carve up the world in the same way as the test makers.

As we can see from the dictionary entries, the signifier *dog* may be used in a number of different systems of meaning. Scientifically it may signify a species of animal (though for accuracy it may be used to refer only to males of the species—with the term *bitch* used for the female). Colloquially, it may participate in several other systems of meaning: it may evoke positive animal images—the dog as faithful, loyal, and true, or negative images—as when people are described as dogs, pigs, wolves. It doesn't just refer to a concept of an animal in the world in a way that would allow everyone to agree on the truth of a statement in which the word was used. Rather, it participates in various meaning-systems, any one or several of which may be evoked by the word. The apparently simple relationship between signifier and signified becomes a relationship between a signifier and many possible signifieds, leaving a great deal of ambiguity and indeterminacy of meaning in the word alone: the word boots might evoke a whole range of understandings, from cowboy boots to snow boots to waterproof Wellingtons, and Melanie has to keep refining and clarifying her terms—shoe boots, combat boot shoes—until her listeners perceive the relevant meaning system and Karen responds, "Oh those?" and begins to participate in the process of naming.

The girls' problem with naming the style of footwear that is the topic of this part of their conversation points to a second source of potential confusion in the relationship between signifier and signified: multiple signifiers (like shoe boots, combat boot shoes, hightops, Doc Martens) may be used to point to one concept or object, and a speaker must anticipate which of these will be understood, and in what ways, by the listener. Molly might hear her dog referred to as a *canine*, a *pooch*, or a *hound* in different contexts, and she'll gradually come to know which is expected by the groomer or the veterinarian.

Modern theories of discourse (particularly those of post-structuralist French philosophers of language like Foucault and Derrida, who followed the work of the structuralist Saussure) focus in part on the ways in which the words we use take part in different meaning systems simultaneously. In post-structuralist terms, the meaning of a word like dog is *overdetermined*, because it participates in so many different systems of meaning. Any use of the word potentially evokes not only the primary meaning intended by the speaker, but all of the other meanings that have come to be associated with the word–and any opposite terms the word might signal as well. This understanding affects the way in which contemporary critical theorists read literature, looking not for one real meaning behind the words or the most accurate interpretation, the way earlier literary critics did, but instead approaching a work of literature as offering multiple, and even contradictory, readings which are present simultaneously, none of which is necessarily more real or true than the others. Post-structuralist discourse theory has also focused attention on the ways in which our systems of categorization both shape our understanding and limit our ability to see something in a different way. Once a term like *dysfunctional family* comes into play in our popular understandings, the categorization of families into the simple, binary opposition of *functional* versus *dysfunctional* tends to obliterate other more nuanced ways of seeing the complex interplay of family relationships.

The ambiguity that results from the fact that words can't be mapped directly onto the world in a one-to-one relationship, but must be understood in relationship to a number of cultural and personal conceptual systems, makes an interesting area of study in the field of semantics or critical discourse theory, but it has immediate consequences in our ordinary interactions.

If I refer to a friend as a black woman, I may be using *black* as a simple descriptor of a physical attribute (Look for a black woman in her forties, about 5'6" with short hair). I may be placing her culturally within the black community (As a black woman she's particularly angry about the way that American history is being taught at the high school). Or the term could be used within a wholly personal system of meaning, with reference to neither culture nor skin color (though perhaps still carrying overtones of American racism), as three-year-old Kenny used *black* to refer to the white teacher he didn't like. At the same time, the public, respectful terms for American blacks as a racial and cultural group keep shifting, with the history of semantic change recorded in the names of such organizations as the National Association for the Advancement of Colored People, or the United Negro College Fund. The elderly Irish neighbor who once used *colored people* as a term of respect may be seen as insensitive and culturally insular, if not prejudiced, when she continues to use the same term today. And the more formal descriptor *African-American*, though not used in informal exchanges in my community, is often the expected term at my university, where noted African–American scholars come to address students in our Black Studies program. Not only do words participate in different systems of meaning, not only can different words be used to refer to particular people or objects or concepts in the world, but relationships between words and meanings are affected by (and contribute to) a constant process of social/cultural change. No wonder any participants in a conversation, even those who know each other as well as Karen, Melanie, and Shanna do, must continually negotiate and affirm shared definitions and references.

Meaning and context: drawing on shared knowledge of the world

In considering the relationship of language and meaning, we've focused thus far on the ways in which language can be studied as a system used to represent the world. Although the system is used by real speakers, a focus on the system does not take into account the ways in which speakers make use that system in their ordinary conversations. Saussure highlighted this separation in his theoretical framework by distinguishing specifically between language (*langue*) and speech (*parole*), stating that language is not to be confused with speech:

> Speech is many-sided and heterogeneous; straddling several areas simultaneously—physical, physiological, and psychological—it belongs to the individual and to society. . . . Language, on the contrary, is a self-contained whole and a principle of classification. (1959, 9)

One consequence of Saussure's distinction in modern linguistics has been to separate the study of the formal grammatical systems of language from the study of the ways language is used. The dichotomy is represented in the distinction between psycholinguistics—the study of the grammatical system as it exists in the mind of an idealized speaker; and sociolinguistics—the study of language as it is actually used in social contexts. Chomsky, the contemporary psycholinguist whose work has been most influential in the United States, echoes Saussure's distinction in his own theorizing of the concepts of *competence* and *performance*, with competence referring to the idealized grammatical system that would exist in the minds of all speakers of a language, and performance referring to any actual speaker's production of the language at a given moment. Chomsky is specifically interested in the study of competence, not performance.

Although Saussure's and Chomsky's distinctions provide useful theoretical constructs, other linguists have opposed this separation, arguing that the grammatical system of a language and the system of social knowledge and meanings embodied in its actual use are not separate and isolatable aspects of language but two interwoven elements. The study of language may be approached, then, from the perspective of the grammatical system or from the perspective of its use in a social system, but both parts need to be seen in relation to each other. Halliday, whose work has focused on integrating these two perspectives in a "functional" theory of grammar, describes language as a "meaning potential:"

> To describe language as a potential does not mean we are not interested in the actual, in what the speaker does. But in order to make sense of what he does, we have to know what he can do. This is true whatever our particular angle on language, whether we are looking at it as behavior, or as knowledge (Chomsky's 'competence') or as art: what is, the actual sentences and words that constitute our direct experience of language, derives its significance from what *could be*. But it is in the social perspective that we are best able to explain what *is*. (1978, 28)

In other words, to learn very much about what speakers like Karen, Melanie, and Shanna are doing as they construct their world through language, we have to know more about the context in which they use the potential that the linguistic system offers.

We can see that Karen, Melanie, and Shanna are engaged not only in representing the world, but in commenting on it, presenting their attitudes toward it while defining themselves in relation to it, signaling a complex set of social meanings, and trying to get each other to respond in particular ways. Halliday sees all of these functions—the ideational (or propositional/referential), the interpersonal (or pragmatic), and the textual (or discourse) function—as a central aspect of language that has to be taken into account in any theory of grammar and meaning.

Karen, Melanie, and Shanna do carry out these functions simultaneously. They are working out their understanding of the world in terms of what objects and events to pay attention to and how to categorize them (what's cool or fresh, and what's not), how things are named and what the logical relationships are between them (16's and 24's); they are expressing a set of attitudes, wishes, and judgements while managing the interpersonal act of conversation; and they are effectively placing their meanings and intentions in relationship to both their situational context, that of long-term friends who are attending different schools, sitting together in my kitchen at the start of the school year, and the immediate discourse context of this conversation. It is, finally, their ability to negotiate the multiple aspects of context—not only conversational and situational, but also the larger cultural contexts these are linked to and imbedded in—that marks their abilities as language users.

It is against the backdrop of these three elements of context that an individual speaker or writer makes choices from the possibilities available within her lexico-grammar. In *Social Linguistics and Literacies* (1990), linguist Jim Gee has focused on the making of such choices, arguing that the production and comprehension of meaning depends on a set of assumptions, or guesses, that both speaker and listener must make about each others' knowledge:

> Context is a mental construct, since whenever we speak, the whole world and everything the speaker knows and believes or has ever seen or experienced are potentially part of the context, so the hearer and the speaker must assume (imagine) just how much of all of this is relevant and so really part of the context and not just possibly so. (83)

When Melanie talks of "shoe boots" and then follows with a variation on the term "combat boot shoes?" (with a rising intonation signaling a question), she is trying to clarify whether such shoes are within her listeners' field of experience, and if so, what terms will evoke for them the concept that she has in mind at the moment. Much of this portion of the conversation is about lexical choices: how to name the items being discussed in ways that show that your terms, as well as the shoes you want, are in style. In this conversation, the semantic field that Melanie brings is extended by Karen, who confirms her understanding with "Oh, those?" followed by a further question, "what do you want?" which Melanie interprets correctly as a question about a subcategory of the style: "the low tops." In confirmation, Karen brings in another word from the possibly relevant semantic field "Doc Martens," but finds that this term is not part of Melanie's context. The mismatch in knowledge that the girls are bringing to this situation at this point is made explicit in the next set of exchanges: "Do they call them that?" "I don't call them that." "Doc Martens is what they call them." Finally, Melanie recovers her authority and reasserts her own term: "Yeah. I know that's what they call them. I just call them combat boots."

Any movement between cultural contexts can lead people to question the assumptions they bring from other contexts, and to reexamine the meanings that they've assumed were shared. Though Karen, Melanie, and Shanna may be having what seems like a trivial conversation about back-to-school clothes, they are engaged in a process of negotiating shared understandings of assumed knowledge that they've brought from other contexts—including their different schools and the other groups of kids they spend time with—and that process gives them practice for examining assumptions and negotiating shared meanings about more charged and difficult issues that arise in their world.

From their other speech communities, the girls bring differences to these conversations, not only in sets of culturally shared meanings, but also in ways of meaning, particularly in how they use the different aspects of context to present, or define, those meanings. At some points in this conversation, Karen refers to a larger, generally shared, cultural context to support the terms she is using, as in the generalized "they" of "Doc Martens is what *they* call them." At other times she takes advantage of the face-to-face speech situation she is in, pointing to the physical world, "up to here" on her leg, to clarify the meaning of the term "24's." And together, in this discourse context, the girls are engaged in a common act of definition and explanation, drawing on each of the other contexts to build, within this text, a shared understanding in response to the evolving context of what has just been said. Though all three girls use a mix of these strategies in each of their conversations, through the larger set of their conversations some differences emerge. It is most often Melanie who draws on assumed cultural knowledge, introducing the topics of styles, T.V. stars, and music videos, presenting a model of the world in which those who understand the right meanings will have this knowledge and will not need explicit explanations. Shanna asks the questions most often, seeking the explicit answers that Melanie does not typically offer. Karen is most likely to introduce those definitions and explanations. Such patterns have partly to do with age and status within this small group. But they also have partly to do with the girls' own cultural backgrounds: Melanie spends a lot of time in black cultural settings where much of the discourse has an interpersonal function—maintaining the solidarity of the group and affirming shared cultural understandings. Karen spends a lot of time in the academic world of her parents and their associates, where meanings are more likely to be discussed and explicitly worked out, rather than assumed.

Within the small speech community that the girls have created, these somewhat different ways are absorbed into the larger, collaborative and cooperative act of meaning-making. They work out ways of using language that are appropriate to this situation, such as knowing when to use a particular dialect, a particular style or "register," and how much of the meaning needs to be put into words. To quote Halliday again, "Language is the ability to 'mean' in the situation types or social contexts generated by the culture. Being appropriate to the situation is not some optional extra in language, it is an essential element of the ability to mean" (1978, 34).

Traditionally, the formal study of semantics has focused on one side of the many aspects of meaning we've been discussing: on the ways in which meaning is defined by linguistic relationships, rather than by the relationship between speaker/listener and contexts. In traditional semantics, meaning is defined in terms of *sense,* the relationship of words *within* a consistent conceptual system; *reference,* the relationship *between* words or linguistic expressions and the concepts they refer to; and *truth,* the conditions under which a statement can be judged true or false—in terms of its verifiability within the world or within the logic of a sequence of statements. However, each of these concepts can also be redefined in terms of the relationship between the speaker and the context. The speaker's *sense* or meaning may be highly idiosyncratic and experiential, like three-year-old Kenny's concepts of black and white, or Molly's distinction between woof and dog. It may depend on a narrowly shared meaning of a term like fresh that will be repositioned in relation to other terms in a conceptual system as it spreads through a wider community. The consistent conceptual system of a language is constantly being reshaped by speakers in speech communities, and new concepts and relationships are continually being developed as a term used by one speaker is shared with others, just as we've seen in the developing set of relationships among terms for a type of shoes in the conversation of Karen, Melanie, and Shanna. The girls are both drawing on larger cultural authority (*they* call them) and asserting individual meanings (*I* call them) in relationship to the understandings of others in the group. While they negotiate speakers' meaning, the girls are also working out a consistent conceptual system in relationship to the larger culture. They are also building a system of reference, by systematically working out the denotation of the words they use, pointing both to their own words (as they repeat and substitute terms), and to objects in the world (like "up to here "on Karen's leg) to indicate their meanings. And they are testing the truth of their utterances in logical terms as well as experiential ones ("They're called 24's cause up to here is 24 holes"). Although speaker meaning is usually treated as an aspect of pragmatics—of speakers' intentions and uses—rather than semantics, these areas of focus are not so easily separable as we begin to collect natural language data.

As my students and I study the conversations we've taped for the class, we find ourselves looking both to the transcribed texts in front of us, and to the information each of us can provide about the context in which we've taped, in order to find patterns of meaning and make sense of the language we see. For each conversation, we need to know something about the larger cultural context in which this conversation, and others like it, take place. We need to know about the immediate situational context: whether the conversation took place outside of a college classroom, after a church service, or around the dinner table, who the participants were, and what their common concern or focus was at that moment. We need to know about the discourse context—what has gone on already in this conversation or preceding ones that have shaped or constrained the exchange that we are looking at.

The participants in these conversations bring knowledge and expectations from each of these contexts, and from the many others in which they participate. They draw on many frames of reference as they elicit, offer, point to, and exchange information, placing prior cultural and personal meanings, and perhaps meanings that have already been negotiated among these participants, into the immediate discourse context, creating a new framework of shared understanding. In the process, they are building and maintaining a set of social relationships and carrying out particular intentions. The shared knowledge they draw on or create in a conversation is shaped by those relationships and purposes. In language, meaning is never disconnected from such contexts and intentions; rather, it is discovered and shaped within them. In the next chapter we'll look more closely at the girls' shoe boot conversation to see how meaning and intention are realized in an evolving text.

CHAPTER 4

Achieving Intentions and Purposes in Discourse

We can see that the conversation Karen, Melanie, and Shanna are carrying on at any moment does not simply involve a set of statements designed to transfer a fixed amount of information from one person to another. Instead, the direction and purpose of the conversation develops as it goes along. One person introduces a topic and another builds on it or from it, responding not only to the explicit statements that are made, but also to the other speakers' implied responses and attitudes. Understanding the meaning of the girls' conversation requires more than understanding the transcribed words on the page; it requires that we know something about their intentions—their reasons for saying what they say—and the implications of each utterance.

KAREN: I didn't do my exercises yet today.

MELANIE: I'm getting back into gymnastics.

KAREN: You told me that already.

SHANNA: Yeah. You said you were going to the Olympics next time [*laughs*].

KAREN: She is! My mom already bought us tickets. No joke. Go ask her. She already bought me tickets.

MELANIE: Karen stop it.

KAREN: No. I'm not lying ... front row, too. I'll be right next to you. I'm gonna be in your coach's stand.

Throughout their conversations, Karen, Melanie, and Shanna are engaging in a series of acts with intended effects on the other participants. This excerpt contains four statements with varying degrees of truth that could be tested in the world. We find a statement of fact, "I didn't do my exercises yet today," a statement of intention, "I'm getting back into gymnastics," two reported statements, "you told me," "you said," and then a complete fabrication by Karen which has no truth value that can be empirically verified. But the intentions behind the words are not stated. In analyzing the girls' conversation we are engaging in our own interpretive act, using what we can see in the words of the texts they produce, the background knowledge I can contribute as a peripheral member and frequent observer of their speech community, and the common cultural knowledge that anyone who spends much time with American adolescents can draw on, to arrive at a plausible reading of their implied meanings and intentions. In the present excerpt, for example, though Melanie clearly asserts her intention to get into gymnastics again, she doesn't state her purpose in asserting this intention. The information that Melanie is presenting here is not new. It represents already shared knowledge (You told me that already) that the others can elaborate on. (You said you were going to the Olympics.). Her purpose in presenting it must therefore be something other than to impart the information. She could be testing out for herself the idea of returning to gymnastics, seeking the approval of the others, asserting her ability in a sport, or trying to reestablish control over the conversation itself. Probably her statement is designed to accomplish a little of each of these purposes.

Although such conversational exchanges are spontaneous, they take place within familiar frames that help to order the discourse and that support roles familiar to the participants. Bringing in my contextual knowledge of the background against which Melanie's particular statement was made, I might contribute the information that being successful in sports is valued in this group: Karen is a serious soccer player and has reminded the others of the significance of that activity to her life by her comment about her exercise schedule; Melanie is a skilled gymnast but has not been competing for a year or two and is probably feeling uncertain about her present ability and somewhat diffident about trying to pick up where she left off. We can see, in the larger context of the whole conversation, that Melanie is usually the leader, the one who introduces topics and controls the others' contributions, so once Karen has brought up sports, Melanie may need to make that topic her own. Melanie's contribution to this segment of the conversation is likely to carry a number of meanings and it might accomplish a number of purposes that cannot be understood from only the words themselves—meanings and purposes that are likely to be altered as they bump up against the purposes and intentions of the other participants. The making of meaning is not a solitary act but a collaborative, interpersonal, and interactive one.

To understand the meaning of such exchanges, we need to look beyond the conventional meanings of their words and the static propositions represented in each of their sentences. We need to see meanings intended by active speakers and listeners as they are created in a dynamic and interactive process, and in a shared context which allows meaning to be assumed or implied as well as stated. Language is used by speakers and writers who have attitudes toward the ideas they are discussing and the propositions they're expressing, who have relationships with their listeners, and who are trying accomplish particular goals through the course of their interactions.

Studying discourse

Linguists who approach language as discourse typically focus their attention on: actual utterances produced by real speakers, rather than on idealized sample sentences; longer texts that these utterances contribute to, not only on sentences and smaller units; the relationship between the texts produced and the attitudes and intentions of the speakers producing them; and the connection between the texts produced and the context in which they are produced.

Beginning with natural language, as it's produced by real speakers in real speech communities, has several implications for how we conceive of the study of language itself, for theories of meaning (semantics), grammar, and competence. Where language has been approached as a *formal system* defined only in terms of relationships within the system and without reference to context:

1. The study of meaning or semantics has focused largely on the propositional/referential function of language—on its use in naming the world and imparting information about it—and on the analysis of propositional content, logic within a sequence of propositions, and the truth of such propositions as tested against general perceptions of the world.
2. The study of its grammar has focused on the smallest and most precisely defined components of that system: its phonology, morphology, and syntax, ending at the level of the sentence.
3. The study of a speaker's linguistic competence has focused on the speaker's knowledge of the grammatical system, described in terms of those components.

In contrast, where language is approached in terms of its *actual use* by real speakers in natural contexts:

1. The study of meaning includes not only the propositions of sentences as represented in the words of those sentences, but also their implications: the often unstated meanings of the speaker and the intentions behind the utterance (the pragmatic or interpersonal function of language), and the ways in which meaning is related to context. Meaning, from a discourse perspective, is not absolute and resides neither within texts nor within the physical world, but in the individual's ongoing construction of understandings within a sociocultural framework.
2. The study of grammar takes into account not only the components of the grammatical system, but the relationship between these components and the functions for which language is used.
3. The study of a speaker's competence includes not only grammatical competence, or the unconscious knowledge of the grammatical system of the language, but communicative competence, i.e., the speaker's knowledge of how to actually use the language to communicate.

Each of these aspects of the study of natural language includes, but extends, the focus of formalist study. But the questions asked in discourse-based approaches to language study are less about how linguistic systems are structured than about the options they provide to speakers and what governs speakers' choices of these options in actual use.

To see, from a discourse perspective, how meaning is created through the interplay of both the semantic/referential, and the pragmatic/ intentional aspects of language (fulfilling what Halliday describes as the ideational and interpersonal functions of language) within an evolving discourse context such as a conversation, let's look again at the excerpt of Karen, Melanie, and Shanna's conversation that introduced Chapter Three—the conversation about the shoe boots that Melanie wanted to buy.

In this conversation we saw the ways in which shared knowledge is established through a set of questions and statements that bring into the common conversation and clarify a variety of terms that are used to refer to such footwear in the several worlds the girls inhabit, creating a common semantic domain. But the propositions put forth here—that Melanie's favorite place to shop is downtown Boston, that she wants to buy shoe boots—and the ensuing clarification of terms, carries only a small portion of the meaning of this conversation. Each proposition carries implications beyond the literal meaning of the words, the meanings that the speaker intends (I know the best place to shop, I know what's in style), and those that a listener may perceive (Melanie is showing off again). We can't, in fact, understand very much of what's going on in this conversation without taking into account the several functions that each statement serves simultaneously. Part of the pragmatic function of the conversation is to show who is an insider and up-to-date with reference to style and teen culture. The question of what knowledge is shared and what terms need to be explained only really begins to make sense in that context.

As well as sharing or not sharing knowledge about shoe boots, the girls share the understanding that Melanie is the leader and initiator of many of their conversations and enterprises. At first the other girls take their usual role of confirming her statements, asking questions that encourage her to continue and expand on her first offerings with the global intentions of pleasing her, acknowledging her leadership, learning more from her about what's really in in teenage culture, and what they should be paying attention to. But in this instance, the tables get turned. Karen turns out to have more specific knowledge about this style than Melanie, and takes on the role of offering the insider information about the 24's. Her intention does not seem to be to cause this role reversal though, and she returns to her former role by asking a question about the color shoes Melanie wants, which gives the floor back to Melanie for the final statement on the topic. Shanna continues her role here as the younger girl who is both a long-term member of this group, but a not-yet insider to a common teenage world, asserting her right to share in the other girls' understanding by asking questions and requiring explanations.

In each portion of their conversation, whether they're recounting events like the encounter at the Science Museum, defining terms like shoe boots and

24's, or presenting future plans, the girls are establishing their roles in relation to the others, by setting forth a set of attitudes or a stance toward the events they're recounting, the objects they're naming, and toward each other as well. With each new utterance, in addition to naming the world and making statements about it, representing what's happened or what they've seen, they're maintaining a complex, interpersonal role—one that's not always easy to interpret.

This interplay of intentions and meanings is being carried out in the course of a rapidly moving conversation, in which speakers have turns and must know when they can take a turn and how long a turn is appropriate, when they might interrupt, what will be perceived as a relevant comment that contributes to the understanding being developed, and what will not. This segment shows short turns and rapid turn-taking between Karen and Melanie, once Melanie has introduced a topic Karen can pick up on, with two questions contributed by Shanna. By repeating, referring to, or offering synonyms for the terms the previous speaker has used, the girls indicate the relevance of their contributions; all of the entries are here related to the topic. Speakers have responsibilities with respect to creating and sustaining this particular stretch of discourse, as well as to placing and maintaining themselves within a set of interpersonal relationships and building a framework of shared meaning. If we return to this text and look at it line by line, we can see how the three functions—the ideational, interpersonal, and the textual—come together in the creation of meaning.

1. Melanie: "My favorite place to shop . . . is *downtown* Boston."
    Melanie initiates the topic; she assumes her role as leader, with the expectation that her interests will be important to everyone. As she names her favorite place to shop, she pauses for emphasis and then stresses *downtown* Boston. The naming of downtown Boston may be intended to enhance her role, since the girls aren't yet allowed to go there on their own, and the others aren't likely to have shopped there.

2. Karen: "Downtown . . ."
    Karen repeats and echoes the term Melanie has introduced: downtown. Her contribution serves as a backchannel, confirming that she has heard Melanie and is encouraging her to go on.

3. Melanie: "They have High Gear down there. . . . Fresh stuff. . . . They have these shoe boots I want. Combat boot shoes?"
    Melanie gives evidence for her first statement, suggesting that downtown Boston offers clothing that is really in style—the brand High Gear. She adds an evaluative comment which makes this explicit: Fresh stuff. She then goes on to cite "these shoe boots I want," as an example of fresh stuff, following with an expansion of terms to assess the others' understanding: "Combat boot shoes?" In introducing this item, she may also be intending to name a style of clothing that the others don't yet know about.

4. Karen: "Oh, those? What do you want?"
    Karen's response confirms that she does know and can participate equally in this conversation. She goes on with a question that offers Melanie another turn.

5. Melanie: "The low tops."
Melanie responds with an appropriate term, indicating continued shared knowledge.

6. Karen: "Doc Martens?"
Karen introduces another term as a question, for confirmation, expanding on the set of terms that has already been suggested. But it is this contribution that turns the tables, suggesting that Karen may have more knowledge about this style than Melanie. The leadership pattern stays disrupted for several more turns.

7. Shanna: "Do they call them that?"
With the disruption of the early pattern of Melanie's and Karen's exchanges, Shanna has the opportunity to enter the conversation. She does so with a question aimed at getting clarification and information about something she doesn't know much about (her usual role). Her words "call them" are repeated through the next several turns, highlighting the importance of being able to use the right name in displaying a knowledge of style.

8. Melanie: "*I* don't call them that."
Melanie echoes Shanna's question, opposing her *I* to Shanna's *they* and implying that she is confident in her role as leader and that a term *she* doesn't use isn't that important.

9. Karen: "Doc Martens is what they call them."
Karen reasserts the importance of the term she has introduced, highlighting the name by placing it in the front of the sentence. Her reference to an unspecified *they* implies that this is common knowledge, though her intention is probably not to *one-up* Melanie here.

10. Melanie: "Yeah, I know that's what *they* call them. *I* just call them combat boots."
But Melanie reads Karen's intention as just that. She affirms her position as the leader who knows at least as much as the others about what *they* call the shoes, and adds a contrasting statement, emphasizing her own authority, what *I* call them.

11. Karen: "My friend has 24 holes, up to here."
Karen tries to defuse the situation by adding some related, noncontroversial information (but also shows that she participates in other worlds where people know what's in style).

12. Shanna: "She has what?"
Shanna again jumps in with a question, showing that she doesn't get the jargon "24 holes," perhaps implying that such a restricted, unshared term doesn't really belong in this conversation.

13. Karen: "24 holes."
Karen repeats as if Shanna didn't hear, rather than didn't understand, her last contribution.

14. Melanie: "Holes of what? Shoelace holes?"
This time, Melanie too doesn't understand and continues in Shanna's usual role, asking a question for clarification, and perhaps implying that

she too finds Karen's contribution too restricted to make sense, but following with another question that expands on and answers her first, to show that she has caught on.

15. Karen: "Mmmm. They're called 24's, cause up to here is 24 holes— [*gesturing*] 16, 9, and 6."
    With "Mmmm," Karen confirms Melanie's understanding, and then adds the explicit explanation, pointing to her leg so there will be no misunderstanding. "They're called 24's, cause up to here is 24 holes—16, 9, and 6. (Her count is off, but no one picks up on that.)

16. Melanie: "Mine are gonna be to here [*gesturing*], for sure."
    Melanie picks up on Karen's contribution, repeating her gesture to indicate the style she'll choose, thus contributing another response to Karen's original question in line 4.

17. Karen: "What color, red or black ?"
    Karen extends the conversation and puts it back on its original footing with a new question to Melanie.

18. Melanie: "Red, black, and orange."
    Melanie gets the final turn in this segment, expanding on the options Karen has offered, again asserting her position. She'll get the shoes that are in style, and she won't choose one color but will have three.

Such conversations demonstrate the speakers' communicative competence, their ability to represent their own knowledge of the world, to assess and respond to each others' likely knowledge, intentions, implications, and to do so appropriately in a conversational context, attending to the several functions of language simultaneously.

Pragmatics—the interpersonal function of language

We can see that natural discourse, as it occurs among speakers and listeners, or readers and writers, is used not only to name and point to the world, but also to establish and maintain the communicative relationship and to accomplish particular purposes within that relationship. The exclusion of the study of speaker intention and meaning from formal semantics led to the development of the field of pragmatics—a way of formalizing the study of other functions of language besides the referential one, and focusing on how people use language to act in the world. In traditional linguistics these areas of study are kept quite separate. But discourse-based approaches focus on how meaning is created as language is used by speakers, listeners, writers, and readers in relationship to their shared knowledge, assumptions, and intentions. The pragmatic effect of an utterance in a communicative relationship, and the meaning of that utterance, are not easily separable, as we can see throughout Karen, Melanie, and Shanna's conversation.

When we begin to look beyond the surface of the sentences speakers utter, beyond the referential/propositional content of the words standing apart from context, we find that it's often difficult to determine a speaker's underlying meaning or intention for words uttered in the flow of a conversation, where the immediate discourse context is changing at every moment and those intentions are shifting rapidly as the meaning of the conversation is shaped by all participants. To begin our study of the interpersonal/pragmatic function of language, we find it useful to start by looking at individual utterances where the intentions seem clear and directly expressed. When Melanie says, "Shanna, be quiet!" she is giving a direct and explicit command; she seems to want Shanna to stop interrupting her story with intrusive questions, and Shanna understands that she means what she says at that moment and does, in fact, become quiet for a few minutes. When Karen asks Melanie what color shoes she wants, her question is a real question and she genuinely wants that information. At other times, even in brief utterances, the speaker's intention may be less directly expressed. If Justine says to her son Matt, "It's time to put your toys away," she's presenting a directive that he is supposed to carry out. But she does so by making a statement, not issuing an explicit command, "Put your toys away!", and so Matt responds by disagreeing with her statement: "Not time put toys way," rather than giving a direct response to the directive she intends. Specific speech acts provide another way into the study of intentions.

The idea that speakers act on the world through language was formulated by the philosopher John Austin, in *How to Do Things with Words* (1962), who pointed out that not only do we make statements with our utterances, we, at the same time, use language to "do things." Austin defined a set of acts called performatives—acts that had "illocutionary force," or the power to get things done in the world. Such acts included stating, asserting, describing, warning, remarking, commenting, commanding, ordering, requesting, criticizing, apologizing, censuring, approving, welcoming, promising, expressing approval, and expressing regret.

In 1965, John Searle published the essay "What Is a Speech Act?" in which he expanded upon the work of Austin, arguing that *all* utterances are also acts, intended to do something as well as say something. According to Speech Act Theory, the basic statement or structural unit of an utterance (the *locution*) not only states a proposition, but carries with it both the intentions of the speaker (the *illocutionary force* of the utterance), and unintended effects on a listener (its *perlocutionary* effects). My next-door neighbor might use the locution "Good day, Mr. Brown!" to greet Melanie's father on the street. The words show the conventional form of a greeting, but even this simple and direct utterance is shaped by the complex interaction of the speaker's intentions, the speaker's assumptions about the listener's likely response, and the listener's actual response. Perhaps the neighbor has chosen the relatively formal address as a sign of respect, so respectfulness would be the speaker's intention or the illocutionary force of the words. But Melanie's father, who is known to everyone on our street as Marvin, might feel that the neighbor is being suddenly standoffish and distant, and so the perlocutionary effect of this greeting would be quite different from the intended effect.

Speech acts and discourse contexts

Conversations, and the sequences of speech acts that contribute to them, clearly take place in a variety of situational contexts, where similar acts may take on very different forms depending on the setting and the participants. Searle argued that "to perform illocutionary acts is to engage in a rule-governed form of behavior." His work focused on analyzing the rules necessary to particular forms of this behavior—to identify the necessary conditions (felicity conditions) for a successful act of making a promise, for example. He saw these rules as universal: "Different human languages, to the extent they are intertranslatable, can be regarded as different conventional realizations of the same underlying rules" (1969, 39).

But while there may be common rules for all examples of an act such as a promise, including the fact that the speaker has a sincere commitment to carry out at a future time the thing that is being promised (see Searle 1969, 57–61 for a detailed discussion of the felicity conditions for promises), what is actually intended or perceived as a promise varies with different participants, in different contexts. "You promised!" my niece shrieks. Did I really say, "I promise we will get ice cream after the movie," or did I say *maybe* or *perhaps?* At Grandma's, *maybe* is always followed by the realization of what was wanted or asked, so my *maybe* seems to my niece (but not to me) to carry the force of a promise, though she knows that her mom's *maybe* does not. We disagree about the rules for this speech act, and I'm learning to clarify my intentions with the explicit statement: "I'm *not* promising anything." But because Grandma's *maybe* has a different meaning than her mom's or mine, with just a small shift in family relations, the assumed and agreed upon meaning of a word, and the speech act it accomplishes, shifts, and these must be renegotiated as new participants arrive on the scene.

With movement from one speech or discourse community to another, words can even come to mean the opposite of their more common meanings, and the intended or illocutionary effect of those words can be quite different from more common expectations, so that "That's bad, man!" becomes a statement of high praise rather than of criticism or censure.

My students study speech acts as they are performed in the many communities in which they live, work, and interact, trying to discover the ways in which language is used to act on the world and what makes communication successful. They choose a type of act, greetings, apologies, requests, and record:

- what is said
- who the participants are: their sex, age, relationship, professional role, and/ or social class, whether they are insiders or outsiders to this community, and any other information that seems relevant
- what the context of the exchange is, both in reference to the setting, and in relation to the discourse if it extends beyond this exchange
- what the intention (illocutionary force) of the initiator of the act seems to be
- whether that intention is carried out directly or indirectly

- what the effect (perlocutionary force) of the act on the other participant(s) seems to be
- whether or not the act seems to constitute a successful speech event

What makes a successful speech act? The obvious answer that emerges from our study is that the speaker's intention (the illocutionary force of the utterance) is achieved. In successful speech acts (even pejorative ones like insults), the speaker's intention and the listener's interpretation (the perlocutionary force of the utterance) will match. In unsuccessful ones, there will be a mismatch between intention and interpretation, though both speaker and listener may agree on the actual words spoken. Such mismatches can occur even in personal relationships where there is a great deal of shared knowledge, as linguist Deborah Tannen's popular book *You Just Don't Understand: Men and Women in Conversation* (1990) shows. My students discover some of the reasons for these misunderstandings. They find that:

> *A single intention or purpose can be realized with different forms of a speech act.* A speaker may carry out her intention directly, using the imperative to give a direct order, the interrogative to ask a question, or the declarative to make a statement; or indirectly, by asking a question to indicate that something should be done. What matters for communication is that both participants have the same interpretation of the act. For example, as the manager of a juice bar, Lisa must remind workers to wear a bow tie that is part of their uniform. Although her intention is always to get them to wear the tie, sometimes she expresses this intention with a question: "Where's your bow tie?" and sometimes with a declarative observation: "Carl, you have no bow tie on." The indirect forms seem to offer a more polite and less confrontational way of indicating what she wants done, but they can also be more easily ignored, and sometimes Lisa can achieve her purpose only with a direct order: "Julie, put on a bow tie *right now!*"
>
> *The same speech act can carry different intentions and meanings.* Lorraine works part-time in a video store where there are many greetings and friendly exchanges, some with multiple illocutionary intent. "What's up?" is often used as a greeting with co-workers and familiar customers. Although its form is interrogative, it's not generally intended to imply a real question, and "Nothing much" is a typical response. But when a security guard who wouldn't usually come into the building unless there's a problem he want's to talk about comes in, "What's up?" presents not just a casual greeting but a real question in a form that won't alarm casual listeners.
>
> *Successful communication and interpretation of intentions depends on shared understandings that arise from personal relationships with other participants, shared knowledge of a discourse frame, or shared cultural background.* In families, underlying intentions are easily understood. Pat knows that her daughter's comment

"Did you bring our chairs home from Margaret's yet?" is not a real question but a reprimand. Sarah knows that when her mother says "I love you," it often signals an indirect request to do an errand. Kerry finds that her husband's question, "Do you want to play chess?" seems direct enough, but many of their interactions are affected by their current roles as students, and she finds that "indirectly I feel as though Kelly is asking for my approval that he take a break from his homework."

In public spaces, like stores, exchanges are shaped by a familiar discourse frame. Many of my students hold part-time jobs in grocery stores, small shops, and fast-food outlets. In such settings, although some customers are regular participants in repeated exchanges, many are not. Yet because the discourse context of a grocery store or clothing shop is familiar and there are common elements to the service exchanges that take place in these settings, even strangers can usually accomplish their purposes successfully, though their forms may vary by the age or other characteristics of the participants, and by how much people seem to feel like insiders or accepted members in the particular context. Kim, a server in an ice cream store, finds that she greets older customers with the more formal "How are you doing tonight?" and younger customers with "Hi. Howya doing?" Liz observes a bouncer at a bar collecting a cover charge and discovers that, though he usually makes only a brief standard request: "$6 cover, ID, please!" he extends this when he's speaking to young, attractive women. "Good evening ladies. That'll be $6 and I need to see an ID." Michelle finds that most of her bookstore customers initiate the exchange, preceding their requests with a brief greeting "Hi . . . I'm looking for a book?" One customer stands around awkwardly until she asks if she can help him, and then responds with, "Yeah, the wife wants this book," suggesting that he is an outsider who is uncomfortable in this setting.

Shared discourse frames often ensure successful communication even across language boundaries. Because the requirements of such exchanges are so familiar, the customer making a purchase or the child sitting in a traditional classroom in another country can usually manage the appropriate interactions within a common structure. Different cultural assumptions can still interfere, however. When I step into a small shop in a foreign country, I am usually trying so hard to remember the words for the items I want that I forget the required politenesses, like "Bonjour monsieur/dame," while my husband, who doesn't usually know much of the language, concentrates on the appropriate forms of polite interaction and is generally much more successful in accomplishing his intentions. In a New York store, on the other hand, the direct request "Give me some brie and two apples" without time-wasting pleasantries is not considered at all rude.

But within any larger cultural context there are also smaller cultural settings where expectations may be shaped by other commonalities, in age or sex, for example, as one student discovered in his visit to a barbershop. There Joe observed several successful interactions—greetings, requests, and inquiries about the services desired—that are typical of such settings. But he also observed one unsuccessful and even rude interaction where a young female barber's direct greeting to an older male customer was ignored, although young male customers responded to her greetings in a friendly way. As the barber, the young woman clearly had a central role in this setting, yet she was probably seen by the older customer as an outsider in a typically male world.

Speech acts that are successful in accomplishing the purposes of the participants in the speech event are most often marked by the familiarity of the participants or their shared understanding of the type and setting of the speech event. Unsuccessful speech acts, like the barber's failed attempt to exchange greetings with her customer, occur most frequently when assumptions are not shared. Without familiarity and shared understanding, successful exchanges are more difficult to accomplish and must be carefully negotiated. The data gathered by Paul, a Boston police officer, show this contrast.

Keeping track of the calls he received on his patrol car radio one night, Paul at first found himself in a familiar environment where assumptions are shared. His dispatcher usually gives direct orders: "Go to _____ ," followed by a statement about the problem that has been reported; on this one evening, several attacks on women by husbands and boyfriends, a threatened suicide by a Vietnam vet, a drug overdose, breaking and entering, public drinking, a report of a stolen car, the accidental shooting of a teenager by a friend, and a call for help in removing a bat from the house. The dispatcher uses few indirect forms, though he sometimes names just the event and location in a declarative statement: "B & E at 165 [W] Street," or a brief narrative account: "We have a report of a woman stabbed at 266 [Z] Street in Jamaica Plain. H & H Ambulance Service is also responding." But the intention or illocutionary force, to have police carry out the order and go to the scene of the problem, is always understood. When Paul arrives at a particular scene, however, he finds much more potential for miscommunication: the woman who called saying her husband was killing her tells the police when they arrive that "everything's fine now," leaving the officers uncertain about the extent of danger; the suicidal Vietnam vet points his gun at the officers saying he "just wants to end it all" and must be talked into surrender; the woman who is revived after an overdose of drugs tells the officers and paramedics to "leave her the hell alone." In each case the officers must respond not just to the immediate statements but to larger intentions and implications that they find difficult to read.

Paul operates in two worlds simultaneously—the shared world of the police precinct and the many different worlds of those whose calls he must answer. In the shared context of the police community many things can be implied without need for direct statement: a report of a stabbing or gunshot suggests to Paul that he should call for an ambulance whether or not that's explicitly included in the dispatch; the nature of the event and the location suggest to him whether he's likely to need backup. But out on the city streets, there is no such shared framework of understanding. Paul is an African-American of West Indian origins who has been raised in Boston neighborhoods, and is sensitive to the possibility of miscommunication across cultural boundaries. But this awareness does not always help him to read a caller's meanings and intentions, particularly in domestic disputes. In terms of his immediate purpose, to end the incident that prompted the call, these speech events are all successful—an arrest is made, medical attention is provided. But a larger resolution is harder to achieve, and he often worries, as he leaves such scenes, about whether there has indeed been successful communication.

Conversation and cooperation

In familiar settings, the success of a speech act is likely to be measured not only by whether the speaker's immediate intention is achieved, but also by whether the act is extended in such a way as to allow ongoing contact and conversation. Many questions or statements in family or workplace exchanges, such as comments about the weather, are intended not to ask for or to convey information but to initiate friendly contact or to elicit further contributions. When Doris's son asks her "Did you get *The Argus* this week?" she understands that her son is not really asking her for that information but is suggesting that the local paper contains a report about her granddaughter's soccer game, and she knows that she should follow his question with an inquiry and with further indications of her interest in her granddaughter's activities. Sandra finds that requests for information by co-workers in her office are frequently intended to begin longer conversations—that while the manager's question, "What's the status on the pension problem?" is really a request for specific information, her project leader's question: "How's pensions?" is really a general invitation to shoot the breeze.

A particular speech act must be understood in relationship to several contexts: the experience and knowledge the participants share, the particular situation they're in at the moment, and the evolving context of the discourse itself. Outside of the brief service exchanges that occur in ice cream shops and video stores, most speech acts take place in, and contribute to, longer conversational sequences, and how we hear and interpret an utterance is shaped by an ongoing conversation that takes place over minutes, and often, in some form, over days, months, and years. Rather than looking at speech acts in terms of whether they follow particular rules, meet particular felicity conditions, and thus can be categorized as promises, apologies, or assertions, the philosopher H. P. Grice has explored the larger principles of human behavior that support communication and make most conversations orderly, purposeful, and efficient—extending the theory of how meanings are developed in the context of language use. He begins with the common sense assumption that participants in a conversation are contributing to a common enterprise that shows some degree of coherence and continuity because they are cooperating in this endeavor. He formulates what he calls the *cooperative principle*:

> Make your conversational contribution such as is required, at the stage at which it occurs, by the accepted purpose or direction of the talk exchange in which you are engaged. (1975, 45)

The *cooperative principle* suggests that participants mean to cooperate in the act of communication. In following this principle, Grice finds speakers will ordinarily make their contributions to the conversation in accordance with four general maxims: they try to make their statements contain as much information as necessary, but not too much (the maxim of *quantity*); they make their statements relevant to the situation or topic (the maxim of *relation*); they make their statements truthful (the maxim of *quality*); and they make their comments direct and clear (the maxim of *manner*). But sometimes, instead of following these maxims and thus stating literally what they mean or intend, speakers will suggest their meaning implicitly by violating one of the maxims. For example, if Kerry asks, "What time is it?" and her husband responds, "I've finished all my homework," there is an apparent violation of the maxim of relation. On the surface, the response might be seen as uncooperative, since Kerry's husband ignores her question.

However, Grice would argue that most such interactions are still cooperative ones—that if a speaker violates one of these common maxims, the listeners will still try to interpret the response as meaningful and to discover what it implies. It's most likely that Kerry's husband has interpreted her question as extending beyond its literal meaning, as not really asking a question about the time but as making an implicit comment about whatever he's doing instead of homework, and his response shows that he is cooperating in an act of *conversational implicature*, responding to what is *implied* by Kerry's utterance, not to her actual words. Such exchanges go on frequently among people who know each other well, as was shown in Kerry's earlier speech act example, where she reads her husband's question, "Do you want to play chess?" as an implied request for permission to take a break from his homework.

The speaker's intended meaning is often different from the literal meaning of an utterance. People interpret these intended meanings based on their shared knowledge of the context in which the exchange takes place. The relevance of the specific words spoken is always being interpreted against the larger framework of the participants' common preoccupations and ongoing interactions. In this case, since Kerry and her husband are both students, they have a shared understanding that their schoolwork should take priority over other activities, and Kerry sees that many of their utterances must be interpreted in that light. Likewise, when Karen uses the eliptical "24 holes," such an abbreviated contribution might be seen to violate the maxim of quantity, but it can also affirm membership in a community where such knowledge is shared. It can be assumed to be understood within the right community of insiders; the quantity of information would be appropriate, rather than an intentional or unintentional violation of the cooperative principle.

In longer conversations, which can be seen as a series of speech acts, there is again an assumption that the enterprise is a cooperative one, and that any violation of maxims is intentional, designed to imply something that's not stated directly. It isn't that the speaker's awareness of these maxims is conscious, or even that the four maxims Grice named are the best way of describing the expectations people have of each other in conversation. But they do have some expectations about the ordinary shape and flow of conversation. If one speaker talks too long (violating Grice's maxim of manner), another speaker is likely to jump in. If a speaker gives too little information (violating Grice's maxim of quantity), she's likely to be interrupted with questions from her listeners. And when the participants know each other well, there's likely to be a lot that can be implied by a violation of these expectations.

If we return to the segment of Karen, Melanie, and Shanna's conversation that opened this chapter, we can see how Karen responds to Melanie and Shanna's expectations. When Shanna laughs as she repeats Melanie's earlier claim that she would be going to the next Olympics, she signals her disbelief that that will happen. Karen follows with the direct, declarative statement: "She is!" and immediately goes on to violate the maxim of quality with her false account of how "my mom already bought us tickets." The implication created by this series of statements is that Shanna has no justification for doubting that Melanie will succeed in participating in the Olympics if she chooses to do so—that Melanie's statement of intention is not something to laugh at. Karen presents the argument most forcefully, insisting that what she is saying is "no joke." When Melanie, somewhat embarrassed by this violation of her sense of the rules for appropriate contributions to this conversation (and perhaps by Karen's unqualified support of an assertion she may not live up to), tells her to "stop it," Karen claims that she is not lying. Her final statements in this series strongly affirm her underlying meaning: "I'll be right next to you. I'm gonna be in your coach's stand." Addressing herself directly to Melanie, she insists on overriding any of Melanie's own doubts or hesitations, declaring her support most forcefully, by implication, for all of Melanie's endeavors. Her apparent violation of a maxim of the cooperative principle serves a larger interpersonal function, contributing in significant ways to her ongoing communication with her friend.

We can see that among family, friends, and co-workers, where people know each other well or interact regularly in a familiar environment, a good deal does not have to be stated directly but is suggested through indirection and implicature. This does not mean that there is no potential for misunderstanding in these contexts. We will see, in later chapters, that expectations based on differences in age, sex, and cultural background can interfere with communication even among people who spend a lot of time together, and that these differing expectations can lead to serious miscommunication in some settings. When people move out of such familiar contexts, whether into a bookstore, another workplace, or a house where a domestic dispute is taking place, they may find that certain acts are accomplished in different ways. In classrooms, for example, where teachers often tend to use the indirect forms that are perceived within some cultural groups as more polite, the teacher who asks a student, "Would you like to write that problem on the blackboard now?" or, "Are your books open to page 150?" does not expect to hear no for an answer. But children who are accustomed to following explicit directives at home may expect to hear "Go to the blackboard," or "Open your books." They often do not interpret these indirect forms as the teacher intends, and when they do not respond as they would to a directive, they are seen as rebellious and uncooperative.

Language study and finding a common language

From our study of how speech acts are accomplished and conversations are carried on in the immediate communities that we participate in, my students and I learn about the different ways in which intentions might be expressed, as well as some of the principles that seem to be common to all communication. We can use our own data to examine or generate formal theories of language use, looking for common patterns across data, discovering categories that help us to rationalize or make sense of the data we've collected about particular acts, and inventing hypotheses about common principles or rules that would explain the patterns we find. At the same time, as we've seen, each speech act is situated in a larger communicative context and can only be fully understood in relation to that context. Once again our study of discourse and language in context leads us away from looking at sets of similar data abstracted from the situations in which they were gathered, and turns us toward studying how these particular examples instantiate patterns of interaction and understanding that occur across different speech acts and throughout the multiple aspects of peoples' lives within a speech community.

When Lisa brings in examples of the different forms she uses for the orders she gives juice bar employees about wearing their bow ties, we can group her orders with similar acts observed by others, label them as directives, list the different forms that appear for acts that seem like directives across our data, and try to generate our own rules to explain the forms that we find. But Lisa can also return to her workplace—to the speech community in which these acts occurred—and study the ways in which these acts are like or unlike other uses of language and like the other nonlanguage behaviors that contribute to larger patterns of meaning within this small workplace culture. Does her indirect observation to Carl, "You have no bow tie on," which Lisa sees as polite, signal a workplace where assumptions about the value of company rules are generally shared and the responsibility for following them rests with the individual employee, with occasional helpful reminders from others? Or is this a workplace culture in which the rules are seen as arbitrary and of no value to the larger enterprise of selling juice, where the manager must directly assert authority and control ("Put your bow tie on *right now!*) or be ignored, and where the need for this form of directive is linked to a larger pattern of assertion of and resistance to authority that may show up not only in other language acts but in other physical acts as well.

Our study of speech acts can lead to other questions about language as a system and about the knowledge and competence of the speakers who use that system, and to questions about the place and use of language in particular contexts. It also gives us a sense of the many possible ways of using the same language in and across communities to express particular meanings and accomplish particular intentions. It suggests that, to communicate outside of our immediate communities, we need to clarify intentions, create shared knowledge across boundaries, move out from assuming that the rest of the world shares the knowledge that is in our heads, and become good observers who can perceive and try out different ways in different settings. Through such studies of differences and similarities, we can gradually extend our own communicative repertoire and our understanding of how other people, under the surface differences of the ways they use language, are participating in cooperative acts of communication in ways that make them fundamentally like-self, how people use language to bring a shared world of experience into being. By studying not only the formal models of the linguistic system but also the ways people use language in particular contexts, we can use our own study of language to find common ground. But to do this we have to understand more about what speakers know—both the resources the linguistic system offers, and how speakers make choices among these resources in the ongoing construction of texts.

CHAPTER 5

Using Structures, Shaping Texts

We've seen that, in their conversations, Karen, Melanie, and Shanna are engaged in a collaborative, and sometimes competitive, process of shaping an extended stretch of discourse—picking up on the topics that the others introduce, echoing and expanding on the words and the syntax that have already been placed into the immediate discourse context, and making choices that highlight their own intentions with each addition to the evolving text. The girls' intended meanings are signaled most obviously by the words they choose, where boys are cute, clothes are fresh stuff, and shoes are 24's or Doc Martens. But these meanings, and their ability to introduce them appropriately into a conversation, depend as well on the rich range of syntactic possibilities available in the linguistic system of English and its variant dialects. The girls' underlying grammatical competence gives these teenaged speakers many of these syntactic resources, providing a large repertoire of possibilities that they draw on, unconsciously, as they represent their meanings and intentions at a particular moment. To see what possibilities are available to these speakers, and what constrains those possibilities as they respond within an evolving discourse context, we need to know something about both the syntactic structures of English, and the larger discourse or information structures that function in coherent, connected texts.

Syntax

Syntax involves the grouping of words (combinations of morphemes) into phrases, clauses, and sentences. When my students and I look at the conversational data we've collected, we see that our informants not only speak in strings of words, but that these strings have a definite organization and structure. Transcribed speech looks messy compared with written text, filled with hesitations and new starts, occasioned by the speakers' attempts to work out what they want to say as they go along. But as we look closely, we begin to see that the nature of its messiness gives further confirmation of the fact that speakers are organizing their thoughts in accordance with a strong intuitive sense of how language should be structured. Both the apparent messiness and the underlying sense of structure can be seen in the transcription of just a few lines of Melanie and Karen's comments as they discuss TV star Luke Perry's appearance at a local mall:

MELANIE: I went to the mall. . . . Did you go there . . .when you . . . when Luke Perry was there? I went there . . . me and my friends went there . . . he was all . . .

KAREN: Nicole went and she got me his signature and everything . . . all they were doing is handing out like . . . some . . . printed signatures. It was stupid.

Even with the false starts and rewordings, a basic structure is apparent here, and Melanie and Karen show a sure sense of what goes where within that structure. In fact, a lot of what makes their transcribed speech look so fragmented is that they keep beginning again as they shift their focus to the different people who were, or might have been, at the mall—*I, you, Luke Perry, me and my friends, Nicole*—and place the new noun or pronoun into what they know intuitively to be the right position. Despite these restarts, the flow of the conversation is generally quite rapid, and despite hesitations and rephrasings, sentence after sentence of English that makes perfect sense to the listeners is produced. When the sentences are printed out of context—the way they'd appear in a grammar book—their structure becomes clearer.

> *I went to the mall.*
>
> *Did you go there?*
>
> *Nicole went.*
>
> *She got me his signature.*
>
> *All they were doing is handing out some printed signatures.*
>
> *It was stupid.*

Several observations can be made about these sentences immediately, apart from describing them using the traditional terms of subject, verb, direct object, indirect object, complement:

1. The words can't be placed in random order: it doesn't make sense to say *went Nicole*, or *me got she signature his*.
2. Some words can be substituted for others: *I went, you went, Nicole went, me and my friends went*, but not *got went*.
3. There are a few ways in which the sentences can be restructured to make the same statement: "She got me his signature" could become *His signature is what she got me.* "All they were doing is handing out some printed signatures" could also be said: *Handing out some printed signatures is all they were doing*, or *Some printed signatures were what they were handing out*. Or they can

be changed into questions *Were they handing out printed signatures?*

When sentences are restructured in these ways, certain groups of words must be moved together: *his signature, some printed signatures.*

From these observations, we might make several hypotheses:

4. Words fall into particular *categories*: *I, you, Nicole, she, me and my friend* can be substituted for one another and therefore seem to fall into one category, with *went* and *got* in a different category.
5. The words from different categories can be combined to form larger groupings, or *constituents,* like noun phrases in which modifiers are placed before nouns: *printed signatures*; or prepositional phrases in which nouns follow prepositions: *to the mall.*
6. There are regular, rule-governed patterns in which phrase structures can be formed and moved around and sentences can be transformed from one structure to another—rules for *phrase structures* and *transformations.*

The terms I am using here are those associated with one theory of grammar that currently dominates much of linguistics: transformational generative grammar, the theory most closely associated with the work of Noam Chomsky. Formal theories of grammar offer hypotheses about the ways in which language is structured. They try to determine how the system of language works, and the rules that govern the system, the way that a mathematician tries to describe a formal system of mathematics. In his book *Knowledge of Language* (1986), Chomsky says that his purpose is to present a general theory of linguistic structure that "aims to discover the framework of principles and elements common to attainable human language"(3). His focus is on describing a language as a formal system, its general principles apart from its actual use, and its syntax (structure) rather than on its semantics (meanings) or pragmatics (intentions and purposes).

Chomsky's is only one of a number of generative grammars, the theories of the linguistic system that focus on how it allows humans to generate new utterances, to produce and understand language. Transformational grammar is a particular theory of generative grammar (usually referred to now as TG theory). In Chomsky's early work on this theory, he described two levels of structure, a *deep structure* or sets of underlying propositions, and a *surface structure,* the actual realization of those propositions in sentences. He showed that the same deep structure proposition can be represented by different surface structures:

They handed out some printed signatures.

Some printed signatures were handed out.

Transformational rules were formulated to describe the ways in which propositions in deep structure could be transformed into different surface structure representations.

Describing such rules is a complex task, and TG theory is constantly being revised. The system described in the formal theory is not part of the conscious knowledge of speakers; rather, it is a formal way of representing that knowledge. Linguists who work on formal grammatical theories try to take into account all of the possible utterances that would be perceived as grammatical by speakers of a language, usually drawing on their own intuitive knowledge of their own native language, but for other languages, asking native-speaking informants whether one could say such and such in the language, whether it would *make sense*. The rules must account for an enormous range of utterances and must explain how speakers can continually create new *grammatical* utterances that they've never heard anyone speak before. Chomsky argues that there is no way that individual speakers (especially children) could derive the rules for producing such a range of new grammatical utterances from the relatively impoverished amount of actual language that they've heard: "Our knowledge is richly articulated and shared with others from the same speech community, whereas the data available are much too impoverished to determine it by any process of induction, generalization, analogy, association" (55).

Chomsky theorizes that these rules are, in a sense, built into the human mind, and that humans have "a 'language acquisition device,' an innate component of the human mind that yields a particular language through interaction with presented experience, a device that converts experience into a system of knowledge attained: knowledge of one or another language" (3). Because an innate component of the human mind would account for the grammatical structures of all languages, Chomsky now refers to his theory as "universal grammar" or UG. Universal Grammar is a theory of human internalized languages, "a characterization of the innate, biologically determined principles which constitute one component of the human mind—the language faculty" (24). Its focus is on biological principles that hold true across languages: "To achieve descriptive adequacy, the available devices must be rich and diverse enough to deal with the phenomena exhibited in the possible human languages" (55).

According to Chomsky, then, speakers like Karen, Melanie, and Shanna have innate capabilities to process language when presented with the real speech data of real communities, resulting in knowledge that, though unconscious, is "richly articulated and shared with others from the same speech community" (55). But Chomsky is not particularly interested in real speech data. Distinguishing between *externalized language* (the actual utterances that linguists can observe, a speaker's *performance*, the actual or potential speech events), and *internalized language* (the structure of language as it exists in the mind of a speaker, or the speaker's underlying grammatical *competence*), Chomsky focuses on competence. Further, he is interested in this competence insofar as it can be described in terms of the structure of sentences and syntax, without direct reference to meaning. To illustrate this point, he offers the now famous sentence: Colorless green dreams sleep furiously. Like the poem "Jabberwocky" from Lewis Carroll's *Alice in Wonderland* ("Twas brillig and the slithy toves/ did gyre and gimble in the wabe.")

such a sentence offers nonsense that still seems comprehensible. In terms of semantics, of the truth value of an utterance as it relates to the world, we can't speak, for example, of something being both colorless and green. But because *colorless* and *green* are both adjectives modifying the noun *dreams*, and because they are grouped together with that noun appropriately (preceding the noun), we process the syntax as if it offers potential meaning. We would not if the word order were changed to dreams green colorless. Indeed, as long as something matches our sense of correct syntactic structure, we work hard to make it meaningful, and if we repeat Chomsky's sentence, it soon comes to offer some meaning to us—to seem profound, poetic even, rather than nonsensical.

We can assume that Karen, Melanie, and Shanna have an underlying competence in their native language that allows them to produce and respond to the grammatical structures that language allows. But can the messy data of their conversation, the sort of *performance* data that Chomsky does not look at, tell us much about that competence in the terms of TG or UG theory? To describe the knowledge represented in those sentences, we need the three concepts we named above.

Categories

To describe the syntactic structures available in English, we need to consider the categories that words fall into and the relationships between those categories. But within a formal system, where we're trying to describe syntactic structures in the terms of that system, our old meaning-based definitions for those categories aren't useful. Instead of defining a noun in terms of what it refers to in the world, as the name of a person, place, or thing, we'll need to describe this category by its properties within the structure of the sentence. The linguist who is focusing on the formal system of linguistic structures and the ways in which the components of that system interact (including linguists working in TG grammar) will describe the categories of words by such principles as co-occurrence, position, and function within the sentence. A *noun,* then, is recognized by several features:

1. It can co-occur with a plural inflection (signature*s,* child*ren,*) and a possessive inflection (Nicole*'s*).
2. It sometimes occurs after a determiner, a definite or indefinite article or the equivalent (*the* signatures, *a* signature, *some* signatures) or an adjective (*printed* signatures).
3. It is positioned as the head word—the essential word—of a phrase that contains the noun along with other possible elements, a noun phrase, and it functions as the subject of that phrase (some printed *signatures*).
4. It can function also as the subject of a sentence (Some printed *signatures* were handed out); as a direct object (They handed out some printed *signatures*); or as an indirect object (They handed out a printed signature to *Nicole*).

Similarly, *verbs* are often recognized by the fact that they can co-occur with the past tense morpheme *ed* (so *hand*, which would be a noun in some contexts, is used by Karen as a verb: hand*ed* out); they can co-occur with *ing* (hand*ing*); they sometimes occur with auxiliaries (*can* hand out, *will* hand out); and they function as the head word or main verb in a verb phrase (will be able to *hand* out).

Other parts of speech can be described according to these same principles, and a particular word may need to be tested against more than one principle to determine its category in a particular sentence. Where, by the principle of co-occurrence, a word might fall in one category (so print*ed* would be categorized as a verb in the sentence "He printed his name"), it may appear in a different category when we look at its position or function in a particular sentence.

Adjectives appear in either attributive position, the position immediately before a noun, or in a predicate position, as after the verb *to be*, so in Karen's sentence "All they were doing is handing out some printed signatures," *printed* acts as an adjective, appearing immediately before the noun *signatures*.

Adverbs often co-occur with *ly*, and function to modify verbs or adjectives, or sometimes the whole sentence (*Soon* they will hand out printed signatures).

Nouns, verbs, adjectives, and adverbs are categories of major words containing lexical morphemes. Although we are not focusing at the moment on their referential meaning—on their meaning as they point to some object or action or idea in the world—they do carry the underlying meaning of the sentence. If we heard *Luke Perry mall* we would guess that Luke Perry is or was or might be *at a* mall or *in the* mall. Minor word classes, serving a grammatical function, include *prepositions* (like *at* and *in*), *determiners* (articles like *a*, *the*, demonstratives like *this* and *that*, sometimes quantifiers like *some*), *auxiliaries* (*will, can, must*), and *conjunctions* (*and, since*). They are necessary to the syntactic construction of a sentence, and they modify the meaning carried by words in the major classes.

A distinction is sometimes made between open and closed classes of words: open classes are the major categories, which add new words as society changes; closed classes are the minor, grammatical categories that tend to remain fixed through centuries. Teenagers like Karen, Melanie, and Shanna often invent new nouns or verbs or adjectives to assert the common values of a peer group and separate themselves from the adult world. As soon as a word gets adopted into common speech a new one is invented. In the girls' community, for example, a "nerd" was, for a while, replaced first with a Barney and then with a dweeb, which will soon be replaced by yet another noun with an equivalent meaning. As we add new words to our lexicon, we seem to mentally store information about their categories and how they can be used. (For a fuller discussion of grammatical categories see Kaplan 1989; Weaver 1979.)

Constituent structure

When we look at sentence constituents, we see that the information we've used to determine categories also describes how categories go together to form phrases: that determiners, and often adjectives, precede nouns and are moved with them (They handed out *some printed signatures* or *Some printed signatures* were handed out), and that prepositions are followed by determiners and nouns (*at the mall*). Whether Melanie says, "I saw Luke Perry at the mall," or "At the mall I saw Luke Perry," the words of the prepositional phrase "at the mall" will be moved around together as a single constituent or removed together and replaced: "I saw Luke Perry *there*." We see that sentences are made up of smaller structures, of noun phrases (NP) and verb phrases (VP): NP "My friends"; VP "saw Luke Perry at the mall". These are made up in turn of smaller structures.

These relationships are typically described in terms of phrase structure rules, showing that a noun phrase consists of a noun plus optional determiners and adjectives (NP— (det) + (adj) + N); that a verb phrase consists of a verb plus other possible elements, like another noun phrase or a prepositional phrase (VP— V + (NP)+ (PP)); that a prepositional phrase consists of a preposition plus a noun phrase which in turn consists of a noun plus an optional determiner and/or adjective(s) (PP—P + NP). (The parentheses indicate that an element is optional.) Or they may be illustrated with a tree diagram that shows the hierarchical relationship of units:

Though formal grammarians may diagram sentences this way, for our purposes it is less important to create such diagrams than to have a sense of these hierarchical grammatical relationships, and to see that elements lower in the hierarchy under a particular branch can substitute for elements higher in the hierarchy. We see that Melanie can make many substitutions for the grammatically required NP + VP of her sentence, from "I went" to "We saw him" to "Two of my friends and I saw the television actor Luke Perry, who appears on the program Beverly Hills 90210, at the mall in Cambridge on Saturday," and that her restarts, as she works out what she means to say and what her audience can be expected to know or care about, all show the same underlying grammatical structure. ("Me and my friends went," a variant on "My friends and I" in the more formal dialect of standard English, is clearly presented and understood as a perfectly grammatical—acceptable and comprehensible—form for a compound subject NP in this informal setting).

Transformations

Another concept that emerges from TG theory is the notion of the transformation itself, the operation that allows us to turn declarative statements (My friends saw Luke Perry) into questions (Where did your friends see Luke Perry?) or passives (Luke Perry was seen at the mall by my friends), or to emphasize certain information in the sentence by changing the usual word order in English and moving something other than the subject of the sentence to the front through a number of alternatives: *fronting*, "Luke Perry I saw at the mall"; *left dislocation*, "Luke Perry, I saw him at the mall"; *clefting*, "It was Luke Perry whom I saw at the mall." (While this latter version is correct in the most formal uses of English, it sounds strange as something the girls might say in their informal conversation, where they'd probably use "that" instead of "whom" or omit the relative pronoun altogether.) Again, native speakers of English know intuitively how to transform one sentence structure into another and to avoid applying transformational rules where they'd result in a sentence that's ungrammatical (as opposed to informal). It's the speaker's unconscious knowledge of what's allowed in the grammar that the theory is trying to describe. But it's helpful to realize that there are a number of different ways to realize the same underlying proposition, and a number of grammatical alternatives open to the speaker and writer, as we consider the effect of particular surface structures within a particular stretch of discourse.

Some of the lessons of school grammar attempt to teach students the syntactic structures of English, but it's clear that in teaching prepositional phrases or gerunds, we're really teaching students terminology for structures they know how to create intuitively, along with a heavy dose of rules about a formal style, like saying "It is I," instead of "It's me," or not ending sentences with a preposition, a rule of formal style that I intentionally violate in this book as I try to create a more conversational tone. These are rules that are appropriate to only a few of the many contexts in which students live their lives. Similarly, though we often spend a lot of time in basic writing courses on teaching sentence boundaries and worrying about fragments and run-ons, what we're really teaching is orthography—the conventions for punctuation in the standard, literate form of a particular language, not anything about the syntactic structures of sentences themselves, which students know unconsciously. Of course, I do think it is useful to have some language for talking about language. But we need to be clear both that we're not really teaching students how to form grammatical structures, and that what we teach in the name of grammar instruction won't have any significant effect on our students' use of those structures in writing. (For a fuller discussion of the pedagogical implications of this understanding, see Hartwell 1985, and Kutz and Roskelly 1991, Chapter 5.)

The basic syntactic structures of a language vary little across dialects. In fact, the world's languages seem to stay within a finite set of grammatical options of all that could be imagined, giving support to Chomsky's notion of Universal Grammar. But within those those acceptable (grammatical) syntactic structures, there is a wide range of stylistic variation of the sort represented in the choice of *whom* or *that* in the example of clefting above, or a decision to place a preposition at the end of a sentence: "It's Nicole I'm getting it from." The picture that emerges is one of both possibility and constraint: a range of surface possibilities may be available for realizing an underlying meaning, but the discourse context narrowly reduces these possibilities for a speaker who must take into account the nature of the setting and its participants, how much they're likely to know, what attitude she wants to convey to the events being described or statements being made, and what has already been said in the earlier conversation. And, in a fast-moving exchange, the participants have little time to attend consciously to any of this. As one of my students noted: "I think that trying too hard to choose the right phrase order takes away from the meaning of the conversation." Instead, speakers must rely on an intuitive sense, acquired through their ongoing participation and interaction in a particular speech community, of what's appropriate to a given exchange in a specific context; they must rely on their *communicative competence*.

Grammatical competence and information structure

Within the rapid flow of ordinary conversation, speakers unconsciously represent their underlying propositions in surface structures that stress particular information and highlight particular intentions and meanings. For example, the most typical (unmarked) sentence structure in English is the one diagrammed on p. 91: "My friends saw Luke Perry at the mall," a "right-branching structure where the initial NP introduces the subject of the sentence and all additional information follows the verb, trailing off to the right of the diagram (S-V-O). Usually old information which has already been introduced to the discourse is placed in this opening, subject position, and new information is added later in the sentence. Any information that is placed before the subject NP or any movement of other information into initial, subject position alters this typical, unmarked order and marks or highlights that information. "It was Luke Perry that my friends saw at the mall." (The same highlighting can also be achieved prosodically through stress and intonation: "My friends saw LUKE PERRY at the mall.") We saw an example of such an alteration in the usual, unmarked S-V-O structure in the last chapter, when Karen said, "Doc Martens is what they call them," instead of the expected, "They call them Doc Martens," and we saw that this transformation of the more common sentence structure served a particular function within the context of that conversational exchange, emphasizing the term that indicates knowledge of the most in-style term for this in-style shoe.

In all of our conversations, we de-emphasize some elements as a kind of background to the important ideas, while emphasizing or foregrounding others. Different languages use different grammatical means to accomplish this task, but similar aspects of the *information structure* of language—showing what we should pay attention to and in what ways—are marked in all languages. The backgrounded-versus-foregrounded information can be described in several ways, each of which is dependent upon our seeing a sentence within a larger discourse context:

Given and new information

Given information is another term for what we have been calling shared knowledge, as it is created within a particular discourse context. Given information is
what is currently in the mind of both speakers and listeners at the moment of the
next contribution: shoe boots, combat shoe boots, and low tops are the given
information at the moment in which Karen introduces the new information
Doc Martens. When the terms are commonly understood and there's nothing
exceptional about the way they are being used, a new lexical item like low tops
can be introduced to refer to the same entity and be seen as referring to given
information, just as pronouns *they*, *it*, and *she* most often refer to a noun that is
already part of given information. When Karen says, "My friend has 24 holes,"
and Shanna responds, "She has what?" both girls know that "she" refers to the
given information "my friend," though Shanna can't recognize the new term
"24 holes" as adding further information on the already-given subject of shoe
boots. Though when Karen uses *they* in "Doc Martens is what *they* call them,
without a specific referent in the preceding discourse, her "they" brings in new
information, the wider general community of arbiters of teenage fashion.
Because the girls are involved in a face-to-face conversation, their pronouns *I*
and *you* also point to given information in the situational context: They know
who's referred to with these pronouns; their face-to-face conversation makes
this information that is shared.

Given information is often evoked first in a sentence: "*They* have *these shoe
boots I want*," "*She* has *what* ?" However, new information may appear in this
position as well, but new information is usually highlighted in some way: most
often, in conversations through intonation and stress within the usual S-V-O
structure, often through specific naming and/or expansion of terms (these shoe
boots I want), and sometimes through the sort of marked transformations of
sentence structure that wrest the new information into the first position (Doc
Martens is what they call them). Passive constructions in English, "The boots
were called Doc Martens," provide a way of placing given information at the
front of a sentence, even when it would not have been the subject of an active
sentence.

Given information is often abbreviated, and when Karen says, "My friend
has 24 holes," her emphasis is on *my friend* as the new element in this conversation, while her eliptical reference to "24 holes" suggests that she expects her listeners to take this as another reference to the already given subject of the shoe
boots—so much so that she simply repeats the term in response to Shanna's
"What?" and doesn't expand on it and explain it until Melanie too asks what it
means. In most conversations, we treat what others have said as given to such
an extent that we don't always even create full sentences when we respond to
their questions and statements; we use their syntactic structures as part of what's
given. Karen doesn't respond to Shanna's "She has what?" with "She has 24
holes," but simply with "24 holes," taking the syntactic structure of Shanna's

query as given information in this exchange, simply adding the appropriate substitution. (Children, particularly those from nonmainstream backgrounds have sometimes been seen as having limited language ability when they respond to questions in this way. Whole educational programs have been shaped around getting them to respond to each question with a complete sentence, though their communicative competence tells them that that's not what is done in natural conversation. See Chapter Eight, and also Labov, "The Logic of Non-Standard English" in *Language in the Inner City*, 1972a)

Topic and comment

The topic of a sentence, like the topic of a conversation, is what it's about. While the topic of the girls' conversation is shoe boots, the topic of most of their sentences is as well, with the addition of a series of comments about the topic. Most often the aspect of this topic that's being named is given information, and the comment is new, but sometimes new information serves as a topic as well. When Melanie says (in reference to her favorite place to shop), "They have these shoe boots I want," the given information (they) is being displaced as the topic of the conversation, shoe boots is being introduced as both new information and as the new topic, and the comment on this new topic appears in the embedded clause "(that) I want." Sometimes we point to the topic with phrases like "*speaking of* combat boots," or "*as for* Doc Martens," particularly when we're trying to get back into a conversation or suggesting the relevance of a not obviously related comment we're about to make, but we don't typically mark the topic in any grammatical way in English, and it's sometimes hard to identify the topic of a sentence very clearly.

Definiteness and indefiniteness

Given information and/or a topic that has already been introduced to a conversation is typically marked as definite through the choice of a definite article (*the*) or other definite forms of the determiner (the demonstratives *these, those*) versus the indefinite article (*a, an*) or other indefinite forms of the determiner (*some*). When Melanie refers to "*the* low tops" she is using a definite form in response to Karen's question, "What do you want?" rather than "*some* shoes" or "*a* pair of shoe boots." The topic of a particular style of shoes has already been introduced in this conversation, and therefore she can refer to the style in definite terms rather than less definite ones. Actually, even in introducing the topic, Melanie has used a definite form "*these* shoe boots I want," rather than "*some* shoe boots"—because her wanting refers to a definite object, even though it hasn't been introduced yet in the conversation. We can see then, that while given information is most often marked as definite and new information is marked as indefinite, the two ways of marking information don't always overlap. Over a stretch of connected discourse there is typically a movement from indefinite to specific reference as topics are established in the discourse context, along with a movement from more general to more specific lexical terms (from shoe boots to Doc Martens).

Referentiality

In our conversations, when we refer to a particular object or person (one that has already been introduced in the discourse context or can be assumed to be shared knowledge) we most often use definite forms: "*these* shoe boots I want," and when we aren't referring to a particular object but to a general category we use indefinite forms: "I need to buy *some* shoes." Pronouns, like proper nouns, are generally referential, pointing to a particular person or object, but sometimes we use them in a more nonspecific, nonreferential way. As we've seen in Karen's "Doc Martens is what *they* call them," a pronoun like *they* or *you* need not refer to something in the discourse context or to a particular person or group of people in the world, but may be far more generalized. A passive construction, "Those shoes are called Doc Martens," might also imply that the action of calling is being carried out by an unnamed entity that cannot be referred to in specific terms but only with the nonreferential *by them*. (Often nameless, faceless institutional authority or powerful public opinion is referred to in this way, and the person who cannot name the *they* controlling what *you* must do, or doing whatever is being done to you, is giving expression to a situation of real or perceived powerlessness.)

Contrast

We frequently highlight our meanings in conversations and in writing by using contrasting versions of the same sentence element. Melanie says, "I know that's what *they* call them. *I* just call them combat boots," and we understand immediately that she is emphasizing the *I* and asserting her own authority, as well as her own term combat boots as contrasted with Doc Martens. Such contrast depends on our understanding of syntactic categories and our ability to substitute an element for a like element, even in an expanded form, such as "She has *the low tops?*" versus "No, she has *the ones we saw at the mall with 24 holes.*" We often stress a contrastive element through our intonation.

The effect of these elements of information structure is to foreground some information (the topic at the moment) while backgrounding other information (the shared knowledge that has already been placed into this discourse context). As speakers and listeners, we can quickly perceive what we need to pay attention to at the moment, versus what we need to be keeping in mind in a more general way.

Cohesion and coherence

The aspects of information structure named above also contribute to cohesion in discourse—the sense that the sentences of the larger discourse are connected and work together. *Cohesion* occurs where the "interpretation of one element in the discourse is dependent on that of another" (Halliday and Hasan 1976, 4) and it is developed sentence by sentence. *Coherence*, on the other hand, refers to the larger sense of unity in a text as a whole: that it has a beginning and ending, a clear pattern of development, a logical pattern of movement from one part to another, and that everything is related, necessary, and placed as it should be. In conversation, a particular segment of a text may be coherent, focusing on one topic such as Melanie's visit to the science museum or the desirable shoe boots over a lengthy turn or a number of turns. But participants who are enjoying their own interaction as much as developing their ideas on a topic may switch topics fairly frequently, and the transcription of the larger conversation that these excerpts of Karen, Melanie, and Shanna's exchange have come from would not appear to readers to be focused and coherent in the way that a classroom discussion or a written text might be. On the other hand, it is cohesive.

Cohesion depends in part on: a system of reference that allows one item to be replaced by another (as nouns can be replaced by pronouns); a system of conjunctions (*and, but, so, therefore*) that act as connecting devices to join main clauses and sentences; and a pattern of related lexical elements (vocabulary): repeating the same word (the shoes . . . the shoes); replacing the word with a synonym (these shoe boots . . . these combat boot shoes); replacing the word with a more general word (the Doc Martens . . . the combat boot shoes); replacing the word with a word the speaker equates with the original (the high tops . . . the 24's).

Cohesion is also created through the repetition of syntactic as well as lexical patterns: "I call them," "They call them," "What do they call them?" Martin Luther King's " I Have a Dream" speech offers an effective example of such repetition. In song and poetry, cohesion may also be created by the repetition of sound patterns, like the alliterative repetition of consonant sounds.

To see more clearly what effect the choice of sentence structures and information structures might have on conversational discourse, let's look back at Melanie's account of her visit to the Museum of Science. To highlight the grammatical structures here, I have listed the contributions by main clauses, or starts of main clauses, even if interrupted.

MELANIE: I was down . . .
  I was at the Museum of Science with my mother.
  I saw these F-I-N-E boys.
  I was like . . . oh my gosh . . .
  I was like . . . I wish my mother wasn't here.
  This boy was so cute.
  The one of them was looking at me and probably wanted to get my number

but my mother was standing right there smiling.

I was like . . . M-O-M . . .

SHANNA: What?

Did he keep looking at you or something?

MELANIE: Shanna.

Be quiet . . .

You don't know nothing you're talkin about . . .

We're too mature for you.

We can see in this segment of conversation how information structure is highlighted by particular syntactic patterns. Melanie's sentences here fall into the common S-V-O pattern. "I" is the subject of most of her sentences, and after the first sentence that pronoun offers given information, with a series of pieces of new information added in relation to "I"—where she was, what she saw, who she was with. But midway in this text Melanie switches the subject to "this boy" and "the one of them," shifting the topic from herself and her feelings to the boy who was the object of her attention. "My mother" is the subject of the subordinate clause that follows, creating a contrast between the boy "the one of them" and the mother, a contrast or opposition that's extended in the next sentence, between "I" and "M-O-M."

This information structure is supported by cohesive devices. "*This boy* was so cute," "The *one* of them was looking right at me," "*He* probably wanted to get my number." These clauses are cohesive because *one* and *he* depend on their reference for the word *boy*. Cohesion is created also through the pattern of repetition: "boy," "boys"; "mother," "mother," "M-O-M"; the reference structure, *fine boys, this boy, the one of them* (moving toward specific and definite reference). It is further supported by intonation patterns—"F-I-N-E boys," "M-O-M."

The pattern of reference also underlines these meanings. When Melanie introduces the boys to the discourse, she uses the definite demonstrative *these* rather than an indefinite, like *some*, speaking as if the boys are already on everyone's mind. As she singles out a particular boy, she continues the pattern with "this boy" and then points out very specifically "the one of them."

Like is characteristic of teenager talk, and seems to serve the purpose of introducing a point where the speaker shifts into the time frame of the events. Melanie moves from telling about a past event, with verbs in the past tense (I was down, I was at, I was like) to reliving it (I wish my mother wasn't here). I wish is in the present tense and moves Melanie back into the moment of the event. Several verbs are in a past progressive tense—"was looking," "was standing"—showing an ongoing state of being in the past, a sort of impasse where everyone just stands and waits for something else to happen, for an opportunity to present itself. That ongoing state is also reflected in Shanna's question: "Did he keep looking at you?"

Shanna precedes that question with "What?" rather than "Why?" Her "What?" doesn't seem to follow directly from what Melanie has just said but seems more global, as if she's asking about the whole event. When Melanie responds she shifts into a Black English pattern of syntax (double negative) pronunciation (nothin, talkin) and intonation (You don't know *nothin* you're *talkin* about). This shift (her only shift into Black English in the whole conversation) highlights the separation between her and Shanna. At this point, Melanie also shifts from "I" to "we," including Karen in her subject frame and setting up another opposition, between "we" and "you," highlighting the new information "we" by putting it first in contrast to the given information "you." The opposition is confirmed in the meaning of her words: "We're too mature for you."

The syntactic choices Melanie has made in this excerpt reflect meanings that are present throughout the larger conversation. Melanie is the oldest of the three girls, and presents herself as the wisest in the ways of the world, leading most of the conversation and introducing most of its topics, while Shanna is the youngest, trying to find ways to insert herself, to find points of contact between Melanie's topics and the things she knows. Karen is really in the middle, included in Melanie's frame but following Melanie's lead. Though she has no part in this particular exchange, she typically comments on topics that Melanie has introduced, placing herself in relationship to what Melanie has said.

Narrative discourse

In this exchange, Melanie is affirming both her individual perspective on the world and her own role in this small group. But she is doing so in a narrative form that is common across languages and cultures. In a study of narratives told by black urban teenagers ("The Transformation of Experience in Narrative Syntax," in 1972a), Labov created a framework of analysis that has been used in many other studies of narrative in a variety of contexts, highlighting common features of narrative discourse across discourse communities (see Gee 1985; Scollon & Scollon 1981).

Labov suggests that any effective narrative must answer the question, So what? The need for an answer emerges, in part, from the demands of the teller's audience, and thus the answer is shaped in part by that audience. In conversation, narrative is governed by the rules of turn-taking. A speaker's turn in a conversation is, in general, very short, so that the teller of even a brief story may be perceived as taking too long a turn, and will need to justify the longer turn which a narrative requires. But the typical narrative, even one as short as the one Melanie tells, is significantly longer than the ordinary conversational turn, and the teller must both communicate her sense of this experience to others and justify her right to hold the floor and to have her listeners' attention for that long. The speaker must show somehow that this narrative is important, that it does have meaning in relation to the ongoing conversation, or that it is so important for some other reason that its telling justifies an interruption of the conversational flow.

With a good conversational partner and a good storyteller, the point and its relevance will be made clear somehow, whether or not it is stated explicitly, and the conversation will go on smoothly. The answer may be stated explicitly from the narrator's present perspective (as when Melanie steps out of her story to comment: This boy was so cute), partly imbedded in the narrative, usually as the thoughts that the narrator or one of the characters in the narrative had at the time of the event (I [was] wish[ing] my mother wasn't here), or deeply embedded in the narrative (I saw these FINE boys). The form of the answer is determined in part by the knowledge shared between teller and audience; where values and meanings are closely shared, as in a family or among close friends, much does not have to be stated explicitly. Writers of fiction are also likely to involve their readers by writing as if a great deal of shared knowledge can be assumed—as if the reader is already intimately involved in a setting and can step into the middle of a conversation.

Whether the knowledge necessary for the communication of meaning is already shared, or whether a world of shared knowledge will be built between narrator and listener, writer and reader, as the story world is expanded, effective communication demands that the listener or reader get the point. Where values and meanings are not shared, the teller must bring the listener into the world of the story or must state the meaning explicitly in answer to an unspoken or stated "so what?" and that's effectively the question Shanna, as the younger child who doesn't fully get the significance of Melanie's story of her encounter with the boys, asks.

It's the demands of discourse that push us to evaluate our experiences clearly in our narratives, whether implicitly or explicitly, and to do so in terms which draw on the knowledge we share with our listeners and the conventions and structures which frame these shared understandings.

In order to answer the "so what?" either explicitly or implicitly, the teller must understand the meaning herself, and often an act of narration represents a process of seeking an understanding rather than the expression of an already determined meaning. Self-initiated narratives or narratives elicited by others in the flow of a conversation almost always do express such a meaning—an *evaluation* of the events, in Labov's terms. But when the task of narrating is imposed externally, as for example, in school tasks where students are asked to recount events for a purpose that's not clear or that they haven't chosen, they're likely to string together a series of events which have no apparent significance. ("I finished supper. John picked me up. We went to the basketball game. I came home and went to bed at 12 o'clock"). Labov, too, found this, when he elicited narratives of vicarious and personal experience. When he asked adolescents to recount episodes of television programs, they most often presented a sequence of events with no evaluation, no hint that these events held meaning. In contrast, when he elicited narratives about an experience in which the tellers felt they were in danger of death, he found that these same adolescents produced highly evaluated narratives which conveyed a clear sense of the meaning and relevance of each detail of the narrative sequence.

So one element that all motivated narratives contain is evaluation, whether it appears as a separate structural unit or embedded in the syntax of the narrative in ways that we'll analyze below. Labov delineates the structural units which he found in the narratives he studied, identifying the common elements of narrative structure as:

1. the *abstract*, which encapsulates the story in a sentence
2. the *orientation*, which provides the listener with necessary background information
3. the *complicating* action, or the narrative sentences per se
4. the *evaluation:* explicit or embedded statements of significance
5. the *result* or resolution: relating the outcome of these events
6. the *coda*, which brings speaker and listener back to the present

The body of the narrative typically consists of a mixture of narration and evaluation, with some ongoing orientation as new background information is needed. According to Labov, the core of the narrative—its complicating action—consists of a sequence of S-V-O sentences in the simple past tense (the preterit), though I would argue that narrative clauses can appear in the historical present as well ("So I go into the store and I say") since many speakers switch into the present tense when they become particularly involved in reliving the action. All else in the body of the narrative—questions, negatives, modals like *could* or *should*—typically serves an evaluative function.

In their narratives, speakers are continually involved not only in stating propositions and offering information, but in showing their own stance toward what they're saying, using the narratives that appear so frequently in conversations to shape and maintain an interpersonal relationship with their listeners and to present their own view of the world. Labov found that the teenagers whose narratives he studied were more likely than older, middle-class speakers, both black and white, to imbed their evaluations in their account of events rather than to step out of the story to state explicitly what they saw as the meaning of those events. In this, their narratives were much like those of the most effective storytellers and fiction writers. As a consequence, seeing how they expressed the implicit meanings of their stories required a careful analysis of the syntax of their sentences, of the grammatical devices that they used (again unconsciously) to highlight their meanings—highlighting that they accomplished in part by departing from the syntax most characteristic of simple narrative accounts. We'll see shortly how some of these devices work in our now-familiar story of the science museum.

In "The Transformation of Experience in Narrative Syntax," Labov names the typical pattern of narrative syntax as including:

1. conjunctions, including temporal indicators like "then," and "when"
2. subjects
3. auxiliary verbs (usually as part of a past progressive: She *was* singing)

4. main verbs in the simple past tense/preterit (jumped, came)
5. direct and indirect objects
6. adverbs of manner or instrument (He hit him hard)
7. locative adverbs or phrases, showing place (in his face)
8. temporal adverbs or phrases: (ever since)

Labov asks: "Given the existence of this simple organization of narrative clauses . . . where, when, and with what effect do narratives depart from it? Since syntactic complexity is relatively rare in narrative, it must have a marked effect when it does occur . . . a marked evaluative force" (378). He finds that the major modifications to the typical syntactic structure of narratives take the following forms:

1. *Intensifiers*: These strengthen or intensify the account of an event, often with a gesture or expressive phonology (emphasizing words by stressing them or drawing them out, as Melanie does with "F-I-N-E boys"), with quantifiers *so* tall or *all* over, and with repetition.
2. *Comparators*: These compare what did happen to what didn't happen, or what might have happened, or what could happen in the future. They include negatives, modal auxiliaries (can/could, will/would, shall/should, may/might, also, ought to, supposed to, had to), and variations in tense structure from past to present (or the future with modal). Questions asked by the narrator are often implicitly comparative, raising the possibility that something else might have happened (Why was he looking at me like that?), and imperatives also implicitly suggest that if a command is not carried out some other consequence will follow. Of course, comparatives and superlatives themselves (bigger than me, the biggest kid) have this comparative effect, and the superlative often appears in a final evaluation (the most important, the scariest).
3. *Correlatives*: According to Labov, while "a comparator moves away from the line of narrative events to consider unrealized possibilities and compares them with the events that did occur, correlatives bring together two events that actually occurred so that they are conjoined in a single independent clause" (387). Correlatives include progressives (be + ing) that suspend the narrative action (such progressives can also occur in orientation sections), and participles that represent sequences of progressives following one auxiliary (he was singing and dancing and laughing). These delay the action and bring in several simultaneous events, often heightening the tension while listeners wait to hear what's finally going to happen. Double attributives (two or more adjectives in sequence like a cold, wintry night) or appositives (a sequence of noun phrases like it was a cold night, and a wintry one) also act as correlatives, placing several features into the foreground at once.
4. *Explicatives*: In this feature, additional, subordinate clauses are added to the main narrative clause, usually with *that*, again suspending the main narrative action, while adding information about other actions that may or may not

have occurred simultaneously (I learned that he had had his eyes closed the whole time).

Other syntactic features may serve similar evaluative functions, and, in analyzing the narratives we collect, my students and I begin with Labov's schema, displaying our data to highlight the basic narrative structure and the variations on it that he has named, but working flexibly with this schema, looking at what doesn't fit as well as what does. Not everything fits neatly, but a chart provides a way of seeing patterns, and often what doesn't fit shows a significant variation in the common pattern.

Looking back at the science museum story, we can see how some of these features work, as we list conjunctions, subjects, auxiliary and main verbs, direct objects, indirect objects and complements, and adverbs showing manner, place, and time, and then look for the evaluative devices Labov has named.

1 Conj	2 Subj.	3 Aux	4 MV	5 DO/IndO/Complement	6 Adv: manner	7 place	8 time
a.	I	was				down—	
b.	I	was				at the Museum	
					with my mother.		
c.	I		saw	these F-I-N-E boys.			
d.	I	was		like . . . oh my gosh—			
e.	I	was		like . . .			
f.	I		wish [that]				
	my mother	wasn't					here.
g.	This boy	was		so cute.			
h.	The one of them	was	looking	at me			
and (probably)			wanted	to get my number			
i. but	my mother	was	standing smiling.				right there
	I	was		like. . .M-O-M—			

Melanie's narrative is then interrupted by Shanna's question.

This narrative is introduced into the conversation without an abstract. Its first sentence serves the function of orientation, showing where the events took place and who two of the key participants were. The complicating action begins with "I saw," the only active past tense verb. Then the action essentially stops, so that the story is more about what didn't happen than what did. Although Melanie often tells her listeners a lot about what she thought about these events as they were happening, using partially embedded evaluation, the larger meaning of the event is more fully embedded and requires closer analysis to uncover.

We can see that Melanie uses many of the features Labov names:

Intensifiers: Her intonation and stress in "FINE boys," the *so* in "so cute," gives her clear evaluation of the boys. With her final "MOM," she uses intonation to stress her frustration with her Mom's presence—really with the whole situation.

Comparators: She uses one negative "wasn't," and this points out the major conflict of the story, the one element that could have led to a different outcome—if only her mother *wasn't* present. She uses no modals but "wish" has a similar function, suggesting a comparison between events as they were and events as they might have been. (She could have used a modal construction to make her wishes more explicit—He might have come over; He would have talked to me.) She doesn't use any imperatives, questions, comparatives, or superlatives.

Correlatives: She uses several progressives: "was looking," "was standing," and the participle "smiling." These suspend the action, while the two areas of events that concern the speaker go on simultaneously: the boy "was looking," but the mother "was standing," and "smiling." The repeated *like* also stops the action, and each time it precedes either an intensifier (MOM), an evaluative statement from the time of the events (Oh my gosh), or her explicit wish about how things might be.

Explicatives: Melanie uses only one. Following "wish" there is an implied "that," followed by an embedded clause, "my mother wasn't here." This pulls away from the narrative event, presenting the alternative possibility on which all of the speaker's sense of the meaning of events depends.

Finally, then, we have a story in which the limited actual events are implicitly compared to what could have been. The evaluation of this experience is based not in what it was, but in what it wasn't—in what it might have been without the mother.

This reading makes sense within the larger discourse frame, where Melanie responds to Shanna's question, "Did he keep looking at you or something?" with the reply, "We're too mature for you."

The Museum of Science story is about the whole question of being mature from the perspective of a young adolescent. She's old enough to notice and be noticed by boys, to imagine that this initial attention might lead to the larger world of dates and relationships, but she's too young to enter into that world—a lot of what she does outside of her own neighborhood is still done with her mother. Her implicit evaluation of these events—her frustration at having her mother present when she wants to be grown up, although she wouldn't have been at the museum where she saw these boys without her mother—is embedded in the perspective she holds in the middle of the events, the perspective of a young girl waiting to get on to a new stage of life, to be mature. And in the end she offers an explicit evaluation of the events in the immediate discourse frame for this narrative: Shanna's inability to get the meaning, her need to ask, "What?" and Melanie's shift to Black English in her response, "You don't know nothin you're talkin about" lead to "Anyway, we're too mature for you" highlighting this placement of the younger Shanna outside of the world Melanie's describing.

The narratives that my students record in conversations in their families, workplaces, and communities help us to appreciate, once again, the rich linguistic resources that all speakers bring to their acts of meaning making. Each narrative is finely attuned to a larger context of personal as well as shared cultural and social meanings, an immediate context in which a particular conversation with particular participants takes place, and the context of an evolving text. Some narratives, like Melanie's, develop spontaneously in conversation. Others are told and retold as part of family history (see Kutz, Groden, Zamel 1993, for a longer discussion of narrative meaning and the role that studies of family narratives can play in the teaching of composition and literature), while still others may be elicited in response to someone's question. Yet each narrator manages the complex interaction of personal meanings and discourse constraints in the immediate and ongoing creation of a text.

When Paul, the policeman who studied the speech acts he encountered on duty, asked his nephew T.J. a question like the one that was asked of Labov's informants—whether he'd ever thought he was in danger of being killed—he got this narrative in response:

> I was at the party at the Y . . . and gang kids came in there . . . and everybody was messing around . . . and it was real dark . . . and somebody snatched somebody's chain and kicked the back door open . . . and there was a whole crowd of boys . . . and one crowd thought that the other crowd stole the boy's chain . . . so they started opening fire . . . shots . . . in the middle of the gym. Everybody started running. Then there was automatic and everything . . . and the bullets going all over the place . . . and people tramping over . . . and big fat girls tramping over people . . . breaking ankles. I tried to get out one side. But more kids be shooting from the other side . . . and just shooting back and forth . . . and everybody almost ran into the bullets . . . and that's all that really happened.

'Again, when we display this narrative to highlight its syntactic patterns, the features Labov identified as significant in evaluation emerge.

1	2	3	4	5	6	7	8
Conj	Subj.	Aux	MV	DO/IndO/Complement	Adv: manner	place	time
	I	was				at the party at the Y	
and	gang kids		came		in there		
and	everybody	was	messing around				
and	it	was		real dark			
and	somebody		snatched	somebody's chain			
and			kicked	the back door open			
and	there	was		a whole crowd of boys			
and	one crowd		thought	that			
	the other crowd		stole	the boy's chain			
so	they		started opening	fire, shots,		in the middle of the gym.	
	Everybody		started	running.			
Then	there	was		automatic and everything			

1	2	3	4	5	6	7	8
Conj	Subj.	Aux	MV	DO/IndO/Complement	Adv: manner	place	time
and	the bullets		going		all over the place		
and	people		tramping		over		
and	big fat girls		tramping		over people		
			breaking	ankles.			
	I		tried to get		out one side		
But	more kids	be	shooting		from the other side		
and			just shooting		back and forth		
and	everybody		almost ran		into the bullets		
and	that	's		all that			
			really happened.				

This narrative has no abstract; it begins with a brief orientation that sets the stage for the action to follow—placing the speaker at the party at the Y, followed by the action that starts when some gang kids come in. Most of the narrative consists of a mixture of complicating action and evaluation, there's no real result or resolution, but there is a final evaluative statement that also serves as a coda, closing off the story in a way that can return the conversation to the present.

In this more extended narrative we can see many of the features that Labov identified as evaluative. There are intensifiers (a *whole* crowd, *all* over the place, *real* dark), with repetition (started opening fire, started running) and contrast (one crowd—the other crowd, one side—the other side). There are comparators (*more* kids, *almost* ran). But this narrator particularly draws on correlatives, bringing together a number of events that actually occurred, and suspending the narrative action to show all of the things that were going on simultaneously, heightening the tension.

Interwoven with each of the simple preterite verbs showing the narrative action (came, snatched, kicked, started) there are many more showing what was ongoing (the bullets *going* all over the place and people *tramping* over and big fat girls *tramping* over people, *breaking* ankles; more kids be *shooting* from the other side, just *shooting* back and forth). The Black English form "be shooting" is a tense structure that doesn't exist in standard English, but that indicates an ongoing action or event, and its use here highlights the constant and continuing nature of the shooting. There's an appositive (fire, shots), doubly emphasizing and clarifying the danger. There's one explicative, breaking the action to say what was in people's minds (One crowd thought *that* the other crowd stole the boy's chain). And there's one modifier at the end that serves as a final comparator (Everyone *almost* ran into the bullets).

The picture that emerges is one of two simultaneous sets of events, each presenting its own dangers: the shooting that's going on back and forth between two gangs with bullets going all over the place, and the running and tramping back and forth that the panicked crowd is doing. T.J. places himself in these ongoing actions just once after the opening orientation. He tells us, near the end, that "I tried to get out one side but more kids be shooting from the other side."

Then the shooting back and forth continues, while everybody (implicitly including T.J.) "almost ran into the bullets." Finally, he offers as a final evaluative comment and coda "and that's all that really happened." How are we to interpret this final evaluation? Though a great deal has gone on, "that's all" again suggests an implicit comparison to something that couldn't be summed up as "all," if someone had been killed or seriously injured. (We know, from T.J.'s response to his uncle's question, that he did think he was in danger of being killed.) As Paul concludes:

> It is impossible for the listener to say "So what?" His point is driven home pure as a diamond. It illustrates in this microcosm, the issues facing inner-city youth. . . . This narrative about T.J. at a party at the YMCA, is about being a teenager in the inner city. T.J.'s evaluation illustrates a cartoon world where life and death have no meaning. In this world, if someone disrespects you, you shoot them. It is a world where life is cheap. As a fifteen-year-old black male growing up in the inner city, T.J. wears this reality as a badge of courage. It is a reality that must change.

Labov's studies of language in the city were a response, in part, to the view that speakers of nonstandard varieties of English were somehow limited in their linguistic competence—that their use of those varieties, like Melanie's and T.J.'s shifts to features of Black English at particular moments, limited their ability to communicate and express their meanings. But we can see, even in these brief examples, that one variety need not be less effective than another, and that a speaker who controls more than one variety, as Melanie and T.J. do, has an expanded, not a reduced, linguistic repertoire, one that allows them to use the the resources of two systems as appropriate to highlight their meanings. The work of sociolinguists like Labov has led to a new appreciation of the comparable worth of all varieties of language and to an appreciation of an urban environment, where many languages and varieties of language come into contact, as a place where linguistic repertoires may be expanded rather than reduced. Or as Halliday suggests:

> A city is a place of talk. It is built and held together by language. Not only do its inhabitants spend much of their energies communicating with one another; in their conversation they are all the time reasserting and reshaping the basic concepts by which urban society is defined. If one listens to city talk, one hears constant reference to the institutions, the times and places, the patterns of movement and the types of social relationship that are characteristic of city life. . . . The man [or woman] in the city street has internalized a pattern that is extraordinarily heterogenous. (Halliday 1978, 154–55)

The ways in which people acquire and use new varieties of language and new languages will be the focus of the next chapter.

CHAPTER 6

Acquiring and Using Varieties of Language

As I walk through my neighborhood on my dog's daily outing to our local park, exchanging greetings with my neighbors along the way, I find myself subtly altering the pace and rhythm of my speech, slowing down, evening out the emphasis on words, shifting from "How are you?" to "How are you doing?" to "How you doin' there?" with several other variations as I check in with neighbors of Irish, Haitian, Jamaican, Cape Verdean, Brazilian, or African-American origin, with whom I may be on more friendly or more formal terms. Although our exchanges take place in a common language—English—each of us tends to speak that language a little differently in our most informal exchanges, depending on our language of origin, the region we grew up in, and the settings where we spend the most time. My range of informal vernacular styles is more limited than that of Karen and her friends, and they're likely to move from their polite greeting to an elderly neighbor (Hello, Mr. Hunter. Isn't it a nice day?) to a full black teenage vernacular that I can only begin to imitate (Yo, how you doin there girl?). In our neighborhood, it is easy to see that there are many varieties of English, even for those who have grown up with it as their first language, and that people draw on these varieties flexibly in different exchanges.

Children, through their interactions with family members and the most immediate members of their communities, not only acquire language, they acquire a particular language and a particular dialect of that language, as well as a range of styles that are used around them. The language they grow up speaking, like the color of their skin and their place in the family birth order, is a fundamental part of their identity—so much a part of them that they are not consciously aware of it. It is wholly rooted in the context of their lives, and it's only when that context changes, when outsiders come into their immediate speech community or they go outside of it, that they become aware of differences in the ways people talk—in the words that are used, in the ways they're pronounced, in a range of idiomatic expressions and in some syntactic structures. But in contemporary society, most people do move outside of their immediate speech communities; they encounter speakers with other accents, other words, other languages. And they encounter others' attitudes toward the way they've been speaking as well, responses that in turn shape their sense of their own language, and of their identity.

In my neighborhood, where people are engaged in ongoing, unself-conscious interactions, where everyone is used to hearing English spoken in many forms, along with other languages as well, these varieties of language seem to be a natural asset, contributing to the rich texture of daily life. But in my classes, students become self-conscious about the varieties of language spoken in their home communities, too often seeing those varieties in negative terms, as poor or filled with errors. Schools play a particularly large role in shaping peoples' attitudes toward the varieties of language that they and others speak, casting one version of a public language as correct and everything else as wrong, paying little attention to either the grammatical and communicative competence students bring to their classrooms or to the ways in which effective communication depends, not on one formal style, but on the ability to vary style in relationship to context. But my students, whether freshmen or graduate students, have been so affected by their school experiences and attitudes that I want them to begin their language study on new ground, looking at the language and languages of their families and communities from a linguistic perspective—describing rather than judging what they find, and at the same time exploring their own attitudes to their varieties of language and the nature of their own experience as they've moved outside of their own language community. It's that study that will be the focus of this chapter.

Varieties of language

We begin our study of varieties of language on the first day of class, when I ask my students, "Do you think of yourself as belonging to a particular linguistic community or as speaking a particular dialect?" In their responses, they typically focus first on the way that their spoken language sounds, often describing how they discovered as they moved outside of their immediate communities that they have a regional accent. Kevin notes:

> I have a strong Boston accent that I have been working on. There is so much I'm not aware of as different because of my community. But when I was in the service I had to put up with "Paaack the caaar" no less than 20 times a day.

As they record conversations, they find that when people from various parts of the city come together, differences other than accent appear. Joan observes:

> While my boyfriend's family thought nothing of saying "mines," my mom would definitely cringe at the thought. I noticed though that when my mom and his mom talked together, they each gave in a bit and moved their levels.

And as they write about their own and others' attitudes toward language—their beliefs and their pet peeves—they often report on disagreements about grammatical form, even within their own families. Joan goes on:

> My mom has always bothered me about using correct grammar. While she says "For what class are you doing this," I say "What class are you doing it for?" She feels and tells me that it's practically a sin to end a sentence with a preposition! I, on the other hand, could care little about this because when I'm with my friends I fit *in*! I place little emphasis on spoken syntax because I think that trying too hard to choose the right phrase order, etc. takes away from the meaning of the conversation. My mom and I have disagreed on this point for years.

Others find that such differences appear across languages. Nilda reports:

> My first language is Spanish. When I was growing up in Puerto Rico among my relatives, almost half spoke Spanish of the country type and half the Spanish from the town . . . even if they lived in the same community. In some families, when a child learned or said the wrong thing, something that wouldn't be said at school, it was corrected by the parents. In other families, where the parents were less educated, the child spoke at home in terms that the parent could understand, but when in school, talking to a big class, the child would speak in a different style, with a higher social status.

Nilda, like Joan's mother, is upset that her children, who have been raised to speak English at home, "do not always speak the English language the way I think they should." She feels that:

> Many times I correct my children, because they are using more slang like "ain't," "gonna," "she don't" instead of "she doesn't." I know this is how their friends talk, even when their native language is English. But as a parent, I don't feel it's acceptable for them to talk to me that way.

Because we *know* the underlying grammar of our native language, having acquired it for the most part before the age of five, we tend not to notice it at all in our conversational interactions with family and childhood friends. It's when we move outside of that group—from one region to another, from one neighborhood to another or from an informal to a more formal setting, that we perceive differences, particularly when these are distinguished by differences of race or of socioeconomic class. Most of these differences are regular and systematic variants in the grammar of a language. They show up as phonetic differences in pronunciation, in a few morphological features like the *s* added as an additional possessive marker to the possessive pronoun "mine", in a few areas of syntax, and in vocabulary. And they appear regularly in the speech of most members of a speech community in particular contexts. Some differences are regional in origin, and some appear in relation to social class, even within one region; they tend to remain relatively constant in communities and to leave their mark on the language of those who have been raised in those communities.

    Other differences are more directly connected to the context of a particular exchange, the styles that people use in informal or intimate settings versus formal or public ones. But the relatively constant elements of regional or social variation and the more fluid elements of stylistic variation tend to overlap, with people shifting to the patterns that are characteristic of their home regions or social groups when they are with others from that group in intimate or informal settings (just as speakers of English as a second language might switch to Spanish or Vietnamese at home), and shifting again to more common, less differentiated forms in public settings.

A language like English is characterized not only by its underlying structural regularity, but by the almost infinite, yet equally regular variations in the ways in which it is spoken by different speakers or groups of speakers in different settings and different circumstances. Because our potential for language is realized only in social contexts, the language we speak is finely tuned to those contexts, whether they are shaped by geography, larger social structures, institutions, or the nuances of our immediate circumstances and relationships. Such fine tuning allows the language we use to be shaped in ways that are maximally efficient for communicating with those closest to us. But fine tuning to immediate contexts works against communication across distance, whether that distance is physical or social, and communication in a larger society requires that the forces holding speakers in distinctive language communities be balanced by forces pulling speakers in toward a common language.

Such forces are provided in part by public media and by educational institutions, but a significant force on individual speakers is exerted by the language attitudes held by the various social groups with whom they interact—by what these groups see as appropriate and acceptable language in a particular context. For each person growing up in contemporary society there's likely to be both a pull toward the original language of home and family or of neighborhood and peers on the one hand, and a pull toward the language esteemed by the public world and the larger society on the other—a tug of war between the need for a rooted identity and the need for public status.

Some, like Richard Rodriguez, consider it necessary to give up the language of home (in his case Spanish) to succeed in the public world, leaving in its place only a "hunger of memory." Others may choose a new language, only to rediscover the value of the old. My student Nilda reflects: "I'm very much aware of the role that language plays in maintaining common values or aspects of a community culture and I'm sorry I didn't teach my children Spanish at an early age. But I'm trying to do so now." Still others like black writer and teacher bell hooks try not to leave their home language or variety of language behind. Hooks describes how, when she came from Kentucky to attend Stanford, she learned, as she writes in an essay called "Keeping Close to Home," "to speak differently while maintaining the speech of my region, the sound of my family and community. . . . To deny ourselves daily use of speech patterns that are common and familiar, that embody the unique and distinctive aspect of our self, is one of the ways we become estranged and alienated from our past" (1989, 106–107). Hooks argues further that we need to encourage others, as well, to bring the languages of home into our educational institutions, where "learning to listen to different voices, hearing different speech" should be part of what is learned, concluding that "Education as the practice of freedom becomes not a force that fragments or separates, but one that brings us closer, expanding our definitions of home and community" (111).

Regional and social variation

When I ask my students to describe their experiences as insiders and as outsiders to speech communities, they usually have clear memories of both. Sandra recalls:

> My most memorable "insider" experiences are from my childhood. I attended the same grammar school in Salem, Mass. from kindergarten through eighth grade. . . . When I was about eight years old, a family from Georgia moved into our building. My neighborhood friends and I thought they were the "Beverly Hillbillies" come to life, because that TV show was one of the few exposures we had to Southern accents. I even remember asking one of the girls in the family if they ate "vittles" for supper every night.

Our most striking impressions of the differences in vocabulary, pronunciation, and to a lesser degree, syntax, that speakers from a different speech community might use are typically responses, like Sandra's, to regional dialect variation—to the differences that arise in a language, over time, when speakers in one area are separated from those in another. Despite the fact that people are relatively mobile in the United States, there still exist deep differences in both the words that are used and in how those words are said from one region to another. Sandra, as a child, rightly associates the accent she hears with differences in vocabulary, and genuinely or mockingly, she offers a word, "vittles," that she associates with the region her neighbors have come from. But the tables are turned a few years later, as she explains:

> My most memorable "outsider" experience came during my first visit to California in the late seventies. . . . I went into a McDonald's on Sunset Blvd. and ordered some burgers and fries. The cashier said, "Shurr, and would you like kewks with that?" I said, "What?" She said, "Would you like kewks?" I just stared at her trying to figure out what "kewks" were. Of course the cashier and the people in line next to me were looking at me as though I was from Mars. Finally, the cashier said, "You don't want anything to drink?" and it came to me that she had been saying "Cokes." Feeling stupid, I ordered two Sprites and walked out of there red-faced. Though most of the pronunciations I had heard in Southern California had not been too difficult for me to decipher, that one word had caught me by surprise and I failed to pick up the contextual clues.

In fact, like Sandra, we all depend a great deal on contextual clues to pick up what's being said by those around us, even in our home territory. It's our familiarity with a larger cultural context, the immediate situational context, and the context provided by the preceding discourse that allow us to recognize and interpret even unfamiliar words and pronunciations within a stream of conversation. But here, although Sandra brings the cultural knowledge that Coke is a brand of soft drink and the situational knowledge that her purchase of fast food suggests the likelihood that she'll want to order something to drink, she nevertheless fails to understand the particular referent of the word she hears as "kewks" until the cashier extends this exchange and recontextualizes her question, making it clear that "kewks" refers to something to drink. Only then is Sandra able to respond appropriately, ordering Sprites so that she won't have to use her own dissonant pronunciation of Coke.

A moment of misunderstanding like this one, encountered by all of us as we move across regions, is generally resolved in the way it is here—by extending the exchange and providing more context to support the understanding of a particular word. Because speakers most often cooperate in such exchanges they generally provide sufficient information to support the listener's understanding. Simple misunderstandings based on differences in vocabulary or pronunciation are usually cleared up quickly, and we aren't seen as speaking a foreign language when we move from one part of the country to another.

People from different regions of the United States are part of a common *language community*. Halliday defines a language community as "a group of people who regard themselves as using the same language" (1973, 11). Within a language community, many varieties, such as those my students have observed, coexist. The term *dialect* highlights the variety of a language that speakers share with others from the same region and/or social class, marked by differences of the sort that Sandra observed. The term *register* points to identifiable patterns of discourse that appear across similar contexts, so that the same speaker is likely to use different varieties as they are called for in different contexts—home, church, the classroom, the workplace—varieties that are less or more formal in style and that are often shaped by specialized vocabulary as well as common syntactic patterns and patterns of intonation.

All speakers who participate in the specialized contexts of various sorts of work or different professions adapt their language, to some degree, to the register called for in those contexts. But many speakers also shift from using more strongly marked features of a dialect at home for example, to what's perceived as a more acceptable, common or standard variety in public. Most shift from using informal or colloquial terms like "kids" to somewhat more formal terms like "children" in some contexts.

Dialects are initially marked by differences in grammar and vocabulary, as well as in pronunciation, but many of these differences are eliminated by ongoing contact with other varieties, so that accent emerges as the most significant sign of regional differences. Linguists who study regional variation typically draw up dialect maps, discovering where the pronunciation of *roof* shifts from r/u/f to r/u/f or where a word like *bucket* stops being used and a counterpart like *pail* begins. We may moderate our regional accents somewhat, like the way I learned to add /r/ to car and to eliminate it from idea/r/ when I went to graduate school in the Midwest. But we rarely lose all traces of that accent. I'm amused that my husband, who grew up in the Midwest and Southwest, but has spent all of his adult life in the Northeast, still can't perceive or represent any difference in pronunciation between merry, marry, and Mary. Yet because we interpret the words we hear in relation to a surrounding context, my husband and I have never had any misunderstanding about which word he means in a conversation.

In the United States, different dialects were originally shaped through immigration and migration patterns, as English speakers brought a variety of dialects, and as speakers of different languages brought to their learning of English as a second language some habits of pronunciation, syntactic features, and even words from their language of origin. (ESL speakers also regularized the irregular grammatical features of their new languages, giving rise to forms like the possessive *mines* that matches *ours* and *yours* and *theirs*.) Regional patterns shaped by early immigrant groups were spread across the United States with westward migration, and they diffused and blended as these groups spread out or intermingled. At the same time, continued immigration from particular countries of origin to particular regions of the United States helped to shape and maintain new patterns, affecting to some degree, the dialect of all who live in a region, so that the English spoken in cities like New York or Boston has taken on some of the characteristics associated with the speech of large immigrant groups. (The dialect map for what we perceive as a Southern accent corresponds with the regions where slavery was widespread, suggesting the strong influence of the Plantation Creole that developed among American-born speakers of African origin on the English of all speakers in the region.) Pat, one of my students, comments:

> I first noticed differences in pronunciation when I was a child. My father's parents who came to America as teenagers were not described as "immigrants" but as people who came "over in the boat." I never saw this as a derogatory comment when I was younger although I have heard it referred to as an insult as an adult. They retained their brogues throughout their lives, but I had little difficulty understanding them. They used to refer to me as "Patty girl" and told me that my exuberant behavior "raised their blood pressure." I knew that this was a criticism and that it meant that I had to calm down or leave. When I was four-years-old, I went to Newfoundland to visit my mother's relatives and I was amazed that her relatives also spoke with a brogue. I was referred to as a "girrdle" and I remember thinking that they had me mixed up with a type of corset.

The language of immigrant families comes to shift toward the regional norm with each succeeding generation, largely because of the strong influence of our peers on our language acquisition. We may hold stereotypes about those who use a different regional dialect, just as eight-year-old Sandra must have considered her neighbors to be "hillbillies" and therefore as unsophisticated as the stereotypical Appalachian family presented on the TV program. We may be embarrassed about our regional patterns, like dropping *r*'s, when we spend much time in other regions. But our stronger emotions about our language experiences are associated with variations that mark differences in social class, differences that we seem to find profoundly embarrassing, in a way that's surprising at first, given the myth of our "classless" society.

Social class and regional variation are somewhat intertwined. People of lower socioeconomic strata generally use the most marked regional variations, perhaps reflecting, in part, their more limited opportunities to interact with others from different regions, but also their strong identity with an immediate, local community. But each speaker varies such features, depending on context, in the way that my neighbors and I make slight alterations to the way we speak even the same words of greeting as we encounter others in our neighborhood.

To look more closely at the distinctive features in the language of speakers around us and at when and how speakers vary those features, my students and I begin with a simple exercise, identifying some common words that we think are likely to be strongly marked in their pronunciation by a regional accent. A stereotypical Boston accent is likely to show up most strongly in words that end in /r/ (car) where the /r/ will typically be dropped, in words that have a /t/ in the middle of two vowels or vowel and a liquid like "l" (potato, bottle) where the /t/ will be replace by a glottal stop [ʔ], and in words ending in *ing* where the [ŋ], is replaced by [n] (talking, talkin'), so we include such words on the list, as we begin to observe how different speakers say them and/or recall our own use of such features. Similarly, we identify grammatical differences that we might expect to appear, like the "yous guys" used by one student's buddies in the North End of Boston. We anticipate that we'll see evidence of the sorts of regional and social variations that we all remember encountering, and we do. The differences in pronunciation and grammar that characterize the language used by speakers from a particular region or a particular social class are systematic and rule-governed, and we can observe their regularity. Justine comments:

> In doing this exercise, I realized that there is a lot of truth to the Boston stereotype. All of the native Bostonians that I spoke with dropped the "r" and the "g" ("pahkin" and "walkin") when they were unconscious of my purpose. In fact, one speaker changed to a typical Boston accent when I asked her to repeat herself, even though she is from Maine.

As they reflect on what they've observed, some members of the class realize that they have shifted their use of such features as they've moved from one speech community to another. As Lorraine comments:

> I grew up in Revere where the letter "r" does not exist. I once had a heavy Revere accent, but after high school I moved to Northhampton, MA. I still remember my sister saying to me that people would think I was stupid if they heard me speak. (I also pluralized the word "you" to "yous"). Being an impressionable person, I listened to those around me and quickly changed my patterns of speech.

In fact, while speakers from a particular region may share a dialect, each has a distinct *ideolect* as well—a unique pattern of features that they've acquired through their own individual experience of language, by being a particular age within a particular peer group, living in different regions, and participating in different speech communities.

But the presence of some of these features varies as well, within a speech community, and within the the language spoken by almost all members of that community at different times. To observe that ongoing pattern of variation, we draw on the concept, set forth in the early work of sociolinguist William Labov (1966), of a *linguistic variable:* a linguistic element that appears in different forms (different variants) in a speech community. Such elements vary in the speech of individual speakers as well as from one speaker to another, so (as Labov found) the same speaker might use *-in'* in one context and *-ing* in another. To look at such linguistic variables, we try to introduce these words into a conversation and observe the speaker's informal pronunciation of them, and later ask the speaker to repeat the words or read them in a sentence, seeing what happens when speakers are more conscious of the way they're speaking. Not surprisingly, we find that the most marked variations associated with peoples' region of origin appear in their informal conversations, and less marked variations in the more conscious readings and repetitions or in more formal contexts. Testing out our word list heightens our awareness of such features, and helps us to observe such variations more carefully in our ongoing conversations. Sandra, for example, observes the informal exchanges of her coworkers, who have comparable educational and social class backgrounds but who come from different regions and finds that most of them "drop 'g's" to some degree in casual conversation, but that "in discussions with managers, almost everyone puts the 'g' back on the end of 'ing' words."

A number of sociolinguistic studies from different regions have turned up the same pattern we discover. (See Labov 1966, on New York City; Trudgill 1974, on Norwich, England; Milroy 1981, on Belfast.) They show that most speakers do tend to shift "up" to what they perceive as the more prestigious pronunciation, when they are paying attention and think others might be paying attention to the way they talk (linguists often have trouble getting accurate dialect data for this reason). They also find that women use prestige pronunciations significantly more often than men. This effect is subtle, and speakers don't notice any difference, but we soon become aware of it in our observations. Joe notes:

> It seems that younger, college educated people, myself included, shift frequently from their native home dialects to the broader, worldly pronunciation where *ing's* and *er's* are more prominent. . . . My first exposure to language/ dialect differences was when visiting with my cousins from PA, who thought dropping "r's" and "g" (in *ing*) was improper. Later, in college, I felt linguistically inferior to my classmates who were from other areas of the state and pronounced their "r's" and "g's." This began my life as a code-shifter.

But speakers also may also shift "down" to the less prestigious features in other situations, particularly when they are expressing solidarity with others who use those features. Connecting to others, or showing that we're insiders who belong to a group, is an important motivation for such style shifting, though again, it's usually not conscious. We've already noted Joan's observation that her mother and her boyfriend's mother "moved their levels" when they were talking to one another. Likewise, Sandra comments, of herself:

> In my social speech community, vocabulary and pronunciation vary depend-ing on whether the friends I'm with in a given situation are those I've known from childhood or high school age or those I've acquired in my adult life. With the "old" friends, everything is very casual—many "g's" are dropped, lots of "you know's," "yeah's" and "I mean's" come out and four-letter words are used. We use the language we first started communicating with I suppose. With "newer" friends, it's a mixed bag. I find that I tend to adopt the vocab-ulary and pronunciation of the person or group I'm with. For instance, the other night I was talking to a group of friends who are all originally from out-side New England. One from Maryland, one from Michigan and one from New Jersey all really burn those "r's" in there. I could hear myself, as the evening wore on, pronouncing my "r's" more and more frequently. I heard myself say "matter," "parking," and "ward," where I know I usually say "mat-teh," "pahkin'," and "wod."

And David discovers:

> I have a Boston accent when I'm hanging with my buddies or my cousins but no real noticeable accent when talking with my parents. I also think to some degree I change my accent when I talk to my "boys" in Boston and when I talk to my friends in Brookline. But I bring threads out of each to the other speech community.

Still others of my students may feel significant pressure from their families or communities not to adopt a different variety, as Andy states:

> My sister is bused to school out in Wayland through the Metco program. I went to a private high school. Every time we talk, our brothers who went to school in the city get on us for talking white.

And they may decide to assert their home identity. Pat adds:

> I grew up with a typical Dorchester accent. When I went to school I began to talk differently, and my older sister accused me of getting too "la de dah." I quickly figured out that, whatever I did at school, I should stick to my real way of talking at home. Now I would never never give up my accent completely.

But sometimes the shift to a different language variety feels less like a matter of choice and more like a forced change, one marked by painful loss and separa-tion. Paul writes:

> When this writer was young, he observed a child who spoke with a West Indian dialect in school. All the children, except one, found it difficult to

understand his accent. They tried at first, but soon gave up. Even the teacher told him that he spoke badly. This made the child feel very sad. The only thing he wanted was to fit into his new school. One day, he started to speak like everyone else. His teacher approved and even put him on the honor roll, yet the only thing that had changed was his West Indian dialect. The child had abandoned his accent in favor of fitting in with the majority. That child is the writer of this paper. This happened over twenty years ago. The question I still ask is, "Should a child be forced to change the way that he speaks so that he can fit in, or should everyone else learn to accept cultural diversity?"

Language attitudes

Paul's question is at the center of our study of language variation. We may begin our study by bringing in our observations of lexical differences from one region to another, laughing over the confusion that people have experienced when they tried to order a tonic rather than a soda or pop along with a grinder instead of a hero or sub, and sharing anecdotes about our trials with strange pronunciations, like Sandra's with "kewks", and then observing the shifts in the language of people around us. But as we begin to bring our more private thoughts about our encounters into the classroom, we discover that each of us has been marked in some way by the experience of language difference: by the attitudes of others toward some aspect of our way of speaking, our own attitudes, and a common attitude in the larger society that marks some accents, some pronunciations, some forms and structures as not acceptable, even though they've worked perfectly well for our friends and family. Others outside of our immediate communities can usually understand what we mean to say perfectly well across such differences, especially since natural communication is imbedded in rich contexts, and our ability to process out variant features, just as we process out the hesitations and false starts of any conversation, is a sign of our underlying grammatical competence. So expressing an intolerance of linguistic differences may really provide a safe way of expressing more deeply rooted intolerance of ethnic, cultural, and racial differences that's not socially acceptable in a multicultural society.

My students recall trying to counter their own negative responses to linguistic differences. Melissa, for example, whose mother always sounded "very proper," has noticed a shift in the opposite direction in her own speech.

> When I heard the kids I went to school with leaving out "r's," I automatically assumed that these kids were not very smart. Apparently the kids at school picked up on the difference too, because I remember in approximately fifth grade being teased for putting such emphasis on "r's" and "ing's" and being accused of being nerdy. Although I don't believe anymore that people who speak without "r's" are any less intelligent or of a lower social class, I still find that when I am around people who speak this way I try not to put such emphasis on my "r's" or "ing's". Perhaps, unconsciously, I'm still worried that they may find me to be nerdy or snobby.

As Melissa's comment confirms, people's responses to the ways others speak are not always neutral. The strongest negative responses to others' language are likely to be associated with morphological or syntactic variants, forms that don't appear in standard English. But if we look at any grammatical form that's used by real speakers in actual conversational contacts, we'll find that it makes sense grammatically, and that the particular pattern is used systematically, in rule-governed ways. In other words, speakers who use a particular regionally or socially marked variety of English are demonstrating their grammatical competence as speakers of that variety, their underlying knowledge of its rules. But as speakers within a community, they are also demonstrating their communicative competence, speaking in the way that will show them to be members of that community.

When I ask my students whether they have any pet peeves about other people's language use (a question suggested by Mark Vogel (1992), whose Appalachian students undertake similar studies to ours of the features of their local dialect and their attitudes toward them) what they find annoying often illustrates such communicative competence. Joan comments on several of her pet peeves:

> The first deals with my mom. I can always tell who my mother is talking to on the other end of the phone because she blatantly imitates the other person's accent. If I didn't know her, I would swear she was from Maine, Maryland, or wherever the other person's from. But I'm beginning to see that it's her way of maintaining a close connection with her old friends and family. It also annoys me when my boyfriend stresses his Italian accent and tends to cut down the number of letters in his words. I know he's educated, but I'm afraid of what others will think. But I also get a kick out of hearing him use different Italian words for objects even though he doesn't speak Italian. And my brother carries on conversations in which he will switch rapidly from speaking in six-syllable words to street talk.

Joan may be bothered by all of this, but her mother's adoption of others' accents, her boyfriend's use of the Italian words that are commonly used in his Italian-speaking family, and her brother's ability to shift from a level of diction that uses multisyllable words to street talk are all marks of their communicative competence.

James and Leslie Milroy, in their study of language prescription and standardization in English (1991), recount the long tradition of complaint about others' use of the language. Standardization is, of course, needed for efficient communication, and is promoted by the spread of literacy, and as they point out: "the movement toward a national standard language in England arose not primarily because authoritarian individuals wished to impose complete conformity on everyone else, but in response to wider social, political, and commercial needs" (36). In other words, standard forms in writing and public language arose out of social needs, and they built on the spoken forms used by those who were in power and at the center of the society's enterprises in trade and politics. But once the written language was codified, an accompanying "ideology of standardization" emerged, in which the standard forms and usages were seen as the only correct ones, shaping what the Milroys call "a transcendental norm of correct English" (38), and deviations from those standard forms were judged to be illegitimate—to be errors.

The Milroys look at the pressures that encourage stability in the forms of a language, in the face of constant pressure for language change, including complex attitudes toward various forms on the parts of their users. High prestige forms—those that are commonly used by speakers who are seen as having high prestige—are typically enforced by institutions such as schools, but also by informal mechanisms, so that many speakers will shift to those forms in at least some situations (as when they're being interviewed by linguists).

But there are other social mechanisms that tend to pull speakers toward the forms that are used by others in their social network, as a sign of solidarity, so that nonprestige forms are also maintained. The Milroys describe a permanent tension between language use that is maintained by solidarity pressures, and usage that is maintained, or enforced, by state-based ideologies. Prescriptive norms tend to be conservative, maintaining older forms that are remnants of older systems in the face of a general tendency for language to change in ways that regularize and simplify the system (leaving anachronistic bits like the *s* morpheme on the third person singular present tense of the verb).

The Milroys conclude that prescriptivism is social, not linguistic, in origin, and that prescriptive comments on linguistic correctness represent, in effect, "a social prejudice that cannot directly be expressed" (100).

So far in our study of language variation, then, we've discovered several things from our observations and recollections:

1. The varieties of English that are spoken in different speech communities are fully grammatical and functional, and there is no linguistic reason to prefer one over another. Speakers of nonstandard varieties are not careless or sloppy or even making errors. They are using the correct forms for the variety they have learned to speak.
2. Being able to vary one's style and to use appropriate features in particular contexts is an important aspect of adult communicative competence.
3. People's choices about the variety of language they use in any context are meaningful, determined by social factors like their desire to be part of a group and not to mark themselves as different from the others they're talking (or writing) to, and, in some instances, to highlight the differences between the group they identify with and the rest of society.

We've also learned, however, that too often people's choices about the varieties of language they use have been made in reaction to the negative judgements of others. Terms like stupid, not very smart, linguistically inferior occur frequently in my students' recollections, and it takes courage and a belief in her own intelligence for someone like Pat to assert her linguistic identity and maintain the accent of her working-class Irish-American community.

In the process of our study, we've also increased our understanding of the formal structures of language. We've discovered, for example, that speakers can understand each other across many different pronunciations, many different phonetic realizations, of the same sound concept like the /t/ that may vary, as different speakers say *potato*, from a precisely pronounced /t/ to something much closer to /d/. And we see that what allows us to understand each other across dialects and to understand children whose pronunciation is different from that of adults is our ability to perceive the important phonemic distinctions in a language and to ignore differences in their phonetic representation (in actual pronunciation) whether spoken: by different speakers; in different social/geographical settings; or in different word contexts (whether the phoneme comes at the beginning, middle, or end of a word, and what other sounds surround it).

We find that adult speakers who say "dese" and "dose" instead of "these" and "those" may not even be aware of this variation but perceive themselves as producing the /th/ phoneme, just as many of our Boston-area informants are unaware of using a glottal stop—a complete stop made in the back of the throat—rather than a /t/ in the word "bottle". Speakers of other dialects will still perceive the meaning of words like "dese" as if they had heard a "th" (though they'll also perceive what the "d" suggests about the person's region or class or level of education, and they may have definite attitudes about this variant).

Our unconscious knowledge of the phonological system of our language allows us to filter out such variations as we process the meaning of utterances, and to communicate across them.

While the mayor of Westfield, as we saw in the Introduction to this book, may feel self-conscious about his own accented English and therefore be unwilling to appoint a first-grade teacher who has an accent, those who listen to him will generally understand him perfectly well, unconsciously filtering out the variant features of his pronunciation as they become accustomed to them, and perceiving the phonemes he intends. Likewise, the accent of a bilingual teacher will have no effect on the language of native English-speaking first graders. They will perceive the phonemes the teacher intends and will gain some important practice in perceiving phonemes across different accents. They may even try out mimicking the teacher's accent and develop some skill in shifting their pronunciation to come closer to that of speakers outside of their community, but they will still be able to produce those phonemes as they always have—as their friends and families do.

We likewise develop a clearer concept of a morpheme when we see ways in which a grammatical concept like indicating possession is reinforced by a form like "mines." Dialects spoken by adults also tend to alter illogical or redundant features of the morphological system of English, so that their morphology is actually more logical and regular. As a language changes, it tends to eliminate such irregularities, and it's only the conservative effect of having particular forms be highly valued that causes them to be maintained, either because they're indicators of a prestigous standard version of the language, or because they're valued as markers of belonging to a particular group.

Although, as my students collect data, they tend to think of their informants as dropping endings (He run) or ignoring the inflected form of the verb *to be* (He my brother) or misusing morphemes (mines) such systematic features of adult language simply show that the adults have acquired a dialect that doesn't contain these forms. We could just as easily say that other speakers stick in unnecessary elements. The differences aren't inherently good or bad, and it is only through comparing their dialects with other dialects that people become aware of the variant features and of the social weight attached to them.

Using what we've learned we can go on to study any variety of English—any dialect or register—analyzing the systematic features of its grammar, pronunciation, vocabulary, and idioms on the one hand, and the ways in which it is used and the social values associated with its use on the other. Some of my students may focus on the register of a particular workplace (a television station, a hospital, a local gym, a computer software company), perhaps extending their earlier studies of speech acts, or on the dialect of a community or the prestige forms of the public, "standard" dialect. Those who plan to teach might examine the prescriptions of school grammar books, analyzing the characteristics of the variety represented there, particularly in terms of the social rules that appear in the disguise of grammatical ones, something Patrick Hartwell refers to as "linguistic etiquette."

What we've learned about various regional and social dialects is instantiated in the case of Black English, a dominant variety in my own neighborhood where it shows a shared set of beliefs and understandings, but a variety that's been the focus of much controversy, particularly around issues of schooling.

The case of one social dialect: Black English

When we turn to any variety of English, we find that speakers of that variety can work out both the underlying grammatical rules governing a variety of English and the social/communicative rules that determine when its use is appropriate, making explicit some portion of the knowledge that represents both grammatical and communicative competence even though, as speakers, we're not usually conscious of either aspect. The poet June Jordan describes a study of Black English begun by students in her college literature class, a class made up mostly of black students. When the class began to discuss Alice Walker's *The Color Purple*, her students responded with comments like: "Why she have them talk so funny. It don't sound right," and "It don't look right neither. I couldn't hardly read it" (1988, 364).

Jordan marveled at the similarities between her students' casual speech patterns and the language they were objecting to: Walker's written version of Black English. But rather than comment on these similarities, she decided simply to write the opening lines of *The Color Purple* on the blackboard and ask the students to help her translate them into standard English, something they could all do adeptly. "*You better not never tell nobody but God. It'd kill your mammy,*" becomes "*Absolutely, one should never confide in anybody besides God. Your secrets could prove devastating to your mother*" (365).

Jordan's students soon discovered that along with the grammar of standard English, they had also acquired through their schooling a set of negative attitudes toward the very language that they themselves would use in their informal conversations—language that conveys a shared sense of identity and a common worldview. They decided to study that language (sometimes referred to by linguists as Black English Vernacular—BEV). They soon found that they could not only describe some of the rules that govern its common structures but they could see why it might be valued. They discovered, for example, that the passive construction is not used in Black English, that someone has to be doing something to someone, so that "Black English is being eliminated" would become "White people eliminating Black English." They hypothesized that this feature might be linked to a cultural attitude in which what's most important is "the living and active participation of human beings in events," and "the expression of person-centered values" (367).

As Jordan's students began to see the representation of Black English in works by writers like Walker as embodying a stance and worldview that's necessary to the meaning of those works, they became increasingly interested in studying the language itself, generating, from their own experience, the rules that govern the language. Beginning with some working rules, like "If it's wrong in standard English it's probably right in Black English," and expressing even these rules in Black English, "If it don't sound like something that come out somebody mouth then it don't sound right. If it don't sound right then it ain't hardly right," they discovered that they could name many of the systematic grammatical features of Black English, as well as the rules governing the use of these features in social contexts.

The syntax of Black English varies from that of standard English in a few ways that are significant, but not all that extensive. The use of Black English syntax by itself doesn't interfere much with communication, but its use evokes both positive and negative attitudes on the part of listeners, even within a family, so that the same student whose siblings complain of his sounding too white may have a grandmother who insists that he "talk right," echoing the sidewalk chant that Melanie loved as a child: "Don't say 'ain't' or your mother will faint, and your father will fall in a bucket of paint." Yet that same grandmother might see his shift to language that contains no markers at all of his black identity as a sign that he is "gettin uppity." Likewise, a native Hawaiian student informed me that she grew up trying to negotiate a fine line between speaking in ways in that would be acceptable in a larger public world and being seen as "haoleized" if she lost the linguistic markers of her Hawaiian identity.

Black English developed from the Plantation Creole created when Africans who spoke different languages were forced together as slaves. At first they would have communicated in a pidgin: with a limited vocabulary drawn mostly from English with some words from African languages, and a simplified syntax.

But the children born to these diverse pidgin speakers developed a fully grammaticized creole language. Over time, because of the dominance of English in the larger society, the original creole would come to approximate English in almost all of its features, and so a recognizable creole remained only in isolated communities, as among the Gullah speakers of the Sea Islands off of the coast of Georgia. Contemporary Black English bears only the remnants of an original creole language, in a few grammatical and phonological features that vary from those of standard English.

The major features that characterize Black English can be summarized briefly. In each case they are wholly systematic and rule-governed—part of a coherent grammar.

1. The deletion of the copula: In Black English the copula, the verb *to be,* is deleted any time it would be contracted in standard English. Thus *he's scared* becomes *he scared.* June Jordan's students offered this guideline: "Always eliminate the verb *to be* when it would combine with another verb" (368). (A misperception of this perfectly regular feature of Black English has caused a lot of trouble in the area of language attitudes, with one composition specialist even suggesting that students whose dialect does not include the full inflection of the verb to be are unable to discuss states of being as well as actions, and are incapable of abstract thought unless they're drilled in the "full deployment of the verb," an argument that's nonsensical to anyone who understands either the underlying grammaticality of all varieties of language or how new varieties are acquired by learners (Farrell 1983). In Black English, the auxiliary *do* is also systematically eliminated so that "What do you want?" becomes "What you want?"

2. The habitual aspect of the verb: Speakers of standard English don't have a convenient way of indicating within the forms of the verb, the sense that an action goes on all of the time. The best we can do is say, "he's always fooling around." In Black English, "he be foolin" gives that sense of an ongoing, habitual action (or "he been foolin" for habitual actions in the past). June Jordan's students stated this rule as "use *be* or *been* when you want to describe a chronic, ongoing state of things" (368).

3. The pronoun *it: It* replaces *there* in standard English: "There isn't any food" becomes "It ain't no food."

4. Multiple negatives: More than one negative may be used in one sentence, while "ain't" replaces all forms of the negative copula: *isn't, aren't, am not.*

Several morphological features of Black English also vary from those of standard English:

1. The plural marker *s* is omitted whenever there are other words in the sentence that indicate a plural: "I got two dog."

2. The possessive marker *'s* isn't used: "Kyeitha hair long."

3. The *ed* ending is not used to indicate past tense: "Paul close the door" for "Paul closed the door." Actually, the elimination of the *ed* ending results, not from any variation in the past tense morpheme, but rather from a regular phonological process of consonant cluster reduction, in which for most speakers, a combination of consonants, as in "he crushe*d the* hat" would be reduced, in speaking to "he crush the hat" with the *d* and *th* combined. But in Black English the reduction of the consonant cluster has been generalized to all *ed* endings.

There are other variant features of morphology and syntax (June Jordan's class came up with nineteen rules), as well as other phonological differences (like [n] for *ng*) [ŋ], but what's important is the understanding that these features are regular and "logical." As June Jordan's students discovered, Black English has its own rules; it's forms aren't errors, though they can be seen as such from the perspective of standard English, just as the forms of standard English can be seen as errors from the perspective of Black English (and despite my twenty years of residence and involvement in a black community, I still make many such errors when I try to give Black English examples in my classes).

While some of these features, like the zero copula, are unique to Black English, others like some of the morphological regularities are common to many dialects of English. They are the forms that children and new speakers of the language would generalize as they developed a logical sense of its rules, and they are fixed and reinforced within language communities. In fact, many non-standard forms are more regular and logical than standard ones. In a system that includes *myself, yourself, herself, ourselves, theirselves*, the form *hisself* is more regular and logical than *himself*. "He walk" follows the pattern of "I walk," "you walk," "we walk," "they walk"; since the third-person singular is indicated with the pronoun he or she, the *s* is redundant and can be eliminated without affecting the meaning. But the reason such forms are reinforced within communities has less to do with the logical regularity of the grammar than with the other element June Jordan's students associated with Black English—a shared understanding among those who share competence in a particular variety of a language that the use of that variety brings with it an expression of a common cultural understanding. As a consequence, those who share a language or a variety of a language that differs from the dominant language of the larger world in which they participate are likely to use that variety, that language, when they're with others who share the same language and values—to become, as my student Joe discovered himself to be, "a code-shifter."

Varieties and values: code-switching

A *code* generally refers to a language, or to different varieties of a language with such significant linguistic differences that a speaker would be likely to use that variety only with others who spoke it also. Joe probably wasn't a code-shifter, but a style-shifter, moving from an informal style with particular dialect features to a more formal, less marked style as he moved from the world of his home-town friends to a larger social world. But Nilda does shift codes as she moves back and forth between English and Spanish, and because she's beginning to see that each code is linked with particular cultural beliefs and values, she now wants her children to have mastery of both codes as well.

Bilingual speakers shift from one language to the other as they move among settings where one or the other language is spoken. But when they are with others who speak both languages, they may engage in conversational *code-switching*: "the juxtaposition within the same speech exchange of passages of speech belonging to two different grammatical systems or subsystems" (Gumperz 1982a, 59). In other words, they may start out a conversation in English, switch to Spanish for a sentence or a part of a sentence, and then switch back to English because they find one language or the other more suited to conveying particular ideas. (See Genishi 1981; Valdez 1981, for studies of code-switching among Latinos in the United States.) Many of my students find evidence of code-switching in their own conversations. Nilda has tried to separate her two languages, seeing the mixing of Spanish and English in informal conversations (like her children's use of informal forms such as gonna) as wrong, yet she acknowledges that she nevertheless will use a Spanish phrase that seems particularly appropriate when she's having a conversation in English with others who will understand. Similarly, Eliot finds that friends of his generation frequently sprinkle their conversations with Yiddish phrases, expressions that just don't seem to translate well into English:

> Using insults or responding to insults is a common manner of expressing humor and good fellowship within my speech community. Although none of us speaks Yiddish as a second language, most all of us retain words that have meanings that are difficult to translate into English. These words are interdispersed into sentences without any awareness until someone who is involved in the conversation and doesn't understand says "What?" After a period of time, these newcomers will also use these words but frequently they're either pronounced wrong or not used in the proper context. This in turn will start a lot of banter, with more insults or insulting responses.

For Eliot's generation, Yiddish is no longer spoken as a complete code, yet the vocabulary is common to a community where most participants are from a Jewish background. Along with particular genres like insults, teasing, and a bantering style, these words contribute to a particular social register in the Jewish community, one that appears across a range of particular social events and contexts.

Finally, Stephanie, whose first language is English but who has been studying French and has recently married a French-speaking husband, comments:

> Our language is interesting because not only do we speak in either French or English, but we also form sentences that include words and phrases from both, therefore restricting our speech community to the two of us only. So, because our language is very personal, the values it maintains also tend to be private.

Speakers who share more than one code are likely to draw on both of them to express meanings that are imbedded in a shared understanding of the world and shared set of values that a particular code (particularly one that's not the dominant language) represents. Within smaller speech communities, the particular mix can come to represent a more immediate sense of belonging, to the point where some speakers, like Stephanie and her husband, create a private language from the pattern of their switches between two public codes.

Black English also functions as a distinct code for most of its speakers; although its features may show up along a continuum of styles from informal to formal, those who speak that variety as well as standard English are likely to use it in contexts where they want to affirm their belonging to a culturally black community and to switch to it within a conversation when they intend to convey particular meanings, the way that Melanie switches to "You don't know nothin girl" when Shanna interrupts her science museum story.

Anthropological linguist Linda Nelson studied code-switching among African-American women whose life narratives she was collecting. She discovered that most of what she elicited from them was presented in standard English, despite the fact that she had contacted many of them through an extended network of friends and family, until she herself switched codes. Her initial question, "How would you describe who you are?" elicits a response from one informant of "I was going to answer in the context of being Black in America, but . . ." until Nelson interjects: "Girl, go with your first mind" (1990, 146). By using a familiar cultural form of direct address ("Girl") and a familiar idiom, she signals her own belonging in the black community and initiates a conversation that draws not only on linguistic features of Black English like deletion of the copula or multiple negation but on common rhetorical patterns, vocabulary, and idioms as well.

Nelson then translates some of these sentences back into standard English, so that "I always had an ear to what older folks talkin bout" becomes "I always listened to what the older people were talking about" and asks her informant what she sees as the difference between the original Black English and the translation. Her respondent replies, "I have to slip into my home tongue to get the message across; it's comfortable, and the words are not enough," suggesting to Nelson that: "in order to talk about Black cultural experience, she needs the language created out of that experience" (151).

Black English provides a rich resource for the women Nelson interviewed, one that adds to, rather than subtracts from, their overall communicative competence. Studies like Nelson's call into question the deficit model with which we've approached speakers' use of such codes, particularly in schools, where they've been seen as something to eradicate rather than as a rich resource to draw and to build on in acquiring new codes, styles, and registers.

To highlight the fact that all varieties of language are imbedded in particular contexts with their own cultures, the linguist James Gee uses the term *Discourse* for any variety of language, whether a code, a dialect, or a register, as it is used by a group of speakers who draw on particular linguistic features, rhetorical, patterns and other stylistic features, and a shared cultural frame of reference. He distinguishes between a primary discourse, "our socioculturally determined way of using our native language in face-to-face communication with intimates," and secondary discourses, those that involve social institutions beyond the family and require communication with non-intimates (1989, 22). In Gee's view, whether or not we acquire a new language—a new code—we are all involved in a process of acquiring new discourses as we move into unfamiliar or public settings and try out the new ways of interacting and functioning with language that are characteristic of each setting.

Acquiring and using new languages and new discourses

Although most of us who have sat in foreign language classrooms in the United States remember the process of learning a new language as one of memorizing vocabulary, lists of prepositions, and rules for subject/verb agreement apart from actually using these in communicative contexts, most of us also remember that we weren't very successful in using these elements when we were faced with a real need to communicate. But our understanding of how a second language is acquired has been reshaped by what linguists have learned about first language acquisition and the nature of both grammatical and communicative competence.

Chomsky's work has suggested that an underlying grammatical potential is shared by speakers of all languages, that this potential is realized through a process of acquisition rather than conscious learning, and it rests in the deeper or more abstract nature of grammatical structure more than in surface features. The idea that people have an underlying sense of grammatical structure that's given particular form as they confront the evidence of particular languages affects the way in which linguists have come to see second language acquisition as well as first language acquisition. It seems that second language acquisition proceeds by a process analogous to the one we saw in Chapter Two for a first language. Second language learners gain competence (both grammatical competence and communicative competence) in their new language as they hear it used and begin to use it themselves in purposeful interactions that take place in meaningful contexts. They develop systematic working grammars for their new language unconsciously, and they revise these grammars as they take in new evidence about the nature of the target language (the new language that they're trying to master).

At any moment, a person who's acquiring a new language has a perfectly regular grammatical system—an interlanguage—which represents her working hypotheses about the structure of the new language. At first this interlanguage will be closer in structure to the first language with some of the new vocabulary of the second language. But this interlanguage is revised constantly as the speaker receives new linguistic data, so that it gradually draws closer to and approximates the structures of the new language. The nonstandard forms speakers produce in their interlanguage won't really respond to correction, because they aren't really errors in terms of the systems they've created, and the "errors" created through the systematic testing of new hypotheses are a necessary part of the process of acquiring a new language. In order for speakers to revise their system, they need the new information that comes from further exposure to the new or target language.

But in order to have appropriate exposure to the target language, learners need to have the opportunity to participate in real communicative contexts. While Chomsky's work altered the way in which the acquisition of grammar was seen, Halliday's perspective on the functional nature of language and sociolinguistic approaches like that of Dell Hymes led to an emphasis on the role of communicative context in acquisition, the pragmatic and meaning-focused nature of language acquisition, and the relationship between acquiring the structures of a new language and acquiring communicative competence in particular social contexts.

In acquiring another language, whether through conversations in the community or classroom writing activities, language users are acquiring the perspectives of a different culture, a different sense of what to say and when to say it, and moving back and forth between that perspective and whatever they've known before.

When second language learners use their new language in speaking or writing, we can see their hypotheses about the language in the texts they produce. The following text from a student in a beginning ESL class was collected by one of my graduate students, Mike Arsenault, at the local community college where he teaches. Mike gave students the task of writing a response to a letter that appeared in an advice column, in which the writer wants to know what to do about the fact that her daughter is going to marry someone the writer objects to. One student, an elderly Russian woman, wrote this response:

> Dear Lady!
> I think you should not to go incide this problem. Most of kids never agree with parents. I fill if you will push to strong they will marryd anyway, but they will move to another city or state and you will lose your girl forever. You should to explane her "Whay?" You should to meet that boy, his family and then decide. In my shoose I would never say anything.

If we look at the features of this text that vary from standard English, we can begin to observe some of the aspects of this student's interlanguage. It appears from her text that one systematic feature at this stage is a construction with a modal *should* plus the infinitive: "should to go," "should to explain," "should to meet." English doesn't use the infinitive after the auxiliary *should*, though it does use it, for example, with verbs referring to desires (I want to go, I wish to go, I hope to go), so the writer's hypothesis is a logical one. In any event, this learner has begun to refine this pattern, because when Mike reads her text back to her (rather than marking errors in red ink), she hears that it doesn't sound quite right, and she crosses out the *to* in to explain and to meet. (The intervening not in "you should not to go" may distract her from perceiving the incorrect infinitive form in that sentence.) When she returns to her text, she also crosses out *of* in "Most of kids," inserts *their* in "with parents," and corrects her spelling from *fill* to *feel*. As with all language learners, her understanding is slightly ahead of what she's comfortably been producing, her competence is somewhat greater than her performance, and the discrepancy allows us to see a moment of alteration in the regular grammatical system that comprises her ever-evolving interlanguage.

But it's not enough to see a learner's language acquisition only in terms of the systematic grammatical features that show her present interlanguage as she moves toward a closer approximation of the grammar of her new language. While she is acquiring the grammar of English, she is acquiring a discourse—both the larger cultural meanings represented in American English and the particular register appropriate to a given context, in this case, the newspaper advice column. In this too, she is testing out and refining hypotheses as she comes to approximate a new discourse. Mike describes her as "an apprentice to American culture" who still "sees life through a Russian-based perspective," and he points out that this shows up in her pragmatic reading of the situation described in the advice column letter.

> She advises the woman not to interfere with the daughter's life too much, or she warns, the daughter and the husband might move away from her. In other words, she partially equates physical proximity of family members to the closeness of the family bond. . . . In Russia, because of government allocation of housing, newlyweds usually lived with their in-laws. For better or worse, families were forced to stay very close to each other and most immigrant Russian families that I know of continue to stress physical closeness to maintain strong family bonds.

But physical closeness may create a pattern of interaction in which discussion of difficult issues is avoided. When the writer concludes "in my shoose I would never say anything," she's trying to draw on an idiomatic expression in American English ("If I were in your shoes"). Although she hasn't analyzed the expression and can't reproduce it accurately, she knows that its purpose is to signal a change in perspective, to indicate that the advice to follow comes from the speaker imagining herself in the listener's situation. Ironically, though "in my shoose" is exactly appropriate here, because it is from the perspective of this elderly Russian woman, standing in her own shoes, with her own experiences, that the advice she gives makes the most sense.

By focusing on communication and trying to recreate in the classroom some of the real communicative contexts that are common to American society, including writing in a genre (the advice column letter) that calls for a conversational style, Mike is supporting his student's acquisition of both grammatical and communicative competence in her new language.

The most influential theory of second language acquisition has been that of Stephen Krashen. Krashen has proposed that we see language acquisition and language learning as "two distinct and independent ways of developing competence" (1982, 10), for second language learners, as for children acquiring a first language. Krashen sees *language acquisition* as accounting for the development of a speaker's fluency and underlying competence, for what learners can use productively in a second language. He argues that learners acquire most of the grammar features of the target language in what he terms a "natural order," the order needed most for communication, and that they acquire them by participating in real communicative contexts, engaging in genuine conversations, reading, and writing.

He sees acquisition as fueled by *comprehensible input* (language that the learner can understand but that's slightly beyond what the learner is already producing), offered by those around the learner in such contexts. "Foreigner talk" (where people slow down, speak distinctly, and use relatively simple syntax and common vocabulary in speaking to those they perceive as not understanding the language well), like caretaker language with children, offers one form of comprehensible input.

Language learning, on the other hand, involves the conscious knowledge of rules and explicit attention to form, and it accounts for learners' ability to monitor their own accuracy and correct their first attempts at an expression, but only under certain conditions: they must have a lot of time, their anxiety has to be low, and they must already know the relevant rule. Mike's student can monitor and correct her utterances (drawing on her most recent hypotheses about the use of the infinitive in English), because her anxiety (her *affective filter* to use another of Krashen's terms) is low—because Mike makes her feel comfortable in class and puts her in control of the changes to her text.

It is through meaningful interaction and attempts with others to make sense of and respond to the world, that a new language is acquired as words and syntactic structures are repeated within the ordinary flow of conversation as part of ordinary discourse cohesion. At the same time, the interactional features of ordinary conversation, in which speakers negotiate shared meanings, help shape comprehension (see Long 1981). In the end, acquisition can't take place unless the learner hears language that's both meaningful and comprehensible. It is contextual information—the learner's knowledge of the world, immediate situational knowledge, and discourse knowledge—that allows learners to interpret and understand what they hear, that makes language comprehensible.

Krashen's model of second language acquisition is often referred to as an input model because it emphasizes what a listener takes in through such communication but not what that same person puts out as a speaker as contributing to acquisition. Others (Swain 1985; Ellis 1990) have argued that learners need the opportunity to produce language as well as to hear it in order to acquire a language to any degree of proficiency. In particular, learners probably also need the opportunity to use various styles of language, both more planned or more formal and unplanned or informal (Givon 1979).

One of my sophomore students, in the course of our study of varieties of language, commented on his growing awareness of differences in style and register in his new language. Antonio writes:

I have always been an outsider. Since I came to the United States a few years ago, I have found myself grappling to understand the way the people around me speak the English language. . . . At this stage in my English-learning process, fortunately, I can confidently say that I can communicate relatively well with any speaker of standard English. What I have not been able to understand, however, is where I stand in the middle of all these dialects.

Since I work in a relatively informal setting, I have noticed significant stylistic variations in morphology, syntax, and phonology. Last week, for instance, I had a brief conversation with a middle-aged man who later described himself as a psychology professor at Harvard University. He was also a researcher, some of whose psychological works I have been studying in my psychology course this semester. Had I not been aware of these facts, and just guided by his phonetic style, I would have never imagined I was in front of my favorite psychologist.

Second language learners acquire, with the language, both a variety and a style appropriate to a particular discourse community. Since many learners acquire their new language, initially at least, in school settings, the style that they acquire is likely to be a relatively formal one, using a standard variety of English. Having acquired a formal school style, Antonio is surprised when he discovers, not only different dialects, but the range of informal styles that native speakers, like the famous psychologist, shift into as they move into different informal contexts.

Other learners, particularly those who arrive in the United States as adults, acquire their new language through their ongoing interaction in a community where most of their exchanges are informal and other varieties of English are spoken. Many of our students at UMass/Boston have acquired English as a second language in just such contexts. They have become fluent speakers of a particular variety of English that is not the standard, and their task now is to learn, not a second language, but a second dialect, along with the formal, public, style associated with school settings, and to do so in writing, using all of the conventions of literacy. In many contexts, such students have been placed in rigidly remedial programs that focus on exercises and limited skills instruction, where students may spend a semester practicing sentences before they're allowed to write a paragraph. At our university they begin their studies in an intensive reading and writing program where they engage in genuine communicative acts, through writing, drawing on all of the communicative strategies that they've developed from their acquisition of a number of secondary discourses.

Here's a paper produced by one such student a few years ago in response to a writing assignment that asked students to describe what they'd learned from a PBS videotape on apartheid.

Apartheid People

We ask ourselves, "Why is apartheid still so wide spread in South Africa."

But after viewing the documentry "Apartheid people" it has become clear, that apartheid will be hard if not impossible to eradicate, for it's a legally sanction practice in South Africa, which has imposed it violence and injustice on black's. Keeping them segragated from the white Afrikaaner.

This documentry has inable us to look at different views of apartheid as it exist today. First we see Peter Hatta an Afrikaaner priest that has openly denounce the injustices of apartheid.

He has express how difficult it has been for him to see the police beat an abuse the children of South Africa as well as the adult.

Yet the contrast view of Mr Laru an Afrikaaner farmer who have benefited from apartheid.

He tell's us he has a good relationship with his workers, yet he felt they were inferior to him. However we look at another view from Rom OHossa a black African lawyer, and his approach to fight apartheid. Rom's dedication has takeing him to different part's of South Africa, where he work with miner's organizing the union to fight against apartheid. For he feel that organization of the union will ultimately bring about the changes necessary to defeet apartheid. However the view of EeMtutu Matshaba a black African in the advertisement industry, one of many who lives in the homeland and makes the journey every day along with 350,000 others to Johanasburg to work and are required to carry with them what is know as the dum past. Which is one of the evil of apartheid. We also see a black catholic nun by the name of Sister Agatha sum up apartheid like this.

The devastation and injustices of apartheid has reduce all black of South Africa to their base.

Finally apartheid has brought the total population of South Africa black's and whites alike to a perpetual war, with blacks paying the blont of it, for no one is at ease as long as apartheid remain in control of the small population of white Afrikaaner's

This writer is in the process of acquiring the discourse of English academic writing, a discourse that is secondary for her in several respects: English is her second language; because she acquired English within a community where Black English was the dominant dialect, standard English is her second dialect of that language; standard written English also requires a new formal style, used in the university in a particular academic register; and as a written discourse, it demands particular orthographic conventions. The text shows how, in approximating these multiple aspects of a new discourse, the writer draws on her existing competence, while trying out new hypotheses about what's relevant to her new context. In the text we can see evidence, not only of an interlanguage, but of what might be termed an interdiscourse—something between a primary discourse and and several secondary discourses.

If we look at the systematic variant features of this text, we discover that two dominant features are the absence of the past tense morpheme *d* or *ed* (missing in *sanction, inable, denounce, express, reduce),* and the *s* morpheme that marks the third person present tense (missing in *exist, work, feel, remain).* However, these are probably not evidence of an interlanguage between Spanish and English, but of the correct forms of the variety of English this fluent speaker has acquired—Black English. She has acquired (rather than learned) that variety through ongoing use of the language, without formal instruction, and she is able to speak it wholly fluently and correctly, using complex syntactic structures to define precise relationships among her ideas. What she faces now is the task of acquiring a new variety—standard English—but not a new language. And from this text we can see that she has begun that process: since neither feature (the third-person present tense morpheme *s* or the past tense morpheme *ed*) is consistently aligned with one variety, the writer is probably already conscious of these differences and is monitoring for them some of the time (so that we find benefited, required, tells, lives). We know, however, that attending to both meaning and form simultaneously may be impossible at some moments for writers working in a secondary discourse, and we can anticipate that, as she gains fluency as a writer and as a speaker of the standard variety of English, she'll both acquire more of these forms and find it easier to monitor for those she has learned but has not fully acquired.

Many of the other variant features in the surface of this text involve orthographic features: spelling, *'s* used for the plural (overgeneralizing the need for an apostrophe that she knows is a feature of written text), punctuation of dependent clauses (so that we find fragments like "keeping them segragated from the white Afrikaaner") and she's equally involved in acquiring the features of written language, or more specifically of written English for this student who acquired her literacy in Spanish. At the same time, terms like "Afrikaaner" and "apartheid" are spelled correctly, suggesting that this writer is also an attentive reader who has had no trouble learning from the new texts she's been encountering. Her misspellings of words she'd ordinarily use are evidence of her earlier invention of English spelling from the literacy she'd already acquired in Spanish—as she applied her prior competence to a new discourse context.

Once we see that this writer has already acquired full fluency in English as a second language, albeit a particular variety, and both literacy in Spanish and strategies for using her literacy in English, we can begin to look beyond the surface of this text to see what it shows about her discourse strategies and her assumptions about the particular act she was engaged in. We'll certainly want to know about the context in which this text was produced, the nature of the task she was responding to, the audience she perceived, and the purposes she was trying to achieve, as well as her sense of the nature of texts produced in this context. We'll also want to know what areas of knowledge and competence she brings to this new setting from the communities she participates in: the discourse practices of those communities, the typical speech events that take place there, the ways in which literacy is used in these contexts, and how those uses of literacy fit in with other discourse practices, with the ways of using language and being in the world that are valued in the community. We might also want to know what strategies for becoming a member of a new community she brings to this new situation from her earlier successful experiences. We can see that she's already acquired many structures that are common in the academic discourse context she's now involved in: a topic-focused title; the rhetorical strategy of an opening question followed by an essay that moves toward an answer; the representation of different points of view, signaled by transitions like *yet, however,* and *finally,* and a concluding statement.

Looking at this text takes me back to my neighborhood, to my sense of the richness of the varieties of language represented there. The writer is, in fact, one of my closest friends, an ally in community struggles since our older children were small. Joann grew up in Honduras with Spanish as her first language, came to the United States after finishing high school in her late teens, married an African American and settled in a black community, raising three children whose home language has been English. There's no doubt about her communicative competence in English—she's been an effective organizer of many common efforts within the community, active in the local church, the NAACP, and youth outreach programs, while remaining involved with a Spanish-speaking Honduran community as well.

In the early years of our friendship we were very involved in our local community center, and we co-chaired the parents' advisory committee of the center's day care. We worked well together: she had terrific community organizing skills and could draw larger groups of people together around common concerns where different priorities (of young parents and senior citizens, for example) were creating deep divisions; I could quickly produce the letters, the reports, the documentation needed for our various efforts. The division of labor seemed a natural one.

A few years ago I encouraged Joann, who had completed high school in Honduras and who'd had no further formal education in the United States, to enroll at the university through a program designed for older students like herself. In the years that we'd been friends, I had received invitations from her for birthday parties, graduation parties, and other such gatherings, but I'd never seen any extended example of her writing. I knew Joann as a very intelligent and highly energetic woman, verbally powerful and convincing; while I, on the other hand, could not approach the powerful oral style that characterized our community events.

My first response to seeing the early papers she produced for freshman courses was one of concern and worry, accompanied by feelings of guilt and responsibility. I had encouraged her to enter a world where I knew she would succeed or fail on the basis of her formal language, her ease with the ways of the academic community, her use of standard English. And though I'd been designing programs for students like Joann and trying to reinvent a freshman curriculum that would challenge and respect intelligent adults, even though they lacked traditional academic knowledge and styles of speaking and writing, until that moment I didn't really get it.

I do get it now. Joann and I switched places, turning around the roles of outsider and insider. As a linguistic outsider to our local community, I was welcomed as a full participant from the time I moved in. I've been accepted with tolerance and some amusement when I've used inappropriate discourse strategies like reading from a prepared text at a celebratory public gathering, and my ongoing interactions have been judged on the basis of my intentions and meanings rather than on the still too formal surface forms of my utterances. But that was not Joann's experience at the university, where despite her extensive range of linguistic and communicative competence, she was expected to prove herself as an insider before being accepted as a fully capable participant. Rather than being allowed to acquire this new secondary discourse through the ongoing interaction that supports full acquisition (like that which supported her full acquisition of English in the community), she was expected to learn the forms of that discourse first, without full immersion in the context that requires them, and to be kept outside of the gate that freshman writing courses are seen as guarding until she succeeded.

Our study of language variation teaches us that, from a linguistic perspective, no one variety of a language is inherently inferior or superior to another, though differences carry significant social meaning. And our study of language acquisition tells us that learners gain fluency in other languages or varieties by participating in the meaningful interactions that take place where those languages and varieties of language are used. We are all at different times, insiders or outsiders to different discourse communities. Our successful participation in those communities will have a lot to do with whether we're invited into the conversation and treated with tolerance and respect as we gradually acquire a new discourse, or whether we're kept outside of the conversations that would support that acquisition until we demonstrate a mastery that we can't achieve without participation. Joann, like many of our adult students, has stepped out of the university for a while, as she juggles the competing demands of work, family, and her own education. But she'll be returning soon. This time I hope she'll find more pockets of the academic community, beyond freshman writing courses, where she'll be brought into the conversation even as she acquires the insider discourse of the disciplines she studies. In the meantime, I will work toward the goal of making our particular academic community a welcoming one.

CHAPTER 7

Extending Communicative Style Across Discourse Contexts

We have seen that most speakers have a linguistic repertoire consisting of the variety (or varieties) of language spoken in their home (what linguist James Gee would refer to as a primary discourse from the perspective of a learner) and other varieties that they've acquired as they've moved into new speech communities and other discourse contexts (what Gee calls secondary discourses), with the features of other dialects, cultural styles, and context-specific registers. Within a discourse community, a shared variety of a language is likely to signal some shared cultural understandings that don't have to be named explicitly—the shared perspectives and shared knowledge common to insiders in this setting, whether it's a neighborhood store or a network of computer hackers. For the learner, the process of acquiring any of these new discourses is similar, and it is best accomplished by having the opportunity to use the variety with others who speak (or write) it, in the ordinary communication that goes on in settings where it's used.

As we saw in our brief look at Black English in Chapter Six, controlling a particular discourse is related not only to features of grammar, characteristic syntactic patterns, pronunciation, or vocabulary, but to knowing how to use such features appropriately. But such differences extend beyond these features to larger discourse structures and ways of signaling what sort of discourse event is taking place. In acquiring a discourse, speakers must acquire discourse competence, in the sense of knowing how to participate in the larger units of any extended discourse event in that setting.

As we've seen, Karen, Melanie, and Shanna know when to take turns, how long their turns can be, when another speaker can be interrupted, how to hold the floor, when to shut up, what topics can be introduced and how, and what words are appropriate to use for talking about them—in a variety of settings or discourse contexts—with each other, at school, with their families, in church, and in a range of other, more public settings. The discourse structures of conversations like the one we've been looking at follow particular patterns that develop over time, shaped partially by the participants' experience with conversation in other contexts, and partially through ongoing negotiation within a particular context. Such negotiation and reassertion of individual styles and perspectives is characteristic of informal, unplanned conversation among participants who know each other well.

In other, more formal or more public discourse contexts, exchanges are less flexibly structured and less easily negotiated. Some of these event structures are relatively fixed across contexts, so that someone entering a store in virtually any setting, even across countries and languages, will know roughly what to expect and will be able to accomplish the purpose of buying what's available, even if awkwardly. Likewise, typical classroom discourse structures are similar enough that non-English speaking children who are familiar with those structures from classrooms elsewhere can get along, offering minimal responses in appropriate places, when they enter a classroom in the United States.

Other structures vary, particularly among different cultural groups. Some are negotiated by the participants in ongoing dialogue. In others, the responsibility for structuring and maintaining the ongoing discourse rests with a person in authority. This is true to some degree even for simple service exchanges in stores, it's often true at the family dinner table where parents tend to play strong roles in shaping and framing the conversation (see Ochs 1979), and it's particularly true in one setting where part of the purpose is to initiate learners into new discourse structures—the classroom. In addition, expectations about discourse structures often transcend the boundaries of speech and writing.

A person who would move from one discourse community to another must know how to participate in the characteristic speech events and discourse structures of the new context, whether these are informal conversations or the formal exchanges that go on in professional journals. But often in public as in private settings, discourse differences must be negotiated. Breakdowns across cultural discourse styles, like the one that occurs when Shanna interrupts Melanie's science museum story, occur in public settings as well. But without the glue of long-term friendship to bring participants back together, moments of miscommunication can foster deeply held stereotypes and mistrust. Communication in a complex society with many varieties of language requires more than the ability to listen to a different accent or to tolerate, if not make sense of, the jargon used by lawyers; it requires a willingness to negotiate the process of interaction, a sensitivity to the ways in which different understandings about the requirements of particular speech events can disrupt that process, and an openness to learning from others' perspectives. Once again we can begin our inquiry close to home.

Speech events in context

If we look at the exchanges that take place in the world around us, we see that similar events are structured to some degree in similar ways, but that those ways are shaped and altered by particular contexts. Service exchanges of the sort that I'm typically involved in, generally look something like this recent one:

SALESPERSON: Can I help you?
CUSTOMER: Yes. Do you carry soccer shoes in women's sizes?
SALESPERSON: No. We only have men's and children's. What size do you need?
CUSTOMER: My daughter wears a women's size 7.
SALESPERSON: I could put her into a boy's 5 1/2. That should fit.
CUSTOMER: We can try it, but it will probably be too narrow.
SALESPERSON: I'll get it for you. Have a seat and I'll be right back.

The focus at this mall store is on an exchange of information, on whether the stock that's available will fit the customer's needs. The language is public and standard, and reasonably explicit. Later references, like "a boy's 5 1/2," point back to information that is recoverable from an earlier part of the exchange where the topic, available sizes of soccer shoes, has been named. An exchange like this is generally direct: there's a clear common goal: to buy/sell a pair of soccer shoes that will fit the player, and since the only real issue here is the fit, the salesperson isn't likely to comment much beyond that topic or suggest that the color is flattering or the style is what all fourteen-year-old girls are wearing.

At my neighborhood gas station, such service exchanges are more likely to fulfill multiple purposes:

CUSTOMER: Hi Gerry! How're things going?
MECHANIC: Oh . . . not bad, El. What about you? What's Ron been up to lately? Still traveling a lot?
CUSTOMER: Yes, as usual. He just got back from Chicago and he's off again for Oregon at the end of the week.
[*After as much as five or ten minutes of catching up about kids, dogs, neighborhood events, the actual service exchange begins.*]
MECHANIC: So . . . got a problem?
CUSTOMER: Yeah . . . the Toyota's leaking oil again.
MECHANIC: A lot?
CUSTOMER: About the same as before.
MECHANIC: I'll take a look. Can you bring it in next week?
CUSTOMER: Ron's leaving again on Tuesday. Is that OK?
MECHANIC: OK, El, see you then.

Here, the larger exchange serves two purposes. One is social/interactional, affirming and maintaining a friendly relationship. The other is informational/

pragmatic, exchanging the information necessary to get the business of a car repair accomplished. But even this part of the exchange differs from that in the mall or at a highway service station: it takes place in relation to an ongoing series of exchanges. The Toyota and its problems are as familiar as the husband's travel, and nothing has to be said about the history of the oil leak. *A lot* and *the same as before* refer to shared knowledge that exists outside of the explicit information of this text (*a lot* is about a quart of oil per week, and *before* is before the head gasket was replaced). Both the structure and the level of explicitness of even a common discourse event like this service exchange are affected, then, by the particular context in which the event takes place.

What participants must know

What makes the event work for both participants in each of these service exchanges is, in part, a common understanding about what they have to do in it—about how to carry out particular discourse functions. John Gumperz, whose studies of discourse have focused particularly on the strategies people use to communicate their meanings and intentions in such spoken exchanges, says that speakers in a conversation have to be able to indicate the following:

1. what the topic or message is and what's foreground and background information in relation to that topic, or what's the main point and what's related but subsidiary or qualifying information
2. what knowledge and attitudes are assumed to be shared
3. what is old and what is new information
4. what their point of view or attitude is toward what is being said

Furthermore, all of this information must be "contextualized"; it must be indicated in such a way that it fits in with the expectations of other participants in a particular discourse context (1982b, 28–29).

In the two-part auto repair exchange, there are really two topics: "how things are going" or the current affairs of kids, family, and neighborhood, and "the problem" of the malfunctioning car. The first part is a prerequisite to the second for any member of our community. We all know that catching up takes precedence over getting down to business, and we also know that keeping in touch should take place with or without the following business. So stopping into the station to catch up is part of a trip past Gerry's corner, even on foot, without a car problem. The shape and nature of exchanges like these is negotiated in a community through long practice.

But it's also through practice in the community that we know how to read and interpret the exchange—to know that Ron's travels are a main point and are foregrounded in the earlier part of the conversation but merely serve as background information (indicating that another car will be available) in scheduling an appointment for car service; to know that the only significant "new" information in the second part of this exchange is contained in the word *still* as in "still leaking"; and to understand the shared assumption that, as long as the car is running, there's no real urgency about the oil leak.

Gumperz suggests that, "any utterance can be understood in numerous ways, and that people make decisions about how to interpret a given utterance based on their definition of what is happening at the time of interaction" (1982, 130), that is, in terms of a familiar frame or schema or type of language activity that they can identify. Participants need to be able to figure out what's an interview, or what's a joke, for example, and then draw on their background knowledge about that particular type of activity: predicting the formats such an exchange will take; what the roles of participants are likely to be; and how to realize their meanings within this framework in linguistic structures that are appropriate to the activity and its context and to the other participants.

Of course, while some activity types or event structures, like the service exchange, are relatively fixed across contexts, others, like jokes, may vary a lot, and most unplanned, informal conversation moves fluidly among different events within a constant process of negotiation among participants. Yet only rarely is anything about the nature or structure of the event or the participants' roles in it stated explicitly, and most often, participants must continually predict and reassess what's going on and what it all means through a process of conversational inference. Here's an example, taped by one of my graduate students, Michael Bradley, in a teachers' lunchroom conversation. As is typical in this setting, the teachers use their lunch time (when they're not on cafeteria duty), as a break from the intense demands of students during the rest of their teaching day, engaging in conversation about current events, both personal and public, moving fluidly from stories, accounts of events, to jokes. At the time this conversation took place, Olympic figure skater Tonya Harding had just been implicated in an attack on her rival Nancy Kerrigan. Four teachers, two men and two women, take part in this portion of the conversation.

SPEAKER 1:   So did you hear? Tonya Harding

SPEAKER 2:   . . . Oh this will be good.

SPEAKER 1:   Was offered a spread in *Playboy* for $250,000? Meanwhile Miss Kerrigan gets offered a Disney contract.

SPEAKER 2:   Disney. Oh, yah. A million dollars.

SPEAKER 3:   She was really offered a spread in *Playboy*?

SPEAKER 2:   Yeah.

SPEAKER 3:   I thought it was the beginning of a joke.

SPEAKER 2.   No.

SPEAKER 1:   It said $250,000.

SPEAKER 3:   You're kidding. Oh, I thought it was the beginning of a joke.

SPEAKER 4:   It was in *The Herald* so it might be a joke.

This conversation, among people who see each other every day, takes place in a framework of shared knowledge. Everyone has read or heard news accounts about the attack that damaged Kerrigan's knee and nearly removed her from

Olympic competition; everyone has read extended profiles of the two skaters that have played up the contrast between good girl Nancy Kerrigan, who lives at home with her parents and is the model of innocence, and bad girl Tonya Harding, who talks and acts tough, and who rebelled against an abusive mother by marrying a young troublemaker.

This excerpt starts off as a report of a newspaper account. But the notion that Harding would be offered a Playboy contract and Kerrigan a Disney contract fits so well into an already shared thematic framework that it could as easily be invented on the spot, and the third speaker, a woman who has not read the news report, assumes at first that the first two speakers (both men) are making a joke—another common genre in this context. Because she can't be sure, she names the sort of speech event she thinks it is explicitly and repeatedly, until a fourth speaker connects the two genres—joke and news account—by suggesting that the particular newspaper in which this account appeared is not necessarily reliable, and that the account itself could be seen as a joke.

Contextualization cues

The signals which speakers use and which allow listeners to read and interpret information necessary to their participation in such speech events are carried through *contextualization cues:* surface features that signal what frame of reference is to be used in interpretation. These cues are conveyed through three linguistic channels: prosody, syntax, and lexical choice, as well as through related (paralinguistic) features like gesture and facial expression. Prosody includes rhythm, stress, pitch, patterns of intonation, and tone of voice. It's through our use of prosody, in spoken discourse, that we most often highlight important information, show what information should be chunked together, and indicate what our intentions are. Here stress is used to highlight the contrasting pairs: "Tonya Harding" and "Nancy Kerrigan"; "Playboy" and "Disney." Similarly, in the girls' conversation, Melanie's words, "You don't know nothin, Shanna," are an explicit put-down of Shanna, but the prosodic contours of her statement—as she speaks these words loudly, directly to Shanna, with stress on the *you* and a second stress on *nothin*, in a tone that's challenging and yet friendly, signal quite a different intent than if they'd been muttered under her breath with a different pattern of stress for only Karen to hear. On the other hand, the light, mocking tones of the lunchroom exchange could highlight either the irony of a true event that fits so neatly into a thematic pattern that it would seem to be fiction, or an account that's actually fictitious—a joke.

Signals offered through syntax include much of what we looked at in terms of the information structure of a text in Chapter Five—surface features associated with discourse cohesion: signaling a topic, foregrounding and backgrounding information through subordination and relativization, establishing perspective, showing contrast, etc. In the lunchroom, Tonya Harding has been a commontopic for a few weeks, and when the first speaker names her and pauses to highlight this topic, the significance is immediately understood by the second speaker, who interrupts to comment "this will be good" even before the first speaker completes the sentence. (The passive construction, Tonya Harding was offered a contract instead of Playboy offered Tonya Harding a contract, allows the topicalization of Tonya Harding.) And lexical choice shapes interpretation as well. "A spread " in Playboy has implications far different from "a story." Typically, these elements work together, particularly when there's a shift of code, as when Melanie combines a shift in accent and intonation with the double negative syntactic structure of Black English Vernacular to strengthen her implied challenge to Shanna. Being able to interpret such signals correctly is necessary for full participation in a particular community.

At the service station, Gerry's "Got a problem?" is not a statement of annoyance or a sarcastic put-down, but a real question intended to shift the speech event to the service exchange. The casual conversation that has taken place thus far might occur any time a customer walks by the station or stops in to get gas, and the question signals, in a fairly direct way, that it's time to move on to business if this is more than a social call, or, if there's no car problem, it's time to end the social conversation and get back to work. A different summary statement like "So same old . . . same old," might also signal the end of the social conversation, but in a much less direct way, and it would not necessarily be read as indicating closure by someone unfamiliar with the shape of the conversations that take place in this setting.

Gumperz points out that such contextualization cues help participants decide what discourse task is being performed, what the goals of this task are, and what the intent of each participant is, that "they are acquired as a result of a speaker's actual interactive experience, i.e., as a result of an individual's participation in particular networks or relationships . . . [and that] they operate below the level of conscious choice" (1982b, 18). Participating successfully in a conversation requires picking up these cues and using them in an ongoing process of drawing inferences and evaluating intentions.

Miscommunication occurs when speakers do not share an understanding of the same system of signals. An outsider to our neighborhood might be expecting a more abrupt exchange with an immediate statement of the real point: the car needs to be repaired, and be puzzled by the nonfocused nature of the first part of our service exchange. But in this context, an opening statement like "Gerry, my car's leaking again!" would violate the conversational rules and might create an implicature like "I'm angry, you didn't do a good job." The larger framework of meaning is embedded in a relationship that goes beyond one car repair, and beyond narrowly defined roles of customer and mechanic, where those roles have taken shape in a larger context of shared involvement in the community center and evolved into a long friendship with implied reciprocity—I'll jump start your old car on cold mornings, and you'll be patient if a repair isn't finished immediately.

Cultural differences and communicative style

The contextualization cues that we all rely on unconsciously show up most clearly where they don't work—where a signal doesn't communicate what the speaker intends. Gumperz' work shows the sorts of miscommunication that can arise between speakers from different cultures. Much cultural miscommunication occurs, not because of a difference in codes or dialects—differences in grammar or lexicon or even pronunciation. They arise, rather, from differences in the more subtle cues of the sort Gerry offered when it was time to get down to the business of car repair. Focusing in particular on communication between Asian or West Indian speakers of English and British speakers in typical exchanges at banks, in job interviews, on committees, and in courtrooms, Gumperz shows repeatedly how different prosodic patterns of stress and intonation—along with different assumptions about how to signal the main topic, what sorts of pleasantries should precede the main point, how directly or indirectly the point should be stated—cause the intentions of the Asian and West Indian speakers to be misread. In service exchanges, for example, Asian speakers might typically use the falling intonation of a statement where British speakers would use the rising intonation of a question. As a result, Asian speakers are often seen as abrupt, demanding, and arrogant by their British counterparts. Likewise, in job interviews or courtroom testimony, where Asian speakers often frame their responses with background information that their listeners don't perceive as relevant, they may be seen as evasive or not well-informed. Similarly, differences in how to highlight or introduce or lead into a topic, in what's relevant and what's not, frequently contribute to misunderstandings between teachers and their students from different cultures about how to shape another discourse event, the written school essay. Helen Fox, in *Listening to the World* (1994), offers a useful discussion of such differences, though she seems to suggest that all of the accommodation must take place on the student's part, and I see communicative differences as something to be addressed in two-way dialog and negotiation.

Different patterns of organizing and presenting information can cause misunderstanding when communication takes place in either a spoken or a written mode, but much of our signaling of how to interpret spoken exchanges comes through prosody alone. We generally use intonation to highlight the information structure of our utterances, creating groupings of words around one idea (tone groups), and placing stress on the key word in the group. Such groupings help listeners to pick out the key ideas and process information quickly within a rapidly flowing conversation. Thus an alteration in the expected pattern of intonation and stress for a typical sort of utterance without any change in the words themselves can cause miscommunication, as in one instance recounted by Gumperz.

As passengers were getting on a London bus on, the driver (a West Indian) said, "Exact *change*, please," with the emphasis on *change*, highlighting that as the relevant issue. But when someone tried to give him a large bill he repeated,

"Exact change, *please*," saying *please* this time with extra loudness, at a higher pitch, and with falling intonation. A passenger then went down the aisle muttering about "why do these people have to be so rude and threatening" (1982a, 168). Gumperz explains that according to the prosodic conventions of British speakers of English, the polite way of marking this directive would be to put the stress on *change* (on the specific information that passengers might not know) as the driver did at first, with *please* left unmarked within the same tone group. Alternatively, the speaker could have used a more indirect, polite marking of *please?* with a rising tone like a question. But, by the conventions of British English, a strong stress on *please* in a falling tone would strongly signal a directive, in the manner used by someone in a position of authority over the listener, like a parent or teacher who might say to a child: "Eat your lunch . . . *please*," and it would be insulting to order another adult around in this way. Within the system of contextualization conventions used by West Indian speakers, however, the emphasis on *please*, even stressing it with a falling tone, would show greater politeness.

Gumperz also shows that miscommunication can occur between members of the same cultural group if they choose different codes in the same context, as when one speaker's shift into a shared, less public code, is not picked up. He reports one instance in which a black graduate student who is supposed to interview a black woman is greeted at the door by her husband, who says, "So y're gonna check out ma ol lady, hah?" The husband expects the student to respond in kind, and when the student replies, quite formally, "No, I only came to get some information," the husband pulls back from the friendly exchange and goes to get his wife (1982a, 133). The student, with his standard English reply, has contextualized this encounter as a formal interview rather than an informal and friendly exchange of information, and has rejected, perhaps unintentionally, the husband's opening to a more extended interaction.

Communicative style

The specific linguistic devices that speakers use as contextualization conventions, as indicators of how they intend their utterances to be interpreted, are elements of a communicative *style*. Even as we shift our styles of writing and speaking in relationship to different audiences and contexts, we tend to feel that we have developed an underlying personal style. But, as we will see in succeeding chapters, style is not a wholly personal and idiosyncratic aspect of speaking and writing. Rather, it develops through an individual's interactions with a number of discourse communities, and even the elements that remain relatively consistent as a speaker moves across contexts, giving us a sense of that speaker's or writer's *voice*, show multiple tracings of where that person has been.

Of course, one place we've all been is in our families and our primary discourse communities, where we've mastered the expected contextualization cues unconsciously, to the degree that we don't recognize either how subtle they are or even that others might not share the same set of signals. Our understanding of how to mean, of how to do things with words, is so strongly formed by those first contexts, that the cues we've learned there continue to shape aspects of our communication, no matter how many other places we've been.

While Gumperz' work shows the difficulty of interpreting these cues across cultural groups, Deborah Tannen's research shows how the misinterpretation of such signals can interfere with understanding among friends from only slightly different discourse communities, and between men and women from the same community. In *Conversational Style* (1984), Tannen analyzes a Thanksgiving dinner table conversation that took place among a group of her friends, some of them from New York and some from California. Building on an earlier collaborative study she had done with Gumperz on the relationship between individual and social elements of style (1979), Tannen is interested in finding out how stylistic strategies are shaped by discourse functions (by the ideational, interpersonal, and textual functions we examined in Chapters Three, Four, and Five). As we saw, speakers are concerned, at once, with representing ideas and propositions and with common human pragmatic concerns about how to place oneself in relationship to both the subject matter (how to maintain an appropriate emotional distance from a subject) and to other participants (how to be polite but not too friendly, how to signal a recognition of the appropriate social relationship, as between peers), while contributing to and maintaining an evolving text. Tannen discovers a variety of strategies that participants use to shape their relationship to one another in conversation and to indicate their relationship to the subject matter being discussed. She goes on to describe a continuum of styles, between those that focus on the message and show little involvement between the speakers or with the subject and those that signal a great deal of involvement between speakers (which she terms "camaraderie") and between them and their subject. Of course, a low-involvement style typically sends a signal about interpersonal relationships—one of distance or deference.

Turning then to people she assumes to be most like herself—the group of friends in the arts and education who have gathered for Thanksgiving dinner—Tannen nevertheless finds a significant distinction between styles that she labels high-involvement and low-involvement. Speakers using these two styles differ in terms of the topics they choose (more versus less personal), the ways in which they introduce or shift topics, the pacing of their speech and their turns, the amount of cooperative overlapping or backchanneling they use, their narrative strategies (including their use of explicit versus imbedded evaluation of the sort we saw in narrative discourse in Chapter Five), and in prosodic features like pitch and stress.

Tannen, who identifies herself as being from New York, with Jewish parents of East European origin, discovers that her conversational style differs in subtle ways from the style of her friends from other parts of the country and even from that of some other New Yorkers of a different cultural heritage. For example, she asks a lot of questions at a rapid pace (what she refers to as "machine gun questions"), many of them fairly personal, with the intention of creating rapport, but while some of the other participants respond to this strategy as a familiar one, keeping up the pace and responding in kind, others are more distant and hesitant, acting as if they've been put on the spot in a way that they're not comfortable with. Likewise, differences in narrative strategies appear, where some speakers don't state the meaning of a story explicitly but embed it in expressive phonology, as in the following exchange:

STEVE: I have a little seven-year-old student . . . a little girl who wears those. . . .She is *too* . . .

DEBORAH: She wears those? [*chuckle*]

STEVE: . . . much. Can you imagine? She's seven years old and she sits in her chair and she goes . . . [*squeals and squirms in his seat*].

DEBORAH: Oh: God . . . She's only SEVen?

STEVE: And I see well . . . how about let's do so-and-so. And she says . . . Okay [*squealing*] . . . Just like that.

DEBORAH: Oh:::

DAVID: What does it mean.

STEVE: It's just so . . . she's acting like such a little girl already. (114)

In this example, the participants have different expectations about even the amount of information to put into words. Steve acts out the meaning of his narrative—that the young girl is too coquettish and flirtatious, too sophisticated for her age—when he squeals and squirms. Deborah immediately understands the point, and shows that she gets it with her reply "Oh God." David, a Californian, still doesn't seem to get it however (even after Steve goes on and repeats the squeal) and finally has to ask, "What does it mean?" (much in the way that Shanna interrupted Melanie's Museum of Science story with "What . . . ?").

In commenting on this exchange, Tannen points out that in her system of communicative values, establishing rapport is especially important, and it's better to make a try at showing you understand someone's meaning, even if you're wrong. In David's, though, understanding the correct meaning is most important, so he won't falsely suggest he really gets the point unless he's absolutely certain he does. These listeners, then, have different responses to Steve's story, depending on the degree to which they share a common communicative style and contextualization conventions with the speaker.

As my students and I look at the conversations we've recorded in our own discourse communities, we too find places where participants have moments of miscommunication because they have different expectations of what's called for in a conversation, shaped in part by their cultural backgrounds. When we analyze these conversations, we find similar and often surprising elements of difference by age, culture, and gender. Florence, for example, who has recorded and analyzed a conversation she's had with her husband and another couple about school committee elections in her town, finds that three of the participants use the intense, rapid speech, with frequent overlaps between speakers, overall loudness, and the general emphasis on rapport and involvement that marks Tannen's New York style. She comments:

Three of the participants share some vestiges of Eastern European Jewish culture, which may account for their discourse style. After reading Tannen, I discovered that my husband finds our speech patterns rude—an amazing revelation after 28 years! As a Virginian and former Air Force Captain, discipline and politeness tend to mark his speech patterns.

Her husband's long-held impression that his wife and their friends talk the way they do out of rudeness, because someone from his home community who interrupted and overlapped with another's turn would be intentionally violating the community's norms for politeness, shows exactly the sorts of larger misunderstandings that can arise from differences in communicative style.

Gender differences in communicative style

In other work, Tannen has shown how men's and women's styles of conversation differ in many of the same ways, with women likely to place more emphasis on creating involvement and rapport as opposed to simply exchanging information, and more likely to expect a high degree of conversational inference as opposed to explicit statements of meaning. Women appear to be particularly concerned about building and supporting relationships; men to be more focused on controlling information and displaying knowledge.

These differences in overall orientation are realized in ongoing conversation through specific features: different patterns of interruption (men interrupt more often to change the topic or oppose a point while women make more interjections designed not to take the floor but to provide supportive overlap), different patterns of intonation (women more often end clauses on a rising tone, opening up their statements as questions), and the use of particular elements, such as tag questions like "isn't it?" (used more often by women and by speakers in a position of lesser authority). Such differences contribute to the multiple examples of miscommunication that Tannen recounts in her popular account of men's and women's experiences in conversation, appropriately titled *You Just Don't Understand* (1990).

Gender differences show up very early in the language of young children, and they're modeled by parents and other adults in the child's community. Home studies show (not surprisingly) that patterns similar to those Tannen describes for adult interactions are also displayed by parents with their children. For example, in extended home studies of twenty-four families that included the recording of family dinner table conversation, Jean Berko Gleason found that fathers used almost twice as many direct imperatives as mothers, with more of these direct imperatives (along with more threats and disparaging names, like "Stop that, you twit, or I'll break your head") especially directed toward their sons. Mothers, on the other hand, were more likely to soften imperatives with polite forms ("Would you take your plate off the table, sweetie?") whether speaking to boys or girls. (1985, 195.)

Children themselves begin to show these differences early on. Jacqueline Sachs (1987) studied boys and girls, ages two and five, engaged in pretend play about a visit to the doctor. At age two, there were larger differences in attitude and stance that showed up in the children's choice of roles: boys most often chose to play the doctor or sometimes the father, but refused the roles of patient or baby, while girls chose all roles, and sometimes negotiated shared roles. And by ages three to five, when children begin to rely more on language in setting up their play, boys tended to use more imperatives and explicit prohibitions ("Do . . . ," "Don't do . . . "), while girls used the language of pretend ("Let's pretend you have a sore throat"), and other mitigating forms like tag questions ("Want to?") to negotiate their play. At this age they were already beginning to sound like their same-sex parents.

Yet differences that show up in the early years become strikingly greater as boys and girls move into older childhood and adolescence. Daniel Maltz and Ruth Borker (1982) offer a cultural model, influenced by the work of Gumperz, to explain these gender differences. Summing up some of the key features of women's speech that have shown up in other research, they suggest that women show a greater tendency:

1. to ask questions
2. to do more of the work of maintaining routine social interaction and facilitating the flow of conversation, so that they use questions, and other utterances that encourage responses from their fellow speakers
3. to use positive minimal responses, like "mm hmm" more frequently (more backchanneling)
4. to respond with only silent protest after being interrupted
5. to use the pronouns "you" and "we," explicitly acknowledging the existence of other speakers.

In contrast, men are more likely

1. to interrupt the speech of their conversational partners
2. to challenge or dispute their partners' contributions
3. to ignore the comments of the other speaker or to offer only a delayed minimal response
4. to control the topic of conversation
5. to make more direct statements of fact or opinion (197–98).

While some explanations for these differences focus on social power, the differences in dominance and control that men and women have in the larger society according to their sex roles (West and Zimmerman 1977), and others focus on the resulting effect of these sex roles on the development of women's personalities (Lakoff, 1975), Maltz and Borker propose a cultural explanation, based in men's and women's experiences in different sociolinguistic subcultures, where they've learned to do different things with words.

According to this explanation, a man and a woman may end up using language differently, not because one is trying to dominate and the other trying to please, but because they've effectively grown up in different discourse communities through many of their formative years. During their early school and teenage years, most boys and girls interact socially primarily with peers of their own sex, even if they are in coed classrooms (where, as we'll see, talk is likely to be limited and constrained). Thus, they have learned and/or strengthened rather different ways of carrying out friendly conversations. During these years, while boys tend to play in larger groups, in more competitive games, and focus their conversations on the things they're doing, girls are more likely to play indoors, in pairs or small groups, in noncompetitive activities, with intense concern for establishing friendships and resolving inevitable conflict.

Maltz and Borker sum up the things that girls must learn to do with words over these years: how to create and maintain relationships of closeness and equality, using inclusive forms like "we," and sharing confidences; how to criticize others in acceptable ways, often presenting criticism in terms of group norms or indirectly as the concern of someone else; and how to interpret accurately the speech of other girls, perceiving shifting alliances and reading the intentions of others (205). At the same time, boys are learning to use speech that asserts their own positions of dominance, including threats and name-calling; that attracts and maintains an audience, despite ongoing challenges; and that allows them to assert themselves when others have the floor, to offer challenges to a speaker and thus assert their own identity, even when another has the floor (207).

After years of practice with these different speech styles, when women and men become each others' conversational partners in mid-to-late adolescence, they've developed quite different implicit systems for carrying out conversations, and they read each others' contextualization conventions quite differently: they have different understandings about how to take turns; how to introduce new topics whether gradually or abruptly, acknowledging what's been said before or ignoring preceding comments to get right to the new point; and the purpose of questions, as part of conversational maintenance or only as requests for information.

From a cultural perspective, then, the difference in the speech communities boys and girls inhabit contributes most strongly to shaping the differences that show up in men's and women's language. And, as we've seen, differences in discourse are not simply variations in surface features but differences in ways of seeing, believing, and valuing. Differences in language reflect and contribute to differences in ways of thinking about and responding to the world.

Studies of the intellectual development of college-aged women, such as that carried out by psychologist Mary Field Belenky and her colleagues and reported in *Women's Ways of Knowing* (1986), show the importance of women's imbeddedness in particular social contexts and relationships to the development of their thinking over the college years, while Carol Gilligan's study of women's moral reasoning, *In a Different Voice* (1982), shows that women tend to reflect such imbeddedness in making moral judgments, taking into account particular circumstances as well as abstract principles. The linguistic features of involvement in women's communicative style are connected to other aspects of their being in the world.

Communicative difference as multidimensional

The picture that appears when we look at people's ways of using language through the lens of cultural or gender differences is powerful but somewhat distorting, and leaves a danger of stereotyping. Human beings participate in multiple discourses, in multiple discourse communities: They are not only male and female, they are a certain age, with experiences and ways of viewing and talking about the world shared by others in their age group: They have a particular cultural background, linked to race, ethnicity, language, religion, and social class that influences each of these other variables. Cross-cultural studies show that differences between men's and women's styles of using language exist across many different languages and cultures. But they also show that such variation is contextual—that styles vary within a culture from the interaction of gender, age, and status, while differences between cultural styles take different forms when they are displayed by men or women, of particular ages, in particular contexts.

When I look back at my own data, at the conversations of young teenaged girls at my kitchen table, I find that the patterns that have shown up in research on women's language don't fit very neatly. In Karen, Melanie, and Shanna's conversations, I can see some of the characteristic features of girls' talk: supportive backchanneling, as when Melanie says, "My favorite place to shop is downtown Boston," and Karen echoes "downtown"; interruptions that extend and confirm the original speaker's comments rather than seize the floor, as in the following exchange on the topic of Luke Perry at the mall, where Karen interrupts to extend Melanie's comments and Melanie comes back in to confirm their common point of view:

MELANIE: But now I think back to myself . . . and I'm like . . . what did I see
    in that guy? Cause I think he's ugly now . . . bald and wrinkled and . . .
KAREN: I know it . . . he looks worse now than he did before . . .
MELANIE: He sure does.

But I also find that these girls are engaged in constant challenges, struggles to hold the floor, conflicts over whether information should be given explicitly or implied, and that they often display features associated with boys' language as well as girls'.

The blend of features in each girl's use of language seems linked to her personality: Karen tends, in general, to be a supporter and a mediator, and to play that role, in particular, with these two friends, but she does so assertively, insisting that she's right about her friends' strengths and successes; Melanie tends to make more assertions and play the role of leader, though she doesn't combine that with using explicit directives, as is more often true of boys and she'll often take on more supportive roles; and Shanna tends to ask questions that require specific information (rather than questions that support another speaker's turn), but she does so to place herself more firmly within the conversation rather than to take it over.

Returning to Heath's research in *Ways with Words*, I find some common-
alties between aspects of Melanie's style and the black discourse of Trackton,
some between aspects of Shanna's style and the white working-class discourse of
Roadville (and I suppose a lot of overlap between Karen's style and that of
Maintown families), so that these styles appear to be more cultural than individual. But again these differences are confounded by the multiple discourses with
which the girls interact.

Neighborhood peer language is certainly one important influence, and in
my own inquiry into the research on difference, I find a study done by Marjorie Harness Goodwin and Charles Goodwin (1987) on the language of
working-class black preadolescent girls (ages nine to fourteen) that shows more
of what I see in my data. The Goodwins found that, while studies of adult black
speakers showed a marked contrast between a female tone of sweetness and a
male argumentative style, the young girls showed opposition through the use of
dispute structures that were much more similar to boys'—structures that
depended on sequenced challenges in clever verbal exchanges, drawing on the
characteristic black cultural form of the ritual insult. Specifically, they found
that, in these exchanges, participants will use what's been given by another
speaker to shape a reply, often with an exact repetition of some of the surface
structure, but adding a clever substitution or reversing the framework of the
utterance so that it is turned back on the original speaker, and frequently adding
a characterization of the speaker (such as "crazy") (207–219).

Here's one exchange between Karen and Shanna that seemed familiar and
typical to me, but that didn't wholly fit the expectations I was bringing from my
study of the research until I read the Goodwins' article. I think of it as playing
around:

KAREN: Melanie . . . you can't go like this [*stomps across the room*]. Melanie . . .
   I'm sorry . . . no . . . don't hit me . . . not with that knife.
SHANNA: She's not going to stab you with the knife . . . she's going to cut a
   slice of pizza with it.
KAREN: Gosh Melanie . . . you're so old-fashioned.
SHANNA: Yeah . . . and gone insane.
KAREN: Like some people we know named Shanna . . . Hey don't spill on
   my . . .
SHANNA: Here's one acting like an idiot.
KAREN: Ha ha . . . look in the mirror and that's what you'll see.
SHANNA: Another case in point.

In my first reading of this exchange, I focused on contextualization cues, both
verbal and nonverbal. Much of this event is carried out through gestures rather
than words. Karen begins by making fun of the way Melanie walks across the
kitchen as she gets a knife to cut the pizza. Melanie turns and scowls at her, and
Karen responds in a high-pitched mock protest, as if Melanie's about to use the
knife on her. Shanna doesn't pick up the signal for such play, though, and her

first response is a literal description of the events taking place: Melanie is using the knife to cut the pizza. Karen responds to the content of Shanna's statement and shifts frames of reference, now commenting on Melanie's using the knife to cut the pizza, but continues the larger playing around event with her strong, measured stress on "so old-fashioned." Finally Shanna picks up the cue and adds her delayed reaction to Karen's earlier pretend interpretation of Melanie's getting a knife: "gone insane."

Shanna (like the children Heath studied in Roadville) tends to focus on the literal and the factual, and is less likely to leap into fiction and fantasy. Despite the cues given by Karen's exaggerated tones, she tries to stick with a factual account of what's going on. But these girls also learn to accommodate each other's styles and to make shifts that will keep the conversation going, as Shanna does here. It's the next part of the exchange that I'm struck by, however, as Karen and Shanna move through the sort of sequenced challenge described by the Goodwins. Building on Shanna's word "insane," Karen directs the comment back to Shanna and they continue on for a few more turns of formulaic responses and reversals, playing out a variation on the familiar ritual insult pattern that's used so often by their neighborhood peers, while Melanie, who's slightly older, steps quietly aside. The girls have acquired a varied repertoire of communication styles to draw on, and although this pattern is most often associated with black male adolescents (see Labov 1972a), I conclude that it is age, not race or gender, that most influences the style of this particular exchange.

Experiencing new discourse communities through literary texts

As my students and I study the communicative styles we find in the discourse communities we inhabit, we use what we're learning to explore communities that lie outside of the immediate experience that we collectively bring to the classroom. Literature provides one point of entry into the experience and the communicative worlds of others, and what we've learned about language and discourse style in our own worlds can help us to enter the imaginative worlds created in literary texts as well. Such an approach can also give us new understandings of the workings of those texts, by turning the questions we've been asking throughout these chapters on both the texts we read and our own reading of them.

We can begin with my favorite starting point for the study of language in any setting—asking who is an insider and who is an outsider to this discourse community (now to the one being created in the text) and how is insiderness shown. Is it marked by the shared knowledge about the world that's assumed or represented? By implicit understandings about how a writer signals and realizes particular intentions and purposes (contextualization cues, including conventions of genre, of rhetorical forms)? By the elements of style, register, dialect, and code—by the lexicon, patterns of syntax, even pronunciation of particular varieties of language as these are represented in the written text? We'll want to consider how these many elements, which shape the discourse context within the text and the immediate context surrounding its production, are shaped in turn by larger contexts—by the knowledge, prior texts, and prior experiences that writers and readers bring to the texts they write and read. Such questions, when applied to literary texts, help us to open up our understanding of those texts in ways that plot, setting, and character approaches of traditional formalist English study only begin (or sometimes close down). They can help us see how the experience of language as literature can move us across some of the boundaries that too often divide discourse communities in the world. More broadly, our questions can help us to see how texts are used, by and for whom, what picture of the world they present, and what's not explicitly represented in that picture. We can see the world of texts as a speech community writ large, with the same competition, conflicts, power relationships, roles, and sometimes negotiation and cooperation that we found in the conversation of teenage girls at the kitchen table.

Literature always invites its listeners and readers into a world constructed through language, whether it's the oral literature continually being created and passed on through the stories told at the family dinner table, the events recounted on the front porches of Piedmont towns, the written literature created in notebooks, letters, and journals, tucked away in a drawer or an attic, or the literature that has appealed to the public tastes of the time as responded to and shaped by the publishing industry. Even conversational tellings are likely to be marked by elements of a common literary or poetic style that appears across languages, tellers, and contexts—a style indicates that the events being recounted are special and worthy of being recounted, that the ordinary rules of conversational turn-taking are being suspended for a while as both speaker and listener (writer and reader) enter a world they'll experience together, a moment being recreated in the present.

In *Talking Voices* (1989), Deborah Tannen explores the elements common to this style, whether in conversational storytelling or written literature. She points in particular to the use of repetition and to the recreation of dialogue, features we found in both Melanie's and TJ's stories, as well as to the use of imagery, and she sees the effect of such features as heightening involvement and contributing to the aesthetic quality of any conversation where the pleasure is in the telling, not only in what's told. Such a style offers in itself a contextualization cue to listeners and readers (when Shanna misses the cue that Melanie is telling a story and should not be interrupted by questions, her violation is met with as much impatience and indignation as was evidenced by the bus passengers Gumperz studied).

As we saw in Chapter Four, any successful act of communication depends on shared understandings about how to cooperate in a speech act. The cooperative principle says that the maxims like those of quantity, quality, and relation, which call for the inclusion of sufficient, reliable, and relevant information to support a shared understanding will be followed, or where those maxims are violated, this violation is in itself intentional and meaningful, creating an implication that should be understood with participants who have sufficient shared knowledge. When Melanie doesn't provide enough explicit information about the boys at the Science Museum to enable Shanna to get the point, she may be violating the maxim of quantity, but that violation is intentional at some level. A true insider in Melanie's world will not only know how to read the cues that she's telling a story and shouldn't be interrupted but will also have enough background knowledge to imagine the events without the added information Shanna asks for–and Melanie's comment "You don't know nothin'" points to Shanna's lack of both types of insider knowledge. But it also suggests that the discourse knowledge about how to participate in this speech event is more important than shared background information: If Shanna had just listened, let the story go on, and entered the world Melanie was portraying, she'd have come to understand. Likewise when we open the pages of any contemporary literary text, we are expected to bring the understanding that a reader may not be treated as an outsider, to be introduced around the community and filled in on what's been going on there, but rather given a seat at a table where an ongoing conversation continues without interruption; the reader will become an insider by attending carefully and trying to catch up with what the others already know. Readers, like listeners, need to assume that the teller/writer is participating in the larger cooperative principle that governs the intentions and meanings of participants in a speech act. (For an extended discussion of these points see Mary Louise Pratt, *Toward a Speech Act Theory of Literary Discourse* 1977.)

The reader who enters new discourse communities through literature gains experience in listening and attending in new contexts, contributing to a communicative flexibility that's increasingly necessary to effective participation in a diverse, multicultural, and even global society. Whether reading the work of Shakespeare or Toni Morrison, part of what we acquire is a new communicative competence that allows us to gain meaning from varieties of language that may be different from those we regularly use, even as we enhance our ability to respond to different discourse strategies and frames for interpretation–to respond at least as potential insiders. To cast a quick look around us at the discourse communities we've experienced through the literature we've read, my students and I each bring in an excerpt from a favorite work that has introduced us to a new variety of English, creating a language medley that seems not unlike the book we put together at the beginning of the semester with excerpts of the conversations we tape. As we read these texts, we take in their language, adjusting to the rhythm created by their syntactic patterns, the framework of meaning shaped by their lexicon, enriching our own linguistic repertoire. At the same time, the texts of our language medley help to highlight much of what we've discovered through our study of discourse.

The discourse of a literary text

While reading the literature of diverse linguistic and cultural worlds extends our experience of discourse, what we've been learning through our study of discourse points to new ways of understanding the literature we read. We select from our language medley a text to analyze in common, using the methods represented in the earlier chapters of this book, but focusing in particular on the ways in which we are invited to become insiders to the world of the text, and the various signals we are given as to the meaning its story should hold for us. Many texts further explore the ways in which the characters are themselves insiders or outsiders to each others' frames of interpretation and meaning, allowing multiple possibilities for the way a reader might be positioned.

One example of such a text is Flannery O'Connor's short story "The River," the story of a child's journey from the apartment of his parents into the world his baby-sitter inhabits, a world of born-again Christianity, preachers, and healings. As with all O'Connor stories, its meanings are ambiguous, and readers' responses are affected greatly by the experiences they bring to the text and the ways they position themselves with reference to the very different discourse communities the story presents. Here is its opening passage:

> The child stood glum and limp in the middle of the dark living room while his father pulled him into a plaid coat. His right arm was hung in the sleeve but the father buttoned the coat anyway and pushed him forward toward a pale spotted hand that stuck through the half-open door.
> "He ain't fixed right," a loud voice said from the hall.
> "Well then for Christ's sake fix him," the father muttered.

With this opening, O'Connor brings the reader instantly into the middle of a world that is defined by competing discourses. "The child" of the story, as yet unnamed, is pushed out of his parents' apartment, out of their world and their ways of using language—their speech community—and into the very different world of a baby-sitter. And as readers we step into the middle of the conversation, so to speak, where everything already seems to have been introduced and nothing is presented as new. Part of the shared knowledge that O'Connor assumes with the readers who implicitly make up her larger discourse community is the understanding that such an opening is meaningful. We aren't told about *a* child, who is named X, is Y years old, and lives with his parents in city Z. The narrator of these events provides no abstract or orientation. Instead, the definite article *the* presents the child as an object that is already part of the given information of this particular world of discourse. And like the child, we are pushed toward a door where a disembodied voice waits to take us from this given world (that we're trying to take in and make sense of) into one that's new and wholly unknown. Like the child, we are being moved around, but by language, by systems of references that the writer has used and that lead us as readers to see the world of the story from one perspective or another. But at the same time, we move with the child through the worlds that are defined within the story, at times observing that world from the child's point of view, and at times observing the child from another's point of view, as we experience the story aesthetically.

Let's look at the worlds within the story first. "He ain't fixed right," introduces one of them, the world of the baby-sitter—one defined in part by linguistic features of social variation. The baby-sitter, who can be assumed to live within the same region as the boy and his parents, is immediately placed in a lower social class through her use of the nonstandard *ain't*. In her brief encounter with the boy's father we find other variants of prestige English in lexical items: *twict*; and in syntax: "This particular preacher *don't* get around this way often." With these variant features comes a different set of values, made explicit in the baby-sitter's comment about the condition of the apartment, "I couldn't smell those dead cigarette butts long if I *was* ever to come sit with you," and in her judgment of the painting hanging on the wall, "I wouldn't have paid for that . . . I would have *drew* it myself," but suggested also by what she does value—going to a healing with a particular preacher. She's sorry to hear that the boy's "mamma is sick," and she'll ask the preacher, the Reverend Bevel Summers, who has "healed a lot of folks" to pray for her. But the mother's call from the bedroom for someone to bring her an icepack suggests, together with the cigarette butts, that her sickness is really a hangover from a party the night before, and that she's unlikely to be interested in the preacher's sort of healing.

Finally, as the boy and his baby-sitter leave the apartment, we, as readers, find some of the orientation we've been waiting for: a description of the boy (with "a long face and bulging chin and half-shut eyes") and his age: "four or five." With this description comes an evaluation from the perspective of an observer of the scene, not a participant: "He seemed mute and patient, like an old sheep waiting to be let out." And we continue to move in and out of the perspectives of the characters.

Once they're outside, the baby-sitter is named—Mrs. Connin—and she asks the boy his first name. We're told: "His name was Harry Ashfield and he had never thought at any time before of changing it. 'Bevel,' he said." In leaving the world in which he is Harry Ashfield, the child assumes the name of the preacher he has just heard about, "a coincident" in Mrs. Connin's words, though of course nothing is coincidental in any of Flannery O'Connor's stories.

As O'Connor's story goes on, the child moves into an unfamiliar world where even the words he knows take on new meanings, and he doesn't know how to interpret what he hears, traveling first to Mrs. Connin's house and then to the healing at the river. He's returned to his house, but the next day he sets out again on his own, to the river where the preacher has said paradise is found, throwing himself in and letting the river pull him under and carry him off. As readers we experience those events, but we also try to sort out the competing meaning systems that shape his experience and guide his actions, and as we step out of the story, the framework we developed for studying the conversations we taped earlier in the semester proves useful once again. By looking at the functions of language as we have throughout this book, we can see the ways in which the discourse of literature, like other discourse, shapes as well as comments on the world.

1. *The propositional/referential function*: systems of meaning. Just as we sketched out the semantic field of terms for shoe boots that the girls were drawing on and negotiating in Chapter Three, we can sketch out the relevant systems of words in this story—both those that are related within a semantic field of connected and overlapping terms and those that tend to appear together (to cooccur), even though they're not systematically related, so that a coherent world is created through a pattern of lexical repetition and substitution. As readers we find the world Harry/Bevel leaves to be marked by ashtrays and cigarette butts and a mother with a hangover. The world he enters is a world where sin and pain and affliction are healed with prayer and where one can be baptized in a river of life and of faith. To the boy, everything seems to be different in this other world. A "pig" is no longer the small, fat pink animal with a curly tail and bow tie that he knows from his storybooks but a huge snorting "hog" or "shoat" that runs him down when Mrs. Connin's children lure him into pulling a board off its pen. Where "Jesus Christ" was a curse at home (as we saw in the father's opening words: for Christ's sake), in Mrs. Connin's world he learns that Jesus Christ refers to the carpenter in the picture on Mrs. Connin's wall. He is told that it was Jesus who made him, whereas at home he thought it was a doctor named Sladewell. But he decides that maybe the story about the doctor was "a joke," because at home everything is a joke. Here, though, it's the "gospel truth." The "gospel truth" is the basis of value to Mrs. Connin for a book she reads him, "The Life of Jesus Christ for Readers Under Twelve," but when he takes the book home, it's seen as valuable because it's "a collector's item." The names "Harry" and "Bevel" are coreferential, referring to the same child, though they apply in different worlds with different values: the mother's response to Mrs. Connin's saying "Bevel" is "My God, what a name." Bevel is also the preacher's name (and it was at the moment that Mrs. Connin told him so that he renamed himself). But the parents aren't named; they're only "the mother" and "the father." And they refer to the child as "old man."

2. *The pragmatic/interpersonal function*. Within the text, Harry/Bevel has a hard time interpreting the intentions and purposes of those around him. He has left home, where nothing is to be taken seriously, where everything is a joke. He's entered a world where "he knew immediately that nothing the preacher said or did was a joke"—the world of gospel truth. But that does not mean that every statement is to be taken literally. Many of the preacher's speech acts violate the maxim of quality (of truthfulness) as he calls for people to enter "the rich red river of Jesus' blood," because "This old red suffering stream goes on, you people, slow to the Kingdom of Christ," but those who are insiders to this community understand the implicature,

believing the words, if not their most literal meaning. But even though he has renamed himself, the child is too much of an outsider to this community, too unfamiliar with its discourse, to comprehend its shared meanings. Yet perhaps for that very reason he understands more than the adults around him realize. As readers, we both share and step back from the child's perspective. Yet in his final actions, his own purposes are clearly named for us: "He intended not to fool with preachers any more but to Baptize himself. . . . He didn't mean to waste any more time."

3. *The textual/discourse function.* All of these features contribute to the evolving text. But some additional aspects of the syntax have a particularly strong effect on the way we process the text as readers. One is the element of *modality.* We saw in Chapter Five, that modal auxiliaries (might, must, would, etc.) serve an evaluative function, suggesting an interpretation of the propositional content of a sentence. "It appeared" and "it seemed" serve a similar function. At Mrs. Connin's, the boy doesn't know how to interpret what's happening around him. When Mrs. Connin's son suggests pulling the board off the pigpen "he appeared to offer this as a kindness." Then the boys' faces "seemed to become less taut, as if some great need had been partly satisfied." What Harry/Bevel had known before "must have been a joke." He "would have thought" Jesus Christ was a curse. None of these indicators of his attempts at interpretation appear as he finally heads to the river, however. There the narrative is presented as a straightforward series of "complicating actions" (to use Labov's term for basic narrative versus evaluative clauses).

Finally, two other features affect our understanding of this text. One is the way in which propositional meanings are realized in the surface syntactic structures of the text—particularly in terms of active or passive constructions. And another related element linking syntax and semantics that I have not focused on earlier in this book, but that's particularly significant to this story, is that of *semantic roles,* the roles that the participants in the actions set forth in the sentences of the text play in those sentences (a descriptive system sometimes referred to as case grammar). Though many roles can be named, the most important for our reading of this story are those of actor or agent (always in the subject position of an active sentence), the experiencer (usually in the subject position, experiencing mental or emotional changes of state), the patient (always in the direct object position and acted upon), and the beneficiary (in the indirect object position). Seeing which of the characters is placed in the agent position, which in the patient or beneficiary position, at various points in the story (seeing who is acting and who is acted upon) can add still more to our reading of this narrative.

As it turns out, the child (still unnamed until he names himself after leaving the apartment) is the patient, who's acted upon in the opening section of the story where his father "pulled him into a plaid coat" and "pushed him forward" toward the door. But once they're outside the apartment, he appears sometimes as a beneficiary, as Mrs. Connin gives him a handkerchief, but more often in the subject position of sentences, as an actor. He puts the handkerchief Mrs. Connin gives him in his pocket, puts pressure on her hand, and soon he names himself Bevel. When he is confronted by Mrs. Connin's sons, he becomes, for a moment, an experiencer (He thought of crawling under the bed), and even an actor again as he pulls the board off the pigpen, but then he's the patient who's acted upon as "something snorted over him and charged back again, rolling him over and pushing him up from behind and then sending him forward, screaming through the field." At the healing, he's again an experiencer (He knew immediately that nothing the preacher said or did was a joke). Then he's acted upon by the preacher who "swung him upside down and plunged his head into the water." Back at the apartment, his mother pulls off his coat, then shakes his shoulder, pulls him into a sitting position so that "he felt as if he had been drawn up from the river" before lowering him onto his pillow. But from the moment he wakes up the next morning, he is the actor or experiencer. He decides to empty a few ashtrays on the floor, then he tiptoes out, goes back to the river, puts his head under the water, and pushes forward. For a moment, the river seems to defeat him as he comes back up, choking: "The river wouldn't have him." And he thinks maybe it's another joke. But then he plunges under again and "the waiting current caught him like a long gentle hand and pulled him swiftly forward and down." And "he knew he was getting somewhere."

Even after we've looked at the story together in this way, we come away with different understandings of its meaning—and different interpretations of the boy's drowning as tragic death or salvation. These are formed in part by our perception of the writer's intentions and purposes as shaped through the text, in part by our prior experiences of other texts, and of different religious discourse communities. But we know much more about how the discourse of the text has contributed to those understandings. There is much more that could be said about the linguistic analysis of literature. (Two helpful guides are Fowler, *Linguistics and the Novel* 1977, and Pratt and Traugott, *Linguistics for Students of Literature* 1980.)

In our study we return to the question of the discourse communities the text presents and creates. Having entered the world O'Connor has constructed for us, we have gradually become insiders to the discourse offered there, with its related beliefs and values. By the time we're used to "ain't that a coincident?" we have become "experiencers" of that world. And that experience leads us to reflect on other worlds we enter through the texts we read and the degree to which being drawn into the language of those texts shapes our experience of the worlds they present.

Conclusion

Communication, and miscommunication, are constant concerns in our complex society, and there's a real need for communicative flexibility. I don't spend my days in a world segregated by gender, weaving with other women while the men are working in the fields, but in one with more evenly shared responsibilities, where common understandings have to be negotiated across gender differences; I live in a neighborhood that's mixed by race, language, and class; I'm raising children who participate in an adolescent peer culture that's different from the one I grew up in and whose view of the world is certainly different from that of people my age; and I teach at a university whose students represent all of these differences of gender, age, race and ethnicity, language and class, some of whom, in turn, are teaching or will teach in schools affected by most of these same differences. I, my children, my students and their students, all need to be able to communicate across these differences. We can learn to do this, in part, by expanding our own repertoire, especially by participating in multiple worlds through our activities and through our reading, acquiring—mostly unconsciously—as much understanding as we can of the styles and strategies that are used in them. We can observe and reflect on our own uses of language and our own moments of miscommunication to discover patterns that contribute to conflict. But we can also use the conscious understanding of the ways in which others use language that we gain from analyses like these to learn new strategies for bridging differences. In all of these ways we can educate ourselves for participation in a multidiscoursed society. In the next chapter, we will turn our attention specifically to educational contexts, to look at the role that the discourse of the classroom plays in such an education, at the ways in which the educational goals of the classroom can be either fostered or shut down by particular discourse patterns, and how we can use the understandings about language that we've been building here to facilitate those goals.

CHAPTER 8

Classroom Discourse I—Encountering School Style

Although exchanges in public settings, such as service encounters, may be adversely affected by the participants' differences in communicative style, and even private conversations among friends may be marked by more subtle differences, schools are typically the site of the earliest extended exchanges between people from different cultural groups with significantly different communicative styles. In the classroom, learners may have their current communicative competence confirmed, learn to understand the communicative styles of others, and come to expand their own repertoire as listeners and speakers, as well as readers and writers. Or, as is too often the case, they may enter a world in which their home ways of using language are denied or condemned, where what is taught in the name of language instruction is a set of attitudes that leads them to dismiss the ways of others as well, and where learning new communicative styles associated with schooling and literacy calls for a contraction rather than an expansion of their own linguistic and communicative repertoire. In the United States, even while education has been seen as a route to success for individuals from any linguistic, cultural, ethnic, or class background, the failed experiences of schooling for many groups has led to a focus on communicative differences, among other factors, as an explanation. While one purpose of schooling is the building and extension of formal knowledge in various domains, schools are also cultural contexts, with assumed beliefs and values embedded in a common discourse. Each classroom, then, becomes a small community, mediating the culture and discourse of schooling and the cultures and discourses of the learners even while it is affected by the attitudes, beliefs, values, and experiences those learners bring. The teacher who hopes to build on and enrich her students' language and learning must negotiate various communicative styles, and at the same time, be attuned to all that's embodied in the discourses that come together in the classroom.

Discourses in the classroom

Rebecca Day, a brand-new teacher in her first weeks of teaching at an inner-city middle school, is having trouble with the male preadolescent students in her bilingual classroom. Her class takes place in a resource room, in a special program for students who aren't succeeding in their regular classes. She is supposed to be working with her students on their reading, in Haitian Creole and in English. But she's discouraged by what she describes as constant pandemonium and worries that she is a failed teacher when she has barely begun. Her goals are "to have the kids learn to love to read and write, and to interact with print in a personal way," but she describes the pattern of discourse in her classroom as "digression-lesson-digression-lesson-digression, with more digression than lesson," and she finds that many of her own utterances are aimed at bringing her students back "on task," rather than providing the sort of open questions and rich scaffold for their own thinking that she aims for. She transcribes this portion of a reading lesson as an example:

STUDENT 1:   [*reads from lesson*] La rivye gen plis dlo . . .
STUDENT 2:   [*screams*]
CLASS: [*laughs*]
STUDENT 3:   [*shouts name of student 2*]
TEACHER: [*calls out name of student 4, admonishingly*]
STUDENT 3:   [*reads from lesson*] Gen plis dlo pase . . .
TEACHER: Put it down. Put it down.
STUDENT 2:   [*begins to read*] M pa . . .
STUDENT 4:   He gaved it to me.
TEACHER: Where's he going? Where's he going?

At this point the lesson breaks down completely and full attention is given over to dealing with Student 4, who has shot a rubber band (an elastic to these Boston-area speakers) at Student 2. A school disciplinary officer, Mr. M., enters the room, and after hearing a brief report from the teacher, addresses Student 4 (while the others continue to comment in the background):

MR. M.:   Come here . . . How would you like it if I shot you with an elastic?
STUDENT 4:   He gaved it to me . . .
MR. M.:   How would you like it if I shot you with an elastic?
STUDENT 4:   Because he gaved it to me.

                                            . . .

MR. M.:   I think this boy . . . gentleman . . . deserves an apology first of all.
STUDENT 4:   He's a gentleman?
MR. M.:   Yes.
STUDENT 4:   Then I'm a gentleman too?
MR. M.:   You're a gentleman too. But you don't need to be snapping elastics at each other . . .

STUDENT 4:   Yeah.

MR. M.:   It's very dangerous.

STUDENT 4:   And a gentleman always says he's sorry?

MR. M.:   Apologizes, that's right.

MR. M.:   OK. You guys are classmates.

STUDENT 4:   Yup.

MR. M.:   Alright?

STUDENT 4:   OK.

MR. M.:   Get in there . . . Gentlemen!

To consider the sorts of learning that are going on in this classroom exchange, we need to consider the functions and purposes of language in the classroom, how these are represented in various elements of school style, and how the secondary discourse of schooling might differ from the primary discourses of learners' homes in ways that can interfere with communication and with learning in the classroom.

School purposes

A predominant purpose of classroom discourse is to foster the expansion and reconceptualization of referential/propositional knowledge—expanding frameworks of knowledge about the world and ways of reasoning within those frameworks. But at least two other purposes make up the pragmatic underpinnings of the classroom: creating an environment that can support the first sort of learning, by defining the nature of this community and the rules, both implicit and explicit, by which its interpersonal interactions will be governed; helping learners to acquire the patterns of discourse in which all of the purposes of schooling go on.

Members of the classroom community, like participants in other discourse communities, are involved, through their talk, in several functions at once: sharing knowledge about the world; interacting with each other and accomplishing various intentions and purposes through that interaction; and building together a common text through which all of this occurs. But, unlike other communities, where members acquire the skill of accomplishing all of these discourse functions implicitly through their ongoing participation, the classroom has an explicit didactic purpose in relationship to all three functions. Students learn not only new information but how to reconceptualize and reframe the old in light of the new, and vice versa. They learn not only how to accomplish their purposes in their interactions with each other, but how to reframe what they know of such interactions so as to develop new pragmatic strategies. They learn not only how to talk the talk, but how to talk about talking the talk. Each of the functions of discourse becomes part of the explicit propositional/referential knowledge being shared in the classroom; each becomes the focus of the intentions and purposes of the participants; and each is accomplished through the conscious and explicit use of new discourse patterns.

In the classroom these multiple discourse functions are likely to be complexly interwoven and hard to disentangle, though they also offer teachers rich possibilities for scaffolding student learning. For example, the primary purpose of teacher questions about the referential content of a lesson would seem to be to help students develop their understanding and frames of reference with respect to that content. But often such questions are really intended to control classroom behavior (and thus they become part of what Courtney Cazden, in her study of classroom discourse (1988), calls "the language of control" versus "the language of instruction"): the teacher calls on students not to check their understanding or to give them a chance to develop their ideas, but to keep them from fooling around or passing notes—or just drifting off. And since boys violate the norms of classroom conduct more often and more intrusively than girls, it is boys who generally get called on the most, and thus have the most opportunity to give voice to their understandings in ways that may support their learning—even in the classes of teachers who are determinedly nonsexist in their approaches and values.

The discourse of many classrooms is dominated by a restricted discourse pattern generally described in terms of Initiation/Response/Evaluation (IRE): a rapid exchange in which a teacher initiates questions, students respond with single word answers, and the teacher in turn offers a brief teacher evaluation— "right" or "no". Despite the fact that this pattern offers students little opportunity for the kind of extended talk that lets them work out their ideas (an important aspect of learning), the IRE pattern predominates in schools, partly as a result of its true, but hidden purpose: classroom control. Other classroom speech events, like primary school reading lessons, may also have purposes beyond those named in a teacher's lesson plan. Many instances have been observed where a teacher interrupts a student's reading to correct his pronunciation and enforce the use of a standard code, as in a lesson recorded by Piestrup (1973) where the teacher repeatedly interrupts the children's reading of the words "What did little duck say?" until she finally gets them to pronounce a final "t" on "what." By that time, of course, any sense of the meaning of the words being read, of the notion that reading is about understanding the meaning of whole sentences and stretches of text, is lost. Sound/letter correspondences are implicitly presented as the only aspect of reading that really matters, and the written word is seen to represent the spoken word only as it is pronounced in the standard dialect. In such a case, the purpose of the lesson is less to support reading than to monitor a different discourse element—the use of a standard dialect.

Becky is aware of all of this. In her reading lessons, she keeps her focus on meaningful exchanges, not on the correction of error. She tries to heighten her students' awareness about language, using a book entitled *Ann Reflechi Sou Lang Nou Pale A* (Let's Think about the Language We Speak) that encourages them to make their own observations about their native language and its structures. She discusses explicitly the discourse structures of the classroom such as keeping focused on the same topic, and following the "one person talks at a time" rule. And she also tries to allow a lot of room for natural discourse, to let students initiate turns and at least some topics. But when she listens to her tapes, she hears everyone "talking at once, trying to gain the floor to read or to answer questions, fooling around, and code switching." In a geography lesson, where students are naming countries on a map, "everyone starts yelling out names of countries at once." And she feels discouraged, wondering whether any learning is taking place.

Of course, learning *is* taking place, though not always about what Becky perceives as the official classroom content. The reading lesson has been sidetracked, but learning about classroom behavior and values, and ways of using language to frame and describe these, goes on, and that becomes the explicit content of the second exchange. At first, the school officer and the student approach their discussion of this classroom event from different frames, with Mr. M. focusing, repeatedly, on individual feelings and a notion of reciprocity: "How would *you* like it . . . ?" while the student responds with the reason for his action and repeatedly asserts a version of cause and effect: "because he gaved it to me, presenting the other student as culpable as well. But when they move out of these competing frames into the question of what should happen next, they come to some common ground. When Mr. M. renames "this boy" as a "gentleman" who deserves an apology, he finally engages this student, and the other students as well, in a process of reconceptualization. It's the student who suggests that "a gentleman always says he's sorry," taking up one of Mr. M.'s terms and relexicaling the other—expressing the concept of apology in his own words. Mr. M. gives an affirmative response to the student's wording and the action it represents: "Apologizes, that's right," offers another way of framing the students' status and relationship as "gentlemen," and then introduces the term "classmates" as a way of extending the notion of "gentlemen" to their present setting and reminding all of the newly shared concept and frame of reference for their behavior.

Here the school officer is playing the role of teacher as well, building on what students know, on their existing frames of reference, and helping them to expand and reframe what they know. The teaching, at this moment, is directed toward the question of how students should interact and includes naming the specific speech act, an apology, that is appropriate to their newly defined, shared intentions and purposes.

Becky appreciates the school officer's efforts here, but she doesn't want to create a sharp division between her role as a teacher and his as a disciplinary authority—or even to have so much of her own classroom discourse directed toward maintaining order. She wants to teach in a style that will be supportive of students' language and learning, yet being nice—polite and friendly—doesn't seem to work. As she raises these concerns, we turn to an article written by an experienced teacher I know who has encountered similar problems. After many years of teaching in other settings, Cindy Ballenger took a position in a preschool that served the Haitian community in Boston. In an article for the *Harvard Educational Review,* (1992) entitled "Because You Like Us: The Language of Control," she describes her situation and how she set about resolving it:

Having had many years of experience teaching in early childhood programs, I did not expect to have problems when I came to this Haitian preschool three years ago. However, I did. The children ran me ragged. In the friendliest, most cheerful, and affectionate manner imaginable, my class of four-year-olds followed their own inclinations rather than my directions in almost everything. Though I claim to be a person who does not need to have a great deal of control, in this case I had very little—and I did not like it.

My frustration increased when I looked at the other classrooms at my school. I had to notice that the other teachers, all Haitian women, had orderly classrooms of children who, in an equally affectionate and cheerful manner, did follow directions and kept the confusion to a level that I could have tolerated. The problem, evidently, did not reside in the children, since the Haitian teachers managed them well enough. Where then did it reside? What was it that the Haitian teachers did that I did not do? (200–201)

At the time, Ballenger was a member of a teacher research group associated with the Literacies Institute—part of a network of people involved in research on literacy. As a teacher and researcher, she identified the problem she was having in her own classroom as one of cross-cultural communication, and she began to study it by systematically observing and recording what the Haitian teachers said to the children in their classes when they were concerned about the children's behavior and finding out what the teachers thought about the things she observed. The Haitian teachers, in turn, pointed out patterns they had observed in North American teachers' classroom behaviors: that North American teachers tend to emphasize the feelings of the individual child, to try to get children to talk about their feelings, and to interpret individual children's feelings for them, while Haitian teachers most often emphasize the group in their control talk, articulating the values and responsibilities of group membership. When they talk about families, Haitian teachers typically emphasize what families have in common—wanting their children to behave properly and respect adults—rather than differences. They don't, like North American teachers, talk about the particular consequences of particular actions, but rather, they assume a shared knowledge about what bad behavior is and that it shouldn't happen. And they often rely on a particular discourse pattern that emphasizes this shared understanding, asking a series of rhetorical questions: "Does your mother let you bite? . . . Does your father let you punch kids? . . . Do you kick at home?" expecting each question to be followed with a chorus of "no" from the children.

In her article Ballenger describes how, in her teaching, she began to adapt her own style to the children's expectations and tried to approximate all aspects of the cultural style she had observed—the Haitian teachers' tone of voice and facial expressions, as well as their actual utterances. In particular, she learned to use a new discourse pattern, asking a sequence of rhetorical questions that would reflect group values and common understandings about expected behaviors, as she did in one instance when some of the children in her class had run across the parking lot alone. When she followed these rhetorical questions with her own nonrhetorical question, "Why do I want you to wait for me, do you know?"

expecting an answer about cars being dangerous, she received the response "because you like us," an answer that reinforced her own sense that she was acquiring an important pattern in the communicative style of Haitian adults, one that affirmed for the children an understanding that she cared about them.

Ballenger writes that she has learned that students expect her to offer support and caring in the context of firm expectations for the group. She has also learned that direct reprimands, which she had avoided in her classrooms, can strengthen relationships. As she herself begins to take on a Haitian frame of reference, she begins to wonder whether it's a problem that North American teachers' language seems to place little emphasis on shared values, on a moral community.

Becky Day, like Cindy Ballenger, is encountering differences in communicative style, differences that assert themselves in the classroom, as in other contexts, creating, and often intensifying, the sorts of cross-cultural miscommunication that Tannen found in conversation and Gumperz studied in various public contexts. In analyzing how the school officer handled the exchange in her own classroom, Becky notices the way each participant goes on repeating the same words: the student repeats, "He gave(d) it to me" five times, to both teacher and officer, the officer twice asks, "How would you like it if I shot you with an elastic?" and the teacher says, "Put it down," and, "Go sit down," three times each—all with little effect:

> It seems that repetition is the main way people try to get things done in this community. . . . No one seems to be listening to anyone else . . . so people repeat and repeat, thinking that maybe that way their message will be heard.

And she sees what's happening in terms of insiders and outsiders:

> As outsiders to each other's definitions of proper behavior, the student and Mr. M. can't seem to get it together until Mr. M. mentions the concept of a "gentleman" and the appropriate behavior expected of one. This is something the student can latch on to. He obviously has a previous notion of what a gentleman is that he can use here: "And a gentleman always says he's sorry."

Note Becky's framing of the problem here. Rather than seeing the student as the outsider who must assimilate himself to the school culture, she sees both the student and the school officer as outsiders with respect to the other's frame of reference. The implication is that the responsibility for learning to communicate across such difference must be shared, rather than resting on the student alone, though she recognizes the possibility that, in this instance, "Mr. M's position of authority in the situation was ultimately responsible for his success in getting control, rather than a shared negotiation of meaning." She sees at least the possibility of a common understanding. And that possibility emerges when the officer stops repeating questions that emphasize how it would feel to an individual child to be hit with an elastic and instead affirms shared knowledge about how people should behave, just the difference between North American teachers' styles and their own that Ballenger's Haitian colleagues pointed out to her.

Where students of diverse backgrounds become effective participants in classroom contexts, they typically have had some culturally sensitive scaffolding of the sort Cindy Ballenger provided, to help them bridge the ways of home and those of a larger community, or else they've been given explicit, nonjudgmental instruction in school ways of the sort that Becky's been trying to offer. Where neither implicit nor explicit supports are given, and learners are dismissed for what they do not yet know, a deep-seated resistance to school language and values is the most common result.

School style

Everyone has to learn new discourse patterns when shifting to new, more public contexts, and learning the relevant discourse of an educational context is part of the work of all students, whether they're entering kindergarten, a college classroom, or graduate study in a particular discipline. But the language of schooling aligns itself most closely with the language of white middle-class speakers of English. For children from that background, school ways offer an extension of language practices already comfortably acquired at home. Children from other backgrounds, however, may have to acquire a substantially new discourse (as well as, sometimes, a second language) when they enter the classroom, and how successful they are in doing so will depend in part on how supportively their new discourse community receives them. Again, as in conversations and exchanges outside of the classroom, cultural and gender differences in style become clearest when there's a problem—when the implicit understandings that facilitate communication among speakers of the same community no longer work and dissonance arises among students or between teacher and students.

School style is dependent on a number of features: its speech acts are characterized by indirectness and politeness (to mitigate the teacher's absolute authority); it depends heavily on specific rhetorical and information structures and uses a style marked by the conventions of literacy, including explicitness and syntactic complexity; it structures the discourse of participants in particular ways, with patterns of turn-taking, ways of initiating turns, and gaining speaking rights that differ from those in many communities; it draws on a particular dialect, standard English, that differs from the primary discourse of many native English speakers; and it embodies a particular set of values. (See Kutz and Roskelly 1991, for an extended discussion of home and school styles.)

Even in their earliest days of schooling, young children know a lot about school style and school ways. One of my students, who was student teaching in a kindergarten class, asked her own students to tell her whether they knew of any differences between the ways they talked at home and at school. The children seemed particularly eager to tell Nicole what was not acceptable language and why. They thought some things were unacceptable at either home or school: swear words "because they are bad"; baby talk "because Dad says I should talk like a big boy"; "mean" words and name-calling "because it's not nice—it hurts a person"; and fighting "because it's mean." At school, they saw additional restrictions though. There they shouldn't use silly words "because the teacher will get mad"; loud talking "because the teacher will get mad"; laughing "unless the teacher says a joke"; back talk or fresh talk "because the teacher will get mad"; or fighting "because you'll get in trouble." From this discussion we can see that when talking about the kind of language that isn't acceptable at home, the children presented reasons that had to do with the effect of their language on the people they were addressing, the immediate perlocutionary force of their utterances, or with their own relationship to the world (that of a "big boy"). There was also a suggestion of common values that made swear words categorically bad. But Nicole was struck by the fact that, for the kinds of language that were unacceptable only at school, the children focused, not on the effect of the words on the people they were directed to, but on the indirect effect on the teacher, who was not part of the conversation, and on the consequences, for them, in terms of the teacher's response. In other words, outside of school they saw reasons for some kinds of prohibitions that had to do with a larger social understanding about appropriate ways of acting toward others, while school prohibitions appeared arbitrary, related only to what the teacher wanted. Using silly words or laughing or talking too loud wasn't going to hurt anyone else, but it would make the teacher mad. Even fighting, which shouldn't be done outside of school because it's mean, was seen as not acceptable in school because it would get you in trouble with the teacher. Clearly then, a striking feature of school discourse, one that's obvious even to very young children, is the presence of a figure who has authority over that discourse by virtue of her role in the classroom, who need not explain larger reasons for the prohibition of particular language behaviors, beyond the fact that she will get mad if these prohibitions are violated.

The role of the teacher as an authority figure who structures, controls, and mediates the discourse of the classroom is significant. Therefore, so too is the teacher's responsibility in facilitating learners' acquisition of school style while affirming their own and their classmates' competence as language users. The teacher who will help students succeed must find ways of bridging home and school discourse, with their different values and frames of reference, defusing the resistance of students who have been constructed and confirmed as outsiders through their earlier school experiences, and discovering and making explicit the implicit stylistic cues and contextualization conventions that can keep even advanced students in the position of outsiders as they move into new areas of study. Such a teacher must learn to provide the scaffolding that will help learners become effective participants in their new educational contexts, and not just silent knowers of particular bodies of information.

Some classroom discourse events are specifically intended to help young learners connect the language of home and the language of school. In these, the teacher models or interprets school ways, helps children translate their utterances into school style, sometimes explicitly (How do we say that?). In her conversations with her kindergartners, Nicole helps them to make their implicit and individual knowledge of school ways something that's explicit and shared. She asks her students to give her some examples of the ways someone might tell you to do something at home, and they offer: "Where are the keys?" and "Clean your room!"; for school they suggest: "We have work to do now" and "Let's see who came to school today," an expression Nicole recognizes as one she herself uses every day. As we've seen, the latter examples are indirect speech acts, substituting statements for directives and questions, and using the suggestion of a cooperative enterprise to mitigate the direct authority of the teacher. Although the research of Shirley Heath and others (cf. Ripich and Spinelli 1995) has shown that such indirectness often interferes with communication across different discourse communities, by talking with them about the language of home and school, Nicole has been helping all of her students to understand the intentions that might otherwise be hidden behind the style of school speech acts, and after only a few months, these children are well accustomed to at least some of the conventions of school style.

Teachers like Nicole and Becky provide scaffolds by making the topic of communicative style an explicit part of the referential knowledge presented in the classroom. Lisa Delpit, in "The Silenced Dialogue" (1985), draws on her own experience as an anthropologist in other cultures, where she found it was much easier for her to adapt when someone pointed out, explicitly, what the rules were. She contends that "it is much the same for anyone seeking to learn the rules of the culture of power. Unless one has the leisure of a lifetime of 'immersion' to learn them, explicit presentation makes learning immeasurably easier" (283). She points out the corresponding disadvantage to students "who ultimately find themselves held accountable for knowing a set of rules about which no one has ever directly informed them" (286). It's not just the naming of the rules that creates successful communication, but cooperation in the enterprise of figuring out what the differences are and how to negotiate communication across them. When Nicole begins, with her kindergartners, the exploration of differences between the way things are said at home and at school, she is helping them to make their experience of communicative difference an object of common inquiry.

As we've seen, much of what Nicole learns about her students' understanding of school style is related to the teacher's control of language in the classroom. Even where children are expected to take an extended turn, the teacher controls their right to speak, and the ways in which they may initiate turns and the length of their turns. Sharing time or show and tell, for example, are speech events common to most primary school settings, ones that are explicitly intended as a scaffold to help children bring in their knowledge and experiences from home and talk about them in the classroom. Children are asked to take a turn in front of the class, telling the class about a favorite object that they've brought in or a story about something that has happened outside of school. In connecting the child's out of school world with the in-school world, this event provides a chance for children to practice translating the ways in which things are talked about in one context into the ways they're talked about in another. But when Nicole observes her class in their version of sharing time—which they call current event, when the children talk about future events or about something that they are going to do—she finds that their statements have a particular pattern of intonation, unlike that of similar statements in their conversations with peers. She reports:

> I noticed a rise in pitch at the end of the sentence. It seems to me that one reason that the children raise their pitch is because they want their message to be responded to with a positive response, and raising the pitch sets up this response. . . . Many of them also say "right?" after every sentence or phrase. I think they do this to involve me in their message. They also watch for me to nod my head as a response.

What children learn from this event falls largely into the pragmatic and interpersonal domain: how to respond to the teacher as authority. There's no doubt here that the children see this sharing time event as teacher-controlled. Its function is less for them to convey information than to do so in a way that will please the teacher, so that she'll ratify their response and confirm that they've given the right answer, as in other classroom discourse events. Just as you don't say some things in school because they make the teacher mad, in classroom speech events you do say what seems to make the teacher happy. That is probably the most salient lesson that students everywhere learn from school.

The ways in which children are expected to participate in the different speech events of the classroom, whether raising their hands and being called on for a brief response as in the IRE pattern, or being nominated by the teacher for an extended turn in front of the class, differ from the ways of many homes. But students from communities with significantly different styles of communication may have a hard time finding their way at all into classroom speech events. The structures that control participation in classroom discourse are shaped by values that are too often at odds with the values inherent in the participant structures for discourse in their own communities.

Classroom discourse structures and communicative difference

Many studies of classroom discourse have shown the exclusionary effect of school discourse practices on students whose home discourse patterns are significantly different. Shirley Brice Heath's extended study of the Piedmont area speech communities pointed out some of the problems. In Chapter One we saw the ways in which the home communicative styles of children from the

rural white community of Roadville and the rural black community of Trackton differed from those of the Maintown community. When Roadville and
Trackton children come to school to study with Maintown teachers who
expect Maintown ways, they immediately become outsiders.

Roadville children are taught explicitly from babyhood that the right to
initiate turns in conversations with adults belongs only to the adults—they're
only supposed to speak to an adult when spoken to, and they must always be
silent before the authority of teachers or preachers. If they are called on to speak,
what's wanted is a limited recitation or display, a brief factual response with no
interpretation or fictionalization. Trackton children learn, implicitly, to compete for attention by interacting freely with adults, initiating turns in ways that
are not only assertive but also inventive and creative (not factual) in order to
insert themselves in adult conversations. But Maintown children, from both
black and white middle-class families, are expected to know when to be silent
and listen to adults, and when and how to initiate turns and carry on their side
of a conversation; they learn how to display factual knowledge and how to
question, interpret, and be creative. They are expected to recognize the authoritative discourse of teachers, but they should also be able to shape, increasingly,
their own authority, backed up by information they get for themselves, from
other knowledgeable people, or from books.

Such discourse practices are embedded in other structures and values,
including the ways children use time and space: Roadville children are used to
doing specific tasks at specific times and places, and won't initiate any change—
they just wait for the teacher's instructions. Trackton children are used to carrying out activities for as long as they are interested in them and in locations that
they choose, and they have trouble accommodating themselves to the highly
structured school setting with assigned seating and strictly allotted time periods
for art, reading, and physical education. Maintown children are expected to
work within established structures, but to be able to adapt those structures to
particular circumstances. And they bring these expectations and practice in
appropriate behaviors from home to school. So Roadville children end up
being silent in most school contexts, responding in those classrooms that depend
on the most limited IRE pattern, but rarely raising their hands to initiate longer
turns or to ask questions, drawing back from more extended interpretive or
creative responses. Trackton children, who initiate and interrupt frequently,
violate the expectations even of teachers who use a more extended IRE pattern,
and are likely to be seen as disruptive troublemakers. While Maintown children,
who pretty much meet the discourse expectations of their Maintown teachers,
are rewarded with school success.

What Heath found in the Piedmont study has shown up again and again in
other communities. Where there are significant differences in communicative
style, particularly in the ways in which people participate in speech events and
in the values associated with those ways, neither the children nor their mainstream teachers negotiate these differences very effectively. The children of the

Warm Springs Indian Reservation, studied by Susan Philips (1983), were more likely to be perceived by their teachers as nonresponsive and failing to understand, than were Anglo children. Philips found that Indian students did talk less in the classroom than did their Anglo peers: they responded less often to teacher-initiated questions; they took more time when they did respond before offering an answer (often losing their turns in this way), and they asked fewer questions. At the same time, the responses they did give were less often seen as correct or coherent in reference to the larger topic, and were less frequently ratified or followed up by the teacher. Their listening behavior was different as well, and so they were perceived as not paying attention: They often looked elsewhere when the teacher was speaking, not directly at the teacher; and they interacted more with their peers, particularly through movements and gestures. Some standard classroom speech events, like show and tell or oral reports where students are expected to step to the front of the class as an authority, were so unsuccessful that they were often abandoned by teachers of Indian children .

Philips describes these problems as resulting from differences in the ways that attention is signaled, in who is attended to, and how, and she offers a cultural account of these differences: "For the Indian students, getting the floor in classroom encounters regulated in Anglo fashion requires them to behave in ways that run counter to expectations of socially appropriate behavior in the Warm Springs Indian community" (115). In the community, Indian speakers control the length of their own turns and aren't interrupted by others, while listeners may offer delayed responses and have greater control over when and whether to speak. Yet this individual control is exerted within a larger cooperative structure where all participants have the same speaking rights, and talk itself tends to be distributed equally. Children of the Warm Springs Indians are not accustomed to having to appeal to a single individual for the right to speak. They're not used to having a speaker address them alone, requiring them to take a turn, nor are they used to responding to one speaker alone. They don't expect to have to respond immediately to a topic initiated by another. Again these discourse practices are reflective of a larger set of cultural practices and values, as Philips explains:

> The children are not oriented toward a single adult authority, being cared for by a number of adults and older children as they are. Partly because of this, Warm Springs children do not compete with one another for parental attention. They are expected to become more self-sufficient at younger ages, and to cooperate with older brothers and sisters and cousins in providing mutual companionship and care. For all of these reasons Warm Springs Indian children are less likely than Anglo children to be motivated to compete with one another for the teacher's attention.
>
> And finally, the children are raised in an environment that discourages drawing attention to oneself by acting as though one is better than another. The efforts children are expected to make to get the teacher's attention to be given a turn at talk require them to draw attention to themselves, to lay claim

to knowing more than their peers, and to demonstrate a desire to display that knowledge, all of which is unseemly by Indian adult standards for behavior. (117–18)

On the other hand, in small group activities where the teacher was not present, where students did not have to select a leader but could structure and control their own talk, there was a high level of involvement by students, because these activities offered a participant structure most similar to the practices of the community. In such structures, Indian children interacted with a greater number of their peers, and did so more equitably, than Anglo children.

Native Hawaiian children also bring patterns of interaction that are different from those valued in the classroom—patterns that are typically seen as problematic, as when children who are used to working cooperatively and helping each other on tasks at home are thought to be disruptive or even dishonest when they try to do the same in the classroom. There too, common classroom discourse structures like sharing time have often been unsuccessful, because they violate cultural norms about cooperation rather than individual performance. Kathryn Au has long been involved with the Kamehameha Early Education Project (KEEP) in Hawaii, where she has been working to develop a "culturally responsive pedagogy" that takes into account and builds on the communicative style of the Native Hawaiian community, using common speech events outside of the classroom as a basis for instruction. One such event is "talk story," a cooperatively produced story, jointly constructed by a number of speakers.

> Seldom in talk story does any one child monopolize the right to speak, as children are asked to do during conventional classroom recitation. What seems important to Hawaiian children in talk story is not individual performance in speaking, which is emphasized in the classroom, but group performance in speaking. Children who are leaders, those who are well liked by others, usually are those who know how to involve others in the conversation, not those who hold the floor for themselves. The value Hawaiian children attach to group—versus individual performance—seems consistent with the importance in Hawaiian culture of contributing to the well-being of one's family or friends, rather than working for one's own well-being. (1993, 114)

Au and her colleagues have been working to integrate the talk story genre into reading lessons, and they've found that a cooperative—versus individualistic— recitation pattern has resulted in twice as much productive academic talk, supporting the propositional and referential function of classroom discourse as learners bring in ideas from the text and make logical inferences based on a text. By varying classroom participation structures to accommodate the discourse patterns children bring from home and using those familiar patterns to support the new learning of the classroom, teachers can use the discourse itself to provide a scaffold for other learning.

Carol Lee's recent study of the ways that the language practices of the black community can be built on in the classroom, *Signifying as a Scaffold for Literary*

Interpretation (1993), offers still another example of such culturally responsive pedagogy, as does the work Heath reports on in the second part of *Ways with Words* (1983), where both teachers and students become ethnographers of community discourse practices. (See also Kutz, Groden, and Zamel 1993, for ways in which such student research into language can provide a scaffold for the work of the freshman writing classroom.) Familiar discourse structures not only help students to feel competent in new settings, but in affirming that competence, allow learners to turn their attention to new learning.

Gender differences in classroom interactions

Although most studies of communicative difference in the classroom, and the ways that such difference can contribute to school problems, have focused on differences of language, culture, and class, recent studies have begun to indicate that the participant structures of classroom discourse seriously affect the learning experience of women as well. Across levels of schooling, girls are called on less frequently than boys, given shorter turns when they are called on, and offered fewer follow-up questions that ask them to extend their thinking and expand on what they've said and engage in the kind of oral reconceptualization that supports real learning. Eventually, many of them stop responding and fall silent. A study by The American Association of University Women from the Wellesley Center for Research on Women has summarized the major research on gender and schooling in *How Schools Shortchange Girls* (1992). Educators Myra and David Sadker have reported on their own research into women's experience in school in *Failing at Fairness. How America's Schools Cheat Girls* (1994).

The Sadkers rely on reconstructed classroom accounts rather than actual recorded examples of classroom discourse to show the pattern of girls' silence and silencing, so their examples are less immediately useful to our analysis, but the pattern they report across their studies of many classrooms is confirmed by specific classroom discourse studies. For example, Joan Swann and David Graddol (1994) studied talk in two classrooms of ten-and-eleven-year olds, where, from an analysis of overall interactional patterns, striking differences by gender emerged—with boys speaking almost twice as many total words, taking about twice as many turns, and participating in almost twice as many total interchanges. The boys' verbal dominance was similar in both classes, even though the participant structure was different. In one, the teacher's authority was relaxed and students offered observations without raising their hands or being selected by the teacher; in the other, students raised their hands and the teacher called on students by name. But even in the first classroom, the teacher's gaze was more often focused on the boys, inviting their participation (and possibly monitoring their behavior). In the second classroom, the boys were more aggressive about volunteering, but again because of the teacher's gaze, they were most often implicitly invited to do so, even though the teacher was selecting the speakers. From a careful analysis of turn exchanges and interactional sequences (which included notations about teacher's gaze), the researchers conclude:

We found in our own transcripts that questions addressed to the girls were less frequently the challenging and open variety typically addressed to boys and more often rhetorical or yes/no questions . . . [And] we suggest that there is a hidden curriculum at work in classroom talk, which provides boys with an important learning experience even in the kind of talk we might want to discard as worthless. Boys, in other words, are acquiring and practicing skills in competitive public speaking: the skill and confidence to seize the floor, control topics, and develop discourse strategies which ensure the flow of talk returns to them. . . . Girls seem to have learnt to expect a lower participation level than boys, and boys seem to have learned that their fair share is a larger one. . . . We have identified, then, two distinct causes of educational concern. . . . One, that girls may—as a group—be given less privileged access to certain kinds of learning experience. Second, that classroom talk forms an important arena for the reproduction of gender inequities in interactional power. (165–66)

School style and the language of literacy

Classroom speech events provide structures for students' participation in the discourse of the classroom, but they also provide what Sarah Michaels, who has carried out extensive studies of sharing time narratives, describes as an "oral preparation for literacy" (1986). Since school discourse depends heavily on the language practices of the middle class, which are themselves influenced by the language associated with written texts, the recognized and acceptable ways of introducing and maintaining a topic, taking turns, and signaling stance and purpose are strongly influenced by assumptions about language carried over from writing as it's produced for common, public purposes. The sharing time event gives one speaker an extended turn (such as a writer would have), with the expectation that the speaker will present a coherent account in ways that are characteristic of literate texts and contexts. Such events may fail, then, not only because a participant structure in which one speaker calls attention to himself through an extended turn may be at odds with the participant behaviors and values that some students bring from their communities, but also because the ways of structuring information within a turn differ.

Michaels studies moments when such sharing time events succeed—when the child gives an account that the teacher accepts and the teacher offers questions that create a scaffold for extending the account. But she also looks at moments when the sharing time event fails—when a child's story is perceived by the teacher as incoherent and as violating the central rule of this event: that the child must tell about just "one thing that's very important." The teacher expects narratives in a style that Michaels calls topic-centered: focused on a single topic, ordered in a linear way, and leading to a resolution. But when one child, Deena, tells her stories, she seems to bring in a number of scattered ideas, talking first about her new coat, then about a plastic bag on the couch, about her baby sister, and then about her cousin—covering what seems like a series of unrelated topics and never making the connections among them explicit—a common narrative style in the black community (and one that Michaels names as "topic associating"). When Deena moves from her first description of the coat to bring in the baby and the plastic bag and her cousin, the teacher interrupts impatiently:

TEACHER: Wait a minute. You stick with your coat now. I said you could tell one thing. That's fair.

DEENA: This was about my c . . .

TEACHER: OK . . . all right, go on.

DEENA: This was . . . and today, and yesterday when I got my coat, my cousin ran outside and he ran to, tried to get him, and he, he, he start . . . an' when he get in, when he got in my house, he layed on the floor and I told him to get up because he was cryin'.

TEACHER: Mm . . . what's that have to do with your coat?

DEENA: H . . . he, becau . . . he wanted to go outside, but we couldn't. [*exasperated*]

TEACHER: Why?

DEENA: Cause my mother . . . s . . . wanted us to stay in the house.

TEACHER: What does that have to do with your coat?

DEENA: Bec . . . um uh Because, I don't know.

TEACHER: OK. Thank you very much, Deena.

CHILDREN: [*talking*]

TEACHER: OK, do you understand what I was trying to do . . . Deena . . . I was trying to get her to stick with one thing. And she was talking about her . . .

CHILDREN: Coat.

TEACHER: New . . .

CHILDREN: Coat.

TEACHER: Coat. It sounds nice, Deena.

As Becky noted earlier in looking at the exchange that took place in her classroom, when two participants keep repeating the same utterance back at each other, as if saying the same words again and again will produce understanding on the listener's part, we can see a complete breakdown of communication, and the participants remain outsiders to each others' frames of reference. The teacher here is making the rules of this discourse event explicit, but simply repeating the rules in a stern and hostile way, without trying to take on the child's perspective in any way, provides no opportunity for the scaffolding the event is designed to provide. No learning takes place here, and, as Michaels later learns in talking to her, Deena is confirmed in her belief that the teacher really isn't interested in what she has to say and is always stopping her (cf. Cazden, 439). Deena is, of course, able to make connections between the events she has named: her cousin was a "bad little boy" with dirty hands, he was trying to touch the new coat, and the plastic bag that was for protecting the coat was dangerous for her baby sister. But under the stress of responding to the teacher's repeated question "What does that have to do with your coat?" she can only respond, "I don't know." And over time, she is increasingly perceived as unable to think coherently.

What differs in Deena's narrative style from the style her teacher expects is not only the extent to which Deena does or does not focus on one topic, but also the degree to which she makes connections and statements of meaning implicit rather than explicit. Because the development of literacy is a primary focus of schooling, the conventions commonly associated with literacy take on particular force in the classroom. Spoken language in schools is judged by standards of style, as well as correctness, that are carried over from written language. Writing is often intended to be read by distant audiences, and it tends therefore to be verbally explicit and elaborated because it cannot assume much shared knowledge on the part of readers and cannot point to things in the writer's immediate context that a reader cannot see. These features, common to writing, have been incorporated into much middle-class speech, resulting in a "literate-style" of oral discourse in contrast to an "oral-style" that depends more on implicitly understood, shared knowledge.

Differences in these styles of discourse were the focus of a famous (or infamous) study carried out in England by sociolinguist Basil Bernstein (1973). Bernstein too was concerned about school failure—in this case that of working-class British children—and was working to develop a social theory of language to account for differences between the ways in which they used language and the ways that middle-class children did. He theorized that the two groups used what he described as different codes, which differed semantically in their orientation toward implicit versus explicit meaning—in how much of a speaker's intended meaning was actually put into words. Those who spoke an "elaborated code" used more verbally explicit language that could be understood apart from the situational context and that didn't assume much shared knowledge on the part of listeners; those who used a "restricted code" left more of their meanings implicit, used references that were dependent on context, and assumed more shared knowledge. When children were asked to describe a picture, for example, they might differ in whether or not they included in their description enough information so that a reader could understand the description without seeing the pictures: Three boys are playing football versus They're playing ball (26). Or when they were asked to sort pictures of lunch foods, they might sort them by categories (They're vegetables) or by their relationship to the immediate context of their lives (What mommy eats). Bernstein found these differences in the ways children realized meanings to be based on the ways families handled key socializing contexts. The parents of middle-class children would typically explain things in terms of larger, universal rules and fully stated logical propositions, for example: "It hurts animals to have their ears pulled. And I know you don't want to hurt your dog, so you mustn't pull on her ears!" while working-class parents would refer only to the immediate situation or context: "Stop pulling his ears." The more universal, less context-bound language was similar to that used in many school speech events, so children who used the particularistic, context-bound code for school tasks were likely to fail in them.

By describing what he observed in terms of codes, rather than styles, Bernstein exaggerated the extent of the differences in the ways in which they were used in the interactions of ordinary speakers, suggesting that the differences he saw were more comparable to the differences between languages, not between the styles that different speakers of one language might use or that one speaker might use at different times. And with the terms "restricted" and "elaborated," he unintentionally paved the way for a deficit model of communicative difference, one that suggested that the language some children brought to the classroom was inferior and limited, while that brought by others was rich and extended.

Bernstein's theory of elaborated and restricted codes became infamous because of the ways in which it was applied to educational contexts in the United States. Restricted language was seen as a sign of restricted thought, and pedagogical interventions were designed to push children with linguistic deficits toward more explicit and fully elaborated spoken discourse. For example, the influential designers of preschool programs for disadvantaged children, Bereiter and Engelmann, insisted that a response like "in the tree" was an illogical, incomplete answer to the question, "Where is the squirrel?" and that children must be trained in the schoolroom to respond only with the full statement, "The squirrel is in the tree" (Labov 1972a, 205). Many well-intentioned teachers, hoping to help their students achieve success, followed programs in which they drilled children to respond to a series of questions only with complete statements, creating artificial interactions that did not take into account the shared semantic and syntactic knowledge that an evolving conversational text builds on.

In fact, everyone uses language that has the features associated with one or the other of these styles in some contexts. In intimate settings with family and friends, we point to objects in the immediate environment, use pronouns without clarifying their referents, and assume the sort of shared knowledge that means we don't have to explicate meanings. We engage in the sort of fast, fluent conversation that affirms what everyone knows and/or agrees on (You know?) and that both depends on and contributes to social solidarity.

At other times, in less intimate contexts, we may assume less shared knowledge, offering explanations, putting more of our meanings explicitly into words, and elaborating on our personal understandings. Deborah Tannen's studies of conversation helped to address the assumption that there were two markedly different styles, oral and literate, that mapped out neatly according to how literate members of a community typically were. The participants in the dinner-table conversations she studied were all well-educated and highly literate, yet some used a conversational style that assumed shared knowledge and was syntactically reduced, with implicit cues as to meaning and the relatedness of any new information that was introduced. Others expected the conversation to be more explicit, elaborated, yet focused. The first group could shift style comfortably as they moved into more formal public speaking or writing contexts, but their dinner-table style was focused as much on involving their listeners as in making a particular point, and they used a wide range of strategies to accomplish both purposes at once. In an article titled "The Oral-Literate Continuum in Discourse" (1982), Tannen concludes that the formulation of a sharp divide between people who use an oral style versus a literate style was misguided, and that the choice of a particular style at a particular moment is partly a matter of cultural difference and partly of communicative purpose.

All normal language users are successful at communicating complex and subtle meanings in their home environments, whether these meanings are expressed in words alone, or in a combination of words, facial expressions, and gestures that point toward features of the immediate environment. And most language users who have had experience in less intimate contexts are able to express their meanings in more elaborated language, to take the needs of less familiar listeners into account. But young children whose families use a more implicit style for more of their interactions often do not recognize the expectation of more verbal explicitness for school tasks, a demand that's somewhat artificial since, in fact, teachers and students do share knowledge of the immediate situational context, as, for example, the number of people in the picture they are looking at together or the author and the title of the work they are talking or writing about. However, school style, in demanding more explicit definitions, explanations, connections, and statements of meaning, does not require greater linguistic competence, or necessarily even greater communicative competence, from its speakers. As Labov's research has shown, the embedded evaluations (statements of meaning) in the oral narratives of black urban teenagers were syntactically more complex than the explicit evaluations of middle-class speakers, while the same speakers were likely to be able to shift through a much greater range of styles as well. The underlying linguistic competence of all speakers of all varieties of a language is the same, acquired, along with communicative competence as they grow up with their primary discourse. It is in the extension of their early communicative competence—to control a range of styles appropriate to a range of contexts *and* to know when and how to use those styles—that speakers may differ, and then the language of the middle-class speaker who controls fewer styles may be more restricted than that of speakers who control more. Again, experience in private and public, informal and formal settings and across cultural contexts, where not all knowledge can be assumed to be shared and different styles are used, can best help all of us to expand our linguistic repertoire.

Finally, if the purpose of the classroom discourse event is to present a spoken version of what would more likely be a written text, fully formulated with each utterance extended and explicit as for a distant or unknown audience, then pedagogical practices that focus on elaborated display are appropriate to that purpose. If, however, the purpose of the event is to encourage exploration, risk-taking, and discovery, while creating a supportive learning community and providing a scaffold that connects everyone's prior discourse experience to the new demands of a community where not everyone shares the same prior knowledge, then the conversational strategies for creating involvement and negotiating newly shared meanings need to have a more prominent role.

Language and school resistance

A common pattern of low school achievement among students from minority and working class backgrounds has been the focus of a variety of studies and a range of theories, many of which center, at least in part, on questions of language, and particularly on the sorts of cultural differences in language and communicative style that have shown up in these studies of classroom discourse. What emerges repeatedly from studies of discourse and communicative competence in the classroom is a picture of unresponsiveness and apparent lack of verbal ability in school, while studies, like those of Labov, focusing on communicative competence in the community, show the same groups of young people to be skilled communicators. Clearly, what's going on cannot be explained by the theories of linguistic deprivation (limited language/limited thought) that informed an earlier cycle of school interventions, and attention has turned to the sorts of communicative mismatch we've been discussing—resulting either from cultural differences or differences in experience with a literate style. But the performance gap increases by grade level, whereas the ability to negotiate meanings across communicative differences might be expected to improve with more years of experience in the new discourse context. So these differences, by themselves, cannot fully explain what goes wrong in schools.

The theory of language differences

One attempt at an explanation for the low school achievement of black students focused on the differences between Black English and standard English as codes. Although these differences don't seem to be significant enough to interfere with communication, some educators, responding to the problem of low school achievement for many black children, have proposed that Black English should be considered a separate language. But are the differences in Black English great enough to justify considering it a separate language? Or are they like other dialect variations—different enough to mark the regional or social identity of the speaker, but not really different enough to interfere with communication?

The question was decided by the courts (not by linguists, though their expert testimony was used) in the 1979 case of *Martin Luther King Junior Elementary School v. Ann Arbor School District Board* (commonly referred to as the Ann Arbor case). In this case, filed on behalf of fifteen black, economically deprived children, it was alleged that the school district had failed to properly educate the children, thus denying their rights under the 1974 Equal Opportunity Act, by failing to overcome language barriers preventing their learning and by inappropriately placing them in learning disability and speech pathology classes. Evidence showed that teachers had failed to recognize the children's Black English as legitimate, and that their "negative attitudes toward the children's language led to negative expectations of the children which turned into self-fulfilling prophecies" (Smitherman 1985).

Black English itself was not found to be a barrier, but the institutional response to it was. Linguist Geneva Smitherman, who acted as an expert witness in the trial, links the implications of this finding to a language/dialect distinction. If Black English is a distinct language, then there may be actual linguistic interferences to communication, while if it is a dialect that is not significantly different from other dialects of English, then the barriers to learning must not reside in the students' use of this dialect but in the teachers' attitudes toward it.

There has been a great deal of research which shows that teachers from other primary discourse communities frequently exhibit negative attitudes toward speakers of Black English. Roger Shuy, for example, recorded comments like these from teachers in urban schools: "The child's vocabulary is very limited"; "I can't get them to make a sentence. Even if I have them repeat after me exactly, they don't do it. They repeat in sentences they are familiar with. They're not really sentences but fragments of sentences . . . they don't realize that they aren't making a complete thought" (1975 169–70). Children who aren't familiar with the vocabulary of school are too often seen as lacking all vocabulary, and those who respond to questions in less than full sentences (as we all do in familiar contexts where knowledge is shared), may be seen as having cognitive deficiencies. Their speech is then seen as needing constant correction and improvement. The King School teachers constantly corrected the children's speech, interrupting their ordinary flow of discourse and causing them to become almost completely nonverbal; because of differences in pronunciation, the teachers sent the children to speech therapy sessions designed to correct genuine pathology, and removed them from the ongoing work of the classroom, setting them farther behind; they gave them limited, remedial tasks to do, and they suspended them from class for trivial actions that they saw as misbehavior. The court concluded that "if a barrier exists because of the language used by the children in this case, it exists . . . because in the process of attempting to teach the children how to speak standard English the students are made somehow to feel inferior and are thereby turned off from the learning process" (473F. supp. 1371, E, D, Mich. 1979, cited in Smitherman, 50).

The attitudes evident in the Ann Arbor case have been altogether too present in other levels of education as well, with a resulting focus on limited remediation rather than challenging learning. The pedagogical implications of the Ann Arbor case are not that schools must teach Black English, or any other variety of English to speakers of that variety (schools don't need to teach what students already know) but that schools should help students see that their competence as language users is confirmed by their ability to respond to the demanding uses of this dialect in their own communities. Learners who know themselves to be competent users of one dialect—able to follow its rules and use it correctly and appropriately—are likely to feel most confident about their ability to master new codes and styles and to venture willingly into settings that will demand them. Students who are invited to discover the rules and work out the systematic structures of the language they use, in the way that June Jordan's students were invited to do, are more likely to understand better not only the workings of their own variety, but the systematic ways in which that variety differs from standard English, ending up in a better position to monitor their use of the standard code when that is what's called for. And seeing the systematicity in all varieties of English is likely to change the attitudes of all learners to nonstandard varieties other than their own.

Differences in communicative styles, goals, and purposes

We've seen, earlier in this chapter, that children from communities with communicative styles that differ from those of the mainstream in their participant structures, as well as in expectations around structuring information and using elaborated language, may have difficulty in classrooms where teachers neither accommodate those differences nor provide scaffolds to help them use those styles as a base for building an expanded repertoire. But such differences in style must be seen in terms of the larger communicative framework of classroom interaction. Successful interactions in any communicative context, including classrooms, depend not only on shared understandings about the world and shared ways of managing discourse, but on shared intentions and purposes. Cooperation in achieving such shared purposes is necessary to any successful speech act. Intentional violations of the underlying principles of communicative cooperation can shape the meaning of the act, creating implications—implied meanings, that can underline a common perspective. But violations of the other participants' usual expectations for cooperation can also highlight differences in stance and perspective—differences in meaning, in illocutionary and perlocutionary force, that the same words can have for speaker and listener.

In conversations, where authority for managing the discourse is generally shared among participants, moments of misunderstanding are easily negotiated and meanings clarified, as we've seen in many instances with Karen, Melanie, and Shanna (who might temporarily cast one of the group as an outsider, but who have a greater investment in continuing to cooperate than in emphasizing differences). But where participants in a discourse event are held there only by the external authority of the teacher or the school, and when that authority is used to manage all aspects of the event—to control who initiates turns and when and for how long and on what topic—then cooperation really depends on how willing the other participants are to accept this authority and to take on the stance and perspective the authoritative participant brings. If other participants don't share that stance and intention, they can't easily negotiate this difference directly where they have little control over their own speaking rights. They can only, through an intentional violation of the cooperative principle, create an implication of disagreement, of a different position or perspective.

Young children, who are accustomed to sharing an understanding about the world and how it works with those who are in positions of authority over them (their parents and community adults), may not understand a teacher's style. Yet responsive negotiation and scaffolding on the teacher's part, along with validation of the children's ways (much in the way Cindy Ballenger responded to her preschoolers), can create a climate of trust and acceptance that can support further cooperation and the development of shared purposes. But where the teacher assumes that a difference in communicative styles signals an intentional lack of communication, as Deena's teacher seems to, an apparently small difference can come to represent a fundamentally different way of seeing the world and, over time, can lead the student to stop trying to cooperate on the teacher's terms. As Deena told Michaels in an interview the next year: "Sharing time got on my nerves. She was always interruptin' me, sayin' 'that's not important enough' and I hadn't hardly started talking (1986, 110). The result is likely to be resistance on the part of a student that extends beyond the lesson into the school year and that may increase with years of schooling and of similar experiences. When a whole group shares such an experience of mismatch and misunderstanding in school and in the larger society, and when school does not lead to social respect, jobs, and progress up the economic ladder for whole groups in the society so that there's a large communicative breakdown about its real intentions and purposes, the result can be a broadly based divergence of attitude and values.

Oppositional responses

John Ogbu, who has studied the effect of social and economic circumstances on the attitudes of blacks toward school achievement, has argued that the effect of cultural differences between speech communities in a mass society is relatively minor compared to the larger experience of discrimination (1978, 1987), and he has come to describe American blacks as a "caste-like (or involuntary) minority" with little hope that real change in their situation will be gained through school success, in the ways that it has for other minority groups. The result, in Ogbu's terms, is an "oppositional culture" whose members distance themselves more and more from mainstream ways—and this too manifests itself as discourse differences and problems. For members of an oppositional culture, the communicative style a teacher demands can become a symbol of oppressive social structures, and resistance will take the form of creating more marked differences—of not talking white.

Labov reported on the linguistic realization of such resistance in his essay "The Linguistic Consequences of Being a Lame" (1973), where he showed that, among teenagers, the "lames," who were most insecure and least respected by their peers, were most likely to shift to the forms of the dominant dialect, while the speakers with the strongest social web (often those who were the brightest and most linguistically skilled) remained vigorous users of their vernacular forms, even in school contexts. They increasingly reject the school's language and the school's rejection of them. As Labov tells us in a later essay,

"Competing Value Systems in Inner-City Schools": "The healthy, well-adjusted youth of normal or superior intelligence is a well-integrated member of the neighborhood peer group" (1982, 155), and, by implication, not a lame. Labov went on to show the extent to which such differences reflected much the sort of conflict in values that Ogbu finds in an oppositional culture. In a study focused on Martha's Vineyard, Labov found a similar phenomenon occurring, where, in resistance to outsider summer people and their values, the language of island youth moved toward more strongly marked features of the local dialect, when without such resistance the strong dialect differences would tend to disappear with so much infusion of a less-marked variety (1972b).

Frederick Erickson, an anthropologist who has focused on the culture of educational contexts, finds some support for what he calls the "communication process explanation" since altering school discourse structures seems to enhance school achievement. But he recognizes the force of the larger inequities Ogbu describes—that such inequities, like communicative differences, can be impediments to the trust that is the basis for school legitimacy. He suggests that there's a distinction between cultural boundaries, of the sorts that occur where there is cultural difference—manifested in the discourse differences we have been considering—and cultural borders, where such differences result in the differential allocation of rights and obligations. He turns for an example to Piestrup's classroom research, where the teacher interrupted the reading lesson until she got the children to pronounce the *t* in "Wha*t* did little duck see?" He sees the teacher as making a special point of the cultural communication style of the black children in a negative way—making a communicative difference or a cultural boundary into a more rigid cultural border:

> This cultural border work—making cultural communication style a negative phenomenon in the classroom—seems to have stimulated student resistance that was manifested linguistically. . . . In those classrooms in which the teacher, whether black or white, negatively sanctioned the children's use of black English vernacular, by the end of the year the children spoke a more exaggerated form of that dialect than they had done at the beginning of the year. The opposite was true in the classrooms in which the teacher, whether black or white, did not negatively sanction the black English vernacular spoken by the black students. In those classrooms, by the end of the year the black children were speaking in the classroom in ways that more closely approximated standard English than did their ways of speaking at the beginning of the year. . . . In the former kind of classroom . . . the use of Black English Vernacular became an occasion for stigmatizing border work by the teachers and for resistance by the children . . . [and] cultural difference was increasing in a situation of cross-cultural contact. (1988, 347–48)

Differences in language, then, whether in phonological features, syntactic variants, lexicon or larger discourse, or rhetorical and information structures, may increase when cultural differences are linked to opposing value systems—or when there's value to be found in opposition.

Conclusion

A beginning teacher like Becky must negotiate a difficult terrain. She's trying to validate her students' home language, Haitian Creole, and support the students in their continuing acquisition of English as a second language and of literacy in both languages. She's trying to create a productive classroom environment, provide an explicit guide to the expected behaviors, both communicative and social, of the classroom, and at the same time alter her own style of communication in ways that will be more effective in communicating her own intentions and meanings to her students. She does not want to turn communicative differences into cultural borders, and she does not want to separate the work of her classroom into distinct teaching and disciplinary functions, with the latter carried out by the school officer.

What she does want is a classroom where genuine learning about language and literacy can take place. She asks her students to write as well as read, she reads with them their own poetry alongside the poetry of John Donne and contemporary Creole literature. She has them keep journals, to allow for the sorts of extended, reflective discourse in English that will contribute to their fluency as readers and writers of that language. She encourages them to write in their journals about themselves as learners, and about their experience of the class.

Partway through her first term, Becky received two journal entries that responded to her own ongoing concerns with creating an effective learning environment in the classroom. One was from a boy who clearly appreciated the validation implied in the fact that this white teacher, surprisingly, spoke Creole and was teaching him to read it:

> Ms. day I think your class is fun because you showing us how to read creole. Ms. day your class is wonderful, perfect, excelent and now thanks to your wonderful class I am getting good in reading Creole. . . . When you first came In my class I was surprise because I didn't know If you knew How to speak creole. . . . Ms. day It is fun when I stay after school with you I can talk with other teachers when you stay after school for them they give you lots of work. Ms. day I wish my other teachers were like you not streke.

But the other was from a girl who had a less positive view of the classroom dynamics, though not of the larger enterprise.

> This class is very nice but the kids are very rude. The only way I think the class should be better is every time they make noise call the office. The reason I say this is because they think you just a little lady the more mean you be the more they will stop their nonsense . . . I'm not saying that your not a good teacher but be more strike. . .I think making the kids learned their language and reading it is nice. I promise you that I won't be rude no more. I think you a good teacher.

The dynamics of Becky's classroom are created through an interplay of many aspects of school style and cultural/gender difference, and the teaching is going on in many directions. The conversation that is going on in and about Becky's classroom involves the sorts of negotiation that might take place in any setting. The participants all have speaking rights, though the rules for exercising those rights must be worked out in relation to common purposes and not everyone will agree. They recognize and acknowledge differences from the communicative style they expect, the students' expectations that Becky will be more or less like other teachers and more explicitly, what behaviors go with those expectations, while Becky talks and writes of what her expectations are and elicits their responses to her rules. Here she receives explicit instruction about effective communicative style for accomplishing her intentions, but the messages conflict: both children value the fact that she knows Creole and is teaching them to read it, but the boy wants his other teachers to be like her, "not streke," while the girl wanted her to be like her other teachers, "to be more strike," because "the more mean you be the more [the kids] will stop their nonsense."

As Becky studies these entries, she observes the surface features that give evidence of the students' hypotheses about written English; she notes the comparative fluency of the texts and the different stylistic strategies the writers are trying out. But she also perceives this writing not only as a response to a school task, but as part of a genuine conversation. She has written a response to each entry, continuing that conversation in writing and asking real questions that show her interest in what they're saying. Her responses will help the writers recognize the demands of written texts. She asks questions when she doesn't know what one writer's referring to, letting him know that she, as a reader, needs more information than he's given her —that writing may require more explicitness. In her comments to the second writer she includes "I am trying to be more strict. Did you like my rules? I care a lot. I hope that shows," because she feels that "this relationship of caring and trust is crucial in the classroom." She also considers the fact that neither of these writers is likely to have had prior experience in directly critiquing and evaluating their teachers in writing, so that this discourse event is a new one for them, and they are applying what they know about writing to this new purpose at the same time that they are using what they know from other contexts to measure this one.

Becky sees how the various texts of this classroom, both spoken and written, draw from and contribute to the evolving common text of the class, where the discourse context includes not only the current text or the immediate classroom, but all of the prior experiences and frames of reference and ways of communicating that she and her students bring: "Obviously there are differences in the way I conduct my class and the way other teachers conduct theirs. Since children are said to desire consistency, it's not surprising that the students should take a stance that either I should change to be more like the other teachers, or the other teachers should change to be more like me." In the end, as a beginning teacher-researcher, as well as a beginning teacher, Becky is able to take her own stance of inquiry in relationship to the many sorts of discourse in this classroom, paying attention to the multiple layers of language and of learning that are interwoven here. Finally, she sees the style of classroom discourse as integral to the stance the teacher takes toward learning:

In relation to my own style as a teacher, it must be said that all students are exposed to a wide variety of teachers and teaching styles. I don't think I need to be nervous that if I don't teach my students form and mechanics they won't get it anywhere else. The same goes for university courses. Some are concerned with the learner as a person, interacting with the discipline. Others deal with the discipline as something outside the student, that is either mastered or not. And still others focus on larger political issues, trying to fit the student and the discipline into this context any way they can. I would place my teaching style in the first category. . . . An understanding of the self as a person and a learner must come before mastery of the discipline, and a healthy synthesis of these two must precede analysis of both in a political framework.

Like any language, school language is not fixed and unchanging but is shaped by the community that uses it. We can choose, through our educational practices, to transmit, uncritically, particular ways of seeing and talking about the world and exclude those who cannot or will not accommodate themselves to those ways. Or we can work to create inclusive communities that engage in the process of creating, together, a common language and a continually evolving text that is shaped from the many prior texts that we and our students bring. In the next chapter, we will look more closely at how that evolving text can support another function of school discourse: building new frameworks of propositional/referential knowledge.

CHAPTER 9

Classroom Discourse II: Studying the Language of Learning

Classrooms occupy an intermediate ground between the private discourse of home and community and the public discourse of the larger society. Participants in any context rely on shared understandings about how to accomplish particular purposes and signal intentions and meanings. But while the shared assumptions of private discourse are privately held, implicit, and immediately negotiable, public discourse operates within a larger framework of commonly shared and frequently explicit societal assumptions about what its purposes are and what is relevant and appropriate to those purposes. This is true for all public discourse—for legal discourse, medical discourse, the discourse of news as reported in papers or on television—and in each of those domains, any particular interaction or text is shaped in relationship to common templates. The typical question and answer sequence of a doctor/patient encounter differs from that of the courtroom cross-examination of a medical expert, which in turn differs from the television reporter's questions outside of the courthouse for the eleven o'clock news. All three will be different from a professor's questioning in a course covering the same topic. The differences have to do with what is understood to be the purposes of these events.

Within educational contexts, the commonly held purposes are for learners to become literate and knowledgeable to a degree appropriate to their present level of education; at higher levels, to acquire disciplinary-specific knowledge, methods of inquiry, and ways of thinking (and, ideally, interdisciplinary ways as well); to acquire related ways of talking and writing; and in the process to take on particular ways of behaving, thinking, and valuing. In other words, to acquire new discourses and become participants in new, academic, discourse communities. But for most students, it's the process of learning to do these things that matters the most, for in that process they achieve some common denominator of literate ways which will facilitate their adaptation to other contexts of work, relationships, and adult participation in the social and political structures of the society. One measure of the success of our classrooms is the extent to which the discourse practiced there prepares students who come from many private discourse communities to communicate across the sorts of differences in conversational style that we explored in the last chapters, and to develop the common strategies that will allow them to operate within multiple public domains.

A freshman writing class is discussing *Hunger of Memory*, Richard Rodriguez's account of his own early schooling, looking for places in the text that will help them understand the nature of the transition he had to make from the private world of his Spanish-speaking home to a larger public world that not only used a different language (English) but used it in different ways and for different purposes:

TEACHER: Or another place in the text, if you see it somewhere else too. Is . . . Is home . . . Is home homey? [*Students laugh.*] For the lack of a better word? Ummm.

STUDENT 1:   Doesn't he have intense pressure? [*Teacher doesn't respond.*]

TEACHER: Is it a dysfunctional family?

STUDENT 2:   No.

TEACHER: Okay. Alright. Home life is what? [*Teacher turns to write "home life" on the board.*]

STUDENT 2:   Cold. It may be dysfunctional in a way . . . without the other two children. . . . He has a regular childhood before he got his education. . . . Well, I kinda developed my own thoughts. [*Students laugh.*]

TEACHER: Hey, he's making meaning, okay? He's making meaning. Okay, um . . . home life is . . . I think he uses the word "intimate" [*teacher writes "intimate" on the board*] . . . and school life is what?

STUDENT 2:   Uhh . . . lonely reason.

TEACHER: Okay. [*Teacher writes "school life" and then "lonely reason" on the board.*] So as a young child, alright, as a young child he, he goes to school and he's told this is the way to act and speak and think. And he goes home and he says, "No, no, no, you know, you're the son of Mexican immigrants. Don't ever forget that." So how, how is an eight year old supposed to deal with that? And what are the alternatives? What could his parents have done? What could his teachers have done?

STUDENT 3:   They could have told him that when you are at school, you know, be like other people. When you are at home, be yourself.

TEACHER: They could have helped him . . . right?

STUDENT 4:   Or they could have gotten together, you know, and just sat down and talked to him, his teachers and his parents . . . that way he would have had both values . . . you know . . . he could have looked up to his parents for one thing and his teachers for another instead of having to choose between one and another.

The class is typical of many at this urban university; the teacher Elaine Hayes, describes the students as bringing:

A wide diversity of culture and experience which makes apparent a wealth of awareness and perspectives. I have a student from Haiti, one from South Africa, one from Russia, one of Asian descent; a former Marine, two mothers of young children, and two mothers-to-be. There is a set of identical twins who play hockey for UMass/Boston as well as some very hip young people. . . . The members of the class are strangers with very different backgrounds from which shared knowledge is formed. The only true shared knowledge is that of being a student within the framework of the academic community. As first-year students, they are all assumed to be outsiders.

The students in this class, then, are engaged in a transition not unlike the one they're discussing, moving from the worlds of their private experiences to the quite different world of the university classroom. But unlike Rodriguez, they are not expected to leave those worlds behind, but to carry them into their present context, connecting their prior discourses and prior knowledge with what they'll learn in this new setting.

All of our classrooms, like Elaine's, mediate the private and public discourse of the larger society to one degree or another, explicitly initiating learners into the appropriate patterns of discourse for new, more public contexts. As we shift our attention from elementary and middle school classrooms like Nicole's and Becky's to high school and college classrooms, we find that, at each level of schooling, the discourse we record in the classroom becomes increasingly representative of public discourse across a number of domains. The scaffolding that we saw parents doing as their young children were first acquiring language (Chapter Two) remains central to the initiatory function of the classroom across levels, as teachers support students' acquisition of new discourses, helping them to build on the discourses they've already acquired, and to situate themselves in relation to the new ones they are acquiring. What changes in effective classroom discourse over the years of schooling can be described in relation to the three discourse functions we've been examining throughout this book.

The propositional/referential or ideational function

When learners enter school, they move out of a world of private discourse where participants share common experiences and a common framework of knowledge about the world, and where, since much knowledge about the world is already shared, it doesn't need to be named or delineated explicitly. They move into a world where people bring different knowledge, from texts as well as from experience. Here the realm of knowledge that's assumed to be shared becomes enormous. (Look at E.D. Hirsch's *Cultural Literacy: What Every American Needs to Know* (1987) to find the range of referential knowledge about Western history and culture—itself a very limited frame—that an educated reader might be assumed to understand.) At the same time, in more public contexts, an equally vast potential realm of knowledge that cannot be assumed to be shared must be defined explicitly.

Texts often provide a means of making a shared body of knowledge available to students, and at higher levels of schooling, classes are typically structured with the assumption that what's in an assigned text is commonly known and understood. (Though of course this is often not true.) In Elaine's class, providing as it does a transition to college-level study, the teacher cannot assume her students will bring a common understanding of an assigned text, so a lot of the classroom discourse is referential in relation to the text that has been read: pointing to particular pages, restating the words that appear there, and working toward both a shared knowledge of the contents of the text and a shared sense of its possible meanings.

The shared knowledge being built in this classroom also includes an understanding of the nature of the course, knowledge initially presented in the first course text: the syllabus, and course description; and captured in a particular lexicon about writing, reading, and thinking (one that includes terms like "making meaning").

The pragmatic or interpersonal function

Again, there are two aspects to this function: the intentions and purposes of the participants in any discourse context, and a participant's stance toward other participants, the discourse context itself, and particularly toward the referential content of the discourse.

Intentions and purposes

The movement from private to public discourse typically involves an apparent shift, first of all, in the extent to which the relative emphasis in any exchange is on an interpersonal versus an ideational function, with private discourse focused in obvious ways on maintaining a set of relationships, while public is likely to be more explicitly focused on ideas of the world. This apparent shift in emphasis may hide the fact that participants in public discourse have particular things they want to accomplish in that realm—positions of power and authority they want to maintain, ways that they want their words to lead others to act or to view the world.

Most of the talk in Elaine's class is focused on the larger topic of Rodriguez's experience, as represented in his book, so the multiple purposes of each utterance aren't as striking as they have been in the private conversations we examined earlier. Yet Elaine, as the teacher, has very definite purposes in mind, and her students respond with their own. She explains her purposes, both immediate and general:

> Within my classroom dialogue, I was pushing for a pattern of thinking, I was
> not striving for a preconceived or produced thought. I wanted my students to

compose their own alternatives to Rodriguez's problems while participating in the composing process that would yield new possibilities . . . I wanted to enable my students to imagine what it was like to be young Richard Rodriguez, the scholarship boy. . . .

[In all of my classes] I perform. I pace, I draw on the board, I tell stories about myself and life in general, I raise my voice for emphasis and illustration, I make my students laugh. I'll do just about anything to engage them in new ways of reading, thinking, and writing.

As Elaine defines her role as teacher, she intersects with students' assumptions, based on their prior experience, about their own roles. When, at the beginning of the course, she asks them to write about their first responses to the course introduction, and to point out places where what is being asked of them is unclear, they point out phrases like "reading, marking, and making discoveries through thought and inquiry," and "composing a meaning of what you have read." Their expectations for a freshman writing course include reviewing grammar and learning to produce particular essay forms, but not "making discoveries" and "composing a meaning" and the student-centered classroom that Elaine is aiming for means "a giving of themselves they were unaccustomed to."

Stance

With any words we choose, we are also expressing our stance toward the propositional/referential content of our utterance as well as our relationship to the other participants and our response to the discourse context, but we gain the linguistic resources to do this more subtly and implicitly in relationship to a wider range of contexts as we grow older. In particular, we come to evaluate the meanings of information and events in relationship not just to our immediate environment, but to a larger and larger framework of knowledge and experience, so that my reading of exchanges among my daughter and her friends may be framed not only in terms of my immediate sense of their relationship, but also in terms of my knowledge about adolescent development and/or about language and discourse. Education facilitates this expansion of our frames of reference, so that, as listeners, we increasingly evaluate the propositional/referential content of an utterance in terms of a wide range of other knowledge, and, as speakers, we express our attitude toward the information we're offering against a broad base of experience and authority, while placing ourselves in relation to that content through a wide range of linguistic choices.

In Elaine's class, the teacher suggests one frame of reference with the words "dysfunctional family," but the students don't fully adopt that framework. Student 2 rejects her term, then modifies it, pointing out that Rodriguez "has a regular childhood before he got his education," implicitly suggesting that the problem lies outside of our usual shared understanding of the notion of a dysfunctional family. Because Elaine's larger goal is to to have students do their own thinking, rather than giving back the interpretations she has suggested, she doesn't reject his interpretation but embraces and applauds his comment that "I kinda developed my own thoughts." But she quickly returns to her own immediate purpose and contributes, herself, the term for Rodriguez's home life that she was looking for: "I think he uses the word 'intimate.'"

The discourse / textual function of language

The evolving texts of our private conversations tend to be negotiated flexibly within some common parameters around turns or expectations for genres like jokes, with a great deal of local cohesion but with less concern for coherence over a long stretch of discourse. Speakers may shift topics by providing a link like "That reminds me of something that happened last week," and after a series of shifts the thread of connection between point A and point F might be lost entirely, but this is unproblematic because of the value attached to the discourse process itself. Being involved in the process serves both referential and pragmatic functions that are more important than the creation of a larger coherent text. But in public domains we are called on increasingly to address our comments to a common point over much more extended stretches, and typically to follow more fixed (though often still implicit) rules about turns and formats as well. The discourse of educational contexts provides an opportunity for learners to practice the different discourse structures and styles characteristic of a range of public contexts.

Most classroom discourse is teacher controlled, but as we'll see in this chapter, the manner of control has a great effect on student learning. Elaine is trying to balance these two poles of control and freedom in her classroom: she is trying to build, with her students, a larger coherent text that is focused on both the immediate topic of Rodriguez's experience and the larger topic of what it means to read, to write, to learn; at the same time, she's trying to leave some of the sorts of space for negotiation and initiation of new ideas that would be more characteristic of informal conversation, in a flexible and inclusive discourse process that won't shut out students with different cultural styles.

When Student 2 shifts the topic from Rodriguez's home life to the process of developing "my own thoughts" that has informed his comments on that topic, he is explicitly referring to the developing text of this classroom discussion and signaling that his contributions to that text are coherent with the larger purposes of the course—the shared course text about reading and writing—even if they're not meeting the teacher's local expectations for adding to the text of the immediate discussion about Rodriguez within a framework she has introduced. Elaine's response about his "making his own meaning" is cohesive with his comment and coherent as well within the larger course text, which again encourages ongoing comment about the discourse process itself.

It's impossible for a teacher to attend to all of these elements of the discourse of learning simultaneously while a class is going on. But through taping and looking more closely at the discourse of her own classroom, Elaine discovers places where her goals and her actual responses in particular classroom moments pull against each other. As a beginning teacher who has been learning how to teach composition through a sequenced internship program (through courses, co-teaching with an experienced mentor, and then teaching her own sections as a supervised intern for two semesters), she has had multiple opportunities to identify goals and to reflect on particular classroom practices in relation to them. But the close analysis of the discourse in her classroom highlights some of the ways in which she has approached her teaching role.

> I carried into the classroom the anticipation that the students would teach me something through their fresh engagement with a text that had ceased to be alive for me. I lacked the understanding that in order to receive a new reading, I would have to be an active participant in the experience instead of sitting back in a state of appreciation as if their work were a painting on a wall. Limiting my role to a facilitator or moderator did not illustrate or further my ideological stance of strong reading and writing. My students were having a difficult time moving from summarizing to analyzing because I was not rolling up my sleeves and investigating and constructing with them. There was resistance all around. . . .
>
> Watching and listening to myself work as I discovered how my students were working has been intellectually exciting. . . . I came to know and appreciate my students as learners . . . and came to realize that the students were also responsible for some of the resistance to new ways of thinking, reading, and writing. . . . When my classroom became a research project it also became a dialectical project. Realizing this . . . helped to re-form my perception of classroom discourse and student writing.

There is value, then, in looking systematically at school discourse both for classroom teachers and for students themselves. The examples of classroom discourse throughout these two chapters were, for the most part, collected by my upper level and graduate students, like Elaine, Becky, and Nicole, in classes where they were teaching, student teaching, tutoring, or sometimes in classes they themselves were attending, including one of my own classes on discourse analysis. They were, in effect, teacher-researchers, identifying something they had found interesting or problematic in the classrooms, observing and recording representative examples, and sometimes involving their students in the collection of data and the analysis and interpretation of what was collected. What they discovered was not a fixed set of answers about how to structure the discourse of the classroom but a method of analysis that they could use, as teachers, to examine the texts of their own classrooms, to see in what ways that discourse reflects their purposes and intentions, and a method that they could use as students (and their students can use as well) to find out what's needed for them to engage more fully in a particular classroom discourse community.

School discourse and the classroom discourse community

A classroom is a speech community, whose members, over time, develop a common discourse that involves: shared knowledge; common purposes, relationships, attitudes, and values; and shared understandings about how to communicate their knowledge, how to achieve their shared purposes (including that of communication) in an ongoing flow of discourse with a particular structure and style. But because a major purpose of the classroom community is to extend students' existing knowledge into new domains, the sort of community that will be created depends, to a great extent, on how knowledge is seen and how it is believed to be developed and/or gained.

If knowledge is seen as a straightforward set of facts about the world and relationships among those facts that can be directly represented in language through its referential/propositional function (cf. Chapter Three), then, when students can re-present a set of referential terms and propositions, they can be said to have the knowledge such terms and propositions represent. However, if knowledge is seen not simply as a set of facts, but as facts shaped by an interpretive framework (one that we may not even be conscious of), even a list of commonly agreed on dates for a set of historical events, or a description of a particular rock will be shaped by what's included and what's left out, by a schema that suggests that some things are important and visible and that others are—for this moment and this purpose—invisible. And the words chosen, perhaps *uprising* versus *revolution* or *sand* versus *silicate*, will not only suggest a particular specialist perspective but also a particular interpretation of the events that are named or features that are described. So if our concept of knowledge includes an interpretive frame that cannot be separated from any representation of the world, then it must include all that goes into and creates that frame—all the ways of thinking, valuing, and believing that go into any discourse, including the discourse of an academic field. And classroom learning, like learning outside of the classroom, becomes a matter of acquiring new discourses, including disciplinary, subject-related ones, through participating in them in meaningful ways, trying on the ways in which they frame knowledge, and seeing how the world looks through those lenses.

Teachers' purposes are likely to differ, then, depending on the notion of knowledge that they hold. If they hold the view that knowledge can be summed up in particular words and sentences and transmitted through those words directly to students, then they will see learning as having taken place when students can give back those words, and their purposes will focus on giving the words and getting them back. (This is what Brazilian educator Paolo Freire describes as a "banking model" of education, one in which the teacher makes deposits of knowledge in students' minds and then reclaims those deposits on a test.)

But if teachers believe that knowledge always involves stance and interpretation, that it's imbedded in a context and a frame of reference created through prior and current personal and shared experiences, and that it is constantly evolving and being reshaped through an ongoing process of interaction with others and with the world, then they will see learning as having taken place when students can represent their evolving understandings in different words from the teacher's, when they can try on different stances and explore different possible interpretations, and can engage in an exchange that involves exploration as well as a display of learning. Such teachers will be particularly interested in the language of the classroom—the language of their students—because it is through a close look at that language that students' development of new conceptualizations and the ways that classroom practices can contribute or hinder that development will most clearly be seen. Teachers like Elaine, who hold the second model of knowledge and learning, are working on altering the patterns of traditional school discourse. But to better appreciate their efforts, we have to look more closely at what those patterns are.

There have been many studies of classroom discourse, carried out by anthropologists, cognitive psychologists, linguists, educational researchers, and teachers themselves. Those who approach the classroom as a cultural/social setting tend to emphasize the culture of the classroom and the nature of the community that is created there; those who focus on the intellectual development of individual learners within that setting tend to focus on the structures of thought that are developed and displayed there. But almost all studies have pointed to several common characteristics of the language of schooling that appear across a range of grade levels and subject areas, drawing on common discourse structures, and a common style. For the most part, because schooling has, over the years, developed its own culture and language, these patterns, though they originated in a different notion of knowledge and learning than is held by many teachers today, remain remarkably dominant, even while they are problematic.

Just as the nature of effective classroom discourse that supports students' learning can be described in terms of the functions of discourse that we've been exploring, what's problematic about much traditional classroom discourse can be described in these terms as well:

1. *The referential/propositional function.* In conversations, shared knowledge is created over time through a gradual expansion of frames of reference, and it is embedded in meaningful discourse. In professional and public contexts, such knowledge is generally developed through years of experience or training, though it might be added to quickly through books or presentations. Only in school contexts do we expect it to come through the memorization of decontextualized bits of information not linked to other knowledge (as in the memorizing of lists of unrelated vocabulary words).

2. *The pragmatic/interpersonal function.* In conversations, knowledge is not seen in isolation, separated from the meanings and intentions and attitudes of the participants. In public and professional contexts, speakers are expected to place themselves in relationship to the authoritative discourse of the field.

Only in school settings do we treat knowledge as only a set of referential facts and propositions that have meaning apart from the intentions and interpretations of a community of knowers.

3. *The textual/discourse function.* In conversations, individual texts evolve. In public and professional discourse, forms of texts evolve, and elements that aren't productive of communication for a particular purpose are discarded over time. Only in classroom contexts do we see texts as fixed, rather than evolving, and teach forms apart from the processes that might give shape to them and the purposes for which they might be used.

The public discourse of educational contexts, effective or limiting, has distinguishing features at several levels, and with reference to the several functions of language we've looked at. For the most part, as we saw in Chapter Seven, it requires a specific linguistic code and variety (standard English), a variety that requires a somewhat common pronunciation and particular syntactic structures. It uses a style that is also more syntactically explicit, and carries more of the meaning in a verbal channel, assuming less shared knowledge. And it depends on a more formal lexicon. Public discourse style is also likely to be characterized by less involvement, more distance, more explicit statements of meaning, and by more politeness features that mitigate authority and save face. Larger discourse patterns like turn-taking are more often conventionally governed rather than negotiated. Participants' roles and relationships are likely to be more fixed.

All of these features affect the ways in which school language shapes learning, and all are controlled to some degree, within the immediate classroom context, by the authority of the teacher. Teachers have some power at least within their own classrooms, to structure a discourse environment that moves beyond the most limited model of school discourse to provide effective scaffolds for their students' language and learning. But to exercise that power, they first need the opportunity to look closely at the ways in which learning goes on in various classroom discourse communities, seeing not only where typical school discourse patterns limit learning, but where these limited models are expanded, extended, and renegotiated to support new learning and reconceptualization.

While the typical class may involve a number of structural units, from teacher-led small reading groups in primary grades to the professor's lengthy college lectures, the most common interactional pattern for actual exchanges between teacher and students at all levels, in large groups or small, is the Initiation, Response, and Evaluation (or IRE) pattern.

The teacher initiates the exchange, usually by asking a question, as Elaine does when she asks, "Is it a dysfunctional family?" The student then responds, usually with an answer to the question: "No." The teacher evaluates the response: "Okay. Alright," and moves on, typically to another question (most often directed to another student), or perhaps first to an expanded comment or mini-lecture on the student's response. This pattern is strikingly different from those of our typical exchanges in natural conversation, where various speakers initiate, others respond, other speakers respond to the responses, and no one explicitly evaluates. But the typical school pattern is so imbedded in our teaching practices that it asserts itself even in the exchanges of a teacher like Elaine, who is trying to change such patterns and the ideas about knowledge and learning that they represent. Even worse, the presence of a pattern like this, in the teacher's unconscious sense of how classroom discourse should proceed, makes it hard for the teacher to hear responses that fall outside of the pattern. When Elaine asks the first question of this segment, "Is home homey?" and the first student to speak doesn't respond with "yes" or "no" before making an extended comment but instead responds with another initiation, "Doesn't he have intense pressure?" Elaine can't really hear that response:

> Because I came to class with a dialogue in my head, my intention and attention is limited. I fail to hear the strong and context-vital student responses that would extend their understandings to knowledge. I am looking for specific answers to my questions, and that closes down discussion instead of opening it up. . . . For example, I ask the question, "Is home homey?" looking for a description of Rodriguez's home life using the language of the text. What I get is a strong student response (Doesn't he have intense pressure?) that's unheard by me, possibly because my agenda does not include new possibilities. And it happens again when a student responds "Cold" to my question, "Home life is what?" The students are interacting with each other and with Rodriguez in a way that I was unprepared for. . . . As the teacher, I control the topic with questions, some open, some not, and then wait for the students to maintain it with their responses. But my intention for the class has been carefully plotted, and a deviation from that is unacceptable.

In a large class, there isn't time for a teacher to respond to every student initiation, and overall Elaine manages quite adeptly to keep students involved in an extended and focused class discussion. As a conscientious teacher, she has carefully planned what she wants to accomplish in this class period, following up on the discussion that took place in the last class. Nevertheless, she has discovered in this exchange a pattern that seems to work against her larger intentions:

> My intention for this class is to guide the students to a strong reading of the text by proposing alternatives to the common sense solutions (to Rodriguez's problems) the class has proposed. . . . And while my questions do probe and provoke the students' thinking, they do not carry the weight I hoped for. . . . Most of the added and expanded knowledge is done by the teacher, not the students.

In Elaine's class, some moments like the one she has recorded interfere with the opportunity for open exchange that she's trying to create, but as she observes such patterns, she learns to hear more of what her students say and to follow up on the starting points for learning that their observations offer. Above all, she keeps the conversation going and all of the students participating. But a more common effect of the teacher-controlled IRE pattern is that the teacher does most of the talking and students have little to say—they're both silent and silenced.

In a recent study of the classroom discourse of another freshman writing class, Glynda Hull, Mike Rose, and two of their colleagues (Kay Losey Fraser and Marisa Castellano) look at a similar set of classroom exchanges. But in the class they study, they find that one student's repeated violation of the IRE pattern doesn't just mean that a particular initiation goes unheard. Rather, the teacher's expectations for the rhythm of the classroom exchange are thrown off so far that she develops a picture of the student as unable to participate in the construction of coherent discourse, perhaps as unable even to think coherently. The teacher constructs a picture of a remedial student, the Queen of the Non Sequiturs, who has thinking continuity problems and is unlikely to pass the next writing class, despite the strong counter-evidence of the student's own writing, and of her prior experience on her high school debating team and as a creative writer who has been working on her own novel. Based on a review of the data they collected, Hull, et al. (1991) comment:

> Maria did, then, seem to initiate more than she responded—asking questions, taking the floor, diverting the course of classroom talk—and hers was not exactly the expected posture for a student in an IRE classroom. . . . Given the way Maria's conversational habits stood out, it seems likely that June's (the teacher's) view of Maria as an inappropriate talker would eventually become salient enough to affect her perception of Maria even when she interjects in a way that is appropriate. Join this perception of a particular student with this teacher's strong predilection for an IRE participant structure, and you won't be surprised that Maria's chances to be heard would be undercut. The cycle continues as Maria's interactional patterns in class become not just an annoying conversational style, but the barometer by which to measure her cognitive problems—evidence that is so salient that it goes unqualified even in the fact of counter-evidence that Maria, in fact, wrote rather well. (311)

The IRE interaction structure exists alongside other structures in the classroom—sharing time or show and tell in primary grades, student reports at upper levels—but where the purpose of such structures is for students to display their knowledge about teacher-initiated topics, within a teacher-controlled form, or risk being seen as unknowing and perhaps not capable of knowing, they offer little opportunity for learners to engage in the sorts of talk that would help them construct new frameworks and richer understandings of the subject at hand. Students who come from backgrounds where the typical exchange structures and roles of participants are markedly different from those of classrooms are at a particular disadvantage, as we saw in the last chapter.

But if the typical IRE pattern lends itself to students' display and teachers' evaluation of pre-set knowledge, what might classroom discourse that leads to richer understandings look like? We'll look next at some moments in classrooms where new understandings are being shaped collaboratively.

Classroom moments 1: scaffolding and reconceptualization

Several studies of classroom discourse have looked in some detail at the ways in which the structures of classroom discourse support the development of students' conceptual knowledge and understanding. Courtney Cazden calls this aspect of classroom discourse "the language of curriculum," focusing on the content or referential/propositional information of such fields as social studies or science, as opposed to "the language of control," the social language of the classroom used to maintain and establish appropriate classroom behaviors and social relationships that we looked at in the last chapter. She adds a third aspect, "the language of personal identity," the expressive language through which participants place themselves in relationship to other participants and to the content—what we've referred to as stance. (The latter two categories are part of what we've been referring to as the pragmatic/interpersonal function of language.)

Cazden does not explicitly name a textual or discourse function, where the focus is on monitoring and shaping the discourse itself. But that function is particularly important in classroom contexts, where what is being taught and learned is not only a particular body of content and not only a way of interacting with others and placing oneself in the world, but also particular ways of doing these things in ongoing classroom interaction—ways that are monitored and sometimes even explicitly discussed.

Cazden analyzes the lesson structures of elementary school classrooms, describing the ways in which particular structures (like sharing time or show and tell, where a child has an opportunity to tell the class about some event that has happened or an object that has been brought in from outside of the classroom) can provide scaffolds to support classroom learning: making it "possible for the novice to participate in the mature task from the very beginning," and "providing support that is both adjustable and temporary" (107). She sees even the IRE discourse structure as offering a potential scaffold, if it is opened up so that more exploratory student answers are accepted. She cites the research of science educator Mary Budd Rowe (1986), which shows that even extending the amount of time teachers wait after asking a question for a student to answer (the usual wait time is one second or less) can affect the learning of all the students in the classroom, allowing more opportunity for all to formulate more complex responses (60-61). Teachers who are interested in having learners reconceptualize will typically not just evaluate their students' answers by saying right or wrong but help them expand their utterances, in the ways we saw parents doing in Chapter Two, or offer new terms (like commenting that a box is a cube, and connecting the object to a reference frame of geometric features), rather than simply evaluating or correcting.

The most effective classroom discourse patterns for student learning are ones that allow students frequent and extended turns, with scaffolding that helps learners extend their frames of reference and build larger networks of referential/propositional knowledge, helps them discover and express their intended meanings and communicate them appropriately to others, and helps them develop particular ways of using language to do all of this within an ongoing discourse process. Unfortunately, such patterns are more likely to be found in classes for the most advanced, most privileged students, and only rarely in the classrooms inhabited by most learners in our public schools.

We can see one model of such scaffolding going on in an honors class in Western Traditions at a suburban high school, observed by Ellie Klauminzer, a graduate student who is, herself, preparing to teach. She describes the content and purposes of the class as follows:

> Both in subject matter and in manner of presentation, in teaching style, the class prepares academically gifted students for university-level liberal arts courses. The course presents the major themes or concepts from a particular tradition, commonly known as Western Civilization, as seen in its literature from ancient Greece to modern times. In this classroom students are seen to be in the process of becoming what the larger academic community defines as literate adults. Pedagogical goals, therefore, appear to include fewer areas of mastery, and more areas of exposure to ideas that will be developed and expanded upon repeatedly in the course of students' university education—and over the course of their lifetimes.

Ellie sees the teacher's practice as exemplifying the sort of scaffolding described by Cazden: "He repeatedly provides material to his students that is above their heads and a step beyond their own experience, and then through generating questions, summarizing, and clarifying, he assists students to internalize as much of the information as they are capable of." The students, clearly practiced at this sort of discourse, are capable of a great deal, as we can see in this segment of classroom talk:

TEACHER: Judeo-Christian culture . . . out of the Old Testament, out of the creation story in Genesis, tells us that God created everything and it is good and it is hierarchical. . . . Whenever we're talking about something that rationality cannot fully understand, respond to, or answer, then there's going to be this element, of . . . even in terms of hierarchy, of *faith*. [*Writes on board.*] And faith goes beyond reason. And *The Tempest*, if *The Tempest* is about anything, and we know it's about a lot of things, *The Tempest* is about *faith*. And where rationality leaves off, and where faith begins. OK? Student 1, is your hand still up?

STUDENT 1:   I think it died! [*laughter*]

TEACHER: mmmm.

STUDENT 1:   Well, there's like, there are now about five things that I wanted to say. But, um, originally, when we were talking about the hierarchy, and, um, and about how it's linear and everything . . . I thought in Shakespeare's time it was more linear because the towns were smaller, the town would have one carpenter, one blacksmith, one teacher, one mayor, or whatever. I think it was easier then, but now I think there are different laws in the hierarchy of function in that it becomes a pyramid.

TEACHER: mmmm.

STUDENT 1:   . . . because there's simply . . . more of, um, the, the trained workers, or whatever, and there's still, there's only one king. You know, I'm, I'm not sure that it's true, but it seems like this is an inherent flaw in the hierarchy of function. And then, and the way it was in Shakespeare's time is all well and good, but it simply can't work that way today. And I mean to say even that someone should be in a trade school that is in the high school, um, we are furthering the idea, we are furthering the idea of the pyramid, or whatever, to have them here to begin with because we are looking down on the trade school, or whatever, but once they're here to say, "Oh, they should be in the trade school," is part of the pyramid again because that . . . what is that but intellectual snobbery?

TEACHER: Student 2 do you want to respond to Student 1?

STUDENT 2:   Yes. OK, I don't know, I guess I do agree to a degree that there is a pyramid structure, but if you look at a lot of occupations, like there are plenty of lawyers, excess lawyers . . .

STUDENT 3:   Yeah, but they're at the bottom.

STUDENT 4:   They're not at the bottom. People may not respect lawyers, but they respect the occupation.

STUDENT 5:   That's true.

TEACHER: Student 6?

STUDENT 6:   Well, I think I see what Student 1 was saying . . . if you were in a small town in the Renaissance or whatever, you had a very obvious dependency on every trade. Whereas now what's considered to be more "up" in the hierarchy is . . . are, tend to be occupations that are more visible and they are more . . . everyone, you know, deals with the plumber, the carpenter, whatever, on a daily basis but not in a way that seems, I guess, as an expert. Like the President, you don't . . . he doesn't come in your house and fix your sink.

ALL: [*Laughter.*]

The most striking feature of this exchange is the length of student answers. The teacher is clearly in control of this speech event, designating speakers and turns. But he models extended turns, extended thought, and the students' turns are as long as his, if not longer. There's plenty of time for each student to explore an idea (with backchanneling *mmmm* by the teacher to provide support without interruption). The teacher doesn't respond to a student's turn with "right" or "I don't think so," but instead calls on another student to respond—to think about what the first student has been saying—and other students get to initiate their own turns and add to the discussion as well. Nevertheless, the longer discourse event is coherent across speakers, focused on a set of topics related to *The Tempest*, and Student 1 has explicitly monitored the evolving text, keeping track of where the discussion has been and the issues that have been raised, while waiting for her opportunity to comment on each of them.

The talk in this class is exploratory, within implicit guidelines established by the themes of the course. The teacher encourages students to use frameworks of understanding developed around one text or one period to generate larger themes about human society and human social experience and to explore the applicability of these themes to different times and places. The students in this classroom have learned to work off of terms offered by the teacher—to explore their meaning and applicability to Shakespeare's world and to recontextualize them in relationship to their present experience. Here the notion of hierarchy that the teacher presents as originating with the beginnings of Judeo-Christian culture and extending to the time of Shakespeare is perceived by Student 1 as exemplified by the existence of a trade school in her contemporary setting.

Students bring to this Honors classroom a great deal of experience with extended discourse of this sort, from both their earlier courses and from the typical sorts of discussions that make up much adult conversation in this community. The style of discourse is familiar and shared, as is a general framework of knowledge about the Judeo-Christian tradition and an implicit set of values and beliefs about society and its structures. Nevertheless, not all students in this homogeneous class participate equally, and the particular model of scaffolding offered here may support the learning of some students more than others. Ellie observes:

> When the pace of teacher/student interaction is so rapid, and when the class is made up of students who excel, even exploratory speech can be engaged in only by students who are assertive and confident of their verbal skills. Presumably all in the class are excellent students, but it was clear that some students were not comfortable talking: a relatively few students did most of the talking. But I also observed the teacher at times changing the environment so that more students were comfortable participating. He did this through occasional changes in his response time, allowing more time for students to speak; by encouraging student questions about the reading material; and by encouraging discussion of an issue with which students have direct experience.

In this honors classroom, the teacher offers somewhat specialized terms and encourages the students to explore and contextualize them. More often, however, the movement goes the other way—and teachers respond to students' answers by reformulating them and offering new terminology. Too often teachers do not sufficiently take into account the fact that the specialized language of a field is linked to a particular frame of reference, one that the teacher may have, but that the students might not share. Douglas Barnes, a British educator and linguist, together with the late James Britton, made extended studies of the language of education in British schools that led to some fundamental reforms of teaching practices around language and literacy (Barnes et al., 1990). Their studies, carried out with classroom teachers of eleven-year-old students across different types of school and different subject areas, focus particularly on the ways in which the language of instruction supports or shuts off students' reasoning.

In his part of this study entitled "Language in the Secondary Classroom," Barnes too distinguishes between two functions of classroom language, functions he calls *conceptual* (propositional/referential content as represented in a person's actual understandings) and *socio-cultural* (what we've been describing as pragmatic/interpersonal). He points out that the specialist language of a field serves both functions at once: conceptually, a specialist linguistic style supports the exchange of messages about a subject matter and provides a means of reflecting on and reordering one's understanding of a topic. But the same style:

> Serves to remind speaker and listener that he or she is speaking as a physicist (perhaps) or more generally as a scientist, or as a committee member, or a participant in a public meeting. The style helps to maintain this temporary identity, and perhaps to hold at the center of our attention this particular mode of understanding the world, in contrast with the other modes at our disposal. This function is essentially social, concerned with sustaining the cultural identity relevant at that moment in that situation. . . . Socio-cultural and conceptual functions are normally performed by one and the same utterance. (55)

Barnes offers examples of what he sees as unsuccessful, as well as successful, classroom exchanges, as in this case:

> T Now I don't know whether any of you could jump the gun a bit and tell me what actually is this green stuff which produces green color . . .
> P Er . . . um . . . water.
> T No . . . Have you heard of chlorophyll? (48)

Here the teacher is so focused on extracting the appropriate term that he offers it immediately after his evaluation of the student's response, without reflecting at all on the answer the student has actually given, not noticing (apparently) that the student's answer shows he hasn't been understanding the lesson at all, and certainly not backing up to discover what the student thinks about what's going on or why the student might think that the "green stuff" is water. Barnes points out that:

> Our literacy-oriented culture induces us to assume that meaning is a characteristic of words rather than a cultural attribute of the people who use those words. This may account for the excessive value given by some teachers to the mere recognition of words by those pupils. . . . This can at worst shroud from teachers' gaze the meanings which provide the only valid justification for teaching the words. The words without the concepts they represent in adult use are strictly useless to pupils. As their grasp of a concept develops, the technical term becomes a useful centre about which can cluster relevant experiences and understanding; presented too soon the term may actually inhibit the process of clustering and abstraction. (49)

In Barnes's view, "a 'form of discourse' is not just a vocabulary and style to be imitated: it is a way of understanding the world."(57) It is a way of understanding the world, not just the definitions of terms like hierarchy and rationality, that the students in the class Ellie observed are learning. The danger, though, in this monocultural classroom is that they'll not have the opportunity to discover that this particular way is not the only way.

Classroom moments II: trying on new perspectives

It was with the notion of revisiting a classroom context that had offered him a profoundly new way of understanding the world that Mike Arsenault, now a teacher of ESL at an inner-city community college, observed the classes on world religious traditions taught by one of his former undergraduate professors. In this brief stretch of classroom discourse, the professor is trying to construct, with his students, an understanding of the concept of Zen, so that they'll have more than just a definition of a term, but will understand the frame of reference that term brings—what Zen means as a way of seeing the world. He focuses on eliciting common experiences and creating shared knowledge about the experience of places associated with the concept—such as a Zen garden.

PROFESSOR: A very important part of Zen, is that when you go into a Zen temple, or a Zen garden, you are not the central object in the garden. . . . Nor is the gardener. What is the central object in a Zen garden? Whether it is a pond . . . or a pebble garden, you know . . . raked to look like the sea . . . You know in some of these little places . . . Umm. What is the central object? . . . [*long pause*] . . . Almost a koan . . . [*very long pause*] . . . Therefore, I should take the stick and hit you, and you go off for three days and come back with the answer . . . and then I ignore you when you come back you see . . . This is the assumption that I know what I'm doing [*laughter*] . . . Ummm . . . What IS the central object of a Zen garden? . . . Student 1?

STUDENT 1:   ahhh . . . Space? [*tentatively*]

PROFESSOR: Space? O.K.

STUDENT 2:   I'm just guessing . . . I mean, from the one at the MFA (Museum of Fine Arts) . . . walking in there, it's . . . that's a Zen garden, right?

PROFESSOR: Umhuhhm.

STUDENT 2:   [*laughs*] Just get that out of the way. It's uhh . . . it seems like the garden itself . . . the kinda, the unity of the whole garden . . .

PROFESSOR: Umhuhhm.

STUDENT 2:   Nothing in particular stands out and everything's kind of . . . it's all one . . .

PROFESSOR: Umhuhhm.

STUDENT 2:   garden. Nothing is the focus.

PROFESSOR: That's right. Yeah . . . How could one say what is the central object?

Here, although the professor is still the knower, the authority, he poses a question (What is the central object?) for which there is no one answer that students can give—a completely open question that pushes students into a process of thinking. He pauses, muses over the question he has asked, suggests that the question is a koan or difficult puzzle—a specialized term, that may be familiar from the assigned reading—offering an instantiation of both the term and its applicability to the present context (and thus commenting on the textual level about the evolving discourse). A lot of purposes are accomplished with this comment, and with the form in which it's made, as Mike explains:

> He throws in a little joke to lighten the situation. . . . A koan is a question used by Zen Masters and mentioned in (the assigned) book, which brings the Zen student to a rational impasse. By comparing the students' silence to the koan answering process, he is making light of the fact that he has posed a difficult question, one which might make it difficult to articulate an answer. He also of course looks to see if the students grasp his reference, which they would understand if they read the text. With this there is also a slight change in tone, and the professor is portraying himself as concerned, empathetic and less authoritarian. The phrasing, in addition, "Almost a koan" is obviously an abbreviated and somewhat less formal form . . . helping to create a more laid-back atmosphere.
>
> After a long pause he continues along this same line with further comment on the koan process. He says, "Therefore I should take the stick and hit you, and you go off for three days and come back with the answer . . . and then I ignore you when you come back . . . " The whole sequence he mentions is modeled after the koan practice as described in the assigned text. With "therefore" he creates cohesion by tying back to his previous comment and means to say, "Because this very question at hand is like the koan process. . . . " In this way he draws on the assigned material while making light of the students' seeming impasse. He is again pointing out that he realizes that the question at hand is not an easy one. He is showing his empathy. He is also pointing out though, that he is willing to wait for the students to critically develop or discover an answer. This relates directly to "and you go off for three days . . . " It shows that he is interested in more than simply evaluating them. If that were the case he would have already called on someone or given the class the answer. Thus it is clear that he wants them to really think about the question.

In response to the problem the professor has posed, a first student responds tentatively with an answer that the professor accepts but not as a final answer. Student 2 is also tentative (I'm just guessing), but makes a connection to a familiar context, the garden at the Museum of Fine Arts, checks to see that it is in fact a Zen garden, makes a discourse level comment on his own utterance (Just to get that out of the way), and then gradually works through a sequence of ideas and rephrasings (the garden itself; the unity of the whole garden; nothing in particular stands out; it's all one . . . garden). Mike comments:

> Finally the student breaks through to his answer. There is no tentativeness in his voice. He has discovered the central object that the professor had asked about. He answers, "Nothing is the focus." This answer relates back to his previous utterance in which he first began to turn his answer around toward the negative (nothing in particular . . .). It seems as if the student has finally seen that the teacher had posed a trick question. All along the student had been looking for a central object, and as he was formulating the various stages of his answer, he came to see that there was no such thing. The phrasing of his answer also related to his own previous answer in which he had pointed out

that no one thing stood out, or essentially was the focus. Although the professor had asked about a "central object," it is clear to everyone that this student has transformed the professor's terms "central object" to his own "focus."

This is exactly the answer the professor had been looking for and now that the student's journey of discovery is over, the professor jumps in to comment . . . "That's right," with which he means to congratulate and affirm the student's effort.

At this point, the professor goes on to muse at some length about the nature of the Zen garden, and the meaning of Zen, finally restating the main concept once more: "The very idea of center has to be removed. And that's the decentering."

Classroom moments III: sharing knowledge; sharing roles

Although the Zen discussion is a wonderful example of the movement of classroom discourse toward the common construction of a new and newly shared frame of reference for the students, the authority over both the process and the knowledge it embodies still rests with the teacher. An exchange in an English as a Second Language classroom for older adolescents shows a subtle shift in the locus of authority in terms of who is the knower and who controls the discourse process itself, though the larger structure of the class is still shaped by the teacher. Florence Banks, who is studying to be an ESL teacher, has been observing the class of a friend who she thinks is particularly successful in eliciting student talk. Although the comments of these beginning ESL students are not extended in the ways that we've seen in the other classrooms, the students' participation in a rapidly moving conversation provides scaffolding for the understandings about participant structures in conversational discourse that are an important aspect of their mastery of spoken English.

Student 1 has just finished reading an essay he's written about the Tibetan New Year, and the teacher has asked if the other students would like to ask him any questions (immediately turning the responsibility for initiations over to the class as a whole). The students continue to expect responses from the teacher, who provides frequent backchanneling, but most of the additions to the referential knowledge that are found here are contributed by the students. The discussion goes on when a second student asks the first: "What kind of mahjong do you play in Tibet?"

STUDENT 1:   Some people, you know, they play, but, uh . . .
TEACHER: Uh huh.
STUDENT 1:   Some people, they play mahjong, you know . . .
TEACHER: Yuh.
STUDENT 1:   And . . . most people, they don't know mahjong how to play . . .
TEACHER: Most people don't . . . yuh.
STUDENT 1:   Some.
TEACHER: Yuh . . . Yuh . . . I remember my mother tried to teach me how to play and . . .

STUDENT 2:   Do you know how to play?

TEACHER: Well, it's too complicated!

STUDENT 2:   No, it's easy!

TEACHER: Well, I was young. [*Several students laugh*] . . . I don't know . . . maybe . . . maybe you guys can bring it in sometime and you can . . .

STUDENT 2:   O.K.! If you want, if you like to learn it.

TEACHER: Yuh. [*Several students laugh.*]

STUDENT 2:   It's my master.

TEACHER: [*Smiling*] You're good? That's your game, J _____ ?

STUDENT 2:   Yuh. [*Several students laugh.*]

TEACHER: You're the mahjong lady? All right! [*Students continue to laugh.*]

STUDENT 1:   Mahjong lady . . . [*laughs softly*].

STUDENT 2:   [*laughing*] Ahh.

While the second student's question takes up and extends a topic introduced by the first student in his essay, the extension of the framework of knowledge about the game of mahjong is not all that's going on here. The referential meanings contained in this excerpt focus on the game of mahjong, where it's played, whether it's hard to play, who's the expert, and on that subject, the teacher is not the expert. In fact, this lesson succeeds because she so nimbly portrays herself as a learner in the game of mahjong, willingly placing herself under the tutelage of the student with the greater expertise—the master, the mahjong lady. As Florence says:

> This segment reveals much about the teacher's philosophy and approach, which is evidenced throughout the two-hour lesson . . . she seems committed to the goal of empowering the students to take control over their own lives and to develop a strong sense of their own worth. She treats them as equals, with respect and dignity. . . . The teacher's speech pattern quickly and significantly affects the interpersonal relationships in the classroom when the teacher presents herself as the failed student and invites her successful students to become her teacher. Once she steps out of her role as teacher, the speech pattern of the discourse changes. It becomes a natural conversation, quick paced, with overlap, informal forms of address, and repartee. The students respond, appropriately, with laughter, indicating their understanding of the teacher's intentions. They appear to understand, perhaps in varying degrees, the implication that she accepts and treats them as equals, that she believes they all have something to offer, and that they all can learn from one another. . . . The teacher is not in *control* of the discussion during this segment. All contribute equally. Students self-select in taking turns. No one raises her hand or is called on. Student 2 is empowered to take the initiative, challenge the teacher, and participate in the role reversal.

The classroom discourse of this ESL classroom contrasts with the typical discourse of most second/foreign language classrooms, which like that of most other classrooms, is characterized by tightly controlled interactional sequences. And more than in other sorts of classrooms, these sequences are likely to be form-focused, rather than meaning-focused, in the ways most of us remember from our own foreign language instruction: "What is this? . . . A pencil . . . What are these? . . . Two pencils." The format of such exchanges isn't much different from teacher initiations recorded by Barnes in science classes (Teacher: What is the green stuff? Student: Water. Teacher: Chlorophyll.). Such a format calls for limited responses—the correct lexical term, and in the second language exchange, the correct form of the morpheme marking plurality.

Conversational negotiation can shape the comprehensible input and pro-ductive output that supports the acquisition of a new language (cf. Chapter Six), while the repetition of patterns without real concern for meaning offers no such opportunity. The discourse strategies that learners develop in ordinary conver-sational interactions, making repairs or reformulating statements or requesting clarifications, push them to extend their grammatical repertoire for the sake of communication. Research on second language classrooms suggests, then, that second language acquisition is fostered by classroom interaction that allows stu-dents to negotiate meanings, to use a range of interaction strategies, to nominate and control topics, to participate in different styles of discourse, and to partici-pate comfortably, so that the affective filter (Krashen's term for the response to stress that keeps us from taking in as much as we might of what's going on around us) is lowered (Ellis, 126–27). In other words, it is the sort of conversa-tion that we see with the mahjong excerpt that's likely to provide the most effective scaffolding for language learners, as well as the most effective support for all learners in developing their own authoritative discourse.

Classroom moments IV: sharing knowledge, roles, and reconceptualizations

One of the most effective ways to discover appropriate scaffolds for students' conceptual knowledge is to begin by discovering what students know, or better yet, to create contexts in which students themselves can discover and build on that knowledge. Conversations that build a common picture of learners' refer-ential knowledge of the world can go on at any level of education and can pro-vide a base for student-guided as well as teacher-guided reconceptualizations. In An Unquiet Pedagogy (1991), Hepsie Roskelly and I showed examples of how teachers worked to draw out from their students a base of shared knowledge about reading, writing, and language study that students together could reframe and reconceptualize. In The Discovery of Competence (1993), Suzy Groden, Viv-ian Zamel, and I showed how freshman writers, starting with their own studies of language in their home communities, could begin a process of conceptualiz-ing and reconceptualizing the nature of language and literacy in ways that could guide their own process of acquiring academic discourse. Even in the earliest years of school such sharing and discovery can go on, as for example in Karen's second grade classroom, where the study of Africa began with a student-generated list of "Things We Think We Know About Africa" along with a list of "Ways We Think We Can Find Out More About These Things," or in third grade where a book-writing project, directed toward having a published book, began with students going to the library and making their own list of the things such a book should have. Similarly, in *Ways with Words* (1983), Shirley Brice Heath describes an extended project in which fifth-grade science learners became ethnographers of applied science practices in their own communities. All of the questions about discourse raised in this book can be explored in a less technical fashion by students at any level, who can tape and transcribe conversations and look at who takes turns, for how long, and how the things said in these turns build in each other. They can interview their parents and neighbors about their own experiences as insiders and outsiders to speech communities, or observe the ways in which their parents and teachers tell them to do things.

Ironically, the fields in which authoritative knowers—researchers and scholars—are most likely to be involved themselves in investigation and exploration are the fields (including linguistics) in which knowledge is most often passed on to students in transmission/banking models. In the sciences, in particular, the learning of specialist terminology and algorithms, and the following of cookbook-like recipes for laboratory procedures and reports too often takes the place of the genuine inquiry on which the knowledge of the field is based. Jay Lemke, a physicist turned linguist, explores the discourse of science learning in great detail in *Talking Science (1990)*. Lemke looks at the ways in which meanings are created within a system of referential and propositional relationships (what he refers to as the semantics of science), but also at the ways in which social conflict, particularly between powerful, authoritative teachers and challenging students, is represented within the argument structure of classroom exchanges. He points out that the way to learn the language of science is by talking science: "Just as with learning any foreign language, fluency in science requires practice at speaking, not just listening" (24).

Efforts to reform science education, like other areas of educational reform, have focused in part on changing the participant structures and authority relations of classroom discourse. Where students have an opportunity to explore and test out their conceptual understandings with other students, for example, they have much more opportunity to try out the talk of science and to build coherent systems of relationships through their own reasoning, than they do as silent partners in the typical science classroom like the ones Barnes observed. Look at this exchange between two college physics students—a male and a female—recorded in a laboratory setting (that of my husband, Ron Thornton) where, instead of following a prescribed set of instructions, they have been experimenting with their own physical movements in front of a motion detector, connected to a computer that graphs their velocity and acceleration:

MALE STUDENT: I think that what we could tell from the graphs is that they were a lot steeper. It's a nice straight line, too . . . Look at that.
FEMALE STUDENT: Right.

MALE: No . . . No . . . No . . . it's a straight line. You can't be accelerating in
a constant acceleration.

FEMALE: No. Because if you're accel . . . Your velocity is constant so you're
not accelerating. When you have a line like this . . . you're going 55 mph
down the highway.

MALE: Acceleration means your velocity is chang . . . is getting faster.

FEMALE: Right.

MALE: But a straight line means your velocity is not changing at all.

FEMALE: Right.

MALE: So you have no acceleration.

FEMALE: Right. That's what I'm saying.

MALE: So it's not a constant acceleration. A constant acceleration could be like
5 all the time. Not necessarily 0 . . . And that's constant . . . right?

FEMALE: Right. The acceleration is 0.

MALE: Right. OK.

FEMALE: When the line is like that . . . the velocity is like 55 mph.

MALE: All right. I agree with you . . . I think we're saying the same thing.

FEMALE: I think we are too.

The students here are engaged in open-ended reasoning, without the presence
of an authority figure to shape the outcome prematurely. The activity they're
involved in depends on both referential and proposition knowledge: understanding the relationship between the referent (the graph) and the physical
world (their own movements) and being able to reason from one proposition to
another within a particular framework. The female student in this case seems to
understand pretty clearly throughout this exchange that the straight horizontal
line they've created on the graph through their movements indicates that there
is no acceleration (something that the videotape of their movements confirms).
But their familiar physical movements have been thrown into a new frame of
reference by an unfamiliar system of representation, and the male student,
although he keeps restating the key proposition, seems not to believe it. Here
the tools act as a scaffold, in much the way a teacher's language might, representing the evidence that can't be explained away, until the student finally
works his way through a series of propositions to full (but grudging) recognition
of the concept that the line on the graph represents constant velocity with no
acceleration. But his utterances also occur within a social context and carry
interpersonal meaning as well. So his final statement, "I think we're saying the
same thing," covers up his slower process of his coming to an understanding,
and recasts the differences in this exchange with his female partner as a problem
of communication versus comprehension.

    The work in classes like these takes place within a larger framework of
course, and institutional structures, and each class is, in effect, a small piece of
an extended conversation. In the book *Conversations on the Written Word* (1990),
Jay Robinson explores, with the classroom teacher, Patricia Stock, the conversation of a composition class. Following the work of Goffman (1981), who has

analyzed interactional units in terms of their referencings (what they pick out and point to in their contexts), as well as by the intentions of the participants, Robinson and Stock suggest that education can be described as a "sustained strip of referencings." Speakers don't step into preexistent discourse contexts; rather, these contexts are "constituted through the verbal exchanges that community members engage in" (183).

Robinson and Stock are particularly interested in looking at the relationships among the many contexts or prior texts these referencings draw together in the classroom: the students' prior texts of memories, general experiences, and knowledge gained from earlier studies, their expectations based on earlier encounters with similar institutional contexts, and the teacher's prior texts as well. The class itself, as a particular context, is also situated in a set of prior related contexts—the course, the curriculum, the institution, the discipline, the general framework of education across levels. Referencing brings all of the teacher's and students' prior texts about these contexts into the classroom to create a new emergent text—one that is constructed by the participants and comes to represent increasingly shared knowledge—while these prior texts, in turn, help to shape what learners make of the common course text.

Robinson and Stock identify a series of "language learning actions: actions in language that function referentially either to draw upon preexistent contexts or to fashion verbal structures that will come into being as context," naming six of them. The first three: *recollection* (recreating prior texts in the present context); *allusion* (referring to prior texts that are assumed to be common and don't need to be fully recreated); and *exposition* (offering information and explanations that might contribute to common knowledge)—call up prior texts and bring content from those texts into the present. Three other actions *exploration* (seeking areas of common knowledge and interpretation/common ground); *enactment* (showing or imagining a process or event, usually by the teacher); and *reenactment* (the same, usually by the student) build toward future texts.

We can see the sort of referencing that Robinson and Stock describe in the classroom excerpts we have looked at in this chapter. The student who read his essay about the Tibetan New Year to his ESL class has brought prior contexts into the present, offering exposition about a set of cultural events and practices (in particular the playing of mahjong), which are then recalled and alluded to in the segment we've seen. Referencings to the prior texts of different students and the teacher—including the prior knowledge that there's more than one style of mahjong and the possibility that the kind of mahjong played in Tibet might not be the kind other students know—are brought into the present, and their meanings are explored in a new emergent text that the class produces together, trying to arrive at a common understanding. Similarly, when the suburban high school class discusses the notion of hierarchy, there are multiple referencings to prior texts, not so much recollected from students' personal experiences as alluded to and assumed to be shared (by the students) or shaped through exposition (as in the teacher's contribution on the relationship of faith to hierarchy in the Judeo-Christian tradition). At the same time, much of the talk in the high school class

is exploratory, with students raising and testing possibilities for common understanding, and exemplifying them by creating illustrative moments in the present:
"The president, he like, he doesn't come in your house and fix your plumbing."
And again, in the Zen discussion, prior knowledge of Zen gardens, and
specifically of one such garden at the Museum of Fine Arts, is evoked through
allusion (with the assumption that once the museum is named, others in the class
will remember the garden there and it will become commonly shared knowledge
within the emergent text of the class). And with "Almost a koan," the teacher's
reference to a prior shared text (the assigned reading) becomes an enactment of
the concept in the immediate classroom context. The physics students, on the
other hand, have engaged in a physical enactment that provides an experiential
prior text, to which they try, through non-directed exploratory talk, to match a
present set of terms and a graphical representation.

    Prior texts also include differences in cultural experience of the sort we
explored in the last chapter, differences that teachers as well as students bring to
the classroom. In reflecting on what she has observed in the discourse of her
writing classroom, Elaine comments on her own upbringing:

> Reading "Language in Context: Home and School" [Chapter 3 of *An Unquiet
> Pedagogy*] prompted a deeper evaluation of my past and present roles as teacher
> and student and led me back to . . . Shirley Brice Heath's work which talked
> about how differing families and communities teach language use to their chil-
> dren. I was able to see my childhood education explicitly detailed in the
> account of the community of Roadville where storytelling was considered a
> lie and a sin, where children were given rigid rules for right and wrong behav-
> ior modeled after Bible stories, and where parents "bring up" their children
> allowing them few opportunities to think for themselves.

Elaine sees her background as the source of the patterns she observes in her own
classroom—her inclination toward an IRE pattern in which she controls student initiations and evaluates student responses—and she observes, from an earlier study of her conversations with her own children:

> At home I had managed to break the chain of undaunted authority in the rais-
> ing of my children by giving them opportunities to think for themselves and
> explore ideas other than my own. In the classroom, however, I was more
> inclined to practice authority and in some ways resisted the practice of a dia-
> lectical classroom even though I claimed to be teaching one. . . . The old man-
> ner of Roadville instruction was still hanging in there even after much time of
> attempting to relearn and reteach my old ways of thinking about teaching and
> learning. But teaching and learning are ongoing processes, with many oppor-
> tunities for us to relearn and reteach by observing and researching ourselves as
> teachers and as human beings in a social world . . . and I look forward to
> growing with the process.

The discourse of the classroom, then, is continually shaped and reshaped, for
students and teacher alike, in relation to multiple prior texts and contexts,

present purposes, and the ongoing, emerging classroom text. As a speech community, the class cannot be walled off from the multiple other communities that students and teachers participate in, to focus on content that is unmarked by those prior texts. Rather, it is a place for conversation that draws on a constant negotiation of meaning around and through these worlds.

CHAPTER 10

Acquiring Literacy

Learners who grow up in the different speech communities of the Piedmonts, Hawaii, the Warm Springs Reservation, or Boston come into classroom discourse communities where they must negotiate across cultural styles and find a common language that can accommodate multiple intentions and purposes. In the process, they acquire the use of a written mode of discourse, and with it increasing fluency in a common literate style (involving a standard code, a style appropriate to writing for distant audiences, and allusion to an broad range of generally shared cultural knowledge). As we saw in the last chapter, at least one of the purposes of discourse in educational contexts is to provide a scaffold for literate-style discourse itself—to help students acquire not only new modes of language use (reading and writing), but also the literate styles of language use that are common to written texts and the understandings about written language that will support their ongoing development as readers and writers.

In a literate society, of course, literacy learning begins implicitly long before school. But because it is a major explicit purpose of schooling, early reading and writing in school (or in school-like contexts, as when your uncle sat down with you and taught you to read the newspaper by sounding out letters) becomes most salient. School is where most people think literacy begins, and the teaching of reading is something everyone has an opinion about.

It's not surprising then, that the crisis in Westfield that introduced our exploration of language in this book, a crisis over moving a bilingual teacher into a regular classroom, erupted specifically over the fact that it was to be a first-grade classroom. Parents feared that their children would not learn to read if their teacher had an accent, and the mayor and others voiced similar concerns. In a society where literacy is essential and illiteracy is constantly being discovered and decried, the parents did not want to risk their children's success. Because we think that learning to read and write is something that only happens at school, parents (and I include myself here) feel largely powerless to ensure their young children's competence as readers, and yet they want desperately to do so. The discourse perspective represented in this book has helped me as a parent to reframe my own concerns, to make sense, in particular, of the relationship between the school experiences of my own two children and the literacy they were acquiring, and it's that reframing that provides the central thread for this chapter.

Learning to read and write

Here's Karen, at nine, talking to students in one of my classes about her early school literacy:

STUDENT: Do you remember when you learned how to read?

KAREN: [*to me*] When did I learn how to read? I have no idea when I learned how to read. Did I know how to read in kindergarten?

MOTHER: First grade, really, was when I think you learned how to read.

KAREN: Oh yeah. We'd have those things that show yellow . . . We'd have a picture of like . . . yellow . . . and then you'd look at the word yellow . . . and then you'd match it . . . and there's red . . . and you'd match them if they were like . . . the right word to go with it . . .

STUDENT: And how did you learn to write?

KAREN: Well . . . we drew a picture and then . . . well . . . in first . . . like in first grade . . . the teacher writes in her own writing . . . like what you tell her to write . . . and then you have to write over it. . . . Or sometimes . . . I remember this. . . . She writes it down . . . and she tells you what she wrote and you draw a picture. See what they do . . . they just write it in pencil . . . what you want. . . . You tell them, and they always make you do it over in crayon. . . . But then they only do it for you sometimes . . . when you get tired or they're trying to show you a new letter . . . And then . . . I guess in second grade . . . we started to write our own . . . And they just gave us . . . like . . . a lot of times we could just choose what you wanted to do . . . but sometimes they gave us a topic. . . . And we wrote a lot of picture story books. . . . And then at the end . . . the teacher or like . . . you . . . would read them out loud and show your pictures and everything.

Karen doesn't really remember when she learned to read, or how. None of my students can remember when they learned either, but they hope she will, since at nine she's much closer to the event. What she remembers, when she tries, is a classroom activity typically associated with reading instruction—a worksheet that called for matching words and pictures—but she's pretty uncertain about the significance of that activity, and her voice falls off as she waits for a new, easier question. When asked a little while later how she learned to write, though, she has no uncertainty and leaps right in with a description of the extended process she remembers, one that moved through several stages: first, drawing a picture, telling the teacher what she wanted to write about it, having the teacher write down her words, and writing over the teacher's writing; then writing her own words, with the teacher's help only when she got tired or didn't know how to write something, and adding the pictures; and finally writing her own picture story books.

If Karen can't remember learning to read, that is not surprising. Reading an alphabetic orthography, with graphemes that represent, though somewhat imperfectly, the phonemes (or meaningful sound distinctions) of a language, draws on the reader's unconscious, intuitive understanding of the sound structure of the language. Since phonemes never appear in isolation, only in larger morphemic units such as words, there's little reason to have any conscious awareness of them prior to using them to encode and decode the spoken language in a written form, where suddenly this smallest unit of linguistic structure becomes the salient unit for representing the flow of sound in discrete symbols on the page. How beginning readers actually gain this particular awareness is somewhat of a mystery, even to psycholinguists who study the reading process. But we do know that the reader brings many kinds of knowledge to this enterprise, and that there are multiple scaffolds to support this learning. In whole language oriented classrooms like the one Karen was in, the process of learning to read is further supported by the reciprocal process of learning to write.

Theories of literacy

What goes on in primary school classrooms like those Karen was in (and in adult literacy settings as well) is shaped implicitly or explicitly by competing theories of what literacy is and how it is acquired. At one extreme is a position that defines reading as a skill that is separate from other uses of language, largely separate even from writing, and isolated from the particular purposes for which reading might be used. Brian Street (1984), in analyzing how different theories of literacy have shaped the way it has been seen in studies carried out around the world, uses the term *autonomous* for this model. Where literacy is seen as an autonomous skill—something that's essentially the same in any context and that can be learned in the same way in every context—classroom instruction is likely to focus on the subcomponents of that skill, particularly on sound/letter correspondences, on the relationship between phonemes and graphemes that's highlighted in the central place given to the study of *phonics* in traditional reading instruction. Classroom activities will typically move in a linear fashion from sounds, to words, to sentences, with many exercises that focus attention on each subskill (like worksheets that call for matching a picture of an object, pig, with the letter that the name of the object begins with, p). They'll often depend on unnaturally simplified texts designed to introduce new skills in sequence, like the many series of basal readers that have been so profitable for publishers. And learning to read will be seen as a separate activity from reading to learn, with early schooling focusing on the first activity before the second can be introduced at about the fourth grade. Karen's teachers were influenced by the autonomous theory of literacy; it's the one that has dominated the preparation of primary school teachers. So she spent time filling out the worksheets she associates with learning to read, reciting the alphabet, and practicing making the sound of the letter *p*. But the teaching of reading in her primary classrooms was being reshaped in relationship to a different model of what literacy is and how it is acquired, rather than learned.

Recently, literacy has begun to be seen, not as an autonomous skill but as an aspect of discourse. In this view, reading and writing are continuous with and imbedded in all other uses of language, and they're shaped by the social contexts in which they are used and the purposes for which they are used. (Street names this model of literacy "ideological" but I prefer to describe it as *situated* to emphasize its strong emphasis on context.) What does it mean for parents and teachers to approach issues of literacy from a discourse perspective? It means that they will see reading and writing as an extension of other uses of language, as something children will acquire through their participation in a literate discourse community where reading and writing contribute in integral ways to the ongoing process of making sense of the world and acting on it. It means that they will see reading and writing, not as discrete skills made up of discrete subskills, but as continuous with all the rest of a child's grammatical and communicative competence. It means that they will seeing reading and writing as social acts, shaped by children's intentions and purposes and by the contexts in which these are realized. And it means that they will be aware of a constant interplay between evolving texts and the evolving meanings and intentions of the readers and writers of those texts.

In reshaping their classrooms, Karen's teachers had their students writing as well as reading and using both for a variety of purposes that were part of the life of the classroom community: writing to record observations about the eggs they were incubating or the seeds they were germinating, to keep track of tasks they were assigned to do, or to prepare cards for classmates who were sick, and reading those notes and cards and stories they wrote, along with favorite books, to their classmates. School literacy, for these children, was situated in their ongoing classroom learning, contributing to it, rather than existing as an isolated subject to be learned separately.

Classrooms like the ones Karen was in typically draw on a mixture of practices—both those historically associated with the teaching of reading and imbedded in the school culture and those that have emerged from more recent understandings about literacy. But in most classrooms, one model predominates. A preponderance of time in early grades may be given to skill-based activities that focus on decoding words (including a strong and discrete emphasis on phonics). More time may be given, on the other hand, to writing as well as reading, to the shared and cooperative reading and writing of whole, unreduced texts like examples of children's literature, to drawing on reading and writing as a way to learn about the world, and to discovering and building on the knowledge about literacy that children bring to the classroom from other contexts. Although the latter approach may be linked to names like whole language or writing to read, such labels do not adequately represent the instructional emphasis of individual classrooms. The current debate about instructional practice in teaching reading overstates the opposition between approaches based on phonics and those based on whole language methods. However, all children, in learning to read, must come to understand the nature of the alphabetic representation of language as well as the functions and uses of the written code, and most classrooms that place reading and writing in the contexts for which they are used attend to children's understanding of grapho-phonemic relationships as well. It is only through observing actual classes, seeing what children are doing in them and what they're making of what they do, that we begin to see how literacy is supported in them—to see whether learning to read is treated only as a discrete and isolated activity, or whether it becomes part of the ongoing conversation of the classroom.

While my students and I observe a variety of classroom settings, we also observe children we know. Many of my students are themselves parents or aunts and uncles, and most of us know children we can follow as they move through a variety of literacy contexts, homes and churches as well as classrooms, turning on the tape recorder while the children read and while we talk with them about their reading and writing, collecting the many examples of their writing on pictures and birthday cards and shopping lists as well as for school tasks. From such observations we begin to develop a richly contextualized picture of the literacies children are acquiring and their processes of acquiring them. One advantage of studying together the experience of the learners we know is that we are most likely to begin with the assumption that they are competent language users, that their readings of texts and the texts they write are meaningful, and that they hold sensible assumptions about the purposes of their reading and writing and how to accomplish those purposes. We're involved then not just in observing such learners but in drawing on their conceptualizations of their own literacy experiences to aid our own understandings.

As a teacher of teachers, I have seen many classrooms, many school literacy settings, at all levels of schooling. I also have observed adult learners in non-school settings involved in the same enterprise. But it is as a parent that I have worked hardest to make the most sense of these positions and the pedagogies they imply, trying to figure out how best to support my own children's acquisition of literacy in relationship to whatever was or was not happening in their classrooms. And because I have two children who have had fundamentally the same home literacy practices, but quite different school experiences, I will draw in this chapter on what I've learned from them, as well as what I've learned from my students and their children or the children in their classrooms, as I explore in a contextualized and situated way, the abstract positions that are represented in today's literacy debate. In particular, because over the past ten years when I've been most interested in these issues the informant who has been closest at hand has been my daughter, Karen, my extended study of a learner later in this chapter will focus on her texts, her experiences, and her perspective.

Early literacy

Before we can decide how best to support children's acquisition of literacy in school settings, we need to know a great deal more about the kinds of knowledge and competence they bring to those settings. That competence, like all language, has both a psychological and a social aspect. We know for example, from psycholinguistic studies of children's language, that children by the age of five have acquired most of the grammatical competence of adult speakers of their native language, but we know that they've also acquired a great deal of communicative competence in using that language in the ways in which it's used by speakers in their immediate community. We can anticipate, then, that their reading and writing will be supported by their knowledge of both syntactic structures and larger information and discourse structures.

We've also seen that children acquire both their grammatical competence and their communicative competence over time, unconsciously, through participation in meaningful interactions with the people around them, and that those who are acquiring a second language, dialect, or any new variety of a language do so through an analogous process, developing approximative systems that are then further refined, focusing first on meaning, rather than on surface features, and discovering the appropriateness of what they've generated for particular contexts and purposes. And we can anticipate that, for beginning readers and writers, at least part of the process of acquiring a new (written) mode of discourse will be similar, particularly as it involves acquiring a new style of discourse as well—a literate style whose features have developed in response to the typical communicative purposes of written texts. As language users, they too are likely to focus on meaning, and to apply what they already know systematically, gradually refining their hypotheses about how written language works as they perceive the appropriateness of their choices for particular contexts and purposes. We'll see, for example, that young Karen, as a preschool writer, had changing theories about how she could use the letters she knew how to form—at first, the letters of her name—to create different texts for different purposes. And like first-and second-language learners, children typically receive scaffolding in this process from those around them—parents or older siblings or teachers.

In homes and communities where they hear lot of oral reading, young children may also acquire a literate style discourse that's connected with the sorts of texts they hear read. Children's books, in particular, have a strong influence on what children see as the language of written texts, something that showed up strikingly in the research of Ron and Suzanne Scollon (1981). While undertaking a study of the language and literacy practices of the Athabaskans in Alaska, the Scollons continued their research into children's language development, focusing particularly on their own two-year-old daughter, Rachel. Although she was far from school age, Rachel was believed by the Athabaskan children to be attending school, because of the ways she used language—in responding to questions and telling stories in much of her talk. She paid a lot of attention to books, "wrote" stories, and "read" them back in a reading prosody—using the patterns of intonation that characterize the oral reading of text rather than oral storytelling. While she often appeared as a character in her stories, she always did so in the third person: "There was a girl named Rachel and there was a boy named Tommy and they went for a walk," a strategy the Scollons described as a "fictionalization of self," distancing the writer from the characters. The writer who can accomplish such fictionalization must be conscious, in some sense, of the multiple roles of author, audience, and character, and must be able to imagine the self in each of them. Rachel, by the age of two, had learned to take on each of these roles in her literate productions, because the literacy practiced by her family through the stories they read to her encouraged her to do so. But she acquired the style of language appropriate to this task because of her underlying grammatical competence and her propensity to acquire the language she heard. (Children who hear a lot of oral storytelling also have a rich foundation for the language and stances of literature, as writers like Leslie Marmon Silko or Any Tan will attest.)

Reading and writing are, to a great degree, social acts, used for particular communicative purposes in particular contexts. In the Roadville community studied by Heath, for example, most adult literacy practices are church-related, centering on reading and reciting the words of the Bible, though other frequent literacy activities include selecting greeting cards and adding brief notes, or using a written text like a recipe or a set of instructions for assembling a toy to confirm an understanding of how to do something. For Trackton adults, reading is more likely to be an informal social activity, where a letter or a news article is shared and its meaning debated with others in the community. Adults also use brief written texts to elaborate and expand on together in church prayer. Most tasks demanding writing, like filling out forms, are also likely to be done socially and collaboratively. Roadville and Trackton children, like those in any literate environment, begin to develop a sense of what literacy is and how it's used by others around them long before they actually learn to read in a conscious way. By the time they get to school, most children have observed a variety of literacy practices and have seen literacy used for a number of different functions, though these vary by community.

Adult literacy practices are often reflected in children's play and in their earliest awareness of reading and writing. For the daughter of friends who live on a farm in rural Maine, the arrival of the mailman marked the most significant literacy event of the day, and whenever we visited she would want to spend hours with Karen, writing notes, placing them in a drawer that served as the mailbox, and having the other person retrieve them and read them. Karen, whose parents were terrible correspondents in a household where everyone was always working on a task for school, was much more likely to play at doing homework or to sneak off with the Dungeons and Dragons books her older brother and his friends spent so much time with, turning the pages and mimicking his lists of characters and powers. Denny Taylor and Catherine Dorsey-Gaines (1988) in their study of the literate lives and home literacy practices of inner-city families (some of whom were in fact homeless) found that they too used literacy for a variety of functions, that these were reflected in literacy activities (like making greeting cards), and that the parents were helping to create a literate environment for the children. Taylor has also been helping parents and teachers to see how the many instances of children's literacy-related productions—their drawings and notes and scraps of writing, along with observations of how they use these productions, can be used to create a "biographic literacy profile" that offers a rich portrait of a child's literacy as it evolves across multiple settings, not only in the classroom (1990).

While reading and writing draw on the grammatical and communicative competence that we use in acquiring any new discourse, and on an understanding of the social uses of literacy for different purposes and in different communities, they ultimately depend on certain kinds of knowledge about a written versus a spoken mode of discourse. Readers and writers must understand, first, that written language is meaningful. They need to understand the specific function of print in particular social acts, for different purposes—storyreading, labeling (as on cereal boxes), giving directions (as on exit or highway signs), communicating with someone who's not present (as in notes and letters). And they need to discover the nature of the orthographic system—its general features (beginning, for English, with the fact that it works, on the page, from top to bottom and from left to right), and what it represents (phonemes in English, syllables in Hebrew or Arabic). Most young children gain a great deal of knowledge about print as it's used in the world around them (sometimes referred to as environmental literacy). They know what print looks like, that it encodes and represents words (as on signs), that it carries meaning. They know that people read to recover meaning from print, and that they write to record meaning in that mode. And they've typically begun to experiment with the orthographic system. Because children come to school with a wide range of understandings about both the function of print and the ways that the written code works, over the last twenty years attention has been increasingly focused on these understandings (as well as on the contextual literacy practices that children learn before they begin school), on what has become known as children's "emergent literacy." The concept of emergent literacy focuses on the psycholinguistic study of literacy as an aspect of language that's gradually acquired through immersion in a literate environment versus a particular skill that is learned at a particular moment in response to instruction in a reading classroom. Across many countries, languages, and cultures, researchers like Marie Clay (1994) in New Zealand, who designed the Reading Recovery Program that's been particularly successful in U.S. inner-city schools, William Teale and Elizabeth Sulzby (1986) in the United States, Emilia Ferreiro and Ana Teberosky (1985) in Mexico, and Clotilde Pontecorvo (1995) in Italy have looked at the reading-and-writing-like activities of young children to discover what they know about encoding language in a written form and interacting with that written code. The children they've studied all typically begin to write by scribbling and/or drawing, then using actual letters in nonphonetic strings, and finally inventing spellings for the words they intend, gradually approximating conventional spelling and word spacing (with quite a few variations in the orthographic systems they create along the way). By the end of first grade or its equivalent, all of these children can produce some connected text that's readable by an adult. If they've heard adults reading, they begin to read from a young age as well, drawing from a text (either their own, even if scribbled, or perhaps a storybook) and using a distinctive reading prosody that's like what they've heard, the way the Scollons' daughter Rachel did. There's a pattern of development here as well, from the child looking at pictures (if they're available) to attending to print as the source of the reading, and sometimes refusing to try to read any more at the moment when they seem to realize that the print represents words in a way that they haven't quite caught on to yet.

In literate contexts, most children develop the concept of using writing to represent speech, along with the idea that the sound stream of speech can be broken into distinct words, early on. (The Trackton children who did not have storybooks at home were nevertheless exposed to environmental print and were able to identify the names on cereal boxes and the words on traffic signs, even though they might not actually have been able to decode them yet). But children, most typically, come to read and write conventionally (to decode the meaning of a written word working from its grapho-phonemic representation and to work phonemically/phonetically to encode words) when they are of school age, and the process seems to be a gradual one, though there's often an *aha* moment when children suddenly recognize that they've mastered this process.

The acquisition of literacy doesn't take place in linear steps or strict developmental stages: movement in one direction may be abandoned for attempts in another. As with the acquisition of any language or discourse, the process involves building creatively on what's known, forming and testing different hypotheses, but proceeding systematically to develop a rule-governed system that comes to approximate, more and more closely, conventional written language. Emergent readers gradually become readers in the conventional sense, in that they can accurately perceive each word of a text and can render those words meaningful. Emergent writers, likewise, become writers in a conventional sense when they can use writing to represent spoken language in a way that allows them and other readers to recover the words of the text, to read back what's been written.

Jerome Harste, Virginia Woodward, and Carolyn Burke, in *Language Stories and Literary Lessons* (1984), offer a model for the study of children's literacy that depends upon these understandings, though they critique the notion of emergent reading because they see it as suggesting that the processes of young children are psycholinguistically different from those used by proficient readers and writers, arguing instead for a continuum of psycholinguistic and sociolinguistic activity. Harste and his colleagues have studied the ways in which children organize texts, what their intentions and purposes are in creating texts, how they use writing in the generation of new meaning, the ways that they take risks and invent new possibilities, and how they use contexts as well as texts themselves to support their meaning-making. They've shown not only the extent to which reading and writing are psycholinguistic processes continuous with the child's other acquisition of language, but how for the child "each instance of written language [is] the orchestration of a complex social event" (11).

Literacy and discourse functions

If written language is continuous with spoken language and imbedded in social contexts and purposes, we can also approach the social event of reading or writing from the perspective of the discourse functions we've been studying throughout this book. This perspective helps us see that the fully realized literacy that young learners are in the process of acquiring must also be understood in terms of complex acts of meaning-making, not as the application of discrete skills that can be isolated from these functions.

The propositional/referential function

Written words might be seen as carrying meaning potential more than a meaning. The work of readers is not only to go from the written representation of words to their representation in the sound stream, but to recover the potential meaning of those words—their referential meanings and the propositions that they put forth, while the work of writers is the inverse. The focus of reading for fluent readers is on the propositions represented in the text, not on the surface grammatical structure, and certainly not on relationships between graphemes and phonemes, though understanding that relationship plays a significant role in our processing of words that are unfamiliar. However, reading does not depend on the phonetic representation of words as spoken, since speakers of different dialects have no trouble perceiving the relationship between a conventionally spelled word and their own pronunciation, or phonetic realization, of that word. Children in Boston may read the printed word car as *ca* or idea as *idear,* and there's no advantage to starting learners off with reading texts that offer a phonetic approximation of any particular dialect, including Black English. And so the accent of a bilingual teacher would not have affected the Westfield children's reading. It might prepare them to understand people who speak varieties of English that are different from their own, but it would not affect their overall comprehension or production of phonemes and therefore not their learning the graphemic representation of those phonemes.

Neither readers nor writers are, at first, principally concerned with the surface realizations of the propositions of texts in particular words or grammatical structures. Readers will depart from the text, making miscues (substitutions of other words for the ones in the text) that make sense in terms of the underlying meaning or propositions the text has been representing, and that make sense in terms of their understanding of the world. They might say "The bird flew out of the field" for "The ball flew out of the field." But they're unlikely to say "The brick flew out of the field." They'll use their syntactic knowledge to confirm the sense of what they're reading, making miscues or substitutions within syntactic categories—a noun for a noun and a verb for a verb, so that the grammar of a meaningful proposition is maintained. Karen, for example, in first grade, produced a series of picture storybooks. In each of her stories, a main character is described in terms of several propositions, representing, for example, the concepts Bear + once + happy. But in the earlier books she realized these propositions in a surface structure with two main clauses (Once there was a bear. He was happy), whereas shortly afterward she began to embed all of the propositional information within a main clause, using relative clauses (Once there was a bear that was happy, or Once there was a elf who wanted to go to the beach). In reading back the sentences with the relative clauses, though, she would sometimes go back to her earlier syntactic structure. (Once there was a elf. He wanted to go to the beach.) She maintained the same propositional content, but apparently the relative clause was easier to produce than to read back consistently for a little while.

Readers' miscues, like writers' errors, suggest their underlying hypotheses and the ways in which both readers and writers work systematically in their comprehension as well as their production of texts. Yetta and Paul Goodman's studies of readers' miscues (1977) suggest that fluent readers use the text to confirm their predictions about what will come next—their hypotheses about the underlying propositions this text is putting forth. The many readers they've studied, at different grade levels and with different reading experiences, all work toward meaning: toward constructing a version of the text that makes sense, both in terms of the rest of the text itself, and in terms of the world. Where they speak a dialect that has different surface grammatical features from the standard English of the written text, a dialect like Black English that does not use particular inflectional endings such as past tense markers (*talk* for *talked*) or the third person singular verb marker (*work* for *works*), they're most likely to translate the surface structure of the written text into their own dialect's representation of that meaning, a further sign that they're not simply moving from letters to sounds but interpreting what they see in terms of their own sense of how language works.

Constance Weaver, in *Grammar for Teachers* (1979), cites evidence that it's the best readers who produce the most dialect-based miscues. She argues that readers use both the syntactic and the semantic context provided by the text to make sense of what they read: good readers tend "to predict what's coming next, to make miscues that preserve grammar and meaning and leave these uncorrected, and to correct those few miscues that don't fit in context" (43). She shows how both semantic and syntactic context shapes our interpretation of a word. In interpreting a word in a written text, we depend on both the semantic context that precedes a word and that which follows it. We can't be sure of the meaning of "There were some *tears* . . . " until we get to the rest of the sentence and learn whether there were "tears in his eyes" or "tears in her dress." We can't read meaningfully by decoding one word at a time, but must rely on the full discourse context. Readers' processing of text also shows that they attend to the syntactic context: it's most unlikely that a reader would confuse the action "She *tears* her dress" with the existence of "*tears* in her eyes" because of the syntactic structure that demands a verb in the first instance and a noun in

the second. Readers also simplify the syntactic relationships between propositions, as Karen did, while maintaining the propositions themselves. This suggests that readers are looking for whole propositions, ones that are both semantically consistent and grammatically appropriate, rather than simply proceeding
word by word through the text.

Writers too tend to focus on the propositional meanings of the texts they
create, even before they can realize these in complex syntactic structures. Just
before Karen began to write texts that she could decode, she "read" from her
own texts and from other storybooks using the relative clauses that she associated with written language. But while she was working on systematically
encoding and decoding meanings with grapho-phonemic symbols, she moved
back to a simpler surface structure for a time.

The pragmatic/interpersonal function

Readers interpret texts in relationship to what they know of the context and the
purposes of such texts/or the writers of such texts. Harste et al., begin their
account of ways to study children's literacy in *Language Stories and Literacy Lessons* (1984) with a vignette that illustrates the effect of context on the interpretation of meaning (though for a listener versus a reader). In this instance, a pas-
tor as part of a children's sermon, asks the following:

> Children, I'm thinking of something that is about five or six inches high; that
> scampers across the ground, that can climb trees; that lives in either a nest in
> the tree or makes its home in a hollowed-out portion of a tree's trunk. The
> thing I'm thinking about gathers nuts and stores them in winter; it is some-
> times brown and sometimes gray; it has a big bushy tail. Who can tell me what
> I'm thinking of?

And a child responds:

> Ordinarily I'd think it was a squirrel, but I suppose you want me to say it was
> Jesus. (xv)

Harste and his colleagues use this vignette to show how language users, whether
readers or listeners, writers or speakers, adjust their language use to meet the
demands of the setting they're in. Readers guess words they're not sure of by
making the sorts of assumptions about what's appropriate to the context and
purpose that this child makes, by what they think the writer's intention might
be. Writers choose their words and use forms and styles that are appropriate to
their contexts and purposes as well, choices that represent their intentions, their
stance toward the propositional knowledge they're representing, their assumptions about the other participants in this act (the readers), about what they know
and what they'll respond to, and about how to create the effect they'd like on
their audience. As we'll see, Karen, as a writer, began with a fairly limited set of
strategies for signaling to the reader (offering a contextualization cue) that what

she was writing was a story: "Once upon a time . . . ," "Once there was . . . " (She also used these forms when fictionalizing the events of her own life: Once there was a girl . . .) But over time she experimented with many different ways of beginning stories.

The textual function

Like speakers and listeners, readers and writers must also attend to the evolving text in shaping meaning. For readers, this involves an interaction (or a transaction as Harste or reading theorists like Louise Rosenblatt [1978] would say) between the words on the page and their predictions, assumptions, prior knowledge—the evolving text in their heads. They keep revising their hypotheses about that text as they read. For writers, it typically means a movement back and forth in perspectives, between that of writer and that of reader, to see whether the meaning of the evolving text as they imagine it might actual emerge that way from a reader's perspective. In a written mode, the textual function is further affected by the orthographic system, the ways of using a particular written code, and by larger presentational formats, like books with chapters. Using capital letters and quotation marks for emphasis is one way in which Karen begins, early on to use the orthographic system to create meaning in her evolving text.

Competence in managing these three functions of discourse in a literate mode, in particular literate discourse contexts, is achieved principally through the use of that mode in such contexts, through actual reading and writing, not through completing exercise sheets, and such competence is acquired gradually, systematically, and yet creatively, as we will see. Just as speakers cannot acquire a first or second language apart from its styles and meanings in actual use, readers and writers can't learn to process and produce language in a written mode as only a technical process, without particular content, style and structures—without signaling a set of meanings and values. Even the most decontextualized school instruction (that most tries to remove the technical skill from any context, so that it's reduced to isolated exercises) carries implicit meaning about what literacy is, about what's valued in this context. And this point brings us back to the looking again at the impact of competing models of literacy as they are played out in the classrooms that young learners inhabit.

School literacy

Few classrooms are pure examples of one approach to literacy, but many are informed explicitly or implicitly by the assumptions associated with the view of literacy as autonomous: that reading is a skill to be taught through focusing on decoding as a narrowly defined activity; that "reading to learn" is something only possible after about fourth grade, when skills are in place; and that writing instruction is secondary and should focus first on isolated skills like spelling and punctuation, rather than on the production of extended and meaningful text. Let me give you three examples:

Example one

I'm visiting a first grade classroom in a Boston school that's reputed to have the worst students in the system, the school with the highest rate of grade retention (where the most children have failed and been kept back a grade). The regular classroom teacher offers a model reading lesson while the student teacher (my student) observes. The teacher stands at the board where she has written out the letter *p* and makes the *p* sound, which the children repeat. She then asks them to give her words that begin with the letter *p*. Many children raise their hands, including one boy in the back row (where I happen to be sitting, and which I learn later is reserved for repeaters), who waves his hand wildly but is never called on. Finally, he settles down in his seat and pulls out the book he's gotten in the library earlier, whispering *puh, puh* under his breath, following the lines of text with his finger until he finds a *p* word, and trying to read out the sentence, slowly and laboriously. At this point, the teacher finally notices him and tells him to put away his book and pay attention to the lesson or he'll never learn to read and will have to stay back again.

In this classroom the lessons about what reading is are both explicit and implicit. Explicitly the focus of the lesson is on the relationship of sounds and letters, of phonemes and graphemes, as these are isolated from texts and, at first, even from words. Implicitly, reading is *not* about seeing these relationships in a textual context—as in a library book. The students in the class are treated as having no prior knowledge to bring to this activity, even if they are repeating the year. And a child who attends to the book rather than the teacher will fail reading.

Example two

Alice, a teacher in a bilingual first/second grade classroom who is taking a course on narrative with me, decides to involve her students in her research. All of her students speak Cape Verdean Creole, and some have begun to read and write in either English or Portuguese. She has noticed that when she asks students to tell a story in the classroom, those who have come from other classrooms tend to tell abbreviated and somewhat empty stories, even in Creole, while the children who can't read tell much richer stories. She asks her students to help her make a collection of Creole stories—to get family members to tell favorite stories and then to tell these stories to the class. When she asks the readers and writers in this class whether these Creole stories can be written in English or Portuguese, they tell her no. So she works with those students to write the stories in Creole, inventing the spelling from what they already know, and then having them work together to translate them into English. Finally she asks the students why they thought these stories couldn't be written in English, and she learns that, because the only stories her students had ever read in English were from basal readers, they thought that the only stories that could be written in English were boring ones, with limited words and limited actions. Good stories could only be told in Creole.

Alice's students have learned the implicit lesson that their earlier classes have offered about language and literacy. Basal readers that are artificially created to introduce simpler words first, that are syntactically reduced and lexically limited, are not at all representative of the natural language that children encounter in other contexts, and they eliminate much of the base of competence on which beginning readers might build, connecting, typically, neither syntactically nor semantically to what the child might know. For these second language learners who have encountered stories in English primarily through such texts, the implicit lesson has been that the linguistically rich Creole world of their homes cannot be carried into the impoverished English texts of school—perhaps even that literacy requires such a reduction in style and meaning. For Alice, the implicit lesson that emerged from this collaborative inquiry was that her students needed to encounter a broader range of English texts, and she exchanged the basal reader for children's literature.

Example three

A parent (who is also one of my students) observes her son's classroom and studies his developing literacy through his first-grade year. On first entering her son's colorful and carefully arranged classroom in a school that's the best in her school system, she expects "an enriching place for education." What she finds is a pedagogy that's not so different from that in the worst urban schools, again shaped by basal readers, worksheets, and other literacy activities that isolate literacy from natural linguistic contexts. She finds that:

> Instead of drawing on the children's previous experiences to contextualize and provide an expansion point for further growth, knowledge is being fragmented, decontextualized, categorized, and otherwise sterilized. Attempts at risk taking are punished with red marks, that is, in those few nanoseconds when the children are actually allowed to compose.

Margaret examines the pieces of writing that her son has produced in response to two assignments for this class "the only, in fact that have been assigned to date, May 22, in this school year."

> In one assignment the class was told to write a story entitled "The Big Noise." The story that my son Timothy brought home used words like *yesterday* and *safetybelt,* as well as coordinators and subordinators to form longer more fluent sentences. There were three sentences, and average sentence length for this paper was 12.5 words. . . . This risk-taking first grader received a total of 15 corrections in 37 words. There were no comments from the teacher, laudatory or otherwise, on the page.
>   The second piece was a description of a car. It lacked the fluency of the first: there were no compound sentences, no words of more than two syllables, no risks. The only punctuation used was a period, unlike the first piece which also used exclamation points and quotation marks. The average sentence length was 5.6 words. For this risk free, error free effort, Timothy was spared the editor's ink and awarded a "Great" underlined twice.

Before even being allowed to compose a miniscule piece of writing these children are being drilled in editing. From day-one lines must be drawn straight and within a prescribed space, curves must touch without overlapping and incorrect omissions or inclusions are deftly circled in red ink. We move steadily from letters to words, spelling, phonics, and more red ink. I was dismayed at the lack of insight on my son's teacher's part, evident in her frustrated statement, "These kids are perfectionists." She bemoans their tendency to put editing, especially spelling, before composing, while all the while encouraging exactly that. It took only once for Timothy to learn that the teacher wasn't the least interested in his composing ability, the fluency or complexity of his syntax and least of all his ideas. She wanted perfection—in spelling, grammar, and punctuation. The next time she got it, never even recognizing what had been lost in the exchange.

Again, the literacies children acquire are shaped by the contexts in which they acquire them. The implicit message about literacy in too many school contexts is that literacy is limited, that it focuses on surface features of texts (and particularly on orthographic conventions), and that it involves language that's reduced from that of the rest of world.

Closer to home, my son's early school literacy experience was much like that of Margaret's son. He attended our neighborhood magnet school where there was support for children with different learning styles and cultural experiences, and the teachers were dedicated and concerned, but much of the explicit literacy curriculum was focused on worksheets, spelling and penmanship exercises, and on the separation of children into reading groups. There the strong readers got to move rapidly through a variety of reading books, while those readers like Kenny who were not as strong had to sit endlessly through the painfully slow decoding of texts by children who were making little sense of them, with constant interruptions and corrections by the teacher that interfered with what little sense was being made. (Kenny, always restless, was best known in these years for the number of times per class that he tipped his chair over.) After our magnet school was closed, his fourth-grade classroom in his new school offered an even more limited literacy experience. There reading was not at all about making meaning or reading to learn, but about following along with a finger, word by word, line by line, and subject by subject for seven hours a day, five days a week, with recess privileges suspended for any student who lost track.

At home Kenny was immersed in a world of literature (I used to prepare for my medieval literature courses by reading the twelfth-century versions of Arthurian tales to him), and he slowly gained a general understanding about the graphophonemic nature of written language, but he did not naturally make the connection as fully as necessary for the fluent reading and writing of new words. Although he was read to a great deal, he was nevertheless a late reader and a somewhat reluctant school writer. By fifth grade, although he was reading at grade level, there was a gap between his reading level and his general level of functioning that pointed to a persistent reading problem. He was very good at drawing meaning from semantic and syntactic contexts, but when he couldn't figure out a word from context, he tended to guess at it from its first letter, or skip over it entirely. After we found a new school where literacy was imbedded in classroom learning, I also sent him to an remedial reading program run by Jean Chall, a prominent reading expert who is most associated with traditional, code-based approaches to reading (1970). With a year of intensive tutoring at her reading laboratory, with his attention focused on the graphemic representation of the insides of words, he made enormous leap in the materials he could read and comprehend—to typical high school and even college texts. In our conversations, Chall chastised me for not bringing him in for this sort of work earlier. I, on the other hand, felt that he was getting enough code-based reading instruction at school, with a heavy emphasis on traditional phonics, and that what he needed in his early years was a sense that reading was valuable and meaningful. So I'd felt it was more important to supplement his classroom activities by reading a variety of literary texts with him in the evening, rather than sending him for more drills. In the end, more specific grapho-phonemic instruction seemed to contribute to his further development as a reader. But I believe it was his general competence in the multifaceted act of reading that allowed him to make use of that instruction in a way he hadn't been able to earlier.

Jean Chall and I continued to hold our competing theories of literacy learning, and we did not come to agreement about the appropriate moment for code-based instruction—or even whether such instruction was always necessary (it doesn't appear to be for many learners). At the same time that my son was being tutored in her lab, he was also in a classroom where he was finally expected to write a lot, and his own attempts to work out the graphemic encoding of words may have done more than the extra decoding practice to catapult him to a new level of reading competence. In any event, Kenny did soon become a strong reader and a terrific writer, and I'm not sorry that we spent our time at home reading together rather than practicing more of the decoding exercises that he got so much of at school. But the questions Kenny's experience raised for me led me to look much more closely at Karen's evolving literacy over her early school years.

One child's literacy

Although Karen's experience at home was similar to Kenny's, her early school experience six years later was quite different. While they still spent some time on worksheets and on decoding words in traditional reading groups, her teachers were trying to create classrooms where reading and writing were not isolated skills but were an integral part of all learning, used in multiple forms and for multiple purposes. Teachers read to the children from children's literature with the full syntax and lexicon of natural language, older children visited the classroom regularly to read to their younger schoolmates and to write down the stories the younger children wanted to tell. Children then read their stories back to their classmates and teachers, so that their knowledge of the stories they'd told became scaffolds for their early reading. And in reading their own stories and responding to their classmates' questions, they began to develop a writer's sense of audience and of how much shared knowledge needs to be established for readers. As they wrote their stories, the teachers would help them make up dictionaries of words for the things they liked to write about a lot, so they could find those words and take control of their own literate productions. Children read each others' names for blackboard attendance lists and chore lists, and increasingly read those lists as well. They soon began to use writing for recording science observations or playground rules.

What did Karen learn about literacy in her early schooling? We can find out by looking at some of the texts she produced and considering what she herself had to say about the process she was engaged in. We can see what her texts tell us about the propositional referential knowledge she's representing in them and the larger framework of cultural knowledge that she's drawing on, her purposes and stance and relationship to an audience, and her hypotheses about how to accomplish her purposes syntactically, orthographically, rhetorically in an evolving text.

As Karen explained to my students, her early writing in school contexts typically involved either drawing a picture and then telling the teacher about it, with the teacher writing down what she said (in preschool and early kindergarten), or telling a story that the teacher wrote down, and then drawing a picture. Over time, she moved from writing over the teacher's printing in crayon to writing some of the words herself and having the teacher assist only when she got tired. The principal genre of such writing in kindergarten through second grade was the picture story book, though a similar process was used for science observation notebooks and for writing about social studies activities. Though there was some teacher editing, it didn't seem to take priority over the child's production of meaningful texts. As nine-year-old Karen explained to my students:

KAREN: What they do is . . . in the first-and-second grades we were like writing how you would think things would be . . . like how you sound it out. They'd say . . . sound it out. And then like third and fourth you'd learn like . . . let's say I was spelling "thought" *t-h-o-t* . . . and then she told me it was like *t-h-o-u-g-h-t*. I'd be like . . . "wait a second . . . but they told me" . . . but see, that's the way you learn it, like step by step. When you're in first and second you don't really matter about spelling it's just like how you write. And then you're in third grade and you matter about how you write and the spelling. And in fourth grade it's like . . . your punctuation and your spelling. And you like . . . edit. And you keep adding something on to it . . . you keep learning more about it . . . as you go along. In the beginning of fourth, I remember, when I made my question marks, I'd make them . . . I'd go like this . . . and then my teacher would say "they're inside" . . .

STUDENT: Oh to put question marks inside the quotation marks?

KAREN: Yeah . . . Yeah. You know you just learn them as you go along. You just keep learning steps every single day.

Among Karen's earliest school literacy artifacts, is a preschool picture of the cookie monster, with "Cookie Monster is blue" written by the teacher, and nERKA contributed by Karen, followed by a number of pictures/texts with the letters KAREN in various arrangements, often labeling a particular object, such as an airplane with the following combination of letters on the fuselage:

KA
R
E
nnERAK
N

Since in most pictures from this period, Karen's name appears with the letters in the correct order in a corner of the picture, it seems that one of Karen's hypotheses about writing at this time is that she can rearrange the letters she knows from her name to name other objects (not a bad hypothesis). The cards she makes for birthdays and such (her favorite out-of-school genre) during this period follow a similar principle: at four, she creates texts by writing the words she knows LOVE, FROM, KAREN, RON (her father) in a number of combinations. At five, in school, she creates "My Family Book," with pictures and labels for DAD, MOM, KENNY, KAREN, and an S for her dog Sadie—a name she probably can't spell. Perhaps because of the emphasis on tracing over the teacher's writing in kindergarten, she doesn't really invent her own spelling at this stage (as many of the children who've been studied do). She repeats syntactic structures that are both generative (in allowing her to add to them indefinitely) and controlled (involving few new words, all of which have probably been spelled for her): "This is my room, This is my brother Room, This is MY dad.ₛ Room, This is MY Mom.ₛ Room, This is my Dog's Room." Although she includes an apostrophe to show possession, she adds the *s* below the word in each case. The apostrophe must be a teacher-introduced feature, because it appears only occasionally for a long time until much later, in third grade, when Karen seems to notice it again and tries to figure out how to use it, putting an apostrophe before every word-final *s* for a while until she works out the correct system.

The sort of experimentation that shows Karen trying to work out her own hypotheses about spelling disappears with kindergarten and doesn't reappear until some time into first grade suggesting perhaps that she had another hypothesis about school literacy and correctness. In the portions of the writing that she takes over from the teacher, there are many erasures, but everything is, in the end, orthographically correct—including capitalization and punctuation. But by the middle of first grade, there's a significant shift toward greater experimentation. The picture storybooks she writes from then on follow certain formulas, but she doesn't hesitate to try out words she doesn't know how to spell. For example, the following text was written under six pages of illustrations: (original versions of corrected words are in parentheses)

(1)	(2)	(3)
Once there	Happy asapfor	The Behca said
was a Elfe tow	the GraMlins'	a litL Elfe so
Thay wEre	TiMe to go to	They all wanto the Behca
(4)	(5)	(6)
and they haD	a Big ElF so	and went HoMe.
a fun. tiMe to go	Thay Grabd	
HoMe said (siad)	There (thier) towalls	

There's a mix of spelling strategies here: "asapfor" is a phonetic representation of "except for" but "Behca" seems to be based on a visual memory of the word "beach", for it contains all five letters but in nothing like a phonetic order. Other spelling (they/thay, said/siad) is in flux. There may be some testing out of a "silent e" since it appears on elf in two places. And *Elf* seems to be intentionally capitalized, since the final *e* is in lower case.

The next book in this series moves into chapters (again with pictures).

Chapter 1: Once there was a ElF hwo was saD I wish I haD a Dog. he said. So he went to the pet sopE and byde a Dog it was very cute he named him cutie he was nice to

Chapter 2: The Tree—Once There was a Tree that Wanted to be a flower he was saD I whet to be a flower he said I am saD

Chapter 3: The ElF—Once There Was a ElF hwo wante to go to the Beach so he weta to the Beach and he had a good tiem.

Chapter 4: The rich Man—Once There was a richman hwo was very nice and he gave all The kids money to go to The store and by cand

Chapter 5: The sun—Once There was a sun that wanted to be like the other sun. so he went to The Store and he bought some suN glasses

Chapter 6: The bear—Once There Was a Bear That wanted to go to The Beach so he weta to the beach and it was fun

Chapter 7: The Dog—Once There was a Dog hwo was saD I wihs I had a flower gardan like the other Dogs so she planted a flower gardan and the next Day it was a Big gardan and she was very Happy and thats the end

Chapter 8: The End—This is the end of my Picture Story Book I HoPe you like it and thats the end.

There is more experimentation with spelling here (beach is correct now), a new syntactic element, a relative clause, has been added, introduced by *hwo* when it refers to people (a category that includes elves and dogs but not bears or trees). But what strikes me here is the limitation of the chapter format. Books are supposed to have chapters, each chapter has a new subject—though generally a continuing theme, as here where almost every character starts off sad but most get happy.

In looking back with my students at her early work, Karen too was struck by how she approached the form:

> It's a picture story book . . . and it has so many pages . . . and you have to fill them all up with like . . . pictures. And you have to write something. And I just wrote like three pages. You just say like . . . the elph dog went to a house. He had a clown friend. The clown friend was funny . . . the end. And then I'm like . . . chapter two . . . and it would be like (laughs) a totally a different story.

The form, at least in young Karen's interpretation (where each chapter starts a new story), doesn't leave much room for more extended development of an idea, and the fact that she was tiring of the form even as a first-grader can be seen in her next efforts where she completes her chapters by extending her endings: "a boy saw a lion and he started to run and run and run and run," (etc. for six pages); "Its the end no it isn't yes it is no it isnt yes it is OK All right you win its over OK OK Bye Bye Bye Bye Bye See you latr alagatr." In this classroom, though the emphasis is on students' writing, they are each expected to produce a specific number of picture story books, and the implicit message about reading and writing quickly becomes one that emphasizes quantity as what's valued more than quality. So Karen's own purposes here seem to be to fill out a number of pages as quickly as possible. Even the beginning of the picture story book comes into question a few books later, when Karen starts off playing with the form (but filling pages at the same time).

> Hi didn't you want to hear a story. Okay, you did so here I go Once there was a . . . What did you say Okay you want to know what they said? They said that stories always begin like that, so they want a new beginning. But I don't know a new beginning so what should I do? You could read a book.

Karen writes many more picture story books through second grade. Her chapters get somewhat longer, she develops conventional capitalization and punctuation, including quotation marks to mark direct discourse, and she makes references to somewhat broader cultural knowledge—having a boy travel to an African jungle after her class has been studying Africa. But after her brief experimentation with the form, she settles back into it, and there's no significant change in the sorts of things she writes about, the stance she takes, or the way she interacts with an audience until she moves on to third grade.

Karen's third grade teacher introduces a range of forms, and Karen writes longer, more extended stories, keeps a daily journal, and participates in a letter exchange with students from a bilingual school. In this classroom, writing is used for multiple purposes, and forms are generative rather than constraining. The picture book genre is not left behind entirely, but here writers focus on the careful development of a finished, published book rather than race through chapters to complete a requisite number of books. Fourth grade (with the same teacher), continues the work of third, and a look at the book Karen published that year, *A+ for Sure*, shows a great deal about the multiple aspects of her literacy acquisition over this time. (She had just completed this book at the time she visited my class.) The text, fully illustrated, reads as follows:

Ding dong. "Mom, I'm home."
  "Come in honey. The back door's open."
  "OK. Hi Mom Hi Dad."
  "Hi honey," Dad groaned.
  "We're going out tonight and we will look forward to coming home and finding you asleep with your homework done and in your folder ready for tomorrow." Mom said in her long lecturing fashion.
  "OK Mom. I'm going upstairs. Bye."
A while later . . . good. They're gone. Now to check my homework assignment.
  1. Finish last weeks homework. "I did that."
  2. Make a puzzle. "I did that."
  3. Do your history. History?
  4. And an essay on a copple of fairy tales "fairytales? I don't know history and I hate fairytales. Just great!
  J-U-S-T G-R-E-A-T! ! !
Ring-ring-ring.
  "Hello" "hi honey it's me"
  "Mom"?
  "Are you doing your homework?"
  "Yes, Mom"
  "Keep it up."
  "OK bye"
  "bye"
Stephaine drifted farther and farther away from her homework. The next thing she knew she was on a giant beanstalk. She climbed up the beanstalk hoping to see the castle, for she had read this fairy tale many times before. But when she got to the top, all she could see were cloud's, except for a little brown object coming closer.
  When it came close enough for Stephanie to see it was a racoon, Stephanie said "Pardon me but have you seen a castle?"
  "No castle around here Sonny, no castle at all."
  "bu—"
  "What's that you say Sonny? What's that you say? I got no time for chit-chat now. There's wood to be chopping. You know, every second that goes by ten gallons of water goes down that waterfall."
  "Sorry. I will have to be going now" said Stephanie.
  She climbed down the beanstalk. But when she put her foot down to get off she started falling. The next place she landed was in Washington. DC next to President Lincoln after the civil war. He was watching a play. Just then a man wearing a name tag that read John Wilkes Booth jumped off the stage and assassinated Lincoln.
  Again Stephanie found her self floating. The next place she landed was in her very own bed. And now she knew so much about history and fairy tale's that she could get an A+. And she did.

What can we see about Karen's literacy development from this text? We see her understanding of orthographic conventions that she has described to my class: the appropriate use of punctuation, capitalization, quotation marks (though periods and quotation marks offer somewhat competing systems, and she often leaves out the former when she includes the latter). We see that in situations where she can edit her work and monitor her own spelling (often checking with a parent or teacher or classmate, or occasionally a dictionary), she can produce a conventionally spelled text (though in her journal there are still many inventions, along with the continued appearance of old nonconventional forms like *siad*). Her syntax is more complex, with embedded clauses as modifiers: "Just then a man (wearing a name tag [that said John Wilkes Booth]) jumped off the stage." But what's particularly interesting is her assumption and presentation of shared knowledge and her placement of this knowledge within a wider cultural framework (of written genres, of fairy tale motifs, of historical events), and her manipulation of the conventions of the picture book frame to create an involving and evolving text that will engage an audience.

Karen no longer begins her stories with "Once there was . . ." or "Once upon a time," an important device for signaling the start of a fictional story in her earlier texts. Rather, she begins *in medias res*, in the midst of the events themselves as the doorbell rings, with no introduction. This is an expansion of her sense of what's possible within this form, an involvement strategy where she treats her readers as if they're already present on the scene. She also creates involvement through the use of direct discourse, punctuated with quotation marks, and through orthographic representation of emphasis: J-U-S-T G-R-E-A-T ! ! ! Her narrative is also firmly situated in the familiar world of her readers, obviating the need for exposition. Her protagonist, Stephanie, comes home, talks to her parents, begins her homework. But the dilemma posed by the homework assignment creates a link that leads her into a fantasy world where she will experience the worlds of the genres she's responsible for in her homework.

In her conversation with my students, Karen makes it clear that while she draws on her own experience, as well as on her familiarity with these genres, her story is about a fictional character, not about herself. When one student asks her whether she likes to put herself into her stories or to have them be completely made up (we'd been reading the Scollons's study of Rachel and talking about fictionalization), Karen responds:

> There's like another book I just wrote . . . this year . . . in fourth grade . . . it's like . . . it's about this girl and her parents go out and . . . she . . . she reads her homework assignment and she's like "I did that, I did that" and she's like "fairytales, history" . . . like she has to write an essay on them. And at one point she like . . . drifts away, and she like goes back in time . . . at first to a fairytale and then to . . . like . . . a history book . . . I don't know . . . It's called "A+ for Sure" cause after she does that . . . she has enough information so she gets an A+ for sure . . . she could . . . and she did. But I don't know . . . I wrote that totally from . . . I wasn't writing about like me or anything or about

how *I* got A+'s . . . I didn't take off from that . . . or how I didn't know something and I drifted off. But that was like totally my imagination.

We can see from the text that Karen has imaginatively constructed the world of
the protagonist out of the world that she knows and the prior texts that she's
encountered and that are part of the knowledge her audience of readers (her
classmates, teachers, and parents) can be assumed to share. And she consistently
presents that world from Stephanie's point of view. We see the things that happen entirely through Stephanie's eyes, as when a little brown object comes
closer and closer before it can be recognized as a raccoon.

It's not only the propositional content—the statements about the experience of a student, the world of the fairy tale, or historical events—that makes
this narrative interesting from my point of view, but also the representation of
multiple styles of discourse: the style of casual conversations between parents
and children, of phone conversations, of school assignment sheets, of the fairy-
tale world where the raccoon responds to her questions with a typical hurried
and distracted response to the intrusion of a stranger, not even recognizing that
this is a girl: "No castle around here, Sonny, no castle at all?" or, "What's that
you say Sonny? What's that you say?" The raccoon speaks in a distinctive style
that combines variant syntax and a particular vocabulary (I got no time for chit-
chat now. There's wood to be chopping.) with a precise scientific presentation
of information: "Every second that goes by ten gallons of water goes down that
waterfall." Though there's no direct discourse in the assassination scene, one of
Karen's illustrations includes the following epitaph: "Here lies Abraham Lincoln. We will miss the way he gave us freedom of the speech and mind for he
was a freedom fighter. God bless him. Amen." This is clearly drawn from the
language of political discourse that she associates with the presidency.

So Stephanie can show that she knows about history and fairy tales, and
Karen has shown that she can venture into these and other frames and use the
discourse appropriate to each of them in representing the stance and perspective
they bring. As she does so, she encompasses all of these contexts and discourses
all within a familiar (though imaginary) world, and, at the same time, she shows
the multiple aspects of the literacy and the language of literacy that she has been
mastering.

Karen comes in while I'm working on this chapter, reading over my shoulder the things she said at age nine about how she learned to write, using
invented spelling. She comments:

> I think it had some advantages and disadvantages. When you're learning to
> write it's better cause you get to use more words. You could write whatever
> word you wanted. Though it's harder to learn to spell after you've been spell-
> ing a word one way and it's wrong. Now . . . if I'm writing at the computer,
> I still write whatever I want cause I know I can spellcheck it later. But if I'm
> writing at school where I have to be sure everything's spelled right, if I'm not
> sure about how to spell a word, I just use a different word, one I can spell, even

if it's a boring word . . . I guess it's better to learn to write the way I did, because it's better to be able to express your ideas better.

Karen's early schooling provided an opportunity for her to discover not only how the written code works, but the ways in which she could use and negotiate that code as a writer as well as a reader. Her acquisition of literacy in these years was continuous with her ongoing acquisition of the discourses of the many communities she participates in, allowing her to place herself in the conversation that goes on in and around written texts, authorizing her as a reader and writer.

Literacy and pedagogy

What, then, are the implications of what we've seen here for parents and teachers and others who are concerned about children's literacy development? The principles are clear enough: learners acquire literacy when they have the opportunity to use it in ways that are meaningful to them and to others around them, when their literacy learning draws on the multiple aspects of their competence as language users, when their literate productions are themselves treated as meaningful, and when their home literacies (their understanding of the functions and uses of literacy in their world outside of school) are valued and built on in the classroom. But effective practices can't be simply codified; they depend on seeing the many elements of the competence that children bring to the classroom and providing meaningful ways of extending that competence into new contexts. I wish I'd saved Kenny's early literacy artifacts as I did Karen's, so that I could discover, in retrospect, more about his hypotheses about written language. What I do have up to his beginning school years includes mostly pictures with his name or with a few other letters used as labels for objects. But the only writing in his primary classrooms involved filling in worksheets and copying sentences, and I threw out all of that because it seemed to have little to do with him. I do have the elaborate and detailed drawings he produced, but for a long time the only words they contained were "For Mom . . . Love Kenny."

In third grade, after a family trip to Chicago, he kept a journal with pictures of the Frank Lloyd Wright houses we had seen and wrote a report that really impressed me with his understanding of the principles of prairie architecture. But his teacher that year was primarily concerned about spelling and penmanship, and although I learned later that she had in fact been impressed with what Kenny had learned and had passed the report around in the teacher's lunchroom, Kenny thought she didn't like it at all because she handed it back to him with red-marked corrections and no other comments.

Now, knowing what I do about the acquisition of language and literacy in a social context, I am amazed that children learn to read at all in classrooms where they have so little opportunity for the risk-taking, hypothesis-testing, and invention of approximative systems that mark the acquisition of any new discourse—where they're expected to be readers but not writers, copyists and spellers but not authors of their own texts written for real communicative purposes or even for real classroom-management functions like maintaining chore lists. For too many children, classrooms still shut down their emerging literacies, rather than building on and extending them, and such classrooms suggest that the forms of literacy, rather than the social and communicative functions those forms have evolved to meet, are all that matters. As teachers, we can alter the practices of the classrooms we teach in, discovering and building on the multiple aspects of children's evolving literacy. As parents, we may not be able to influence classroom practices, but we can help our children place these in a wider literacy context. I'm sorry that I didn't do more to support Kenny's writing as well as his reading (and in the process, offer the very opportunity to experiment with the grapho-phonemic system that he needed as a reader), to involve him in meaningful acts of writing that would have countered the form-based focus of his classroom—writing letters, writing down the funny family stories he loved to tell: nowadays perhaps I'd try to get him into an e-mail conversation.

But parents are not to blame for the failings of schools. And, as my colleague Elsa Auerbach (1995) argues from her work on family literacy, parents in almost all settings in a literate society are already involved in their children's literacy acquisition in ways that are situated in their family life and cultural experience. The families in our neighborhood are diverse linguistically, socioeconomically, racially, and ethnically, and their home literacy practices, like all of their home discourse practices, reflect this diversity. Yet all of the children who started school with Kenny came to the classroom with rich understandings about reading and writing that could have formed the basis for school instruction. Instead, despite the magnet school's overall responsiveness to differences in cultural style, reading instruction came in a one-size-fits-all form that didn't really fit anyone and that left parents feeling that whatever they might have been doing at home wasn't really contributing to their children's learning.

Parents in this community continued to be active in their support of the school. We fought hard to keep the magnet school open in the face of severe cuts in the school department budget. When we lost that battle, we fought on to have the school our children would be sent to designated as a magnet school—eligible for special teacher development and curriculum support funds under a state desegregation act. And we worked with the desegregation team, even as many of the teachers, hostile to both the magnet school concept and the magnet school children, refused to participate in the workshops it offered. And when the team finished its term at the school and withdrew, its members personally voicing despair over the hope for reform, parents continued to struggle to do what they could to support their own children's education, sending them to live with relatives in a different district, working two and three jobs as my friend Joann did to send her children to a nearby Catholic school that was reputed to be fairer in its treatment of all children, though more rigid in its teaching practices, setting up informal networks to help parents apply for the few scholarships available for local private schools that were trying to diversify their own student populations.

When Kenny entered the high school four years later, he found almost none of his bright, energetic friends from his magnet school days in his honors classes. Those whose families had been able to piece together the resources had left the system for private schools, some had moved, but many had gradually been defeated by the combination of rigid school practices and the lack of cultural sensitivity. Tracked into the lowest ability groups and offered even more limited remedial programs, they gradually withdrew from any real involvement in the educational world presented to them (like the adolescents in Labov's and Ogbu's studies that we looked at in Chapter Nine). The lucky ones—including those who hoped to attend college—found a haven in the high school's vocational wing (where Melanie's mother teaches science and where Shanna is now enrolled), to wait out their high school years in a more open and supportive environment where they could continue their learning, even though that route meant that they would have to move on to the next level of their education once again at a disadvantage, without courses like advanced placement calculus that their peers in the honors track were completing. In the meantime, parents in my community have continued to work for change in schools: through their efforts a new developmental school, more sensitive to learners' pedagogical needs as well as their cultural differences, has recently opened in the building that once housed the old magnet school, and there is hope that its success will have some impact on other parts of the school system.

Auerbach calls for placing all literacy work within a context of social change, and she argues that "change comes about through a gradual process of struggling with inequities wherever they occur; the struggles in the more immediate domains (family, classroom) are both part of and a rehearsal for struggles in the broader domain" (655). Parents and teachers who have only a traditional model of how children learn to read and write are likely to see any mismatches between individual children and school practices as a problem inhering in the child, even as they struggle for school change. But as my students and I have studied the literacy acquisition of the learners who were closest to us, we have discovered that what we learn about the process for each learner (even for a child like Karen who comes from a privileged educational background and was in a supportive school setting) tells us more about ways that schools can be changed to support all learners. Auerbach recommends that teachers who want to best support children's literacy development discover what their parents already do (including drawing on their culture-specific literacy practices): that they learn from students and their parents, taking a stance of inquiry as they approach the multiple experiences with multiple literacies that children bring to their classrooms. We need to maintain that stance as we look at children's school literacy acquisition, seeing how each child moves into new secondary discourses and learns to participate, through reading and writing as well as speaking and listening, in a larger public discourse community.

CHAPTER 11

Writing in School Discourse Contexts

As we've seen, literacy involves not just reading and writing but all the ways of using language and of interpreting texts and the world that are associated with a culture which is in turn formed, in part, by those activities. Our literacies are acquired within particular contexts, and they are shaped by those contexts; each literacy moment is situated within a larger cultural context, an immediate situational context, and an evolving discourse context. We can see the effect of these aspects of context, as well as of prior experiences and prior texts, on the literate productions of an individual reader or writer, not only in an early period of literacy acquisition but throughout that person's literate activity. Nevertheless, writing has most often been seen as a neutral tool or skill that exists apart from the contexts in which it is used, and once mastered, apart from the backgrounds and experiences of those who use it. Such a view affects how we understand and approach all literacy learning (and whether we approach it as a process of learning or a process of acquisition). It affects how we see our own enterprise in the writing we do, and it shapes our ability to respond critically to the texts we encounter. We can discover the implications of these competing views for our pedagogical practices in the teaching of writing by studying the texts produced by a particular writer as she responds to specific contexts.

Intersecting contexts: teachers and writers

We left Karen, at the end of Chapter Ten, as a nine-year-old writer and reader who was beginning to use literacy for multiple purposes, in relationship to different audiences and goals. We'll pick up her literacy story briefly at twelve, and again when she's fourteen, in ninth grade, and consciously trying to learn a new style of discourse—the academic discourse demanded of college-bound students in her new high school setting. Throughout this time she has been developing what might be called her own style or voice. But this style is like an ideolect— the unique yet systematic patterns of language variation that individual speakers develop by age, sex, experience in other communities or being offspring of parents from other communities, separating each of them in small, yet significant, ways from other speakers of the same dialect in the same discourse community. Karen, as a writer, has been influenced by the spoken language and by the literacy practices, uses, stances, and styles of the family, peer, and school worlds she inhabits, and each element has left its imprint on the texts she now produces, even as she produces those texts in response to new moments in new contexts. Her literacy at any moment is a richly textured weaving of these multiple threads, some of which we've seen, and only a few of which we can take time to trace here.

One important thread for Karen, is, of course, a stance toward literacy: a notion that a person's literate productions are valuable and worth the attention of readers and listeners but also that the variations and evolving forms of particular texts, reflective of a writer's knowledge and priorities and choices, are an interesting object of inquiry. This stance might be termed aesthetic, combining the pleasure of immersion in the the text from both writer's and reader's perspective with an appreciation of how the effect of the text was accomplished, in relationship to particular contexts and purposes. It's a stance that has been fostered for Karen at home, in the many times she has been interviewed by my students, and in some of her own schooling. It contrasts with an efferent stance (to use Rosenblatt's contrasting term) that perceives a text only as a source of information, and it contrasts as well with an evaluative stance that judges a text as good or bad according to preconceived notions of style and form, apart from purpose or context. It is the stance of a writer.

School contexts strongly affect a writer's stance even for beginning writers, as we saw with Margaret's son in Chapter Ten, who learned in first grade to limit his writing to short sentences and the words he was sure he could spell, so that the teacher would respond with *good* rather than red pencil marks. Many teachers try to create contexts that contribute to a writer's stance—opportunities for students to write to real audiences, for authentic purposes, particularly in early grades. Writing for academic purposes at more advanced levels can be an equally authentic act of communication where the audience is not just the teacher but a peer group of interested learners, and the purpose of the writing is to present propositional/referential content and create new shared knowledge in a way that will involve listeners/readers, not just a product prepared for the teacher's evaluation of the student's learning. But as students move along in their academic work, more of school writing, like classroom discourse, is likely to be directed toward display of learning not toward the creation of shared knowledge and the negotiation of meanings that are more characteristic of discourse in other contexts. One major study sponsored by the National Council of Teachers of English showed that 85 percent of the typical writing tasks given by nearly eight hundred *good* high school teachers was intended to display information about the subject, while only 3 percent called for theorizing or reconceptualizing; and 88 percent of the writing in the samples was addressed to the teacher, in the role of examiner and evaluator, as the primary audience (Applebee, 1980).

Among the multiple threads woven into a writer's developing literacy, then, are those of the many school contexts in which a student writes, each shaped in large measure by the teacher's stance, which has in turn been shaped by the multiple contexts of the teacher's own literacy experience. (It is the recognition of this effect that has informed the efforts of the National Writing Project to improve the teaching of writing by offering workshops that first ask teachers to become writers themselves.) Karen's English teacher in the seventh-and-eighth grades created a literate discourse community, a culture of literacy, in which the stance of writer, versus that of evaluator, prevailed. Because her teacher, Kevin Dotson, had been my student (and had, in fact, been part of the group we saw interviewing nine-year-old Karen about her early literacy), I know something of the contexts that shaped his own stance in ways that in turn led him to create a particular classroom context for Karen as a learner—one of these being our study of language and literacy from the discourse perspective suggested throughout this book. Like other undergraduate students in my class on language and literacy, Kevin had made a retrospective inquiry into his own literacy acquisition. In constructing their own literacy profiles, interviewing parents and older siblings, and frequently uncovering artifacts of their own early writing, my students often discover salient patterns to inform their own teaching—to help them take on the perspectives of the learners as they move into their own classrooms.

In the account produced for my course, Kevin describes his early literacy experiences. He reflects on his early exposure to environmental literacy when as the youngest of six children in a poor family, he accompanied his widowed mother (who had not herself had the opportunity to complete high school) on errands and read the signs on buses and in stores. He recalls his preschool experiences in Head Start. And he remembers the fun he had with an older sister who liked to play teacher and ask him questions about the Dr. Seuss books they read together. He, like a number of writers (including Eudora Welty), describes also the influence of the spoken language he heard around him—particularly the gossip he heard as a child—on his sense of language: "My mother and my eldest sister, Vanita, were the gossipers of the house [and] the community at large, mainly comprised of men and women near my mother's age, and, like her, from the South, also used language for gossiping, and for the small talk that was the precurser to the gossip." (James Britton calls such language, used to evaluate or comment on the participants' experiences, *spectator language*, and he sees it as providing the underpinnings of poetic discourse [1982].)

Kevin also describes the extended, creative language games he and his siblings would play at home, and, in contrast, the formal school language of his Catholic elementary school, where speaking rights were restricted and he was expected to respond only with limited answers to the teachers' closed, evaluation-oriented questions. And he comments on his own difficulty in learning to offer more extended responses in later school years and to integrate his early, playful experiences of language and literacy with the structures of schooling. He also remembers "devouring" superhero comic books, looking up the new words he found there, and then imagining new adventures for his super-hero dolls, commenting: "It was perhaps this creation of comic book scenarios which got me started in writing fiction stories: instead of manipulating actual tangible characters, I began to create them with my mind and my pen."

It was Kevin's creative writing, more than his early school instruction, that helped him learn to write for academic purposes and to approach the work of other writers. He grew to love Shakespeare. On the basis of his academic work in Renaissance and Elizabethan literature, he had recently won a departmental prize for study at Oxford. But he also continued to write fiction and was a regular contributor to UMass/Boston's literary magazine. As a young black man he had learned to negotiate a range of discourses in a variety of contexts, and to integrate multiple aspects of his own literacy experience, but this had seemed like a very individual process to him, and he couldn't imagine how to apply it to his own teaching. Then, as a student teacher at an urban high school, he discovered a mentor teacher he could identify with: "a Black male who specializes in Shakespearean theater, dance, and music." In this classroom, he finds that students are not taught "by the rote learning which I became accustomed to in school" but all classes are conducted "like workshops, where the students are not being drilled with technique so much as being allowed to develop their own. They all read each others' pieces as well as read the fiction, poetry and essays of published writers. And they critique each others' works in very professional and constructive ways."

So, having begun his teaching in a setting where diverse learners have come together to form a community of readers and writers, he sets out, as a beginning teacher, to create such a community in his own classroom—which happens to be Karen's seventh grade classroom. His students read and write in a range of genres, they write for different purposes, and always for a community of peers and for the teacher as reader/responder, not as evaluator. He teaches both creative writing and academic writing and helps his students see the similar issues these different genres present for the writer. He encourages the learners in his classroom to think like writers, not like students writing for the teacher. And he responds with a reader's comments, not with typical teacher comments or a grade.

Karen, at twelve, talks to another group of my students. When one asks: "Do you feel as if you can't go your own way with your writing in school? That you have to do what the teacher wants?" Karen just laughs:

> Never! . . . Never! Oh sometimes he'll give you a little topic, for a little report or something, but basically you can always write about it the way you want. Whatever you want to do. In creative writing, he might give you a little tiny outline . . . or maybe a picture, like this famous picture of a guy and you have to write a story about him. I have a lot more fun writing now.

In this class, where all students write for each other, Karen describes the process of finding something to write about as a blending of her own interests and those of her friends. For an research report she describes how she started:

by listing what things you're interested in, what things you know a lot about, what things you know a little, what you want to find out more of. . . . So I was thinking about things that I was interested in a lot but also what things would interest other people. I looked at the reports in the library that the seventh graders wrote last year. . . . And I remembered, when you're in fifth-and-sixth grade you listen to the seventh graders' reports, so I was remembering last year . . . what I didn't like and what was really boring . . . and I knew I didn't want to do that. I thought about writing about cancer research and DNA, but I didn't think I could make it interesting enough for other people to listen to. I wanted to find something that you might not know you're interested in but if you hear it you'll stop and listen.

Both Karen and Kevin see this classroom, and to some degree the school, as a writing community, and the writing Karen produces there is shaped most strongly by the sense of an audience that such a context provides. She reads her drafts to her classmates, she responds to their comments, and she develops an understanding of how to anticipate their needs and hold their attention. Her writing for academic purposes is direct and clear, offering specific information and new understandings, and it's addressed to an audience of peers in a style that attempts to involve them by addressing them directly and anticipating their responses. We can see these characteristics in this short sample from the middle of the extended research paper she wrote finally on advertising:

> You may be surprised to hear it, but the most important concern of car manufacturers has been to improve the style of the car instead of the safety of the body, and this shows up in advertising. They think people will buy cars for style, but not always for safety, so they make changes in style to get people to think they need a new car. This wasn't always true. When cars were first being manufactured, people weren't offered much choice of styles. Henry Ford once said that the consumer could have any car in any color he wanted as long as it was black. But in the 1920's General Motors began paying more attention to style and their sales soared. (Pope, 260)

With this paper, Karen succeeded in her goal of interesting her classmates. When they voted on the research report they found most interesting, the one that would become the first assigned reading of a follow-up elective on the report's topic, this was the paper they chose.

During these years Karen continues to be inventive and playful in her creative writing, writing fiction and long, narrative poems in school and out of school as well. Her birthday card for her father's birthday that year begins: "It was the night before his birthday and all through the house not a creature was stirring, not even our mouse," goes on to provide a hilarious commentary on the doings of all members of the family as they fulfill the father's fantasy wishes, and ends: "Well that is the way he would of liked it to happen/ but this is no fairy tale, no story like Aladdin./ This is just a story his young daughter wrote/ on a piece of white paper in her old school notebook." Like her teacher Kevin, twelve-year-old Karen writes for fun.

Same writer/new context

The advantage to following the experience of one writer over time is that it gives us a chance to see how different contexts, with different demands, influence the writer's texts, strategies, and stance. In a high school classroom, with a different culture of literacy, Karen tries on a new discourse, and a new set of strategies for learning and using it. I want to make it clear at the outset of this, that Karen's high school English teacher is a thoughtful, intelligent, and energetic young woman. She genuinely wants to help Karen and her classmates to become better readers and writers, to facilitate their progress in the academic world. She works hard and she asks them to do a lot of reading and writing (and, unfortunately grammar exercises and spelling and vocabulary exercises that take time away from those enterprises). But the discourse of her classroom is shaped by the pervasive culture of high school English. What goes on in her classroom is typical of the "best" teaching within that culture.

This high school English classroom, like many for college-bound students, emphasizes varied and substantial reading and the writing of a number of longer essays in response to the reading. (High school classrooms for other students still tend to require a lot of limited skills exercises, removed from any meaningful context.) There's a focus on the extension and elaboration of ideas in both speaking and writing, much as there was in the spoken discourse of the class on Great Ideas in Western Civilization that we saw in Chapter Nine. There's some drafting and revision: a draft of the opening paragraph of a paper is due some time before the paper itself, though it's usually just checked by the teacher to make sure students have begun their work. Students then have a chance to alter their completed text, based on the teacher's markings, after it is first graded. There's also an occasional opportunity for peer review, where students read each others' texts and respond in writing to a list of questions presented by the teacher. Here's one list:

1. What is the point of the essay?
2. How is the essay organized?
3. Identify transitional expressions.
4. Is the point of the essay clear and does every element contribute to it?
5. Is the organization clear?

The questions direct readers toward issues of form, asking them to take the perspective of an evaluator of the writing rather than the perspective of a real reader, who would certainly be unlikely to step back and identify transitional expressions or even to focus on the essay's organization unless there was something confusing about the way the parts went together. But all writing in this classroom, like that in the classrooms Applebee studied, is for evaluation—here focusing on the form of the written product itself—and students learn to read each others' writing as if they were the teacher. Since in the end all writing is really for the teacher as sole evaluator, despite peer reviews, students typically make changes in their texts only when the teacher requests them.

Most class time is spent discussing assigned readings: some of the discussion does ask readers to draw on their own efforts to make meaning from the texts; the rest focuses again on forms and terms (the conventional analysis of literature in the formalist terms of plot, setting, character). Much homework time is spent memorizing long lists of vocabulary words (which, I'm surprised to find, Karen loves), and students are responsible for assigned units in a grammar book, which are tested more than studied. There are one or two creative writing assignments throughout the year, but Karen no longer enjoys such writing in a school context, fearing that she doesn't have good ideas—though she continues her writing at home for family events.

Writing in Karen's new classroom is aimed at having students extend and elaborate on their arguments while using a discourse style associated in a generalized way with academic writing—with an elevated vocabulary, complex and embedded syntactic structures, and formal rhetorical structures. Writing in this classroom is treated as focusing primarily on the propositional/referential function, supported by the memorization of some new words and of some rules of linguistic etiquette, with little direct attention to the interpersonal/pragmatic elements of stance or audience or the relationship of writers and readers to an evolving text. Texts are seen as a series of discrete units: an opening paragraph containing a thesis, followed by a particular number of paragraphs in the body, followed by a conclusion, with each unit easily isolated from even the larger textual context. To further explore the nature of written language and its relationship to context, we'll look at some samples of writing Karen has produced in this classroom shortly.

As we saw in Chapter Ten, differing school literacy practices often represent opposing models of literacy. These are based on theories of reading and writing that place emphasis on the different discourse functions as a locus of meaning. The *autonomous* model not only approaches literacy as an isolated skill, but it focuses on the text itself, on its propositional/referential function as represented only in the words themselves apart from the intentions and relationships of readers and writers in a discourse context. One spokesperson for this model, David Olson, in an influential article, "From Utterance to Text" (1977), describes alphabetic literacy in Western society as developing, historically, away from a dependence on context for meaning and toward the creation of texts that can stand alone, that contain all of the information that any reader, at any time or place, would need to know to understand them—that are "decontextualized." He argues that there is a fundamental difference between utterance, or spoken language, and text, or written language because, while in oral contexts, "the listener has access to a wide information with which to recover the speaker's intentions" (103)—that is, a shared knowledge and a shared context—written language does not (ideally) depend on any implicit shared knowledge that exists outside of the text: "To serve the requirements of written language . . . all of the information relevant to the communication of intention must be present in the text . . . [so that it becomes] an autonomous representation of meaning" (104). The writer's task is "to write in such a manner that the sentence [is] an adequate explicit representation of the meaning, relying on no implicit premises or personal interpretations" (95).

Olson's position depends a great deal on the idea that there's a radical difference between speech and writing as modes of using language, a premise that we'll explore some more in this chapter. Although he would agree that writing takes many different forms and is often used in context-dependent ways, his position is that the ideal of a context-free text can and should be realized, that the "western essayist tradition" has come to approximate that ideal, and that our school practices should focus on teaching learners how to write (and read) in that tradition and to approach that ideal. For Olson, "schooling, particularly learning to read, is the critical process in the transformation of children's language from utterance to text"(105), from language that is context-dependent to language that is decontextualized. Olson's theoretical position is aligned with the code-based approach to the teaching of reading long advocated by Jean Chall (1970), where the emphasis is put first on instructing young readers in the grapho-phonemic code in a way that's independent of the other kinds of knowledge that they can bring to bear on their reading of a text, so that they are forced to depend on the code alone. (It is also congruent with text-based literary theories like that of New Criticism, where a text has one meaning and the object of reading is for the reader to extract that meaning from the text alone, apart from any considerations of the context in which it was produced or the background the reader brings to it.)

Traditionally, primary classrooms that emphasized code-based approaches to reading did not allow for the creation of extended written texts but focused on copying of letters and words, on spelling, and on writing discrete sentences. But traditional writing instruction at upper levels that emphasizes the mastery of particular written forms and formats—the five paragraph essay, the comparison and contrast paper—apart from considerations of audience or purpose emerges from a similar, text-oriented, theoretical perspective.

Karen's ninth-grade English class presents a somewhat modified version of a classroom oriented toward a decontextualized view of literacy. Students sometimes write and discuss personal responses to their reading, but there's little attention to the ways in which a reading is constructed through the interaction of reader and text. Writing instruction emphasizes meaning as well as form, but writing is largely presented as existing apart from real readers, purposes, and contexts. As a writer, Karen is sensitive to the implicit views of writing that are offered here, and some, at least, of the texts she produces are strongly shaped by this context. The following text is the rough draft of an opening paragraph Karen wrote for a paper on *The Joy Luck Club* (with original spelling, capitalization, and punctuation—the teacher, sensibly, does not ask that rough drafts be edited, and

Karen is uninclined to pay attention to orthographic features at this stage in her composing process, though she always spell checks and edits at the end):

Joy Luck Draft

The book The Joy Luck Club by Amy Tan represents the great cultural, generational and emotional differences between Chinese mothers and their Chinese-American daughters strugling in the persute of happiness.

These chinese mothers' ancient ways of teaching were new to their americanized children, and the cultural differences were often put to blame for their misscommunication. Although they caused some problems, the main set back for the acceleration of their mother daughter relationships was not because of sociatel or cultural differences but was presented because of the daughters incomprehension of the experiences and lessons so important to their chinese mothers. In able for them to finally fully understand their mothers' expeiences and put to use their morals and lessons, they first needed to experience a prototype or similar situation to what their mothers had gone through. Until each daughter regressed back in their mothers' footsteps and experienced something of much less magnification, but of similarity to what their mothers had gone through, then and only then did the bond start to grow, being that it was the differences in culture and cultural barriers began to diminish.

What has Karen been doing in this classroom? One thing she has been doing is memorizing vocabulary words, and she's determined to use as many of them as possible in the writing she's producing for her teacher, even to echoing the definitions on the backs of her vocabulary cards: "a prototype" or "similar situation." She has learned these words out of context, so they're sometimes used inappropriately (each daughter regressed back in their mother's footsteps) or seem slightly wrong for the textual context (experienced something of much less magnification), but Karen, as a writer, is continuing to test out hypotheses about how to achieve the discourse she's aiming for, and here her hypotheses about the text she wants are correct, though her assumptions about how to achieve it may not be. She wants to create a text that will sound the way she thinks her teacher wants her to write—that will make her seem educated and knowledgeable—and she hypothesizes, correctly, that one feature of such texts is their vocabulary. Another is syntax, and Karen repeatedly uses her intuitive knowledge of morphology and syntax to create grammatical structures characteristic of the most dense literate style (though she also creates a few tangles along the way).

Spoken and written language

The linguist Wallace Chafe (1982) has studied the ways in which we present ideas in speaking and in writing. Writing allows ideas to be presented more densely and compactly (Chafe's term for this quality of texts is *integration*), because the writer has more time to place those ideas in precise relationships to one another, and the reader has time to process that integrated information. Inspeaking, the idea units are typically spread out and added on one at a time as they come to mind (Chafe's term is *fragmentation*), and the separation between idea units also helps the listener, who doesn't have time to unpack densely integrated ideas while attending to the flow of speech. Idea units in speaking carry a coherent intonation contour (often rising at the middle and dipping at both ends), and are typically bounded by pauses. When nine-year-old Karen is telling my class about learning to read, we can see from her pauses how she breaks her ideas into such units: "We'd have those things that show yellow. . . . We'd have a picture of like . . . yellow . . . and then you'd look at the word yellow . . . and then you'd match it." Chafe suggests that they represent the information that is active in a speaker's mind at the time they are uttered. All speakers tend to present one idea at a time, and in informal conversations where they're negotiating meanings and thinking about what they want to say and how to say it as they go along, they tend to pause more frequently between ideas. As they become more sure of what they want to say, they tend to move more quickly across idea units, focusing less attention on each one and pausing less frequently. We can see this whenever Karen is talking to my students. She typically pauses or inserts *like* most frequently in her early responses on a topic, and then offers larger syntactic units such as whole clauses without a pause once she gains a clearer sense of her larger idea or direction. In writing, we use punctuation to signal units of information, but intonation translates into punctuation only imperfectly.

In another study (1986), Chafe describes several constraints on spoken language. The "one new concept at a time" constraint is related to our concept of shared knowledge; it suggests that each intonation unit can express only one concept that is being newly introduced to the discourse and is not already activated in the consciousness of both speaker and listener. The "light subject constraint" relates to typical given/new information structure: in speaking, the subject of a sentence most often represents given information that's already active in the minds of speaker and listener, with new information (which both participants have to pay more attention to) added later.

Writers can, and do often, write in a style that adds one idea on to another in the ways we typically do in speaking, but writing for professional and institutional contexts, including academic writing, typically involves greatly expanded punctuation units that contain more information. Writers are likely to subordinate one clause to another or embed clauses within other clauses, for example, instead of adding new ideas in separate clauses strung together with *and,* or isolating separate phrases or individual words as speakers do with pauses. Chafe (1982) finds that the following linguistic devices occur significantly more in such writing than they do in speaking: nominalizations, participles, attributive adjectives, conjoined phrases, series, sequences of prepositional phrases, complement clauses, and passive constructions. Written texts also tend to use a different vocabulary from spoken ones, shaped partly by the nature of these integrative devices, partly by the availability of a more formal Latinate vocabulary for many public and professional contexts, and partly by a concern for expressing precise meanings where shared knowledge can't be confirmed. Let's look back at Karen's draft paragraph for examples of these integrative devices:

Integrative features

Nominalizations (and other category changes)

A nominalization involves adding a derivational morpheme (such as *tion*) that changes a word from one grammatical category to another, from a verb to a noun (so that nominalize becomes nominalization). According to Chafe, a nominalization allows the verb to be inserted into the idea unit as a noun, allowing a place for another verb and compressing two verbal ideas into one unit.

Karen's paragraph contains a number of nominalizations: *misscommunication, acceleration, incomprehension, magnification,* and these, along with the other features we'll look at, compress the information she's presenting significantly, compared with full clauses like "they weren't able to communicate."

Other words that have changed category contribute to both the integrated structure and the stylistic effect: "American + *ize*, generation + *al*, happy + *ness*, relate + *tion* + *ship*, similar + *ity*.

Participles

The participles of verbs can be used as nouns or adjectives, allowing them to be integrated into a nominal or modifying function (again letting another verbal idea be added). The present participle with *ing*, in addition to forming part of a progressive verb construction (as in she was *struggling*) can also be used as:

a noun (a gerund), as in "the daughter's *struggling* was over";
an adjective, as in "the *struggling* parents worked hard"; or
a postposed modifier (one that comes immediately after the word being modifed), as in "the mothers and daughters *struggling* in the pursuit of happiness" (an abbreviated form of a relative clause). It is this last form that Karen has used.

The past participle (with *ed* or a stem change like *found*) forms part of the perfect tense of the verb (as in "The problem was *presented*") , but it can also be used as a adjective or post-posed modifier:

"The presented problem," or "a problem presented in the book." Karen contributes "their *americanized* children," combining the adjectival use of a past participle with a category change of an adjective to a verb. (Such an effort should certainly be worth two points in the integrated style game.)

Attributive adjectives

Attributive adjectives precede a noun "the *old* house," while predicate adjectives follow the verb "to be" and other linking verbs: "The house was *old.*" Karen uses a large number of attributive adjectives in her draft: "*ancient* ways" (instead of the ways were *ancient*), "*cultural* differences" (instead of the differences were *cultural*), "*mother daughter* relationships," "*cultural* barriers," and, again, "*americanized* daughters."

Conjoined phrases and series

Two or more elements can be joined together in an idea unit, as in "the daughters incomprehension of the *experiences or lessons*" or "the great *cultural, generational and emotional* differences."

Sequences of prepositional phrases

Karen sometimes strings two prepositional phrases together: "The main set back *for* the acceleration *of* their mother daughter relationships," but longer sequences often occur in written texts.

Complement clauses

Complementizers like *that* and *to* allow one clause to be embedded in another: "She found *that* her daughter didn't understand"; "In order for her *to* understand her mother's words." Karen uses *because of* (the main set back . . . was not because of sociatel differences) and *being that* (being that it was the differences in culture . . .) to embed clauses in this way.

Relative clauses

Relative clauses introduced by "who," or "which," or "that" appear frequently in spoken discourse, but Chafe finds them to be twice as prevalent in his samples of writing. Karen used them a lot in her early writing (Once there was a bear who was sad), but she doesn't use any here, perhaps because she is experimenting with new syntactic structures. In some positions, they allow the speaker/writer to add on one new idea at a time, so they aren't always as complexly integrative as the other devices we've been looking at.

If we were to write just one sentence of Karen's draft in such a way that we undid these integrative effects and separated out each of the ideas into separate propositions, we'd have to create a long sequence of clauses to express the same information. For example, "These chinese mothers' ancient ways of teaching were new to their americanized children, and the cultural differences were often put to blame for their misscommunication," would become something like:

These mothers were Chinese.
They taught in ways
    that were ancient.
The ways were new
  to their children.
The children had learned
  to be American.
They had a culture
  that was different.
The mothers and children weren't able
  to communicate.
The mothers blamed the differences on culture.

Such a sequence looks much like the sentence combining exercises that were popular a few years ago as a means of helping students develop a syntactically mature writing style. (See, for example, Strong, 1973.) These exercises, which called for students to reintegrate the separated out information, probably helped writers become aware of the integrated nature of much written language, but since they were artificial and they took time away from the students' own writing; they didn't contribute much to students' acquisition of a new discourse style. (See Moffett, 1968, for a critical response to this approach.)

Using a maximally integrated style is not necessarily a desirable goal for writers. Chafe makes the best case for it (and we'll examine his view), in contrasting the speaker's and writer's relationships to their audience:

> The speaker is aware of an obligation to communicate what he or she has in mind in a way that reflects the richness of his or her thoughts—not to present a logically coherent but experientially stark skeleton, but to enrich it with the complex details of real experiences—to have less concern for consistency than for experiential involvement. The situation of the writer is fundamentally different. His or her readers are displaced in time and space, and he or she may not even know in any specific terms who the audience will be. The result is that the writer is less concerned with experiential richness, and more concerned with producing something that will be consistent and defensible when read by different people at different times in different places. (1982, 45)

According to Chafe, the consequence of a more distant relationship with an audience is seen, in a written text, in its quality of *detachment*. One device that contributes to this quality is the use of the passive voice, as in Karen's text: "The main set back for the acceleration of their mother/daughter relationships was not because of societal or cultural differences but *was presented* because of the daughters incomprehension. . . . " The sentence goes on but it is rather tangled up syntactically. Karen has tried to present many ideas here, in complex relationships; she even crams a lot in between the subject "setback" and the verb "was presented." All of this complexity, which makes it hard to see exactly whois doing what, contributes to the detached quality of the text. But that detachment increases with the use of the passive, where we no longer see an active subject, the author, Amy Tan, who is presenting her story in a particular way, offering the possibility that she might have chosen to present it in other ways, but only the outcome: "the setback was presented." Devices like nominalizations also hide the notion that someone or something is acting: "misscommunication" becomes a state of affairs, not specific instances caused by individual people who don't communicate.

In contrast to the detachment of written language, Chafe finds *involvement* in spoken language (a quality shaped by many of the features that Tannen found in the talk of at least some of the participants in the Thanksgiving dinner conversation). In the following transcription, Karen is talking to me, after having written her first paragraph, about what she wants to prove in this paper. She continues to focus on what Chafe refers to in written text as "producing something that will be consistent and defensible." She's primarily concerned here with the propositional meanings she's presenting, not with an audience. But her language is quite different from that in her written draft:

> You learn from experience. The mothers . . . I'm basically proving that the mothers . . . well . . . the mothers always thought . . . that these American children . . . you know . . . that they wouldn't listen to their lessons . . . Well . . . I could use lessons as a point . . . You know . . . they always gave lessons to them . . . when they were young and stuff . . . and then . . . they . . . um . . . and the American children never understood. . . . And they also told them about their experiences . . . and they never seemed to understand. . . . But it wasn't so much just because they were American. . . . Some things they didn't understand because they were American . . . but most of it was because . . . they had never really experienced what their mothers were talking about. . . . They really had *no* . . . I mean . . . it partly *was* culture because they were American so they had never experienced this thing . . . but it was because they hadn't *experienced* it. . . . That might have to do with culture that they didn't experience it. . . . you know . . . they might not have experienced this because they were *American* . . . and they never went through this war . . . but it's because they hadn't *experienced* it . . . The fact that they didn't understand it was because they never experienced it.

Here there are virtually none of the integrative devices we saw in the written text: "The Chinese mothers' ancient ways of teaching" has become "the mothers gave lessons to them." "Americanized daughters" has become "they were American." There are no nominalizations, no participles, few attributive adjectives. Idea units are added as they come to mind. The text also displays the distinctive features that Chafe finds to be characteristic of the speaker's involvement, features that did not appear in the written text.

Involvement features

First and second person references

"*You* learn from experience," and "*I'm* basically proving" point to the fact that individual speakers and listeners are involved in this act of communication.

References to the speaker's mental processes

"I'm basically proving" and "I could use lessons" show that the speaker is actively involved in thinking through what's being said as it is said.

Monitoring of information flow

"You know" and "well" and "*I mean* . . . it partly was culture" offer pauses in which the speaker can make sure the listener is following what's being said, and that it's clear. (Karen seems recently to have eliminated "like"—which was ever-present in earlier recordings— almost completely.)

Emphatic particles

Words like "just" and "really" create emphasis and show the speaker's enthusiasm: "They really had no . . . "

Fuzziness

Speakers who know they share knowledge with their listeners can use less precise terms and assume the listener's involvement in filling in the details: "they were young and stuff"; "they had never experienced this thing."

Direct quotes

Direct quotes make an account of an event more immediate, more involving. Karen doesn't use any in this excerpt, but she does as she goes on to discuss the particular events of the novel.

Differences are likely to appear between spoken and written language, even when produced by the same writer, on the same topic, who is focused on the same larger purpose (in this case, working out a thesis for a school essay). But such differences between spoken and written language aren't necessarily due to the mode of communication, but to the difference in the contexts in which they've been produced: one where the reader is distant and is assumed to have certain stylistic preferences, and where the reading will take place in the future;

the other in which the listener is present and her attention is focused on meaning, not on style. Each text, once started, is further shaped by the evolving text itself and takes on a kind of coherence through a continuity of style—one nominalization leads to another. Spoken texts can, of course, be produced without the features of conversational involvement that we see here: public speakers often eliminate first person references and fuzzy terms and avoid expressions like "you know" that Chafe associates with monitoring the information flow. But a speaker generally plans such presentations in advance (and has, perhaps, engaged in a similar performance many times). Elinor Ochs (1979) suggests that the most significant distinction in discourse style arises between *planned* and *unplanned* discourse, regardless of whether it is presented in a spoken or written mode. But most of the time we do not carefully plan what we'll say in advance, and most of our speaking, even when we're focused on creating logical relationships among the propositions in the text we're producing, will include involvement features that reflect the interactive nature of this discourse event.

The devices Chafe names, especially when labeled with terms like fuzziness, suggest that involvement might be reduced to a kind of messiness in speaking that can easily be cleaned up in writing, that it arises from the immediacy of face-to-face interaction, and is perhaps inappropriate to most written texts. Yet if we clean up Karen's spoken text, we get something less immediate, but not very involving, despite its spoken origins:

> People learn from experience. The mothers thought that the American children wouldn't listen to their lessons. They gave them lessons and and told them about their experiences, and the children never seemed to understand, because they had never experienced what their mothers were talking about. . . .

The real challenge for the writer is to create, not just an unfuzzy text, but a text that will draw the reader in, as if to a conversation, to create a framework of shared knowledge and a sense of the common participation of reader and writer in the construction of an evolving text. To participate in the implicit conversation of a written text, readers have to have a way to engage in that text. They need to be drawn into the process of imagining and predicting what will come next, to be invited to interact with the text in a way that allows them to sense how it is developing. They also have to be given enough information that they can think along with the text but not be told everything so explicitly that their own thinking is closed off.

Deborah Tannen, in her book *Talking Voices* (1989), defines texts that invite readers in this way in terms of their aesthetic quality, and she names several features that contribute to that quality in both spoken and written texts. One of the most important is *repetition*, including repetition of sound, of words, of syntactic patterns (like the three prepositional phrases I've just written); such repetition allows readers and listeners to pick up the rhythm and the sense of what has been said and to predict what might follow, while creating cohesion and ultimately contributing to the sense of a coherent whole. Another is *dialogue*, the direct representation of speech, which creates a sense of immediacy through the reenactment of a scene rather than the reporting of it, and allows readers and listeners to perceive it as if they are present. A third feature is *imagery*, which Tannen defines to include not only striking visual or aural images, but the sorts of specific details that again create a sense for the reader or listener of being on the scene. While these are usually thought of as features of literature, Tannen sees aesthetically satisfying conversation as depending on their use as involvement strategies. I would go further and argue that such features appear not only in literature but in any text, spoken or written, that's engaging and aesthetically satisfying.

Karen knows unconsciously, from her many hours of conversation with Melanie and Shanna, how to keep participants actively involved in a conversation. In her storytelling, she has developed openings that create greater immediacy for her listeners and readers than does "once upon a time." Her correspondence with students from another school has helped her to understand how to manage a conversation with a distant partner. And her seventh-and-eighth-grade classroom experience, which encouraged her to write directly to an audience of peers, has helped her discover some ways of extending her conversational strategies into her academic writing—such as addressing her readers directly and highlighting in an almost narrative form the information she's found that will interest them. But her challenge now is to apply what she knows as a speaker and writer to a context that demands the most formal style of academic discourse—where she can't address her readers directly as "you" or explicitly guess at what they might be thinking. She has to figure out how to create a shared context within the text in such a way that the reader will step into that context and become involved in constructing meaning from it.

After Karen had finished talking out what she wanted to say, while I offered occasional backchannel comments like "I see what you mean . . . " or, "I'm not quite sure . . . can you say it again?" and after she had reread her thoroughly marked up copy of *The Joy Luck Club* for parts that seemed to confirm what she was trying to show, she went to work on her next draft. Though she still likes to try out her text on an audience—at home to anyone who'll listen now that she doesn't really have a writer's group at school—she closets herself with the computer when she's actually writing. When she emerged with her next draft, which with spell checking and some editing for punctuation, became the version you see here, I was amazed. I'd made no comment about her first draft—in fact I'd been delighted to see such a great example of how my own child was actively constructing a model of academic writing in the ways I'd long argued that students did—with syntactic tangles, misused words, and other infelicities to be seen seen not as problems but as a sign of growth (1986, 1991, 1993), and I expected to see a somewhat (but not wholly) cleaned up version of what she had already shown me. But after working her way through the paper, she had created an entirely new beginning.

The Joy Luck Club

The story of *The Joy Luck Club* begins with June, a Chinese-American daughter whose Chinese mother Suyuan has just died. June is asked to take her mother's place at the regular gathering of her mother's friends, her "aunties." The aunties are sending her to China to see the other daughters her mother had left behind there. They tell her: "Tell them stories she told you, lessons she taught, what you know about her mind that has become your mind." But June says. "I don't know anything." June always thought of the stories of her mother's life as a Chinese fairy tale. She has rejected her mothers' criticisms and her Chinese ways. But now she sees that the other mothers are frightened because they see their own daughters as being like June, "just as ignorant, just as unmindful of all the truths and hopes they have brought to America."

The Americanized daughters aren't really unmindful of their mothers stories. They have listened to them and can tell them. But they haven't always understood them. The Chinese mothers have taught their children sometimes through ancient Chinese stories and superstitions, and sometimes through their stories of their own lives in China. They think the children can't understand these stories because of the cultural differences that come from growing up in America. They think their daughters can't hear their teaching because they have "American" ears, and that they can't understand the dangers they warn of because they have "American" eyes. But the mothers have accepted or rejected the meaning of the ancient stories based on their own experiences, and even when they seem to accept them, like Ying-Ying, or reject them, like An-mei, they have worked out their own understanding. The daughters, like Lena and Rose, can come to understand the meaning of their mothers' Chinese stories when they begin to grow up and have their own experiences to bring to them, so that they can see beyond the literal level of the stories to see how they might relate to their own lives.

In creating this text, Karen seems to have used all of her experience of writing to different audiences to imagine a world of possible readers, because she's clearly no longer just anticipating what she has inferred to be the concerns of the teacher. Nor is she focused now on her own need to clarify her ideas and work out their relationships, putting forth only her thesis as shared knowledge. Now the shared knowledge she creates first is the knowledge of the book she's writing about, and she creates a context, within her own text, for the thesis she'll present. She begins by bringing her readers into the story of the book and recounting its opening event, reminding them of it if they've read it and giving them a sense of it if they haven't. To make this introductory event more immediate, she quotes the words the characters speak, recreating the event that illustrates her point by showing, with one daughter's own words, that she hadn't fully understood her mother's lessons: "I don't know anything." But she explores and questions and complicates that daughter's response, inviting the reader to do so also. She takes the term offered in the book for the Americanized daughters' responses, "unmindful," and repeats it to open it up, exploring the nuances of what it might mean. She uses repetition throughout, creating thematic contrasts lexically, "mothers" versus "daughters," "Chinese" versus "American," "stories" versus "experiences," and repeating syntactic structures "sometimes through ancient Chinese stories and superstitions, and sometimes through their stories of their own lives in China." She adds details that highlight the problem, replacing the term "miscommunication" in her draft with the images the book offers: "They think their daughters can't hear their teaching because they have 'American' ears, and that they can't understand the dangers they warn of because they have 'American' eyes." And finally she makes the point she will try to prove in the rest of the paper, that the daughters only come to understand their mothers' stories when they have some experience of their own to bring to them.

As I look closely at what Karen has done here, I am newly amazed. "Where did she suddenly learn to do all of this?" I wonder. Perhaps she too has not been "unmindful" of the lessons she's heard, talking with my students and listening to our class discussions about reading and writing, sitting at the dinner table while I recount the best and the worst of my students' stories about their experiences with writing. Perhaps now, with more of her own experiences, even, ironically, the experience of a classroom that draws from a different, non-contextual model of writing (though they read and discuss interesting literature that provides other models, and have apparently acquired some language for talking about something beyond the "literal" meaning of a text), she has come to see how the literacy stories she has heard might relate to her own context as a writer in this classroom. In any event, when this paper is returned to her for final revision with the comment on the opening that it is too long (that it should have been one paragraph instead of two), and that she should have stated her thesis much earlier, in one sentence, Karen firmly declines the opportunity to alter her text. This event marks a turning point in her work for the course. She continues to work hard on each paper, but no longer to please the teacher, and though she's disappointed to receive B's instead of the A's she thinks she deserves, she will respond only to the revision suggestions that make sense to her in terms of what she's trying to achieve.

The context of school writing: teacher's responses

While several intersecting contexts shape the texts that students produce for their classes—the background and experiences both teachers and students bring, and the larger culture of the methods and purposes of school writing instruction—it's the responses that teachers make to their students' writing that provide the most compelling context to which student writers respond. Studies of teachers' responses to students' texts show that most responses, however well-intended, contribute little to students' sense of how to improve those texts, in part because the responses themselves are so decontextualized. The same comments or types of comments are likely to appear on paper after paper, no matter who the writer is and what the writer's purpose is or what contexts frame the particular act of writing. Nancy Sommers, in her study of teachers' responses to their students' writing (1982), found that "Most comments are not text-specific and could be interchanged, rubber-stamped, from text to text" (152). Where comments do respond to a particular text, they are likely to respond to the teacher's context and purposes, more than the student's, so that they "take students' attention away from their own purposes in writing a particular text and focus that attention on the teachers' purpose in commenting" (149). They also typically focus on multiple and conflicting purposes at once, commenting on textual features on the surface of a text at the same time that they ask students to find meanings and develop ideas.

Vivian Zamel (1985), in her research on teachers' responses to the texts of ESL students, found that teachers misread students' texts, were arbitrary and inconsistent in their reactions, provided abstract and vague prescriptives, responded to all texts as fixed and final products, and attended primarily to surface level features rather than to larger discourse concerns. They rarely offered specific strategies that would help students to resee their texts. And in revising, students typically changed only the surface features of their texts while, in turn, these corrections were accepted by the teacher as representing an improved paper. Though many writing teachers bemoan students' apparent unwillingness to undertake revisions that involve a genuine reseeing of an earlier draft, they are inadvertently creating a context that implicitly excludes such reseeing from what's really valued.

Zamel recommends that the questions teachers raise in responding to a text take into account two crucial dimensions of composing: the author's intention and the audience—the propositional/referential and the interpersonal/pragmatic dimensions of the discourse functions we have been exploring. She suggests that teachers play different roles as readers of student writing, taking on the role that's appropriate to the particular version of a developing text. While a writer is still working through her ideas (as Karen was in her conversation with me about her *Joy Luck Club* paper), it is distracting and counterproductive to do anything but support the working out of those ideas. At a later stage, where the writer wants to know whether a reader might be drawn into what she's written, a genuine reader's response (like that which one might note in the margins of a literary text) is appropriate. And when a final copy of a text is being prepared for the class, an editor's response may be what's needed, not a comment that asks the writer to rethink the underlying premises of this piece of writing. Zamel also reminds us that writers acquire new language, new uses of writing, through a process of acquisition—by being involved in a community where they are pushed through ongoing communication to take in and try out new structures, not by memorizing rules and monitoring for their use. And she calls for those of us who are teachers (or for any readers of a writer's evolving text) to participate in the making of meaning, "to establish a collaborative relationship with our students . . . [one marked by] dynamic interchange and negotiation" (96–97), becoming, in fact, participants in a conversation like those that we've studied in earlier chapters of this book.

So what about Karen's teacher? What sort of responses did she make to Karen's papers, and to what degree did her comments initiate cooperation and negotiation between reader and writer like that which goes on among participants in a conversation? In response to the final, edited version of the *Joy Luck Club* paper (after commenting on what she sees as the problem with the two paragraph introduction without an opening thesis statement), she asks questions like "What is the significance of Lena seeing and believing (her mother's) stories?" These are questions that would have been useful at an earlier stage, in a written conversation about Karen's ideas, but are less helpful on this final text. She makes frequent surface level corrections, adding commas (some that I would say are incorrect), though Karen has done a pretty good job of editing and this printed text is quite clean (thanks especially to the computer spellchecker). And she makes a kind of change that drives Karen (and me) crazy, replacing Karen's perfectly good way of phrasing something with her own: for example, in "It's only now that Lena can understand those stories and the true story behind them," "the true story" is crossed out and replaced with "the truth"; in "An Mei's mother had been a concubine who had no power," "who had" is crossed out and "with" written in. The changes don't contribute to the meaning, and they don't correct a word that was misused. But they do show the intrusion of the teacher's discourse into the student's.

The comments at the end of the paper are more substantial, but hard for me to apply to the text I've just read: "You've included a great deal in this piece which you may not have needed in order to prove your very interesting/complex point. You've almost relied too heavily on the traditional Chinese teachings when, in fact, that is not the emphasis of your analysis. Instead, you gravitate towards what those teachings prompted in the various mother-daughter relationships." Since I find Karen's discussion of the traditional Chinese teachings necessary to understanding their effect on the mother-daughter relationships, I find it hard to imagine how to respond to this comment, and if I were the writer I would want the opportunity to explain why I had chosen to include what I did. Finally, there is a grade, a circled, very precise, "86."

A book report that Karen wrote at about the same time is marked by similar sorts of responses, though ones that I find even more intrusive. She has chosen Samuel Freedman's book about a high school English teacher, *Small Victories*, from my shelf, after asking whether I thought she'd find it interesting. And she has given what I find to be a wonderfully insightful picture of what Freedman was attempting to do and how he approached his task, beginning with her old seventh-grade strategy of asking a rhetorical question in the opening paragraph to gain her readers' attention. The teacher doesn't like this paper much. She hasn't read the book and has misunderstood that the author is male and the teacher is female, so she has changed the pronouns inappropriately throughout Karen's paper. She again intrudes with her own discourse in many places, as when she crosses out Karen's characterization of Jessica's childhood in the next to last paragraph and substitutes "Jessica's *privileged* childhood," a word Karen would never use. And her only substantive comment is a disbelieving "what

about slow learners, uninterested students?" This time there are no end comments, and the paper has earned a less precise B+. I can't resist reproducing the
entire paper here (and I've ignored the teacher's many markings in favor of
Karen's original text), because Karen has so well described what this chapter of
Language and Literacy is ultimately about . We'll see that Karen was in fact writing this paper to her English teacher as her real audience, trying to initiate a
conversation about the purposes of English teaching and ways of achieving
those purposes that there was no real space for in this class. But it speaks to all of
us and provides a fitting close to this chapter.

> In *Small Victories* Samuel G. Freedman tells the story of what education is like
> for students and teachers at an inner-city high school. Seward Park High
> school in Manhattan was ranked among the last 10% of America's high
> schools. It was old, overcrowded, and falling apart, but it remained, even
> through constant struggle, serving America's newest immigrants. How is it
> then that over 90% of the graduates from Seward Park are continuing on to
> forms of higher education? This book suggests that it is because of dedicated
> teachers like Jessica Siegal, the central figure in the book.
>
> Freedman, a former investigative reporter for *The New York Times*, fol-
> lowed Jessica Siegel throughout the 1987–88 academic year. The author takes
> us through a violent struggle of one teacher's ultimate dedication to better
> educate the lives of America's inner-city youth. As she and her students
> explore amazing classroom lessons on Martin Luther King, *The Great Gatsby*,
> and the American dream, the reader is given an in depth perspective of Jessica
> Siegel's teaching of journalism and advanced literature. She attempts to get her
> students to care about their education through an open-minded classroom
> style, in which students are allowed, or more so encouraged, to speak up for
> their thoughts, ideas, and beliefs. She asks them to do a lot of writing, getting
> them to think their ideas through and helping them discover what they think
> before they correct their grammar and put their writing into final form for
> others to read. By studying the ways in which her students write and figuring
> out with them what they're trying to say, she develops her own teaching style
> and technique in which she helps students improve by teaching them to exam-
> ine and explain new concepts. If something is not clicking or is misunderstood
> by a student, Jessica is quick to change her strategy, the students' understand-
> ing her main concern.
>
> One of the ways in which Jessica Siegel really draws her students into want-
> ing to learn is by bringing up and supplying informational background on
> subjects which are ultimately important for their education in English and then
> having her students ponder the relevance the subject has to their own lives. A
> clear cut example of this is one of Jessica's classroom teachings of how racial
> attitudes are established and the retribution, punishment, and the absolute loss
> of rights that African slaves faced. She had her students enter in their journals the
> day before whether they have pets and how they take care of them. As she brings
> up and discusses yesterday's writing assignment with the class, she winds in and
> connects what is a seeming ridiculous subject but one that maintains some
> relevance in their lives, to help them better grasp and understand the presented
> treatment of slaves, in comparison to their pets. Ultimately she connects the

treatment of pets to the ways in which racial attitudes are established, and she links the position of slaves to the question of the choices people have in their lives. She and her students discuss the idea that the one choice the slaves had at the worst of times was to die or not to die and then she brings the class back to thinking about the choices they have in their own lives. It is the kind of interacting, connecting teaching that is believed to contain the most hope for the fast learning and grasping of conceptual understandings in the classroom.

As Jessica works to educate these students, she builds personal relationships with them, becoming an advocate for each of her students and pushing them to the highest level which they can perform at. She helps them to see new choices and possibilities for their future. She works hard to help them to get into college, helping them with their application forms, calling admissions officers and taking them to different schools.

This books makes effective, transitional skips from Jessica's childhood, to the classroom, to her two favorite students' poverty stricken childhood in the Dominican Republic and China. Freedman contrasts Jessica's own childhood, in which learning was important and she and her siblings read books and played the piano and presented plays, with the difficult and dangerous experiences her students have faced. Freedman not only presents a master teacher at work and gives an inside view on public high school systems, but also shows the social problems affecting the lives of these students on the drug-ridden streets of Manhattan.

This is an inspirational book which leads you through the personal stories of the teachers, students and administrators who make up Seward Park High School. Freedman has done an excellent job of presenting the real lives of people in an urban high school. Above all, he has presented a moving portrait of Jessica Siegel, a devoted, dedicated master of her field who will stop at nothing to educate, influence, and ultimately better the lives of her students.

AFTERWORD: AN END AND A BEGINNING

In reporting on *Small Victories,* Karen draws on ways of participating in and contributing to a discourse community that have been shaped by all of her experience of language in the many sorts of communities we've explored in this book: at home, in the neighborhood, in different classes at different schools, and in a number of other settings as well. She uses what she knows both to create her own text that will respond to and implicitly shape a community of readers and to comment on Freedman's attempt to do the same. She's acquired the uses of language that allow her to do this unconsciously as well as consciously, so she's not necessarily aware of the very discourse strategies she's using, but as we look at the text she's created, we can see their presence. As reader, writer and reporter, or critic, she's involved in multiple roles in relationship to these two interrelated texts. And to perform those roles, she has to see something about the discourse communities each text implies and the way those communities are shaped.

One community is the one represented in Freedman's book, that of the high school teacher Jessica Siegal, her students, and the classroom and school they inhabit together and to which they bring the discourse of many other communities in turn. Another includes Freedman and his larger audience of readers: a public that's interested in non-academic accounts of what's going on in schools: a readership drawn by the investigative reporting of this former *New York Times* journalist; as well as the teachers and others who work in schools and whose experience is to some degree represented in the book. Still another community is that of Karen's own classroom—the teacher who will read Karen's text and perhaps engage in the new conversation about English teaching and learning that Karen's paper implicitly invites, and the students who probably won't read the paper but will hear her talk about the book and who may be drawn to read it themselves. Finally, there's the larger community of people in Karen's life who are constantly discussing schools and teaching practices: her parents to whom she'll most certainly read her paper, and the intersecting layers of her mother's students, some of her own teachers, and her parents' colleagues whom she's heard and talked to in ongoing conversations on these topics and whose language clearly merges with her own, when she writes: "It is the kind of interacting, connecting teaching that is believed to contain the most hope for the fast learning and grasping of conceptual understandings in the classroom." Now Karen's text and all of the discourse communities represented in these many intersecting layers are being re-presented in the book I'm writing, to yet another audience of readers I'm imagining to be interested in the questions of language and literacy that I've been discussing here. Through our texts we are constantly encompassing and creating discourse communities, including those created through other texts (an understanding represented by the term "intertextuality" in current critical theory).

When Karen reports on *Small Victories*, she re-presents the events that Freedman represents, but not the words he has used in presenting them. Though his book is rich in the language of teaching and learning he has heard in Jessica Siegel's classroom, it is language that is familiar to Karen, that merges with what she hears all of the time. (Much of the language of the urban communities Siegel's students inhabit is also familiar to Karen, but what they bring from those settings is not the focus of her attention here). She doesn't need to enter a significantly new discourse community as she writes about the world Freedman portrays, and the familiar discourse of conversations at home and school serves her needs in conveying the world of the book to her own readers. But Karen's experience in moving through a number of different discourse communities also allows her to enter, even in texts, those that are unfamiliar.

The Joy Luck Club presents a much less familiar world for Karen, and the register of academic written discourse that she first tries to approximate in writing about the book distances her (and her implied readers) even more from the text. Yet, as she works on the drafts of her paper for that book, she gradually leaves behind the language of the classroom where she's been memorizing vocabulary words and takes on the language of the novel she's been reading and rereading. Rather than stating that Tan "represents the great cultural, generational and emotional differences between Chinese mothers and their Chinese-American daughters," she shows us those differences, drawing on Tan's own words, the words the mothers in the novel use for their daughters: "ignorant," "unmindful," with "American" ears and "American" eyes. Through her reading, Karen has entered, for a time, a new speech community, the one Tan has created in her novel. In fact, entering this speech community, taking in its language and with it the values and ways of seeing the world that its discourse implies, is necessary to understanding the novel, and it is only when Karen the writer returns to the book, drawing its language into her own, that she is able to recreate that world and its meanings for her own readers. The language of Amy Tan's novel, in turn, is shaped by the prior texts—both spoken and written—that Amy Tan the writer has participated in shaping, the texts she's heard and read as well as those she has written, and the experiences that underlie all of those texts, in particular her own mother's stories, the language of those stories, and the values and beliefs and ways of seeing the world that discourse represents. But Tan, like the daughters in her novel, is of a different generation and has grown up in a new, English-speaking language community, and it is that experience of difference within a culture, within a family, that her novel explores.

Language is at the heart of Amy Tan's novel and of readers' experiences of that novel—language that divides the generations, that keeps the women of each generation as outsiders to each others' worlds and represents all of the "great cultural, generational and emotional differences" that Karen was trying to explore and understand. The Chinese-American daughters in Tan's novel speak a different variety of English from that which their mothers speak, and that difference, often a source of embarrassment to the daughters who wish to be fully Americanized, also reflects their differences of culture, experience, and ways of viewing the world. As it does for the mother who is waiting to tell her daughter about the meaning of her own experience "in perfect English."

My goal in each of the courses represented in this book has been not only to show how the study of language can be approached through various analytical frameworks and theoretical lenses, but for us to experience the language that underlies the conversations we hear and the texts we read, to see how multiple discourses, many varieties of language and languages—informal and formal, public and private, distant and personal—merge and mingle in the world around us, and to understand that our schooled notion of a single, standard, authoritative discourse leaves out most of the actual language of the worlds we inhabit. The meanings of the diverse cultural worlds we enter through the conversations we tape and the literature we read depend on language as it is used in those worlds and sometimes on words that can't be translated. Like anyone acquiring a secondary discourse, we, as readers, begin to understand the unfamiliar language of such texts by becoming engaged in the world in which it's used:

> "A mother is best. A mother knows what is inside you. . . . A psyche-atricks will only make you *hulihudu*, make you see *heimongmong*."
>
> Back at home I thought about what she said. And it was true. Lately I had been feeling *hulihudu*. And everything around me seemed to be *heimongmong*. These were words I had never thought about in English terms. I suppose the closest in meaning would be "confused" and "dark fog."
>
> But really, the words mean much more than that. Maybe they can't be easily translated because they refer to a sensation that only Chinese people have.
>
> Amy Tan, *The Joy Luck Club*, 188

Amy Tan, in a talk she gave at a meeting of English teachers (1993), spoke about her own ambivalent attitude toward her mother's English. On the one hand, she tells us, "Her language, as I hear it, is vivid, direct, full of observation and imagery. It's the language that helped shape the way I saw things, expressed things, made sense of the world." On the other hand, "I have described it to people as 'broken' or 'fractured' English . . . as if it were damaged and needed to be fixed." Tan presents herself as going through a process, as a writer, that's much like the one we've seen for Karen, beginning by writing what she thought were wittily crafted sentences, like: "That was my mental quandary in its nascent state." And she explains how her development as a writer came about through her coming to use "all of the Englishes I grew up with." She goes on:

Fortunately . . . I later decided I should envision a reader for the stories I would write. And the reader I decided upon was my mother, because these were stories about mothers. So with this reader in mind—and in fact she did read my early drafts—I began to write stories using all the Englishes I grew up with: the English I spoke to my mother, which for lack of a better term might be described as "simple"; the English she used with me, which for lack of a better term might be described as "broken"; my translation of her Chinese, which could certainly be described as "watered down"; and what I imagine to be her translation of her Chinese if she could speak in perfect English, her internal language. (182)

In the end, the power of language for the students in our courses will come from their appreciation of all of their Englishes, of all of their languages and discourses. The work of writers like Tan who try to reconcile and be faithful to the many voices they hear around them is personal but also implicitly political. They remind us that the world doesn't come only in standard English, that its many meanings can't be represented only in the wittily crafted sentences we might learn to write in our English courses, and that our public language too often hides relationships of power that the many voices of our writers and poets but also our students, expose, question, and even subvert.

There are many more questions about language to ask, many more discourses and discourse contexts to explore. The work represented in this book is only a beginning. The exchanges that take place in homes and neighborhoods and schools—in speech and in writing—will continue, contributing many episodes, many voices, many contexts, to conversations that can enrich our understanding of both the nature of discourse and the nature of community. My students and I will return again and again, gathering what appears around us: the exchanges we hear, the storybooks our children and grandchildren produce, the writing and reading and talk that goes on in the speech communities we find in our kitchens and classrooms. Our study of language is not confined to the classroom but embraces the many discourse communities, the many ways of communicating and meaning, the many Englishes as well as other languages, that we find in the worlds we inhabit.

APPENDIX: A GUIDE TO STUDYING LANGUAGE IN SPEECH COMMUNITIES

The student work that appears in the chapters of this book has been drawn from my courses at various levels, from a sophomore introduction to the English language to graduate work in discourse analysis. In all courses, the object of inquiry is language as it is used in our most immediate contexts, whether in our classrooms or in some random moments of ordinary interaction at the kitchen table, and the approaches to our study are drawn from my work with communities of other researchers who are studying language and literacy in a variety of contexts. As in such research, we start with the actual data of language as it is spoken or written by participants in ongoing discourse communities. As we study those data, we begin to see how speakers' underlying grammatical competence is realized in their communicative competence as participants in different communities. We look at the rich variety of linguistic resources that are potentially available to them in the communities in which they are participants and at the ways in which they demonstrate their competence in those communities. We see also the ways in which those communities, whether homes, classrooms, or professional journals, confirm and maintain the discourse of insiders, and how they respond to participants who bring different forms and different communicative styles.

In this section, I have included examples of the sorts of instructions I provide for students as they undertake their study of the issues addressed in the various chapters. In turn, those students who are teaching have directed their own students toward modified versions of the sort of data collection and analysis represented here. As evidenced in the account in Chapter Eight of one teacher's work with her kindergarten class, even very young children can observe and make generalizations about the ways in which language is used around them. Teachers in upper grades link such observation/generalization with the building of a shared vocabulary for more careful analysis, imbedding the study of parts of speech and grammatical structures that's emphasized in most school grammar in the meaningful study of language as it is used in the world.

In each of my courses, we begin our study with conversational data, taping and transcribing those data, and contributing two or three pages of data per student to a class data set. I add a table of contents that includes the name of the student researcher, the topic(s) of the conversational segment, the context in which it was collected and a brief characterization of the participants. Such data books allow us to make comparisons—to see some of the ways that children of different ages interact with their grandparents, to see how women and men discuss the same topic, to see similarities and differences in workplace exchanges. Natural conversation also provides samples of discourse where meanings and intentions are likely to be negotiated among participants, and thus it offers a comparative base for studies of classroom discourse, which is most often controlled by one authoritative speaker—the teacher. At the same time, examples of spoken language used among immediate participants in a conversation provide a counterpoint for the study of the more formal written language that addresses distant or unknown audiences.

To initiate the collection and analysis of data, I offer the following instructions:

Conversational data:

Please tape-record at least 30 minutes of a conversation. The conversation can take place in any setting in which you ordinarily spend time and people interact regularly and comfortably with each other, and it should be a conversation that would have taken place whether or not it was being recorded. The participants should be informed that you are recording the conversation for a class assignment. (Most participants forget the tape recorder and converse naturally after a minute or two.) Transcribe a short segment (about 3–5 minutes), one that contains lively exchanges between two or more participants. In transcribing, try to get down the actual words as they were spoken, including repetitions and pauses and interruptions. Choose a two-page section to contribute to a class data book, and bring in a copy of your tape to play a portion for the class. I'll distribute copies of the data book and keep the tapes on file so that we can listen to them again throughout the semester.

Chapter 1: studying speech communities

Speech communities are formed when people are engaged in ongoing communication with one another (most often when they gather regularly for ongoing and sustained interaction.) The term *discourse community* is also used, particularly when reading and writing as well as speaking and listening play a significant role in communication. (Some discourse communities, especially professional ones, interact almost exclusively through written exchanges.) Speech communities include families, schools, churches, workplaces, neighborhoods.

1. What are the characteristics of the speech community in which you taped this conversation (location; age, education, occupation, sex, social position of participants; racial/ethnic identity; other significant characteristics?) Who are its members? Does it exist within a larger definable community?

2. On what occasions do people in this speech community engage in conversation or other acts of communication of the sort you taped? Do they often focus on particular topics (like the dinner-table question "What did you do in school today?" that's common in some families?). Do they use identifiable genres (stories, jokes, prayers, admonitions, insults?).

3. What community values or aspects of community culture seem to be represented in its conversations? Are you aware of a role that language plays in maintaining these?

4. How are new members (or children) socialized into this community? Do particular practices around language and literacy play a role in that socialization?

5. How would you characterize the discourse of a speaker who gets attention and respect in this community's conversations? What does such a speaker have to be able to do to demonstrate the expected communicative competence of an insider to the community?

You'll probably want to proceed by describing the community from your general knowledge, then making new observations, and finally listening again to the specific data you taped and finding places that point to the larger picture you've given.

Chapter 2: studying the language of young children

Collecting Data:

Please spend 20–30 minutes in a setting where you can hear the language of a young child under five. If you don't know a child from the larger speech community where you taped your conversational data, you might choose a more public setting that a variety of children might inhabit (a fast-food restaurant on a Saturday is a good setting if you don't have other access to a child). Record on tape or in writing as much as you can of the language that you hear from the child or children. Whether you are taking notes or transcribing a tape, do so as accurately as possible, trying to get down the actual words spoken (and not inserting any that the child leaves out), noting distinctive features of pronunciation and of intonation. Make some notes also about the context—who else is with the child, what the setting is. And observe any ways in which the adults and children use aspects of the context as a prop to support the communication of meaning.

Analyzing Data:

For the data you gathered, try to determine the child's stage of language development in terms of both the child's linguistic or grammatical competence and communicative competence as you study the following features.

A. Grammatical Competence

Intonation

Young babies in the babbling stage, before they produce distinguishable words, acquire the information contours of the adult language. As they begin to produce words, they will continue to rely on these contours to indicate how an utterance is to function—as a question, for example—even though they cannot yet represent that function grammatically.

Syntax

1. Length of sentences. A child goes through a one-word stage and a two-word stage of acquisition. The next stage is multiword, beginning with nouns, verbs, adjectives, adverbs (the free lexical morphemes, the content words). Gradually children add grammatical morphemes, both free and bound. (Free grammatical morphemes include articles, prepositions, auxiliaries, conjunctions; bound grammatical morphemes are attached to words and include inflectional verb tense endings, plurals, and comparators like bigg*er*.) Sentences are measured in terms of Mean Length of Utterance (MLU), and all morphemes, inflectional as well as free grammatical and lexical, are counted in determining that length. For "The boy hitted the doggies," the MLU is counted as 7 because it includes the past tense morpheme on "hitt*ed*" and the plural morpheme on dogg*ies*. Typically by age three children have moved past the two-word stage into the multiword stage.

2. Presence of free grammatical morphemes, such as prepositions, auxiliary verbs, articles (moving beyond telegraphic speech).

3. Presence of inflectional morphemes (plural *s*, possessive *s*, comparative *er*, superlative *est*, verb tenses and participles: present *s*, past *ed*, present particple *ing*, past participle *en*).

4. Overgeneralization. Plural and past tense morphemes are overgeneralized for a time showing the child's acquisition of a consistent grammatical principle that overrides inconsistencies in the language, (goed, feets).

5. Word order:
    a. Negation
        With two words: "no" or "not" precedes the other word: "No bed."

With three words: "no" or "not" typically comes between the subject and verb: "Matt no want." "Can't", "don't" appear.

Later: some irregularities in negation with verbs "to be," "to do." Double negatives: "Don't nobody go."

b. Questions

Early questions: subject (S) + verb(V) + intonation: "Daddy shoe(?)"

or V + Object + intonation: "Tie shoe?"

S or V + location + intonation. "Shoe gone?" "Go home?"

Then: Wh word + S + V + intonation: "Where shoe is?

Finally: Wh + inversion of V + S + intonation: "Where is the shoe?"

Phonology In general, vowels are produced in an order proceeding from those pronounced in the back of the mouth to those in the front, consonants from front to back and from more closed to more open in airflow. The acquisition of distinctive features which show phonemic contrast (that show differences in meaning: *pat* vs. *bat*) is regular. Children recognize phonemic distinctions even though they can't yet reproduce them phonetically (e.g. *baf* for *bath*).

Semantics Children often produce unusual lexical items (e.g. upside-over, for upside-down; alligator for elevator). They overextend word meanings (e.g. dog for all living, four-legged animals). And they show a systematic pattern in acquisition of opposites (e.g. understanding and using *more* earlier than *less*).

Review your data and

a. List and count examples of recurrent features.

b. Describe the patterns you have found.

c. Make whatever general observations you can about this child's acquisition of grammatical competence.

B. Communicative Competence

At the same time that they are acquiring the grammatical structures of their native language, children acquire competence in using that language for communication in their particular speech communities. Typically this includes the following:

Accomplishing Speech Acts (getting things done). Were there things that the child you observed seemed to want or want done in the world, and how did the child use language to accomplish those things?

Carrying On Conversation. How did the child get a turn to speak? What can you observe about the turn-taking pattern of the conversation? If you observed two or more children together, did they have different strategies for getting and keeping the floor? If you observed an adult and child in conversation, were there ways in which the adult supported and extended the child's contributions?

Using Discourse Frames. In much of our conversation we draw on patterns that are appropriate to the particular context we're in (like ordering food). Familiar frames support much of a child's conversational interaction (beginning with early games like peekaboo.) Did you observe ways in which the child drew on familiar patterns from a familiar environment to accomplish acts of communication?

How would you describe this child's communicative competence? In comparing samples of children's discourse contributed by others in the class, what patterns do you find that seem to change in a predictable way with children's ages? Are there other patterns/features that seem to vary for children of the same age in a way that suggests that these are characteristic of a particular speech community?

Chapter 3: studying the sharing of meanings

Please take a small section of your original conversational data and do the following:

> Sketch out the semantic domain of meaning (referential/ideational) being brought into or created in this conversation. Each content-bearing word (lexical morpheme) carries links to prior knowledge that is socially-shaped and shared. What are the key words that appear here? What areas of knowledge do they presuppose (e.g. a knowledge of current fashion from a teenager's perspective), and to what extent is the relevant domain of knowledge shared among the participants? What are the propositions (the underlying statements or assertions) that are stated or implied in the text? What immediate situational knowledge is drawn on and how? How is such knowledge added to and expanded on within this discourse context? What part does the level of lexical choices (e.g. technical, formal, informal, slang) play in eliciting (or interfering with) a common understanding and/or signaling that a participant is an insider to a particular speech community (whether that in which the conversation takes place, or a different one)?

Chapter 4: studying pragmatics: speech acts and the communication of intentions

A. It is often easier to perceive a speaker's intentions in a relatively isolated speech act than over the many speech acts that typically flow together in an ongoing conversation. To begin your study of speaker's intention and listener's response, choose a particular type of speech act that is common in the speech community you are studying—a greeting, an apology, a request, an instruction, a reprimand or correction, etc.—and gather 10–15 examples of the act in that community (and perhaps outside of it as well). Record:

- what is said
- who the participants are, (their sex, age, relationship, professional role and/or social status, whether they are insiders or outsiders to this community, and any other information that seems relevant)
- what the context of the exchange is, both in reference to the setting and in relation to the discourse context if the exchange extends beyond this one speech act
- what the intention (illocutionary force) of the initiator of the act seems to be
- whether that intention is carried out directly or indirectly
- what the effect (perlocutionary force) of that act on the other participant(s) seems to be
- whether or not the act seems to constitute a successful speech event

Does your brief study of speech acts suggest any characteristic ways in which intentions are signaled in this community?

B. For the segment of conversation you analyzed for its semantic domain, give an overview of the pragmatic knowledge—interpersonal understandings and intentions, both shared and conflicting, that you see affecting the conversation. What interactional roles do the participants play and how do their contributions contribute to those roles?

C. Do a sentence by sentence analysis in which you comment in as much detail as possible about the role that each utterance (including partial, incomplete, interrupted sentences, and briefer utterances like ohhh or well . . .) contributes to the evolving text (as well as to the semantic/ideational, and pragmatic/interpersonal functions that are being carried out simultaneously in this conversation). Include any observations you have about how contributions are being understood and interpreted by others (discourse processing).

Terms that are roughly comparable: in general linguistic terminology:	in Halliday's functional grammar:
semantic (propositional, referential, logical)	ideational
	interpersonal
pragmatic	textual
discourse, textual	

Chapter 5: studying grammatical structures, lexicon, and the structuring of information in discourse

A. Using a small segment (approximately 10–15 sentences or turns) of your conversational data, analyze the ways in which its grammatical and lexical elements contribute to its information structure and to discourse cohesion. Take into account each of the following sets of questions.

1. What is the central topic of this discourse? Is the topic always in the subject position of the sentence? Does the topic shift as new information is brought in? How is backgrounding/foregrounding of information accomplished? Is there a focusing in from general to specific or indefinite to definite reference? Is anything treated as given information, as if it's already understood, even if it hasn't been said explicitly?
2. Are there any variations on the typical subject/verb/object word order of English sentences. Is any information emphasized or fronted through a less common sentence structure?
3. What elements of cohesion do you find (pronouns, conjunctions, patterned substitutions of one lexical item for another)?
4. What meanings seem to be linked or placed in opposition (contrast) through the various elements of this text?
5. Is there anything else that you notice about these sentences that seems to contribute to their larger meaning (shifts in verb tense, shifts between more formal and more colloquial expressions, etc.)? How do these elements of information structure seem to contribute to the meanings and intentions of the participants in this conversation?

B. Narrative Analysis

Transcribe a narrative section of your conversational data, or elicit (tape and transcribe) a narrative account from someone in the same speech community. Then, using Labov's framework of analysis (pp. 99–106), analyze the narrative. Begin by identifying the major structural units commonly found in narratives (the complicating action—the basic narrative clauses—will by definition always be present, as will the evaluation in any self-initiated narrative):

abstract: a brief initial encapsulation of the story.

orientation: any background information.

complicating action: the sentences containing the basic narrative action. By Labov's definition these are always presented in the preterit (simple past tense), but narrators often shift tenses to tell the events in the present, as if they are currently happening.

evaluation: explicit or embedded statements of the meaning or significance of the events.

result: a statement of the outcome of the events.

coda: a comment that takes the listeners out of the frame of the story and brings them back into the present moment.

Next, extend your analysis by laying out the clauses on a chart to highlight their structural elements, as on p. 103–105, listing the following categories: conjunctions, subjects, auxiliaries, main verbs, direct objects/objects/complements, and adverbs of manner, place, and time.

Look for evidence of the following evaluative devices:

intensifiers: elements that intensify the account of an event, including gesture or expressive phonology but also quantifiers (*so* big) and repetition.

comparators: elements that compare what did happen to what didn't or might have happened. They include negatives, modal auxiliaries (can/could, will/would, shall/should, may/might, along with ought to, supposed to, had to), variations in tense, questions, and comparatives and superlatives.

correlatives: elements that suspend the narrative action, such as progressives and participles, and double attributive adjectives.

explicatives: subordinate clauses added to the main narrative clause, usually with *that* , adding additional information.

Summarize what you discover in your analysis of these evaluative devices and any other features that strike you. What do they point to as the meaning of the story for the narrator, and what does your analysis add to your understanding of both the narrative itself and of its place in the larger conversation?

Overview assignment: chapters 1–5:

Look back at the conversational data you transcribed, your description of the speech community the data came from, and your description of dialect and register. Try to discover an overall pattern in the conversational language of this speech community that is particularly interesting to you. These patterns might be composed of clusters of individual features:

- what is talked about (ongoing daily events vs. big topics, personal vs. impersonal subjects, light vs. serious subjects, current events vs. past)
- how it is talked about (the way the conversation is shaped through patterns of turn-taking and interruptions, of shifts between one language and another, even of silence; the genres like jokes or stories that appear)
- the attitude or stance of the participants (teasing or joking vs. serious, an underlying concern with maintaining the interpersonal relationship versus exchanging information)

Describe the pattern you find emerging in your own data, discussing the features that contribute to that pattern, giving examples of those features from your data, and supporting your description with any other observations you've made. (Patterns often emerge around male/female, parent/child, old friend/new acquaintance, or sibling relationships.)

Then select an example of conversational data collected by another student that seems to resonate in some way with your own. Perhaps the participants and setting are like yours—another group of male friends sitting around someone else's house—or perhaps they're quite different: a group of female friends, a mixed group, a group of adolescents while your group is older. Look carefully at the transcription of that conversation and see what similarities/differences you can find with what you recorded.

Finally, return to your own data and see if you understand anything more about it after this comparison.

Chapter 6: studying differences in language, dialect, and register

A. The experience of language variation.

1. What is your first language? Your first dialect within that language? How would you describe that dialect in regional terms? In socio-regional terms (taking social class into account)? Is your first language or first dialect the same as that of the speech community you recorded? Does that community include speakers of different first languages or dialects? Can you identify differences between your particular patterns of informal, intimate speech and those of others in your current immediate speech community and/or your home community? What characterizes your own ideolect (an individual's variant of a larger variety), and what experiences linked to age, education, regional background, and/or cultural experience account for your unique language patterns?

2. How would you describe the *register* of the conversational data in the speech event you recorded? Is this the typical register used in this context. According to Halliday, register includes the *field of discourse:* the subject matter or the nature of the event like classroom discourse or a doctor/patient exchange; the *mode:* particularly spoken or written but also including genres like stories or jokes; and the *style:* informal/formal, intimate/polite.

3. What *dialect* features of vocabulary, pronunciation, idiomatic expressions seem to you to be distinctive of this conversation; of the speech community you grew up in; of a larger regional area such as Boston?

4. Do the speakers in this exchange shift style (from informal to formal, from more pronounced to less pronounced markers of their regional dialect) or code (from one language to another or from a significantly different variant of English like Black English to standard English)?

5. What are your attitudes toward the language in the speech event you recorded? Are there features that appeared in this conversation that you found puzzling, annoying, embarrassing, particularly pleasant or desirable? Are there features that you think the speakers might change in another context? Are there any features that seem necessary to the particular character of this speech event in this speech community—positive markers of identification and membership in this community?

6. What are your general pet peeves about the language you hear around you? Or things that you find particularly interesting or pleasant (like special vocabulary within a close group)?

7. How would you characterize your own experience as an insider/outsider to various speech communities whose language has marked characteristics? When did you notice that people pronounced words differently or used different vocabulary? Were there times that you felt that you were judged negatively or found yourself with prejudices against others who speak differently from you? Give examples.

B. The acquisition of a second language or code.

Analyze a spoken or written text produced by someone who is acquiring English as a second language or standard English as a second variety of English. (If you don't have access to such a text, you might return to one reproduced on pp. 133–34.) Note all of the features of this text that vary from the standard. Look for:

1. use of inflectional morphemes (e.g. markers of tense, plurality, possession)
2. variant syntactic patterns
3. variant lexical items (vocabulary and idioms, category changes in which a word that is used as a noun or verb, for example, would not be used in that category in standard English
4. variant orthographic features (spelling, punctuation, capitalization) if the text is written
5. unusual features of pronunciation if the text is spoken

What systematic patterns of variation appear and what do they tell you about the speaker's/writer's current interlanguage, about the person's working hypotheses about the language/code being acquired? Where are there variations in the person's own characteristic patterns, suggesting an area where an aspect of the interlanguage may be undergoing revision? Do any features indicate that the target language the writer or speaker is acquiring is in itself a dialect that varies from Standard English? In a written text, what do orthographic features suggest about the writer's hypotheses about how English is written and about literate strategies that may be being transferred from a first language literacy. Look at rhetorical features of the text as well, and comment on what they tell you about the speaker's/writer's communicative competence as a participant in a particular English-speaking discourse community.

Chapter 7: studying communicative style across differences in culture, gender, and age

A. Contextualization cues and the signaling of meanings

Observe a common speech event in a familiar speech community. How do speakers convey the following information:

- what the topic or message is and what's foreground and background information in relation to that topic
- what knowledge and attitudes are assumed to be shared
- what is old and what is new information
- what the participants' attitudes or points of view are about what is being said

What "contextualization cues" (conveyed through prosody—rhythm, stress, pitch, patterns or intonation, tone of voice; syntax; and lexical choice) signal such information and show how listeners are to interpret the actual words being said?

What seem to be required elements of this speech event in this community? How are turn-taking and interaction patterns negotiated?

B. Conversational discourse style

Return to your initial conversational data or look at a segment of another taped conversation. Do all participants share a common conversational style, a common understanding about how meanings are to be signaled? Can you identify any moments when communication seems to break down momentarily, where meanings are misunderstood and utterances are misinterpreted? What differences in conversational style seem to contribute to such breakdowns, and might differences in communicative experiences according to the age, gender, or cultural/ethnic background of the participants be the source of the differences in style? (Do you find female speakers, for example, to show evidence of the characteristics that have shown up in various studies of "women's speech" such as a tendency to ask questions rather than make statements, to make contributions that facilitate the flow of conversation, to use backchanneling—positive minimal responses like "mm hmm"?)

C. Analyzing Literary Texts from a Discourse Perspective

Choose a literary text that focuses on a particular discourse community as marked by a particular variety of language or style. Short narrative texts can be analyzed through the sort of Labovian narrative analysis applied to conversational narrative in Chapter Five, but they can also be studied from a broader discourse perspective. Read through the following questions and reread the story, keeping the questions in mind and noting any details which would help to provide answers. (The study of literature with the methods of linguistics is commonly referred to as stylistics.)

1. Speech communities and language variation: What are the characteristic features of the language spoken by various characters in the story? Is more than one social or regional variety of language represented? Are there features of a register associated with a particular discourse context? Where there are differences within the story, how might they be significant to the interactions of the characters? To the story's meanings?

2. Shared knowledge and systems of reference: Writers create worlds and place their readers in relation to these worlds, in part, by the amount of background information they offer and, in part by using aspects of a system of reference. One way to push the reader into an active role is to offer little orienting information: how much orientation is provided at the beginning of this text, and where else is it provided, if at all? Another is to use forms of reference, at the beginning of the story, which would ordinarily only be used to refer back to previous discourse. Look at definite and indefinite articles and at pronouns in the first paragraph of

the story? What is their effect? Where do they place you, the reader, in this scene? Is there other evidence to suggest that the reader is being treated as an insider, rather than being introduced to an unfamiliar context?

3. Lexical coherence: Just as cooperating participants in a conversation establish and maintain a common focus with words which are related in meaning to those of other participants (lexical coherence), the writer of literature establishes a coherent domain of meaning by the repetition of key words and cognates. In addition, the writer may cluster different sets of words and meanings around particular characters, creating different world views. (In "'The River,'" for example, Flannery O'Connor repeats key words in different contexts, at different critical points of the story, and she builds related sets of words to represent the world and values of the boy's parents on the one hand and of his baby-sitter on the other.) Using your text, note examples of lexical (and thus thematic) coherence. What lexical items and lexical substitutions keep reappearing, and when? Then sketch out the semantic fields (key words) associated with the main characters and/or settings. Finally note any examples you find of lexical ambiguity, where different speakers use the same words but with different meanings. Comment on what such lexical/semantic elements contribute to your understanding of possible interpretations of the story.

4. Syntax and semantic roles:
   Sketch out the subject/verb/object pattern of the sentences in the story, and note whether the words referring to the main character(s) occur in positions that mark the character as taking the role of the agent or actor (subject position), the patient (direct object), or the beneficiary (indirect object) in key portions of the story? Does the pattern (and thus the semantic role) change at any points?

   Another way to see roles within larger units of text is to summarize the plot in simple noun + predicate sentences. What do you list as the basic structural elements of the plot? Do you see a pattern to the appearance of various names or other nouns in agent position in your list?

   Modality qualifies the truth of a proposition, with verb forms such as may, might, should, must, questions, negatives (anything other than simple present or past tense forms) and suggests alternative propositions. Where do you find modality, expressing such qualifications, in the story? Is it linked to evaluation? (It would be for Labov). Who is evaluating in these instances? What is suggested about the meaning of the story for the narrator?

5. Do you find other signals or contextualization cues (tone such as sarcasm, genres such as jokes or parables) that suggest what frame of reference the reader or the characters within the story might use in interpreting its events?

Comment on how each of these elements contributes, finally to your reading of the text.

Chapter 8: studying classroom discourse and school styles

The next several investigations are focused on the study of discourse in one context that is more public than those in which most of the conversations among family members, friends, or coworkers studied earlier take place: the classroom. In the classroom, as in other more public contexts, participants from different home discourse communities come together for purposes beyond the immediate building of interpersonal bonds and sharing of knowledge that helps to support the relationships of family, friends, and community. More formal and predictable discourse structures mediate the styles of different small and intimate communities, while a wider and more public world of shared knowledge may be assumed and built on. The discourse of the classroom shares some features with the discourse of other more public settings with distinct purposes such as courtrooms or health care settings, and the following guidelines for the study of classroom discourse be applied to the study of other public or semi-public settings as well.

A. Observing patterns of classroom discourse.

Choose a classroom setting in which you can get permission to tape a 30–minute segment of classroom interaction, and schedule at least two visits, so that you can observe general patterns on one visit and follow up with closer observation in another. The class may be one that you are teaching or attending (including this one). During your visits, in addition to taping a portion of the class, observe and make notes on the following elements:

1. the types and purposes of speech events that occur in this setting
   Classroom discourse is often most broadly characterized in terms of lecture, discussion, group work, etc., but often the boundaries of those categories are fuzzy, and each category typically includes a sequence of smaller events: in the course of a lecture a teacher may read from notes, expand on those notes, ask questions, take questions from students, etc. Considering the pragmatic purpose of each smaller event may help you to more clearly define its type. (In elementary and secondary classrooms one purpose that emerges in most activities is controlling class behavior.)

2. the sequence or structure of these events
   You can generally see a distinct movement from one type of event to another. In classrooms these shifts are typically controlled by the teacher and their boundaries are usually marked explicitly: the teacher closes a book and moves to the black board, or moves away from the desk and walks around the room, or asks students to move their chairs or to get out particular materials.

3. the amounts and sorts of talk contributed by different participants
   Who takes the longest turns, and who controls these turns and determines what they will be about? In classrooms, teachers typically control

the larger discourse patterns, but there's a lot of variation in the amount and kinds of student talk that are allowed/encouraged.

4. the patterns of interaction

   In some classrooms all allowed interaction takes place between teacher and students. In others, student to student interaction is encouraged in various ways.

5. levels of address, politeness, and other indicators of social relationship and/or authority

   In most public school classrooms, the teacher is referred to by Mr. or Ms., the student by first name. Yet teachers often use the polite or indirect forms which characterize relationships between relative equals (Please take out your books! Can you add to what you have just said?) Tone of voice is as important here as the actual words spoken.

Your notes can be rough (and if you're focusing on a classroom in which you're teaching they're likely to be very rough). You'll want to draw on them for other parts of this investigation.

Next, transcribe a short segment of your tape, showing a typical or interesting small speech event.

B. How would you characterize the communicative style of this classroom?

From your observation notes and/or your transcribed sample of classroom discourse, is there evidence of misunderstanding or miscommunication between any of the participants? Look in particular for evidence of differences between this particular school style and the styles of communication that learners may be bringing from their home communities and/or their prior experiences of schooling. Where there are communicative breakdowns that suggest significant differences between a learner's understanding of contextualization cues from another context and the signals that are given in this context, you may want to do as Cindy Ballenger did (cf. pp. 170) and consult informants who are part of the discourse community that the learner is most at home in to gain a clearer understanding of what the learner's expectations might be.

Chapter 9: studying the language of learning

A. Analyzing classroom discourse.

Analyze a 10 to 15 line segment of your transcribed data, keeping in mind the three perspectives from which you analyzed your conversational segment:

1. the referential meaning or propositional content that is created in the context of this speech event through building on key words and propositional relations. What prior/shared knowledge is presupposed? What immediate situational knowledge is drawn on and how? How is such

knowledge added to and expanded on within this discourse context?

2. the pragmatic purposes embedded in this event, and the ways in which the participants' roles and their interpersonal understandings and intentions affect this interaction.

3. the process by which an evolving text involving both referential and pragmatic meanings is created in this context. Here take into account the ways in which the evolving information structure of the text signals both referential and pragmatic purposes: the ways in which a topic is introduced, maintained, brought into the foreground, the things that are treated as given information, the elements used to create cohesion and to mark the relevance and connection of particular contributions to the preceding discourse, the role of any shifts in register or code (from more formal to colloquial, from one dialect or language to another). Consider also the ways in which the participants' shared knowledge of the nature and purpose of this event is signaled (or where and how differing assumptions come into play).

How do the discourse structures of this portion of a typical lesson in this classroom support (or detract from) the teacher's goals and students' apparent goals and shape the learning that goes on here?

What prior texts and contexts are referenced and brought into the present text, and what larger framework of knowledge is being created in the emergent text of this classroom?

B. Discourse styles, structures and purposes.

Next, move from the evidence of a small segment of discourse, taken out of context, to re-seeing that segment (or another segment) in relationship to the larger structures, purposes and contexts of classroom (or other public) discourse. Public discourse (particularly classroom discourse, but also legal discourse, medical discourse, news, etc.) operates within a larger framework of commonly shared and frequently explicit societal assumptions about its purposes and what is relevant and appropriate to those purposes (in contrast to the shared assumptions of private discourse, which are more privately held, implicit, and immediately negotiable). For educational contexts, those larger purposes have to do generally with having learners become literate and knowledgeable to a degree appropriate to their present level of education, but also have to do with acquiring disciplinary-specific knowledge/methods/ways of thinking, acquiring new linguistic resources, being socialized into particular ways of behaving, thinking, valuing. And the discourse in such contexts is structured in particular ways to achieve these purposes. Drawing on your observation notes, and your transcription analysis, describe what seem to be the larger purposes of the setting you observed, the sorts of activities or speech events that took place during your observation, and the ways in which the larger purpose was enacted within the particular interactions that took place in the setting. Consider how well matched the larger purposes and the particular events and interactions you observed seem to be. How would you finally characterize this classroom or other setting as a discourse community?

Overview #2

Looking at your analyses of your two transcribed texts, one from a conversation among intimates and the other from a segment of classroom or other more public discourse, and drawing on your knowledge of the context in which each was produced, describe the most striking similarities/differences that emerge in the texts you have been studying (or in other portions of your data) produced in two discourse contexts : in ways that meanings are created and shared, in the relationship between referential/ideational and pragmatic/interpersonal purposes, in the ways in which the underlying values of the discourse community are represented, highlighted, and maintained. While one text is from a more private/personal conversational context and the other from a more public setting, people also have personal/private relationships to and within public discourse contexts, and in many such settings—particularly classrooms—the negotiation between personal and public meanings and purposes is particularly complex. What do you observe about such negotiation, about the role that effective communicative strategies from home discourse styles might play in helping or hindering more public communication, and about the ways in which the structures and cues of the more public context might mediate different strategies and/or close off some strategies that could be effectively brought into play in those contexts?

Chapter 10: studying a learner's literate productions and acquisition of literacy

The next investigations shift the focus of inquiry from the study of spoken discourse—whether personal and informal or more public and perhaps more formal—to the study of written discourse and the acquisition of the written discourses of schools and academic communities. We won't really be leaving our early study behind, but rather extending it to follow through its implications for writing, writers, and the teaching of writing (and reading). For the next set of investigations, then, please collect a portfolio containing several written texts produced by the same writer over time (over several weeks, several months, or many years), including writing at different stages of completion (from rough drafts to revised final versions) and for different purposes. The texts may be those of any writer, of any age. (The texts may be your own if you choose, either collected over earlier stages of your life as a writer, or from your recent and current work, since we are always learners and are always in the process of acquiring the literate discourses of the communities for which we write).

Texts

A. Studying the literate productions of young children

Children begin to acquire literacy long before they enter school, and it is possible to learn a great deal about the understanding a child has about how literacy works from looking at carefully at the texts a preschooler produces for different purposes (drawing a picture that's the basis for a story, making a greeting card) even as she just begins to make marks that represent letters. Once a child is of school age, that child's literate productions are likely to look more like the texts we recognize as writing, but important texts for understanding the child's hypotheses may be produced as often outside of school contexts as in, and favorite genres like greeting-card writing may continue to give evidence of important understandings that aren't as clearly evident in prescribed school texts.

Begin by examining one text, and then extend your analysis across texts produced at different times, across stages toward a completed text, and/or across texts produced for different purposes. What do you find about the state and development of the child's knowledge in the following areas?

1. Language: What syntactic features stand out? What constructions are commonly used? Is there evidence that new ones are being tried out? What about vocabulary? Style? (Is there any evidence of style-shifting? How would you name the dominant style?) Do you find features that you would consider to be more characteristic of oral language? of written language? Do you see changes across the texts you examine?

2. Orthography and features of written language: From the evidence of one text, what kinds of knowledge does the child seem to have about features of the written language—the formation of letters, word spacings, spelling, capitalization, other text conventions like (in English) writing from left to right in lines that move from top to bottom? Does all of this knowledge appear to be systematized, or is some in flux? Does it change across texts?

3. Grapho-phonemic relationships: From the earliest text you've collected, what evidence do you find of this child's hypotheses about the relationships between letters and sounds? What invented (nonstandard) spellings do you find, and is there a pattern to them that continues throughout the text? Do you find change and/or development of more standard patterns from one text to another? (Children typically build on what they know about the letters in their names or in other words they see written frequently—like stop—and they're likely to build words with consonants at first, adding vowels more irregularly for a while.) If there's a chance to read with a child, what relationship do you find between the sounds the child decodes confidently and the ones he/she encodes predictably in texts?

4. Written texts and their conventions: From the evidence of one text, what does the child seem to know about genres of literate discourse and the

conventions that represent them? (These conventions may be linguistic structures: past tense for stories; phrases like "once upon a time" for placement in time; text structures: chapter books, marking of beginnings and endings: "the end"; or relationships between text structures and particular genres: greeting cards, letters, picture story books.)

5. Shared knowledge: What shared knowledge is assumed in a text? How is shared knowledge created and maintained? Do you see any indications that the writer is aware of a reader, either in the explicit introduction of information that the writer has but the reader might not, or in any other features that would elicit the reader's involvement?

6. Cultural literacy, other domains of knowledge, and the world of other texts: What references, if any, are made to the knowledge of a larger literate community? To knowledge represented in other texts?

7. The literate context and the uses of literacy: What evidence is there in the text of the child's sensitivity to the context for which the text is being produced? (What can you learn about the texts that are valued in that context, by interviewing the child, the parent, the teacher or by observing the context?) Such evidence can show up across all of the above categories, in choices of particular words, styles, genres, in what's assumed as shared knowledge and what literate references are included. Does the text seem to be shaped wholly in response to the demands of the context, such as fulfilling a school task?

8. Pragmatic functions: What are the child's intentions and purposes with this text and how are they signaled and achieved? What interpersonal functions might the child be carrying out through this text and how? If the text is not shaped wholly by school purposes, does this child make use of the text-event for other purposes (to discover and express his own meanings, to respond to another child's productions, to please a parent, to offer an implicit critique of a classroom event)? Have the several texts you've gathered been produced for different primary purposes? Do they show the child's awareness of some of the different functions and purposes of literate activity (even in how they are edited, presented)?

B. Studying the literate productions of older writers

Begin your study of an older writer by analyzing the categories above (Once literacy is firmly established, #3—the writer's understanding of graphophonemic representation—will be fixed for a first language, but writers typically hypothesize about spelling in a second language based on the rules of their first, many of which do not apply in English, and such hypotheses also undergo gradual refinement.) In applying these categories, look at the texts your writer has produced, commenting on what they tell you about each of these aspects of the writer's understanding, across tasks and purposes and/or over time. For adult writers, you may find more variation in how these sorts of knowledge are manifested across texts produced for different purposes and audiences, and less variation over time. Each time a writer begins to produce texts for a new discourse community, the process of testing out hypotheses about linguistic and rhetorical forms, text structures, and shared cultural knowledge begins again, and texts will show evidence of approximations that are gradually refined toward the norm of the new community.

Chapter 11: context and written discourse: studying spoken and written texts

While precisely the same text can be represented in speech or in writing, the contextual demands of speaking versus writing lead to some frequent and regular patterns of differences. To analyze those differences, you will need to tape the text produced by a speaker—telling a story, responding to interview questions, engaged in conversation—and to elicit a written text on the same subject, or vice versa. Asking a conversationalist to provide a written account of what was said in the conversation, or asking a writer to talk about the points she/he was making with the written text, as we see Karen doing in Chapter Eleven, are useful ways to elicit comparable texts. (At other times, having asked my students to tape interviews with each other about their acquisition of literacy and/or about the occasions on which formalized oral language, such as prayers or storytelling, were used in their families or communities and/or in school, I ask them to present a written account of what they said or learned, and then compare the transcription of the oral version with the written. (See Kutz et al, *Discovery* 1993, for ways of building on such activities in a freshman writing class.)

According to Chafe (1982), spoken texts are most often characterized by *fragmentation* or loose stringing together of ideas that occurs frequently in spoken language versus the *integration* or compacting of ideas densely that's most often seen in written texts. Likewise spoken texts show syntactic features associated with *involvement*, where part of the linguistic expression of the speaker serves to maintain a personal connection with the listener as opposed to the *detachment* associated with written texts, where the producer of the text may be more concerned about the accurate representation of ideas and less concerned about maintaining a personal connection with the reader or listener. While formal spoken texts such as lectures typically have the integration and detachment features more typical of writing, and informal written texts (or literature) may have the involvement, if not the fragmentation, features of spoken texts, spoken and written texts produced for comparable audiences and purposes nevertheless tend to differ in predictable ways.

Look for occurrences of the following features in each text:	*Spoken*	*Written*

Features associated with fragmentation:
Incomplete sentences

Coordinators
Repetition of words
Predicate adjectives (The house was *old.)*

Integrative features:
Subordinators
Series of repeated elements, e.g.. infinitive
phrases: he like to run, to jump, and to ride
Attributive adjectives preceding a noun:
The *old* house
Nominalizations (verb forms, like
"nominalize," made into nouns)/other category changes
Participles (with *ing, ed, en*)
Relative clauses (with *who, which, that*)
Complement clauses (He learned *that . . .*)
Conjoined phrases

Involvement features:
First and Second Person References
References to the Speaker's Mental Processes
(I think)
Evidence of Monitoring of Information Flow
(You know?)
Emphatic Particles (just, really)
Fuzziness (that stuff)
Direct Quotes

Detachment features:
Passive voice (The window was broken.)
Detachment is primarily characterized by the absence of involvement features

Consider the effect of these features on the texts in question, looking particularly for aesthetic qualities like the rhythm created by repetition, the immediacy created through dialogue, and the sense of being on the scene that's created by imagery (cf. Tannen, 1989).

After you have completed your count, reflect on the patterns you see. What would you add to or alter in the picture of linguistic differences between spoken and written language that Chafe has presented?

The relative prevalence of features of involvement vs. detachment and of fragmentation vs. integration in each text may not correspond wholly to the mode of communication (speech or writing). What is the speaker/writer responding to, in the context for which these texts were produced, in creating a text with these features? To what extent is he/she focusing in each text on each of the three functions of language we've been studying—the propositional/referential (ideational), the pragmatic (interpresonal), and the discourse (textual) functions.

Afterword: Final Reflections

Reviewing your studies of language in different discourse communities and contexts over the course of the semester, comment on any themes that appear across
your studies, any new understandings that emerge from the juxtaposition of
different texts and or contexts, any further questions that you hope to explore.

GLOSSARY

affective filter: in second language acquisition, the affective states, like anxiety, that can interfere with a learner's ability to take in or produce the new language.

abstract: an introductory portion of a conversational narrative, providing a summary or overview.

accent: the distinctive pronunciation of a language within a regional or social dialect or by a non-native speaker.

acquisition (versus learning): in some theories of second language learning, the process by which the new language is taken in without conscious effort or formal teaching.

active sentence: a sentence in which the agent is encoded as the grammatical subject of the sentence.

adjective: a lexical item that modifies a noun.

adverb: a lexical item that modifies a verb.

affix: a bound morpheme attached to a root morpheme (as a prefix, suffix) and modifying the meaning or syntactic category (e.g. *indecipherable*)

agent: in the action represented in a sentence, a thematic role borne by the entity that initiates or performs the action.

antonyms: words with opposite meanings.

appropriateness conditions: the conditions necessary to accomplishing the intentions commonly associated with a particular speech act, such as an apology.

aspect: a grammatical category of verbs used to mark the way in which a situation described by a verb takes place in time (continuous, repetitive, instantaneous).

attributive adjective: an adjective that precedes a noun and functions syntactically as part of the noun phrase.

auxiliary verb: a verb used with (or instead of) a main verb to carry grammatical information such as **tense** and **aspect** or **modality**.

backchannel: in conversational discourse, the utterances that echo what the principal speaker is saying or affirm that it has been heard (e.g. "mmm-hm").

bound morpheme: a morpheme that must be attached to another element (that cannot constitute a word by itself, e.g. *ed* in *walked*).

case: an inflectional category that marks the grammatical function of a noun phrase as subject, object, etc.

caretaker language: the language that parents and caretakers may use with young children, often somewhat simplified with a particular pattern of intonation.

categories: groupings of words by semantic and grammatical functions. **Lexical categories** include the primary meaning-bearing words (nouns, verbs, adjectives, and adverbs). **Functional categories** include words that primarily serve grammatical functions (prepositions, conjunctions, and auxiliaries).

clause: a unit of syntax that includes a noun phrase (NP) and a verb phrase (VP). A clause can stand by itself as a simple sentence or function as a constituent of a coordinate sentence or complex sentence.

coda: a final portion of a conversational narrative, closing the frame of the narrative action and creating a link to the topic or theme of the larger conversation.

code: a language, or variety of a language with significant linguistic differences, such as Black English.

code-switching: shifting from one language to another or one variety to another within a conversation or speech event.

coherence: the overall thematic and structural unity of a larger spoken or written text.

cohesion: connections made within a segment of discourse through patterns of reference, repetition, substitution—sentence by sentence.

communicative competence: a speaker's underlying knowledge of both the linguistic system of a language and the ways to use and interpret the language appropriately in particular discourse contexts.

competence (versus performance): the idealized grammatical system as it exists in the minds of all speakers.

complicating action: the core sequence of events in a narrative.

comprehensible input: in second language acquisition, whatever the learner can understand and make meaning from in what is heard or read.

conjunction: a category of words that serve to join like elements.

constituent: a syntactic unit in a sentence, such as a noun phrase.

contextualization cues: surface features that signal a frame of reference to be used in the interpretation of an utterance, such as a sarcastic tone.

conversational maxims: the maxims of relation, quality, quantity, and manner, which govern aspects of a speaker's contribution to a speech act, suggesting that such contributions should be relevant, truthful, as informative as necessary, and delivered in a way appropriate to the context.

cooperative principle: the underlying assumption that participants in any conversation or speech act intend to cooperate in an act of communication and therefore will offer and interpret utterances in accordance with the four conversational maxims.

copula: the verb *to be,* used to equate the expressions on either side of it, e.g. He *is* old. In Black English the copula is deleted wherever a contraction is allowed in standard English ("He old'"="He's old").

creole: a fully grammaticized language that develops from a pidgin in an area where two or more languages are in contact and is then spoken as a first or native language in some speech community.

decoding: in reading, the recognition of words through the translation of letters into corresponding sounds.

deixis: marking place or time relative to the speaker's position (here/there; now/then).

dependent clause: a syntactic structure in which one clause is subordinate to another.

determiner: a category of words that combine with nouns to form noun phrases and specify whether the noun is definite or indefinite (includes articles: *a, the;* demonstratives: *these;* quantifiers: *some*).

dialect: a variety of a language that speakers share with others from the same region or social group.

discourse: linguistic units composed of several sentences; a sequence of utterances that form a larger speech event.

discourse analysis: the study of language as it is used by speakers and writers in actual communicative contexts.

encoding: in writing, the use of letters to represent the sounds and words of the spoken language.

error analysis: an approach to research in second language acquisition and in composition in which a learner's errors are studied to discover developmental patterns.

evaluation: an structural element of narrative in which the speaker states or suggests the meaning he/she gives to the events being narrated.

free morpheme: a morpheme that can stand by itself as a word.

function words: words such as prepositions or conjunctions whose main function is to specify grammatical relationships rather than semantic content.

generative grammar: a description of the rules of a language whereby an infinite set of sentences in the language can be generated.

given/new information: given information is that which has already been provided within the discourse event or that can be assumed to be known by speaker and listeners; new information is not known by all participants at a particular moment and must be stated.

grammatical competence: knowledge of the grammar of a language and the ability to produce and understand grammatical structures.

grammatical morphemes: those morphemes, whether free (as words) or bound (as elements of a word) that serve primarily a grammatical versus a lexical function.

graphemes: the symbols of an alphabetic writing system; the graphic representations of the phonemes of the language.

grapho–phonemic system: the systematic relationship of graphemes and phonemes within an alphabetic writing system.

ideational function: the aspect of a functional grammar that describes the ways in which language allows us to name and make statements about the world.

ideolect: the unique pattern of features that an individual speaker acquires through his/her own experience of language.

iconic signs: signs that offer a non–arbitrary relationship between meaning and its representation, as when a computer icon uses a visual image associated with the thing it stands for (such as a tiny sketch of a printer).

illocutionary force: the intentions of the speaker in producing an utterance.

implicature: the implied meaning conveyed by the intention violation of a conversational maxim, such as the violation of the maxim of quality (truthfulness) in sarcasm: "The coach is *so kind* to her players."

independent (main) clause. A clause that contains an NP and VP and is not embedded in or subordinated to another clause.

indexical signs: signs that arise from an observed connection to their referents (smoke/fire).

indirect speech act: an utterance whose literal and intended meanings are different. "Can you get out your books?" is literally a question but is likely to be intended by the teacher as a command to his students.

inflection: a morphological process that modifies a word's form in order to mark its grammatical subclass (such as singular vs. plural).

information structure: the way in information is introduced and foregrounded or backgrounded within a unit of discourse, showing what should be attended to and what aspects are related to one another.

intensifiers: elements such as adjectives and adjectives that intensify the experience being conveyed of the narrative action.

interlanguage: the systematic but idiosyncratic and ever-changing system of grammar that a second language learner has in place at any moment in the acquisition of the new language, typically combining features of the native language with those of the new or target language.

interpersonal function: the aspect of a functional grammar that describes the ways in which language allows us to act, maintain relationships, and place ourselves in the world through language.

intonation: the pitch contour of a phrase or sentence.

invented/inventive spelling: a characteristic phase in the development of literacy in which the writer uses what he/she knows of sound/letter correspondences to represent words, rather than using the spelling conventions of the standard written language.

IRE (initiation, response, evaluation): the most common pattern of teacher-initiated classroom discourse.

jargon: a vocabulary that is peculiar to a particular speech community, particularly a professional community.

language acquisition: the process by which a child's underlying grammatical competence is realized in his/her native language; the process by which the ability to speak and comprehend a second language is gained through exposure to the language versus direct instruction.

language community: a group of people who regard themselves as using the same language.

language variation: how a particular language varies among the different communities that use it .

lexical ambiguity: the use of words with multiple meanings.

lexical field: a set of words with related meanings.

lexical morphemes: those morphemes that primarily carry meaning versus primarily serving a grammatical function.

lexicon: the component of a grammar containing a speaker's knowledge of words and morphemes–both their meanings and how they can be used grammatically; a speaker's internalized dictionary.

linguistic variable: a linguistic element that appears in different forms (different variants) in a speech community.

locution: the literal meaning of an utterance.

major word classes: the categories of free lexical morphemes: nouns, verbs, adjectives, adverbs.

marked and unmarked: marked features or terms are those which stand out against the common background. In general use, "dog" is an unmarked term applying to all dogs, male or female, while "bitch" is marked for the sex of the animal. Used as a pair, "bitch" and "dog" both become marked.

maxims (conversational): of quality (making one's contribution true), **of quantity** (making one's contribution as informative as required), **of manner** (avoiding ambiguity and obscurity), **of relation** (making one's contribution relevant).

mean length of utterance (MLU): the total number of free morphemes and bound lexical and grammatical morphemes in a child's utterance.

minor word classes: categories of free morphemes that primarily serve a grammatical function (such as prepositions, conjunctions).

modal verbs: auxiliary verbs through which a speaker conveys attitudes or other suggestions about their assertions (*can, will, shall, may,* etc.).

morphemes: the minimal units in a language that in themselves carry meaning or serve a grammatical function.

morphology: the study of the structure of morphemes and the formation of words.

native language: a person's first language, the one first spoken as a child.

new information: information that is introduced into the discourse for the first time.

non-standard dialect: a variety of language that differs from the standard dialect in systematic ways.

noun phrase (NP): a unit of syntax containing some form of a noun.

orientation: an introductory portion of a narrative that orients the listener with reference to the time and place of the events being narrated.

orthography: the written form of a language, a spelling system.

overextension: a child's extension of the meaning of a word (e.g. "dog" to include all large animals).

overgeneralization: a child's or second language learner's generalization of a rule of syntax to apply to more instances than would be the case in the adult, native language grammar (such as always using "s" to mark the plural, even where plurality is indicated in another way: "those childrens").

participle: the form of the main verb that occurs after an auxiliary: "I am *going.*" "I have *gone.*"

passive sentence: a sentence in which the thematic object is placed in the subject position, while the thematic subject or agent may appear in a prepositional phrase (The shoes were bought by Melanie).

performance (versus competence): a speaker's (writer's) actual production at a given moment as opposed to the speaker's underlying knowledge of the grammatical system of the language.

performance error: an deviation from the underlying grammatical knowledge of a speaker or writer that appears in an actual utterance—as when a speaker omits a word or morpheme that would be required in the grammar of the speaker's dialect.

performatives: speech acts that have the force of action in the world: a promise, a resignation.

perlocutionary effect: unintended effect of a speech act on a listener.

phoneme: a sound difference that is meaningful within a language, because it distinguishes one word from another (as /d/ and /p/ distinguish "dig" and "pig").

phonemics: the representation of the sounds that are meaningful in a given language.

phonetics: the study of all of the sounds that have been identified as occurring in human languages, how they are produced and perceived.

phonics: the study of sound/letter correspondences in the teaching of reading.

phonology: the study of the sound system of a language and the rules that govern the perception of sounds as meaningful elements of words.

phrase–structure rules: a rule that specifies how a syntactic constituent is formed out of other smaller syntactic constituents (e.g. S=NP + VP).

pidgin: a simple language that develops in multilingual contact situations in which the words of one language (usually that of the dominant group, most often the colonizers) are used in very rudimentary grammatical combinations: pidgins are not spoken natively by anyone.

pragmatic function: that which allows us to act, maintain relationships, and place ourselves in the world through language.

pragmatics: the study of how language functions as a mode of communication, a way to get things done in the world, and how context influences the interpretation of meaning.

predicative adjective: an adjective that follows the verb and forms part of a verb phrase. "The shoes are *new*."

prescriptive grammar: a set of rules prescribing the forms a language should have as opposed to describing the forms actual speakers use.

propositional/referential function: the function of language which allows us to name and make statements about the world.

prosody: the larger qualities of sound in a language, beyond phonemes: including qualities of duration, stress, pitch, loudness.

reference: the relationship between words and the concepts to which they refer.

referential meaning: the meaning that an expression has by virtue of the ability to refer to a particular entity in the world.

register: a language variety or identifiable pattern of discourse that appears across similar contexts (e.g. baby talk).

relative clause: a clause that is embedded in a noun phrase and serves to modify a noun.

repair: a turn in a conversation whereby an earlier utterance is corrected or clarified.

resolution/result: the portion of a narrative in which the outcome of the complicating action is presented.

scaffolding: the process by which one participant in a conversation supports the contributions of another, as when parents or teachers work to extend the utterances of a child.

school grammar: the mixture of rules of linguistic etiquette, prescriptive grammar, and descriptive grammar that is typically taught in schools.

semantics: the study of the systematic ways in which languages structure meaning in words and sentences.

semiotics: the study of signs and the representation of meaning, including, but extending beyond, language to culturally significant areas like styles of clothing.

sense: the relationship of words within a consistent conceptual system.

semantic field: a domain of words that may have different referents but a common association, as with a person or setting or event.

sentence (S): a syntactic unit consisting of a noun phrase and a verb phrase.

sign: a form related to a meaning: a word, gesture, etc.; a unit of communicative structure comprised of a signifier (such as the sequence of sounds forming a word) and a signified (such as the concept of an entity in the world).

sociolinguistics: the study of how language is used in and affected by social context.

speech community: a group whose members share both a particular variety of language and the norms for its appropriate use in a social context.

speech event: a sequence of utterances or series of speech acts that take place within one encounter.

Speech Act Theory: the theory that the basic statement or structural unit of an utterance not only states a proposition, but carries with it both the intentions of the speaker and unintended effects on a listener.

standard: the variety of a language that is considered to be the norm, generally used in government and the media and taught in schools.

style: characteristic variations in a language across different speech communities, such as casual versus formal speech.

surface structure: the final syntactic form of an utterance.

symbolic signs: signs that offer an arbitrary relationship between signifier and signified, dependent on convention within a community–such as the relationship between the sounds that make up a word and the concept to which the word refers.

synonyms: two words or expressions with identical meanings.

syntax: the ways the words of a language are combined in phrases and sentences; the component of the mental grammar that represents speakers' knowledge of how to create and comprehend such structures.

target language: a second or non-native language that is being learned.

telegraphic speech: a phase in children's language development in which several words are strung together but grammatical morphemes are omitted.

tense: the representation in syntax and morphology of the time of an event or action relative to the moment of speaking.

text: any set of utterances, spoken or written, that can be represented in writing.

textual function: the function of language that allows speakers to attend to and structure discourse and to carry out the ideational and interpersonal functions simultaneously in a discourse context.

textual reference: a reference recoverable from the text itself.

tone groups: the grouping of words in spoken language through changes in pitch.

topic/comment: a discourse or information structure in which a topic is introduced and then commented on, generally by one speaker within a sentence, but sometimes across speakers.

transformation: a rule that moves a category within a syntactic structure to create a new syntactic structure.

transformational generative grammar: the theory of grammar that focuses on the rules by which syntactic patterns are transformed to generate an infinite variety of new sentences.

tree diagram: the diagramming of a phrase or sentence in terms of the hierarchical relationships of its constituents.

truth conditions: the truth or falsity of a statement with reference to the real world.

Universal Grammar: the proposed set of genetically transmitted categories and principles common to all human languages.

unmarked: terms or features that are most common and least specific or noteworthy.

utterance: any instance of language produced by a speaker.

variable (sociolinguistic): a feature that is realized in different ways in speech, depending on sociolinguistic factors (such as the pronunciation of *ing*).

variety: the forms of a language used consistently by any group of speakers; any language, dialect, or register.

verb phrase (VP): the phrase built around a verb head.

vernacular: the common language or variety of language used in speaking. French, German, etc. evolved as the vernacular languages spoken in Europe, while Latin was the written language.

Wh question: a question beginning with a *wh* word such as *who, where, when.*

whole language: an approach to the teaching of literacy that emphasizes the connection between reading, writing, and speaking, the purposes for which reading is used, and the larger structures and meanings of texts rather than the decoding of words in isolation .

REFERENCES

Applebee, Arthur. 1980. *A Study of Writing in the Secondary School: Final Report.* Urbana, IL.: National Council of Teachers of English.

Au, Kathryn H. 1993. *Literacy Instruction in Multicultural Settings.* Orlando: Harcourt Brace Jovanovich College Publishers.

Auerbach, Elsa. 1995. " Deconstructing the Discourse of Strengths in Family Literacy." *Journal of Reading Behavior* 27, no. 4: 643–661.

Austin, John. 1962. *How to Do Things with Words.* Cambridge, Mass.: Harvard University Press.

Ballenger, Cindy. 1992. "Because You Like Us: The Language of Control." *Harvard Educational Review* 62 (summer): 199–208.

Barnes, Douglas. 1990. "Language in the Secondary Classroom." In *Language, the Learner and the School*, edited by Douglas Barnes, James Britton, and Mike Torbe. Portsmouth, N.H.: Heinemann Boynton/Cook.

Bates, Elizabeth. 1976. *Language and Context: the Acquisition of Pragmatics.* New York: Academic Press.

Belenky, Mary Field, Blythe McVicker Clinchy, Nancy Rule Goldberger, and Jill Mattuck Tarule. 1986. *Women's Ways of Knowing: The Development of Self, Voice, and Mind.* New York: Basic Books.

Bellugi, Ursula. 1980. *Signed and Spoken Language.* Weinheim: Verlag Chemie.

Bereiter, Carl, and Siegfried Englemann. 1966. *Teaching Disadvantaged Children in the Preschool.* Englewood Cliffs, N.J.: Prentice Hall.

Berko-Gleason, Jean. 1985. *The Development of Language.* Columbus: C. E. Morrill.

Bernstein, Basil. 1973. *Class, Codes and Control: Applied Studies Towards a Sociology of Language.* London: Routledge.

Bickerton, Derek. 1981 . *The Roots of Language.* Ann Arbor: Karoma.

Biklen, Douglas. 1993. *Communication Unbound. How Facilitated Communication is Challenging Traditional Views of Autism and Ability/Disability.* New York: Teacher's College Press.

Britton, James. 1982. *Prospect and Retrospect: Selected Essays*, edited by Gordon M. Pradl. Portsmouth, NH: Heinemann.

Brown, Roger. 1973. *A First Language: The Early Stages.* Cambridge, MA.: Harvard University Press.

Bruner, Jerome S. 1983. *Child's Talk: Learning to Use Language.* New York: W. W. Norton.

Carroll, Lewis. 1969. *Alice's Adventures in Wonderland.* New York: Maecenas Press.

Cazden, Courtney. 1988. *Classroom Discourse. The Language of Teaching and Learning*. Portsmouth, NH: Heinemann.

Chafe, Wallace L. 1982. "Integration and Involvement in Speaking, Writing, and Oral Literature." In *Spoken and Written Language: Exploring Orality and Literacy*, edited by Deborah Tannen. Norwood, NJ: Ablex.

———. 1986. "Writing in the Perspective of Speaking." In *Studying Writing*, edited by Charles Cooper and Sidney Greenbaum. Beverly Hills: Sage.

Chall, Jeanne S. 1970. *Learning to Read: The Great Debate*. New York: McGraw-Hill.

Chomsky, Noam. 1986. *Knowledge of Language: Its Nature, Origin and Use*. New York: Praeger.

Clay, Marie M. 1994. *Reading Recovery: A Guidebook for Teachers in Training*. Portsmouth, NH: Heinemann.

Cummins, J. 1981. "The Role of Primary Language Development in Promoting Educational Success for Language Minority Students." In *Schooling and Language Minority Students: A Theoretical Framework*. California State Department of Education. Los Angeles: Evaluation, Dissemination and Assessment Center, California State University.

Curtiss, Susan. 1977. *Genie: A Psycholinguistic Study of a Modern-Day "Wild Child."* New York: Academic Press.

Delpit, Lisa. 1988. "The Silenced Dialogue: Power and Pedagogy in Educating Other People's Children." *Harvard Educational Review* 58 (August): 280–98.

Ellis, Rod. 1990. *Instructed Second Language Acquisition: Learning in the Classroom*. Oxford, UK: B. Blackwell.

Erickson, Frederick. 1988. "School Literacy, Reasoning, and Civility: An Anthropologist's Perspective." In *Perspectives on Literacy*, edited by Eugene R. Kintgen, Barry M. Kroll, and Mike Rose. Carbondale: Southern Illinois University Press.

———. 1987. "Transformation and School Success: The Politics and Culture of Educational Achievement." *Anthropology and Education Quarterly* 18: 335–60.

Farrell, Thomas. 1983. "IQ and Standard English." *College Composition and Communication* 34 (December): 470–84.

Ferreiro, Emilia, and Teberosky, Ana. 1985. *Literacy Before Schooling*. Portsmouth NH: Heinemann.

Fowler, Roger. 1977. *Linguistics and the Novel*. London: Metheun.

Fox, Helen. 1994. *Listening to the World: Cultural Issues in Academic Writing*. Urbana, IL.: National Council of Teachers of English.

Freedman, Samuel G. 1990. *Small Victories: the Real World of a Teacher, Her Students, and Their High School*. CITY: Harper Perennial.

Freire, Paulo. 1969. *Pedagogy of the Oppressed*. Trans. Myra B. Ramos. New York: Continuum.

Gee, Jim. 1989. "Literacy, Discourse, and Linguistics: Introduction." *Journal of Education* 171 (1), 5–10.

———. 1985. "The Narrativization of Experience in the Oral Style." *Journal of Education* 167 (1), 9–36.

———. 1992. *The Social Mind: Language, Ideology, and Social Practice*. New York: Bergin and Garvey.

————. 1990. *Social Linguistics and Literacies: Ideology in Discourses*. London: Falmer Press.

Genishi, Celia. 1981. "Codeswitching in Chicano Six-Year-Olds." In *Latino Language and Communicative Behavior*, edited by Richard P. Duran. Norwood, NJ: Ablex.

Gilligan, Carol. 1982. *In a Different Voice: Psychological Theory and Women's Development*. Cambridge, MA.: Harvard University Press.

Givon, Talmy. 1979. *On Understanding Grammar*. New York: Academic Press.

Gleason, Jean Berko. 1987. "Sex Differences in Parent-Child Interaction." In *Language, Gender, and Sex in Comparative Perspective*, edited by Susan U. Philips, Susan Steele, & Christine Tanz. Cambridge, UK: Cambridge University Press.

Goffman, Erving. 1981. *Forms of Talk*. Philadelphia: University of Pennsylvania Press.

Goodman, Kenneth S., and Yetta M. Goodman. 1977. "Learning about Psycholinguistic Processes by Analyzing Oral Reading." *Harvard Educational Review* 47, no. 3 (August): 253–68.

Goodwin, Marjorie Harness, and Charles Goodwin. 1987. "Children's Arguing." In *Language, Gender, and Sex in Comparative Perspective*, edited by Susan U. Philips, Susan Steele, & Christine Tanz. Cambridge, UK: Cambridge University Press.

Grice, H. P. 1975. "Logic and Conversation." *Syntax and Semantics* 3: 41–58.

Gumperz, John J. 1982a. *Discourse Strategies*. Cambridge, UK: Cambridge University Press.

————, ed. 1982b. *Language and Social Identity*. Cambridge, UK: Cambridge University Press.

Gumperz, John J., and Deborah Tannen. 1979. "Individual and Social Differences in Language Use." In *Individual Differences in Language Ability and Language Behavior*, edited by Charles J. Fillmore, Daniel Kempler, and William S. Y. Wang. New York: Academic Press.

Halliday, M. A. K. 1978. *Language as Social Semiotic: The Social Interpretation of Language and Meaning*. London: Edward Arnold.

————. 1975. *Learning How to Mean: Explorations in the Development of Language*. London: Edward Arnold.

————. 1973. "Users and Uses of Language." In *Varieties of Present-Day English*, edited by R. Bailey, and J. Robinson. New York: MacMillan.

Halliday, M. A. K., and Ruqaiya Hasan. 1976. *Cohesion in English*. London: Longman.

Harste, Jerome, Virginia Woodward, and Carolyn Burke. 1984. *Language Stories and Literacy Lessons*. Portsmouth, NH: Heinemann Educational Books.

Hartwell, Patrick. 1985. "Grammar, Grammars, and the Teaching of Grammar." *College English* 47 (February): 105–27.

Heath, Shirley Brice. 1983. *Ways with Words: Language, Life and Work in Communities and Classrooms*. Cambridge, UK: Cambridge University Press.

Hefner, Nancy Smith. 1988. "The Linguistic Socialization of Javanese Children in Two Communities." *Anthropological Linguistics* 30, no. 2, 166–198.

Hirsch, E. D., Jr. 1987. *Cultural Literacy: What Every American Needs to Know*. Boston: Houghton Mifflin.

Hodges, John C., and Mary E. Whitten with Suzanne S. Webb. 1956. *The Harbrace Handbook*. San Diego: Harcourt Brace Jovanovich.

hooks, bell. 1989. "Keeping Close to Home: Class and Education." In *Talking Back: Thinking Feminist, Thinking Black*. Boston, MA.: South End Press.

How Schools Shortchange Girls. 1992. Washington DC: American Association of University Women Educational Foundation.

Hull, Glynda, Mike Rose, Kay Losey Fraser, and Marisa Castellano. 1991. "Remediation as Social Construct: Perspectives from an Analysis of Classroom Discourse." *College Composition and Communication* 42 (October): 299–329.

Hymes, Dell. 1972. *Directions in Sociolinguistics: the Ethnography of Communication*. New York: Holt, Rinehart and Winston.

Itard, Jean Marc Gaspard. 1962. *The Wild Boy of Aveyron*. Translated by George & Muriel Humphrey. New York: Appleton-Century-Crofts.

Jordan, June. 1988. "Nobody Mean More to Me Than You And the Future Life of Willie Jordan." *Harvard Educational Review* 58 (August): 363–74.

Kaplan, Jeffrey P. 1989. *English Grammar*. Englewood Cliffs, NJ: Prentice Hall.

Kessel, Frank. 1988. *The Development of Language and Language Researchers: Essays in Honor of Roger Brown*. Hillsdale, NJ: Erlbaum Associates.

Krashen, Stephen. 1982. *Principles and Practice in Second Language Acquisition*. Oxford, UK: Pergamon.

Kutz, Eleanor, Suzy Q Groden, Vivian Zamel. 1993. *The Discovery of Competence*. Portsmouth, NH: Boynton/Cook Publishers.

Kutz, Eleanor, and Hephzibah Roskelly. *An Unquiet Pedagogy: Transforming Practice in the English Classroom*. Portsmouth, NH: Boynton/Cook Publishers.

Labov, William. 1982. "Competing Value Systems in Inner-City Schools." In *Children In and Out of School: Ethnography and Education*, edited by Perry Gilmore, and Allen A. Glatthorn. Washington, DC: Center for Applied Linguistics.

———. 1972a. *Language in the Inner City: Studies in the Black English Vernacular*. Philadelphia: University of Pennsylvania Press.

———. 1973. "The Linguistic Consequences of Being a Lame." *Language in Society* 2: 81–115.

———. 1972b. "The Social Motivation of a Sound Change." In *Sociolinguistic Patterns*. Philadelphia, University of Pennsylvania Press.

———. 1966. *The Social Stratification of English in New York City*. Washington, D.C.: Center for Applied Linguistics.

———. 1972a. "The Transformation of Experience in Narrative Syntax." In *Language in the Inner City: Studies in the Black English Vernacular*. Philadelphia: University of Pennsylvania Press.

Lakoff, Robin. 1975. *Language and Women's Place*. New York: Harper and Row.

Lee, Carol. 1993. *Signifying as a Scaffold for Literary Interpretation: The Pedagogical Implications of an African American Discourse Genre*. Urbana, IL.: National Council of Teachers of English.

Lemke, Jay L. 1990. *Talking Science: Language, Learning, and Values*. Norwood, NJ: Ablex.

Long, M.H. 1981. "Input, Interaction, and SLA. In *Native Language and Foreign Language Acquisition*. New York: Annals of the New York Academy of Sciences, 259–278.

Maltz, Daniel N., and Ruth A. Borker. 1982. "A Cultural Approach to Male-Female Miscommunication." In *Language and Social Identity*, edited by John Gumperz. Cambridge, UK: Cambridge University Press.

Michaels, Sarah. 1985. "Hearing the Connections in Children's Oral and Written Discourse." *Journal of Education* 167: 35–56.

———. 1986. "Narrative Presentations: An Oral Preparation for Literacy with First Graders. In *The Social Construction of Literacy*. Ed. Cook-Gumperz, Jenny. Cambridge UK: Cambridge University Press.

Milroy, James. 1981. *Regional Accents of English: Belfast*. Belfast: Blackstaff Press.

Milroy, James, and Leslie Milroy. 1991. *Authority in Language: Investigating Language Prescription and Standardization*. London: Routledge.

Moffett, James. 1968. *Teaching the Universe of Discourse*. Boston: Houghton Mifflin.

Morrison, Toni. 1973. *Sula*. New York: Knopf.

Nelson, Linda Williamson. 1990. "Code-Switching in the Oral Life Narratives of African-American Women: Challenges to Linguistic Hegemony." *Journal of Education* 172 (3): 142–55.

Ninio, Anat, and Jerome Bruner. 1978. "The Achievement and Antecedents of Labelling." *Journal of Child Language, Reading* 5: 1–15.

Ochs, Elinor. 1979. "Social Foundations of Language." In *New Directions in Discourse Processing*, edited by Roy O. Freedle. Norwood, N.J.: Ablex.

O'Connor, Flannery. "The River." *The Complete Stories*. New York: Farrar, Straus and Giroux, 1971. Pp. 157—174.

Ogbu, John. 1978. *Minority Education and Caste: The American System in Cross-Cultural Perspective*. New York: Academic Press.

———. 1987. "Variability in Minority School Performance: A Problem in Search of An Explanation." *Antahropology and Education Quarterly* 18, 4, 312–334.

Olson, David. 1977. "From Utterance to Text: The Bias of Language in Speech and Writing." *Harvard Educational Review* 47, 3, 257–81.

Philips, Susan. 1983. *The Invisible Culture: Communication in Classroom and Community on the Warm Springs Indian Reservation*. New York: Longman.

Philips, Susan, Susan Steele, and Christine Tanz. 1987. *Language, Gender & Sex in Comparative Perspective*. Cambridge, UK: Cambridge University Press.

Piestrup, Ann. 1973. *Black Dialect Interference and Accomodation of Reading Instruction in First Grade*. Berkeley (UC): Language-Behavior Research Laboratory.

Pontecorvo, Clotilde. 1995. *Children's Early Text Construction*. Hillsdale, N.J.: Erlbaum.

Pratt, Mary Louise. 1977. *Toward a Speech Act Theory of Literary Discourse*. Bloomington: Indiana University Press.

Ripich, Danielle Newberry, and Francesca Spinelli, eds. 1985. *School Discourse Problems*. San Diego: Singular Pub. Group.

Robinson, Jay L., and Patricia Stock. 1990. "Literacy as Conversation: Classroom Talk as Text Building." In *Conversations on the Written Word*, edited by Jay Robinson. Portsmouth, NH: Heinemann Boynton/Cook.

Rodriguez, Richard. 1982. *The Hunger of Memory*. Boston: Godine.

Rowe, Mary Budd. 1986. "Wait Time: Slowing Down May be a Way of Speeding Up!" *Journal of Teacher Education*. 37: 43–50.

Rosenblatt, Louise. 1978. *The Reader, the Text, the Poem.* Carbondale: Southern Illinois University Press.

Rymer, Russ. 1993. *Genie: An Abused Child's Flight from Silence.* New York, Harper Collins Publishers.

Sachs, Jacqueline. 1987. "Preschool Boys' and Girls' Language Use in Pretend Play." In *Language, Gender, and Sex in Comparative Perspective,* edited by Susan U. Philips, Susan Steele, & Christine Tanz. Cambridge, UK: Cambridge University Press.

Sadker, Myra, and David Sadker. 1994. *Failing at Fairness: How America's Schools Cheat Girls.* New York: C. Scribner's Sons.

de Saussure, Ferdinand. 1959. *Course in General Linguistics.* 3d ed. New York: Philosophical Library.

Schieffelin, Bambi. 1990. *The Give and Take of Everyday Life. Language Socialization of Kaluli Children.* Cambridge, UK: Cambridge University Press.

Scollon, Ron. 1976. *Conversations with a One Year Old: A Case Study of the Developmental Foundation of Syntax.* Honolulu: University Press of Hawaii.

———. 1979. "A Real Early Stage: An Unzipped Condensation of a Dissertation on Child Language." In *Developmental Pragmatics.* Eds. Ochs, Elinor and Schieffelin, Bambi. New York: Academic Press. Pp. 215–227.

Scollon, Ron, and Suzanne Scollon. 1981. *Narrative, Literacy and Face in Interethnic Communication.* Norwood, NJ: Ablex.

Searle, John. 1965. "What Is a Speech Act?" In *Philosophy in America,* edited by M. Black. Ithaca: Cornell University.

———. 1969. *Speech Acts: An Essay in the Philosophy of Language.* London: Cambridge University Press.

Shostak, Marjorie. 1981. *Nisa: The Life and Words of a !Kung Woman.* Cambridge, MA.: Harvard University Press.

Shuy, Robert. 1975. "Teacher Training and Urban Language Problems." In *Black American English,* edited by Paul Stoller. New York: Dell.

Smitherman, Geneva. 1977. *Talkin' and Testifyin': The Language of Black America.* Boston: Houghton Mifflin.

———. 1985. "'What Go Round Come Round': King in Perspective." In *Tapping Potential: English and Language Arts for the Black Learner,* edited by Charlotte K. Brooks, Jerrie Cobb Soctt, Miriam Chaplin, Delores Lipscomb, William W. Cook, and Vivian Davis. Urbana, IL.: Black Caucus of NCTE.

Snow, Catherine. 1977. *Talking to Children: Language Input and Acquisition.* Cambridge, UK: Cambridge University Press.

Sommers, Nancy. 1982. "Responding to Student Writing." *College Composition and Communication* 33, no. 2, 148–56.

Street, Brian. 1984. *Literacy in Theory and Practice.* Cambridge, UK: Cambridge University Press.

Strong, William. 1973. *Sentence Combining: A Composing Book.* New York: Random House.

Swain, Merrill. 1985. "Communicative Competence: Some Roles of Comprehensible Input and Comprehensible Output in Its Development." In *Input in Second*

Language Acquisition. Eds. Gass, Susan and Madden, Carolyn. Rowley, MA: Newbury, 235–253.

Swann, Joan, and David Graddol. 1994. "Gender Inequalities in Classroom Talk." *Researching Language & Literacy in Social Context*. Clevedon & Philadelphia: Multilingual Matters/Open University, 151–167.

Tan, Amy. 1989. *The Joy Luck Club*. New York: Putnam's.

Tannen, Deborah. 1984. *Conversational Style: Analyzing Talk Among Friends*. Norwood, NJ: Ablex .

———. 1982. "The Oral Literate Continuum in Discourse." In *Spoken and Written Language: Exploring Orality and Literacy*, edited by Deborah Tannen. Norwood, NJ: Ablex.

———. 1989. *Talking Voices: Repetition, Dialogue, and Imagery in Conversational Discourse*. Cambridge: Cambridge University Press.

———. 1990. *You Just Don't Understand. Women and Men in Conversation*. New York: Ballentine.

Taylor, Denny. 1990. "Teaching Without Testing." *English Education*. February 1990. Full Issue.

Taylor, Denny, and Catherine Dorsey-Gaines. 1988. *Growing Up Literate: Learning from Inner-City Families*. Portsmouth, NH: Heinemann.

Teale, William H., and Elizabeth Sulzby. 1986. *Emergent Literacy: Writing and Reading*. Norwood, NJ: Ablex.

Traugott, Elizabeth, and Mary Louise Pratt. 1980. *Linguistics for Students of Literature*. New York: Harcourt Brace Jovanovich.

Trudgill, Peter. 1974. *The Social Differentiation of English in Norwich*. Cambridge, UK: Cambridge University Press.

Valdes, G. 1981. "Codeswitching as Deliberate Verbal Strategy: a Microanalysis of Direct and Indirect Requests Among Bilingual Chicano Speakers." In *Latino Language and Communicative Behavior*, ed. R. P. Duran. Norwood, NJ: Ablex.

Vogel, Mark. 1992. "My Students as the Content in a Language/Dialect Community." Paper presented at Spring Conference, National Council of Teachers of English.

Watt, Ian P. 1964. *The Rise of the Novel: Studies in Defoe, Richardson, and Fielding*. Berkeley: University of California Press.

Weaver, Constance. 1979. *Grammar for Teachers*. Urbana, IL.: NCTE.

West, C., and Zimmerman, D. H. 1977. "Women's Place in Everyday Talk: Reflections on Parent-Child Interaction." *Social Problems* 24 (5): 521–9.

Zamel, Vivian. 1985. "Responding to Student Writing." *TESOL Quarterly* 19 (1) (March): 79–100.

473F. supp. 1371, E, D, Mich. 1979, cited in Smitherman, 50

INDEX